Negotiated Settlements

UNIVERSITY PRESS OF FLORIDA

Florida A&M University, Tallahassee
Florida Atlantic University, Boca Raton
Florida Gulf Coast University, Ft. Myers
Florida International University, Miami
Florida State University, Tallahassee
New College of Florida, Sarasota
University of Central Florida, Orlando
University of Florida, Gainesville
University of North Florida, Jacksonville
University of South Florida, Tampa
University of West Florida, Pensacola

NEGOTIATED SETTLEMENTS

Andean Communities and Landscapes under Inka and Spanish Colonialism

Steven A. Wernke

University Press of Florida

Gainesville | Tallahassee | Tampa | Boca Raton

Pensacola | Orlando | Miami | Jacksonville | Ft. Myers | Sarasota

The publication of this book is made possible in part by a grant from Vanderbilt University.

Printed in the United States of America on acid-free paper

All photos were taken by the author unless otherwise noted.
Frontis: Aerial view of the settlement of Uyu Uyu (YA–050) and surrounding terracing, from the
south. Plaza (*center-left*) is flanked by an Inka kallanka structure (*left*) and chapel (*right*). *Source*:
Shippee-Johnson aerial expedition, 1931, Image #334671, American Museum of Natural History Library.

This book may be available in an electronic edition.

First cloth printing, 2013
First paperback printing, 2014

Library of Congress Cataloging-in-Publication Data
Wernke, Steven A.
Negotiated settlements : Andean communities and landscapes under Inka
and Spanish colonialism / Steven A. Wernke.
p. cm.
Includes bibliographical references and index.
ISBN 978-0-8130-4249-7 (cloth: alk. paper)
ISBN 978-0-8130-6093-4 (pbk.)
1. Indians of South America—Peru—Colca Canyon—History. 2. Indians of South America—
Peru—Colca Canyon—Social conditions. 3. Colca Canyon (Peru)—History. I. Title.
F3451.A5W47 2013
985'.32019—dc23   2012031681

The University Press of Florida is the scholarly publishing agency for the State University System of Florida,
comprising Florida A&M University, Florida Atlantic University, Florida Gulf Coast University, Florida International University, Florida State University, New College of Florida, University of Central Florida, University
of Florida, University of North Florida, University of South Florida, and University of West Florida.

University Press of Florida
15 Northwest 15th Street
Gainesville, FL 32611-2079
http://www.upf.com

For Tiffiny and Livia

CONTENTS

FIGURES

TABLES

PREFACE AND ACKNOWLEDGMENTS

I arrived in Yanque for the first time in June 1996, an anthropological novice, bearing my backpack and letters of introduction. I first stopped by the convent behind the village's impressive church to meet (the now late) Sister Antonia Kayser, a Bronx-born Maryknoll nun who had lived and worked in Yanque since the 1970s, and (the now late) Sister Sara Kathaithara, a Medical Mission Sister (and nurse) from India who ran a medical post at the convent. Leaving my bags at the convent, I crossed the plaza in the blinding midday light, feeling a bit winded from the altitude by the time I arrived at the corrugated tin door giving entrance to the house patio of don Gerardo Huaracha Huaracha, the president of the Urinsaya irrigation commission, former governor of the district, and grandson of the last *kuraka* (native lord) of Yanque. Knowing I had to ask him the preposterous favor of sharing his home with me—a total stranger—over the next couple of months, I was nervous but exhilarated to have finally arrived. After a few raps on the door, a slight man in an outsized cowboy hat greeted me. After I introduced myself as an anthropologist and archaeologist from the United States and clumsily produced a letter of introduction from María Benavides, an old friend of don Gerardo's who has worked for many years as an ethnohistorian of the Colca Valley, he introduced himself as Teodoro Huaracha Huaracha, Gerardo's brother.

"Ay, come in, come in."

The patio was a construction zone. Teodoro and a few other men were setting stones in mud mortar for a new building. One of them, wearing a dusty suit coat and armed with a shot glass and Coke bottle of *trago* (cane liquor), was looking especially cheerful and seemed more a spectator to the heavy lifting than a participant. Thinking this must be the don Gerardo I had heard so much about, I stiffly introduced myself.

"I'm number 14," he said in return, shaking my hand with a wry smile.

Had I misheard? "How's that?"

The men working on the wall paused and chuckled.

"I'm number 14, the fourteenth Inka in the great imperial dynasty."

Teodoro clued me in: "His last name *is* Inka; he's the son of don Inka Inka, the eldest man of Hanansaya."

"Yes, we of the Inka family are descendents of the legitimate Inkas, from Cuzco. *Salud, pues,*" he said, handing me the shot glass and Coke bottle. "Can you drink *trago*?"

I poured myself a shot and, after spilling a few drops to *pachamama,* tossed back the firewater. Smiles all around.

Don Gerardo eventually arrived (I don't recall if he was attending to business in the plaza or if he returned with the burros from a day in the fields) and, after hearing my request, granted that I could sleep on the floor next to the sacks of recently harvested potatoes in the *sala*—one of the few thatched houses left in Yanque, with colorful bands of plants and animals painted on its mud-plastered walls.

•

At the risk of starting with what might seem a cliché in the anthropological trope of "first encounters," these formative experiences in Yanque left in me lasting impressions of the kind of place that the people of Yanque inherited and built, but more important, they reflect upon and are historically connected to the themes explored in this book. The outsider, seeking entrée to community leaders via privileged (and historically colonial) institutional connections is drawn into local practices of sociability, labor, and the routines of daily life by dwelling in the built environment of his hosts. The savvy play on the wide-eyed stranger's sensibilities ("Here before you is a real Inka!") is clear, even as its logic of prestige valorizes imperial power over local autonomy. Lines of power (though it's not all about power, either) are not so clearly drawn. The outsider gets schooled in the first engagement of a longer encounter that produces a certain commensurability of shared experience.

This book traces such processes of (inter-) cultural negotiation in the local experience of colonialism in the Andes through archaeological and ethnohistorical exploration. I insist on the local perspective—both because it provides a unique view of the tangible effects of colonial rule and because I think that "community" and "landscape" are critical mediating structures in the negotiation of colonial power.

It seems apt, then, to start with this experiential core of my research and to acknowledge the tremendous debt of gratitude I owe the communities of Yanque, Coporaque, and Tuti for hosting me and my teams of researchers, who have invaded their villages pretty much annually since that initial stay in Yanque. The field projects this book draws from wouldn't have been possible if not for the goodwill and graces of the people of Yanque, Coporaque, and Tuti, who embraced us, educated us, and often even fed us and slaked our thirst with *chicha* as we stumbled ponderously through their fields. My debt to my *padrinos* in Yanque, Gerardo Huaracha Huaracha and Doña Luisa Cutipa de Huaracha, is greater than I can repay.

During the Yanque-Coporaque survey, when in Arequipa I lived and worked in the research house of the Centro de Investigaciones Arqueológicas de Arequipa (CIARQ), a true home away from home in sunny Sachaca. I thank Karen Wise and Augusto Cardona Rosas, co-directors of CIARQ, for all manner of logistical and bureaucratic support. My knowledge of the archaeology and ethnohistory of Arequipa owes much to the many stimulating conversations with the late Máximo Neira, pioneer of Colca Valley archaeology, and with Félix Palacios Ríos, the late Guillermo Galdos Rodriguez, and Augusto Cardona Rosas. I thank Luis Sardón Cánepa and Franz Grupp, directors of the National Institute of Culture (INC) in Arequipa during the course of the research for this book, as well as my friends on the staff of the Department of Archaeology of INC Arequipa—Pablo de la Vera Cruz Chávez, Lucy Linares Delgado, Marko López Hurtado, and Cecilia Quequezana—for helping me through the permit and inspection process.

The early research for this book began at the University of Wisconsin–Madison. I warmly thank my colleagues, Frank Salomon, Jason Yaeger, (the now late) Neil Whitehead, Sissel Schroeder, and Karl Zimmerer, for all of their advice and always-constructive criticism. My work benefited tremendously from the input of such a diverse group of great scholars. I am particularly indebted to Frank Salomon for my scholarly formation. His intellect and incredible depth of knowledge of the Andean cultural world are inspirational. Jason Yaeger was tireless and selfless in providing feedback, and his work on the archaeology of communities has significantly shaped my own thinking on the subject.

I owe a particular debt of gratitude to William Denevan, who (long ago now) pulled out his maps and air photos during an office visit and, with infectious enthusiasm, encouraged me to go to the Colca Valley to explore research options. Another incredible individual and dear friend, Maria Benavides, profoundly affected my ability to undertake this project by so generously providing me with her collection of archival documents related to the colonial history of the Colca Valley, including photocopies and transcriptions of the *visitas* that are the centerpiece of the ethnohistorical portion of the study. In Lima, Krzysztof Makowski, who took an interest in my project from the first time I met him, opened his home to me and assisted me through the National Institute of Culture permit process. Special thanks to Luis Jaime

Castillo Butters for his support in seeing my proposal through the proper channels at the INC. The archaeological field research for this project was carried out with the authorization of Resoluciones Directorales 615 (1999), 1096 (2006), and 828 (2007) from the National Institute of Culture, Lima.

My heartfelt thanks go to Willy Yépez Alvarez and Erika Simborth Lozada, who assisted in all aspects of the Yanque-Coporaque archaeological survey and postfield analysis. We developed a special bond that only working and living together in the field can create. Many thanks to Ericka Guerra Santander, co-director of the Colca Valley Regional Survey Project and the Tuti Antiguo Archaeological Project, for her able co-directorship and the major contributions of time and effort that our collaborations have entailed. Teddy Abel Traslaviña Arias contributed major efforts to the excavation project at the Malata site in Tuti in the form of mapping, planning, debating, and being an all-around great team member, colleague, and friend. The work of collaborating colleagues on the excavations at Malata—Susan DeFrance (zooarchaeology), David Goldstein and Lizette Muñoz (paleobotany), Nicholas Tripcevich (GIS), and Tiffiny Tung (bioarchaeology)—enabled a multidimensional view of the past that otherwise would have been impossible. I thank Lauren Kohut for the many long hours she spent with me working on GIS projects for this book.

The field research for this project was made possible through funding from the Wenner-Gren Foundation for Anthropological Research (Grant No. 6431), a National Science Foundation Senior Research Grant (grant number 0716883), an NSF Research Experience for Undergraduates (REU) grant supplement, a Vanderbilt University Center for the Americas Faculty Research Fellowship, a Vanderbilt University Research Scholar Fellowship, and a Vanderbilt University Undergraduate Summer Research Program. Spatial analysis was supported by the facilities of the Vanderbilt University Spatial Analysis Research Lab.

Initial postfield analysis and writing was funded by a Lita Osmundson Grant from the Wenner-Gren Foundation. I also gratefully acknowledge the support of a Dumbarton Oaks Junior Fellowship in Precolumbian Studies. I am especially grateful to Jeffrey Quilter, then director of pre-Columbian studies, for his wise advice and input on the project. George Lau, Allan Maca, and Carolyn Tate, my colleagues at Dumbarton Oaks, all helped me formulate my ideas in the early stages of this project.

My work writing the book manuscript was generously supported by a Hunt Postdoctoral Fellowship from the Wenner-Gren Foundation. Editing and production costs were defrayed through subvention funds from the College of Arts and Science and the Office of the Vice Provost for Research at Vanderbilt University.

I am grateful to my parents, Grace and Arlyn Wernke, and my sister, Suzanne Bautz, for their unconditional support of my academic pursuits, no matter how impractical they may have seemed.

Finally, I owe my deepest gratitude to my wife, Tiffiny Tung, who has been a selfless partner through the process of writing this book. Her formidable intellect and keen observations have also fortified it immeasurably.

Any shortcomings are purely my own.

1

COLONIALISM IN THE ANDES

An Emplaced Perspective

In the short span of just a few generations, the peoples of the Andean region of South America engaged the colonial projects of two imperial powers—Tawantinsuyu (the Inka "Fourfold Domain") and the Kingdom of Spain—each bent on extracting their wealth and reshaping their societies according to their own ideal self-images. Andean communities were serially colonized and exploited, as labor, land, and produce were expropriated by these conquest states. But in the everyday interactions and enduring features of landscape and the built environment that constituted the ongoing conditions of life under Inka and Spanish rule, colonizing ideologies, institutions, and practices were also transformed and made to articulate with a great diversity of Andean cultural postulates and practices. In their colonization of the Andes, the Inka and Spanish states were also colonized.

In this book, I contend that community and landscape constituted primary sociocultural interfaces through which such mutually constitutive processes of colonization occurred. It examines how it occurred through an *emplaced* archaeological and ethnohistorical study of how particular Andean communities experienced, adapted to, and transformed successive colonial projects by the Inka and Spanish states. By an emplaced study, I mean a detailed, in situ, empirical rendering of the historical and material ramifications of social practice over varied temporal and spatial scales. It adopts a holistic methodological approach, integrating a range of archaeological and documentary data in a common spatial framework using geographic information systems (GIS) as a central analytical toolset. The chronological scope of the study spans the 500 years between the twelfth and early seventeenth centuries. It begins by tracking the development of two major late prehispanic ethnic polities—the Collaguas and Cabanas—in the Colca Valley of southern highland Peru and then investigates how their incorporation into the Inka and Spanish

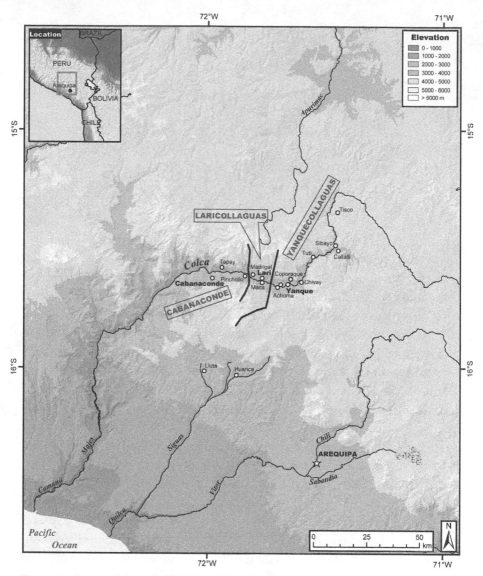

Figure 1.1. Regional map of the Colca Valley, showing provincial subdivisions and their approximate boundaries.

empires was related to the reproduction and transformation of community organization, land-use practices, and the physical configuration of the landscape and built environments of local settlements.

The Colca Valley (Figure 1.1) is an ideal context in which to carry out such a project. On the eve of the Spanish invasion, the valley landscape had already been transformed by some 400 years of autonomous rule, followed by about a century of Inka imperial administration. This history is manifested in the built forms that today make up a spectacular mosaic of anthropogenic landforms, irrigation systems, well-preserved settlements, cemeteries, fortifications, and other archaeological sites (e.g., Figure 1.2). This book traces the construction of that landscape and the occupations of the peoples who built and dwelled in it through a spatial synthesis of archaeological and ethnohistorical data sources. The archaeological component centers on two primary elements: (1) a systematic survey that I conducted in the political nucleus of the Collagua ethnic group, an area surrounding the later Inkaic and colonial provincial capital of Yanque and the neighboring village of Coporaque in the central part of the Colca Valley, and (2) excavations at the site of Malata, a small Inka outpost in the upper reaches of the valley that was transformed into a Franciscan *doctrina* (doctrinal settlement) during the first generation after the Spanish invasion and subsequently abandoned with the establishment of colonial planned towns—*reducciones*—in the 1570s. Appropriate to

Figure 1.2. Agricultural terracing surrounds the settlement of Uyu Uyu (site YA-050). (Source: 1931 Shippee-Johnson aerial expedition, Image 334671, Special Collections, American Museum of Natural History Library.)

the study of Andean community organization and the excellent architectural preservation of late prehispanic sites in the Colca Valley, I designed the survey to collect data of intermediate resolution—more detailed than a regional survey but broader in scope than a site-specific survey or excavation. Also, unlike most archaeological surveys in the Andes, I did not truncate data collection at the point of Spanish invasion; this permits a more seamless view of the transition from Inkaic to Spanish rule up to the forced resettlement of the local populace from their prehispanic settlements into European-style reducción villages in the 1570s.

The ethnohistorical component uses detailed Spanish colonial *visitas* (administrative surveys) from an area overlapping with the archaeological survey to reconstruct how *ayllus* (named, ancestor-focused, resource-holding kindreds) structured regional- and local-scale land-use patterns. The core innovation of the approach presented below lies in its detailed reconstruction of ayllu land-tenure patterns from visita landholding declarations. This methodology uses GIS to reconstruct the land-tenure patterns of local ayllus by matching toponyms from agricultural field declarations in the visitas with their counterparts on the landscape today (derived from ethnographic field mapping and modern cadastral sources). This enabled precise mapping of a large sample of the agricultural fields declared in the visitas in the same area as the Yanque-Coporaque archaeological survey. By spatializing patterns of land tenure otherwise obscure in textual form, this methodology enables reconstruction of colonial-era land-use practices and provides a historically continuous, homologous source for augmenting the interpretation of the settlement pattern data from the archaeological survey in the same area.

The Resistance of Culture: Improvisational Order in Colonial Encounters

Though this is a locally situated study that places Inka and Spanish colonialism in the same analytical frame, it should not be taken as a retreat to particularism. Rather, it strives for a local accounting to enable a view of the negotiation of the conditions of everyday life under colonial rule as a continuous process across the Spanish invasion. Nor should the trans-conquest perspective taken be read as a tacit denial of the uniquely exploitative, oppressive, and transformative effects of Spanish colonialism on indigenous societies of the Americas. The research presented here puts the local manifestations of those exploitative effects at the center of analysis. But it is also in line with the productive turn to the conceptual broadening of archaeological exploration of colonialism beyond the initial global spread of European hegemony in archaeology (see, e.g., Given 2004; Gosden and Knowles 2001; Stein 2005). These expanded archaeological approaches to colonialism contribute critically to a historical anthropology that relativizes (or, sensu Chakrabarty 2000, "provincializes") European hegemony. An unfortunate side effect of contemporary anthropology's deconstruction of the culture concept and the attendant emphasis on (post)modern global webs of power is that it relies on the implicit, opposing caricature of a static, isolated, "cold" premodern social world (Cobb 2005; Ortner 1995). As Charles Cobb puts it (2005:563), "A pre-Columbian Other has been constructed, who now serves as a historic baseline for investigating the impact of the world system from the 1400s C.E. onward." The archaeology of colonialism (broadly conceived) can expose the assumptions behind the persistent myths of this tradition-bound, premodern Other. These trends, however, have not been carried through to transhistorical investigations of the in situ negotiations of successive waves of colonial rule. Despite frequent calls for interdisciplinary research, what happened before and after the Spanish invasion of the Americas has remained largely divided as separate histories, shaped as much by different disciplinary paradigms as by differences in the nature of the information at hand or lived experiences in the past (Lightfoot 1995; Silliman 2005).

In archaeology, the analytical separation between pre-Columbian and historic eras traditionally derives from the approach to the native societies of the Americas—separated from Old World societies for at least 15,000 years—as independent case studies in the comparative study of social evolution and the emergence of complex society. Thus even as most archaeologists of the pre-Columbian past chafe at the postmodernist foil of the tradition-bound premodern Other (and empirically demonstrate its falsity), the boundary that defines the field is undergirded by the same assumptions of qualitatively different pre- and post-"contact" pasts. This is doubly regrettable, since it reinforces archaeology's place in the "savage slot" (Trouillot 1991; Cobb 2005) even as archaeology unearths just how dynamic and interconnected pre-Columbian societies were.

But from a comparative perspective, the institution of Inkaic and Spanish colonialism shares much in common with processes of secondary state formation. Here issues of how the (remnant) institutions of prior states were variously recycled and transformed are in the fore, especially in the case of Spanish colonialism, when there was no prolonged intervening post-collapse period and the institutions of the Inka state were still basically functioning as a new branch of the Spanish state was instituted. How secondary states were imagined and built into being is in large part a question of which elements from prior polities (in this case, from both Andean and European sources) were deemed analogous, then salvaged and repurposed. But this was not (or at least was not *only*) a question of state building "strategies," as the problem is often framed. How the state is conceived in the center/metropole (which is never so homogenous and agreed upon as the monolithic term "state" would imply) and how it manifested and was received outside it is often very different and linked in complex recursive relationships. Thus, as I argue below, the cultural entanglements of colonial encounters produce new kinds of societies that are the product of both colonizer and colonized but controlled entirely by neither.

Before going further, it is necessary to define "imperialism" and "colonialism" as used below to make more explicit what might be only intuitive distinctions in their common usages. Are their distinguishing characteristics qualitative? Chronological (does one generally precede the other)? Spatial (as in an imperial project as it manifests in a remote colony)? I draw on discussions by Loomba (2005:7–14) and Dietler (2005:52–54) to help differentiate terms for the interrelated social processes by which expansionist states extend and institutionalize political and economic control over other societies. Imperialism (derived from the Latin *imperium*), if it is to resonate with the core sense of its common usage, refers to "an ideology or discourse that motivates and legitimizes practices of expansionary domination by one society over another" (Dietler 2005:53). The emphasis here is on "the phenomenon that originates in the metropolis, the process which leads to domination and control" (Loomba 2005:12). In both, the emphasis is on the *intent* or impulse by state agents to dominate and control—whether as a motivator for expansionary policies or a legitimator of them. Colonialism, on the other hand, is a process of social engagement between an imperial state and subject peoples as it occurs away from the metropole; it is a set of "projects and practices of control marshaled in interactions between societies linked in asymmetrical relations of power, and the processes of social and cultural transformation resulting from those practices" (Dietler 2005:54).

This last point linking colonialism to social and cultural transformation is crucial, since colonialism as I conceive of it (as distinct from imperialism) implies an attempt to implant a vision of an ideal hierarchical social order in which the colonizer is dominant and the colonized is subordinate. The *form* of colonialism can vary widely, as it may involve (to list a few of its potential dimensions) religious indoctrination, education, trade, revalorization of prestige and status, warfare, and so on. Its *effectiveness* can similarly vary contextually, since the social transformations of colonial projects are not entirely of a colonizing power's making; they "always entail a host of unintended consequences for both indigenous peoples and alien colonists. Both parties eventually become something other than they were because of these processes of entanglement and their unintended consequences" (Dietler 2005:54). Thus, as pointed out by Peter Gose, even as colonialism is founded on ideologies and discourses of the cultural superiority of the colonizer (per Said 1978), "the practicalities of colonial rule, extraction, and sociability *require collusions* that partially blur and undermine the distinction between colonizer and colonized" (Gose 2008:7; emphasis added).

Such collusions are required because of what I call the dilemma of "analogy or erasure" in the practicalities of colonial rule (see also Wernke 2007a). That is, colonial projects aimed at the erasure and replacement of indigenous practices must—if the introduced foreign practices are to find cultural purchase—resonate with indigenous analogs. In so doing, they (wittingly or unwittingly) partially reproduce the practices they intend to replace. Of course, the resources brought to bear on a colonial project (and their variance over space and time) factor also in this general relationship, and they will influence the degree to which coercion and the threat of violence may forcibly institute a colonial program. But as a general rule, I suggest that the greater the analogical emphasis in a colonial project, the greater its cultural purchase will be in practice, and conversely, the greater the eradicatory impulse of a colonial project, the less its cultural purchase. By "cultural purchase," I refer to a hegemonic process: the degree to which a given set of colonial policies penetrates local commonsensical categories and everyday routines. As John and Jean Comaroff have shown in colonial South Africa, the most enduring effects of Christian evangelization have been in its insertion into such commonsense meanings and routine activities rather than in explicitly "political" realms, even as its articulation with the locally commonsensical transformed Protestantism into a dizzying array of local variants (Comaroff and Comaroff 1986).

To paraphrase Sahlins (2005:4), then, whether or not a "culture of resistance" develops in opposition to colonialism, the "resistance of culture" necessarily entangles colonial rule in local practices—structures and durable material features of daily life—producing new kinds of societies. Thinking about the "resistance of culture" makes some headway toward a perspective that can scrutinize the processes through which social reproduction leads to social transformation in colonial encounters (see Sahlins 1981, 1985, 2004), but it lacks analytical specificity (Sewell 2005). Focusing on the reproduction and transformation of community and landscape provides such specificity by grounding the resistance of culture in everyday practice. As discussed in the following chapter, this is not to reduce community or landscape to residues of conditioned behavior. Rather, this book traces out how each was an emergent structure of social practice. Each was also highly tangible on a daily basis: The stuff of community and landscape enveloped agents in material forms, even as it was a product of and transformed by their labor. Such materiality also accounts for the inertial effects of community and landscape on colonial projects. It also means that archaeology is uniquely equipped to provide insights into the working out of colonial power, meaning, and practices in (and through) their material contexts.

So to the extent that a colonial state manifests social order, it is not only a question of the implantation of a civilizational ideal from above but also an *improvised order* consumed by a welter of interests, understandings, practices, and material worlds of subject peoples. Since such interests and understandings manifest in dialogue with official policies, discourses, and institutions, from a statist point of view, ironically, the work of improvising order was largely consumed by cleaning up the messes that earlier policies created and not a grand design in the usually imagined, strategic sense. Thinking about colonialism as an improvisational order helps to resituate analysis from a top-down perspective toward one that explores the working out of power in situ rather than prejudging power relations as defined by dominant-and-subordinate or core-and-periphery positions.

This approach carries forward several broad trends in models of expansionist states and their relations with subject peoples in archaeology over the last few decades. Research questions have generally shifted from tracing the local "impacts" of imperial rule (a one-way model) to charting the necessary compromises between high-control/high-cost "direct" rule and low-control/low-cost "indirect" rule (also referred to as "territorial" versus "hegemonic" rule; see D'Altroy 1992). Direct control involves a penetrating reorganization of incorporated polities, permitting centralized administration and hierarchically integrated surplus extractive systems, but at the cost of major investments in personnel, infrastructure, resettlement, military securitization, and accounting and surveillance mechanisms. Indirect control implies relatively minor state investments and changes to local political and economic organization, but at the cost of low control and extractive potential. Most archaeologists emphasize how imperial integration should be viewed as a continuous spectrum between these two heuristic types of control, and indeed the model has been highly productive in documenting a regional-scale "mosaic of control" in large imperial formations such as Tawantinsuyu (Schreiber 1992). They advance a more dynamic understanding of imperial politics than core/periphery models, since they provide a model for understanding how state-local articulations can vary diachronically, as "peripheral" areas that were initially subject to indirect rule can become more directly administered and become part of an expanding "core" as imperial rule is consolidated (for review, see Stanish 2001).

Such models, however, are still premised on how a state manages its costs and benefits in an overarching imperial strategy. They are, as Goldstein calls it, "metrocentric" in orientation in that they "assume 'underdeveloped' and politically weak societies on the state's periphery with less complex forms of political, social, and economic organization. . . . Regardless of the terminology, metrocentric views of state expansion imply strategies of power that flow from the top down and from the center out" (Goldstein 2005:8). Also, as Morrison points out, sustained scrutiny shows that most locales of an empire do not conform to the heuristic categories of either "indirect" or "direct" rule (Morrison 2001:258). Rather, when studied in detail, the social arrangements observed in most imperial settings are more accurately described as co-constituted in the engagements between expansive states and subject peoples.

The spatial integration of archaeological and documentary data is critical to understanding how this worked, because, as we will see, the two evidentiary sources produce contrasting visions of Inka and Spanish colonial rule in the Colca Valley, and therefore neither "direct" nor "indirect" models are entirely appropriate for understanding the improvisational orders produced. As discussed at length in subsequent chapters, colonial documentary sources on first examination would seem to reflect a situation of more or less direct imperial rule by the Inkas in the Colca Valley. It would seem that there was a fundamental restructuring of local community structures of the ayllu, recasting them in a nested, hierarchical structure organized according to bipartite, tripartite, and decimal administrative categories. In contrast, the archaeological evidence that seems at first to point to a more or less indirect regime of rule in which the imprint of imperial administration is relatively light. The usual indices of direct imperial rule are not present in the Colca Valley: There was no major reorganization of settlement but instead overall continuity of occupation from autonomous rule, no administrative center dominates the settlement pattern of the valley as a whole, and no major imperial storage complexes are present in the valley indicating the extraction of large amounts of surplus agricultural production.

When turning to the early Spanish colonial era, the evidentiary relationship is almost the reverse. Archaeologically, the near total obliteration of the terminal prehispanic settlement pattern with the establishment of the reducciones would seem to indicate rule by imperial fiat, as has often been suggested. It is only by spatializing the agricultural landholding declarations of local households in the visitas to the valley that it will become evident how the reducciones and the administrative regime that was instituted in them were, quite literally, negotiated settlements that accommodated longstanding patterns of community organization and land-use patterning, some even pre-dating the Inka occupation. Rather than erasing prehispanic practices, then, reducción and colonial administration was built on and worked through an analogical arrangement that balanced local interest groups and systems of land tenure and production with Spain's royal mandates for tributary extraction and religious conversion.

Improvised Orders in Tawantinsuyu and the Viceroyalty of Peru

In the case of Inka imperialism, the negotiation of the dilemma of analogy or erasure is evident in a spectrum of colonial programs and their relative durability after conquest. As discussed below, these range from the ephemeral, as in the case of many ethnic colonies resettled to remote locales by the state, to the long-lived, as in the case of the basic logic of kin-based obligations of tribute and mutual responsibility.

By 1532, the Inka Empire had expanded to encompass a vast area spanning some 4,000 km from north to south, was home to some 10 million inhabitants divided among scores of ethnically and linguistically distinct polities, and possessed an ecological diversity ranging from the humid tropical rainforest in the east to the alpine zones of the high Andes and the hyper-arid deserts of the Pacific Coast. The great rapidity and scale of Inka imperial expansion is now generally understood to be the result of flexible policies of more or less indirect rule: Outside regional imperial administrative centers, direct involvement of ethnic Inkas from Cuzco was usually limited to high-order administrators who oversaw the levying and collection of labor tribute, the mobilization of which was left largely to local *kurakas* (ethnic lords) (D'Altroy 1992). Imperial realpolitik thus played out through varied measures of coercion and violence, ceremonial commensalism, patronage of local elites, and the subordination of local deities to the state pantheonic religion. Ideally, all within the realm were to be self-reliant, while the political economy functioned by siphoning surplus labor from subject peoples (Murra 1980). Though Tawantinsuyu expanded explosively over just a few generations, by the eve of the Spanish invasion, the process of consolidating rule to a semblance of the colonial order envisioned in Cuzco was very much an ongoing project at various stages of development in different areas of the empire (see, e.g., Salomon 1982).

The logic of rule-by-analogy in Inka imperialism is thus evident: kurakas served as intermediate elites, at once recognized as legitimate local authorities, while the state represented its extractive demands as mere extensions of traditional, kin-based relations of reciprocity (Murra 1980). As a result, the form of imperial administration—and thus the form of the state as it actually manifested in daily life—varied significantly as distinct orders were locally improvised. Heterodoxy was partially mitigated through an ideological program that trumpeted the primacy of the Inka solar deity (Inti) and primary descent of the Inkas from it. This ideology of Inka supremacy, however, found cultural purchase through its common, kin-based logic of legitimacy-by-descent and because the resolution of local and imperial religious practices was not generally eradicative in nature. Rather than extirpating local religious practices, local *huacas* (landscape deities) were resituated within an imperial pantheon, and the Inkas thus laid claim to be the kin—indeed, the ancestors—of their subjects:

> The Inkas spoke the language of kin—kin terms, kin idioms, and kin expectations.... One prospect of their kin-phrased cultural acrobatics was to refashion Andean histories: Lords would project a shared past with the tribute-bearing enclaves under their dominion. The Inkas would attempt to accomplish such historical reconstruction by capturing their subordinates' ideologies of descent, the ideologies that voiced social time and gave human significance to the past. Selecting and reworking those histories—along with the widespread custom of deifying ancestors—Cusco was intent on transforming the familiar into a flatter, novel, imperial fantasy in which kings became kin of those they ruled. (Silverblatt 1988:85)

And so the Inkas contended with the dilemma of analogy or erasure. They tried to naturalize the extraction of tribute through an analogical logic that likened the relationship between subject communities and the state to kinship and its attendant obligations. From a local point of view, the Inkas could be drawn into the mutually obligatory relations of reciprocity: As the Inka received tribute from subject peoples, so they were *responsible* to return the gift. In a fundamental way, then, Inkaic "dominance" depended on its antithesis, the communitarian ethos of kinship. As the logic of kinship enabled extraction, the bonds of autonomous kin groups were strengthened (a point also made by Salomon 1995:327 and Silverblatt 1988:86). As we will see, the Inkaic colonial project in the Colca Valley was structured by the logic and idiom of kinship, as local ayllus were resituated in an intricate though incompletely executed, nested hierarchy according to the same categories of kin reckoning that governed the royal ayllus (*panacas*) of Cuzco.

Of course the Inkas also actively sought to produce regimes of value that made asymmetrical redistribution appear as if it were balanced or even favoring subject communities, thus indebting them to the state. The staging of elaborate, public commensal events was a primary medium through which this trick of imperial ideology was enacted. Several archaeologists have observed how the Inkas masterfully manipulated the built environment to produce stage sets for such events, most fundamentally through the construction of large central plaza spaces and associated great hall structures—common features in Inka settlements (Coben 2006; Hyslop 1990; Moore 1996; Morris 1982; Morris and Thompson 1985). These central complexes were used as staging grounds for elaborate processionals and commensal ritual events in which imperial representatives reified an imperial ideology of state beneficence through the conspicuous redistribution of staple and prestige goods in reciprocity for subjects' loyalty and labor services. The performance of staged commensal ritual was a primary idiom of state-subject relations, as the Inka was presented as a living ancestor-deity, cosmological center, and father-provider to his subject "children" (see, e.g., Bray 2003; Coben 2006; Dillehay 2003; Ramírez 2005). Though the material and labor embodied in the redistributed goods paled by comparison to the labor services provided to the state, such rituals engaged core Andean constructs of personhood and community, defined by varied conceptions of reciprocity between people and between people and animating cosmological forces. These cultural archetypes, enacted in the built forms of these standardized architectonic complexes at Inka provincial centers, imbued standardized built forms throughout the empire with a specific, normative model of state-subject relations. Outside provincial centers, however, such models were more often accommodated to existing settlements, producing improvised built environments of both autochthonous and imperial forms. This was the case in the Colca Valley, where there was no major reorganization of settlement with Inka occupation but state investments were still quite significant. We will see a repeating pattern for accommodating certain Inkaic architectonic spaces to local settlements— especially the great hall and plaza couplet—which I argue was used to enact the ideology of state largesse through commensal events.

The durability of such improvised orders was so basic that it formed the basis for tribute extraction at the local level under Spanish colonial rule as well (see below). As Peter Gose (following Abercrombie 1998) has argued (2008:6–7), the "pact of reciprocity" was the guiding logic by which Andean communities engaged the Spanish: by rendering tribute Andean communities sought to *oblige* the Spanish of their well-being. His diagnosis of the intercultural making and unmaking of Spanish colonialism in the Andes is compelling: "Torn between the expediency of indirect rule and a profound will to reform Andean society, Spanish colonialism never achieved political coherence" (Gose 2008:3). Even taken on its own terms, the Spanish colonial project was built on a contradictory ideological foundation. On the one hand, Spanish colonial power supposedly derived from conquest and was based on an assertion of absolute difference from the colonized, but on the other, the legitimacy of colonial rule was based on conversion to Christianity—it was assimilative. The assimilative goal of conversion was thus contradictory to the assertion of moral superiority. To the extent that conversion occurred, it undercut the grounds that morally distinguished Indians from Spaniards and rationalized conquest and the tributary subjugation of the República de Indios (Gose 2008:10–11).

The exigencies of improvising a new order and the particular form of Andean political engagement with the Spanish in the early years following the invasion further complicated the coherency of colonial rule. As elsewhere in the Spanish Americas, initial colonial rule, when peninsular Spaniards were vastly outnumbered, was a hybrid arrangement that inserted Spanish conquistadores in an analogous structural position to their Inka administrative antecedents, working through paramount ethnic lords to call on their subjects' labor for their own enrichment and the fulfillment of tributary obligations. They functioned as feudal trustees (*encomenderos*) of Crown interests, theoretically responsible for the well-being and conversion of their native charges in exchange for access to their labor. Without an organic basis of authority vis-à-vis local communities, however, encomenderos remained dependent on their partner kurakas to make demands. Ethnic lords had their own interests in such alliances, initially to rid themselves of the burdens of Inka rule but also as a means of forwarding their ethnic interests. Over the long run, however, the legitimacy of kuraka authority was increasingly undercut by their alliances, as encomenderos seldom fulfilled anything resembling reciprocal exchange (in contrast to their Inka-era predecessors, however asymmetrical such exchange may have been) and their role was (rightly) regarded as essentially parasitic (see Spalding 1984:125–35; Stern 1982:28–35). Thus even (or even especially) at the outset, as the Spanish sought to exploit and colonize Andean communities, so they were colonized and the form of their authority was hybridized through its dependency on Andean practices and institutions.

Following the initial period of plunder, civil war, and indirect rule, the comprehensive reforms mandated by Phillip II and enacted by Viceroy Francisco de Toledo were aimed at curbing the excesses and independence of the increasingly belligerent encomendero class, systematizing the collection of tribute, and fostering the conversion of the populace to Catholicism. The centerpiece of the reforms was the reducción program, a massive resettlement project that displaced some 1.5 million native Andeans from their aboriginal settlements to gridded colonial towns. Reshaping the built environment of the peoples of the Indies was considered of paramount importance since the earliest years following the Spanish invasion. The Spanish Crown and colonial policymakers considered the replacement or restructuring of indigenous settlements as the key to creating a new social order. As *urbs* (the built form of the city) was to produce *civitas* (urban community), so too was civitas to produce *policia* (social order) (Kagan 2000:1–39). As Tom Cummins (2002:200) writes,

> Bestowing Christian order on the New World was a royal obligation. Its fulfillment was first a philosophical and then a pragmatic problem. It meant, philosophically, the formation of a civilized community of men, the *consortium hominium*. This was to be achieved, as Anthony Pagden has described, by creating a *civilis societas* of which the *civitas* (the city) was the most natural and perfect community; where the practice of virtue and pursuit of happiness were possible and man could achieve his purpose, his *telos*.

Shedding light on this topic, then, requires analysis of the actual built spaces of reducciones and their precursors, an endeavor undertaken in this study. A handful of important projects have conducted site-level mapping and excavations at reducciones (Quilter et al. 2010; Van Buren et al. 1993), but the antecedents of reducciones—that is, highland settlements dating to the transitional period between the Spanish invasion and the first four decades of colonial rule prior to reducción—remain almost entirely undocumented. Chapter 5 explores this question in detail through analysis of the growth and changing spatial organization of Malata, a well-preserved doctrina in the upper reaches of the Colca. In particular, GIS-based spatial network analysis reveals the ways that local elites may have monitored the individuals living at Malata.

Chapters 6 and 7 carry the analysis forward by analyzing spatial relationships between local reducciones and regional- and local-scale land-use patterns as reconstructed from colonial censuses. These chapters will provide a distinct perspective on this transformative era in colonial history. Often referred to as a historical watershed (Stern 1982:71–79) and even a "steamroller" (Abercrombie 1998:223) that brought many ancient Andean practices and institutions to their definitive end, the Toledan reforms would seem a case of an eradicative colonial project if there ever was one (Gade and Escobar 1982; Hemming 1983:392–410; Málaga Medina 1974; Murra 1972). But chapter 6 explores how they were also deeply *compromised*. They were built on analogies between native and Spanish institutions of economic extraction and political administration. Both sources of state revenue in the Toledan system—tribute levies and *corvée* labor drafts—were to be mediated by ethnic lords with oversight by Spanish magistrates (*corregidores de indios*) such that taxes were levied at the provincial or subprovincial (*repartimiento*) level, but their actual collection throughout Peru was still left to native lords. Both were also modeled on Inka imperial analogs of proportional tribute and rotational labor, but with the crucial difference that taxes were levied in kind or cash, not in labor (Murra 1956). Here again, the assertion of dominance ran up against the practicalities of enacting an extractive program that depended on the vested authorities of native elites, as most Andean communities were not alienated from their means of agricultural and pastoral production (Spalding 1982).

These kinds of compromises extended to the actual emplacement of reducción villages in local landscapes as well. Some were situated atop prior Inkaic administrative centers, thus minimizing disruption and systems of settlement and production. In chapter 7, I show how even in the case of a reducción that was established in a locale that was virtually unoccupied previously (the village of Coporaque), it was emplaced in such a way that balanced indigenous interests and structures of community and land use (which themselves were improvised orders from Inkaic times).

Thus as the Spanish exploited and colonized Andean communities and landscapes, so they were colonized and the form of their authority was transformed by its dependency on Andean practices and institutions. The emplaced perspective of this book opens a view to how colonialism in the Andes was a profoundly two-way relation—more than postcolonial theory, which is premised on a defining frame of colonizer/colonized, would admit.

The Colonization of Community and Landscape in the Colca Valley

An emplaced perspective on the colonization of community and landscape requires concerted engagement between theory and data. Chapter 2 is a sustained exploration of both the central theoretical concepts of the book—community and landscape—and how they are specifically informed by and mobilized through the spatial integration of archaeological and ethnohistorical data sets used in the chapters that follow. Taking a practice-oriented perspective, chapter 2 first explores how each constitutes an emergent *interface* between households and states on one hand, and between communities and their socionatural environments on the other. My approach to the study of ancient communities builds on recent interactionist archaeological approaches that conceive of communities as matrices of social interaction that both create and emerge from a sense of common interest and affiliation (Goldstein

2000, 2005; Isbell 2000; Joyce and Hendon 2000; Yaeger 2000). I approach communities as variably constituted collectivities that are "imagined" (sensu Anderson 1991) and reified through social practice. This approach admits to the importance of patterned social interaction, itself partly a function of the spatial organization of the built environment (Bourdieu 1977), but also recognizes that community is continually negotiated and made anew in daily practice (Giddens 1979). In colonial contexts, the potency of "community" as an ideological and political currency is particularly evident, as colonialist attempts to impose new ideals of community are refracted through local schema and in the process expose formerly unquestioned doxa (Bourdieu 1977) to scrutiny, potentially destabilizing them (Ohnuki-Tierney 1995; Sahlins 1995; Sahlins 1981). I argue that it is in these local, two-way negotiations that new, contested social arrangements emerge.

These points are especially apt in the late prehispanic and early colonial Andes, where the multiscalar, territorially discontinuous, kin-based community formation of ayllu mediated political, economic, and ecological relationships. As a political-ecological interface between households, states, and the environment, ayllus not only articulated the production and exchange of diverse produce from vertically distributed Andean ecological tiers (Murra 1964, 1968, 1972) but also constituted the primary building blocks of empire in both the Inkaic and Spanish colonial states (D'Altroy 1987; Julien 1988; Murra 1980; Pärssinen 1992; Pease G. Y. 1981, 1989; Spalding 1982, 1984; Stern 1982). In contrast to functionalist approaches, which view ayllu organization as an adaptive response to the risks posed by the Andean environment, I conceive of the diverse ecological complementarity practices documented throughout the region as recursively related to the emergent structures of landscape and ayllu organization. My approach to landscape thus draws on recent approaches that highlight how humans not only adapt to but also transform the environments they inhabit (Crumley 1994b; Erickson 1999, 2000; Lentz 2000; Mayer 1985; McGlade 1995) through culturally specific practices (Ashmore and Knapp 1999; Balée 1998; Crumley 1999; Gelles 2000; Knapp and Ashmore 1999; Scarborough 2003; Schama 1995; van de Guchte 1999). In the rest of the book, I present both a long-term view of the transformation of the Colca Valley and a detailed synchronic analysis of how culturally specific practices are shaped by the built environment of landscape, even as they transform, even as they were structured by, the built environment of landscape.

Chapter 3 introduces the land and peoples of the Colca Valley. It first describes the physiography and climate of the valley and region, assessing its risks and endowments for human occupation and agro-pastoral production.

While mindful of the broad parameters that such ecological factors set on human adaptation, I argue that it is the *synergy* between the natural endowments of the valley and the ingenuity of the peoples that dwelled in it that accounts for the remarkable anthropogenic landscape observed there today. Drawing on an extensive body of prior research on the human-engineered landforms in the valley (Brooks 1998; Denevan 1986, 1987, 1988a, 2001; Gelles 1990, 1995, 2000; Guillet 1981, 1987, 1992; Guillet et al. 1995; Malpass 1986, 1987; Malpass and de la Vera Cruz Chávez 1986; Paerregaard 1993; Sandor 1987b, 1988, 1992; Sandor and Eash 1991, 1995; Sandor and Furbee 1996; Shea 1987; Treacy 1989a, 1993, 1994), the extent, types, and chronology of these anthropogenic landscape features are discussed in detail, especially the extensive agricultural terrace and irrigation systems. The chapter then provides an overview of the peoples of the Colca Valley, including an overview of their population sizes and zones of occupation and their political and economic organization. I discuss the place of the Collaguas and Cabanas in Andean historiography, both in colonial demographic research and historical monographs. Lastly, I describe the core documentary corpus used for the ethnohistorical component of the project—a series of unusually detailed colonial visitas spanning the years 1591–1617, part of one of the largest series of colonial visitas for any single locale in the Americas.

The results of my archaeological survey, presented in chapter 4, provide a long-term view of the reproduction and transformation of settlement and landscape organization, setting the stage that both structured and was transformed by interactions among local and colonial actors that become visible in the ethnohistorical portion of the book. The survey registered a suite of changes signaling Collagua and Cabana ethnogenesis during the Late Intermediate period (LIP; AD 1000–1450). Along with a marked growth in population, the appearance of distinctive local architectural and ceramic styles suggests an overarching unity of ethnic identity, but the settlement pattern and landscape data from the survey also reveal how autonomous political organization was segmentary in nature, oscillating between coordination and competition. On the one hand, analysis of hydrological relationships between canals that carry water to terrace complexes surrounding settlements illustrates that water apportionment was coordinated at a supra-settlement scale. On the other hand, frequent violent conflict within the valley during the LIP is also apparent in defensive site locations and hilltop fortifications. Thus I argue that varied scales and dimensions of "community" were salient in different contexts—ranging from micro-scale of settlement and mortuary cult to varied hydraulic communities (likely in conflict with each other) and, probably in a mostly latent sense, in an overarching sense of common ethnic affiliation.

Indeed, one of the contexts in which the highest order of local community identification and their associated boundaries—the ethnicities of "Collagua" and "Cabana"—likely would have been most salient was in engagements with aggressive outside peoples, such as Inka imperial agents and their backing forces. As appears to be a general outcome of Inka imperial politics, I argue that ethnic identities hardened through such initial imperial encounters and more or less stable hierarchical political structures emerged over the course of the Inkaic occupation. Changes in settlement patterning during the Inka occupation of the Late Horizon (AD 1450–1532) reflect local processes of negotiation by which communities were integrated within a centralized but locally coordinated form of imperial administration.

Most LIP settlements continued to be occupied during the Late Horizon (LH), but the Inkas established a primary administrative center in each of the three provincial subdivisions (Yanquecollaguas, Laricollaguas, and Cabanaconde; see Figure 1.1), either in the same locations of what later became the eponymous reducciones or adjacent to it (in the case of Cabanaconde). My analysis of local settlement plans also shows that Inka rule was mediated by local elites through an idiom of state-sponsored commensalist ritual at formerly dominant Collagua settlements. The stamp of Inka administration at these secondary administrative centers is evident in the prominent placement of great hall structures alongside central plaza spaces.

Such hybridization of site layouts continues into early colonial times. The Spanish invasion was locally marked not so much by the belligerent presence of conquistador as by a handful of mendicant friars, as the Colca Valley was one of the earliest locales of Franciscan intervention in the southern highlands. In chapter 5, analysis of archival evidence regarding the early Franciscan presence in the valley and documentation of rustic chapels alongside Inkaic plazas and great hall structures reveals how the first friars to enter the valley recognized and mapped onto these spaces of state integration. The logic of evangelization by analogy is thus evident: Friars appear to have leveraged assent to conversion through spatial analogies that linked the Inkaic architectonic unit of great hall/plaza to the Spanish counterparts of chapel/atrium and plaza. A more nuanced view of the manipulation and use of space within one of these doctrinas is provided through analysis of data obtained from extensive mapping and excavations at the Late Horizon and early colonial site of Malata, located in the upper reaches of the valley. There, the excellent architectural preservation afforded detailed registry of the site layout, which in turn permitted reconstruction of the growth and extensive remodeling of the site during its short use life as a doctrina. This growth and remodeling included the construction of a formal atrium around the chapel, a central plaza and public building, along with the introduction of new neighborhoods and new house forms, signaling an incipient form of settlement consolidation that prefigures the more radical displacements of the Toledan reducción. GIS-based spatial network analysis simulating movement through the doctrina shows how foot traffic was specifically rerouted away from its small Inkaic great hall structure and its associated plaza to literally form a processional past the likely house of the kuraka and through the single entry into the plaza and chapel beyond. There is thus significant evidence for surveillance in the funneling of traffic through the doctrina to its plaza and chapel. The *intent* to monitor and regulate ritual practice through such reshaping of the built environment is thus evident. On the other hand, as I will argue, the *effectiveness* of these changes is less clear but surely not as total as intended, since they must have depended at least in part on their congruence and resonance with cognate prehispanic spaces and practices that were present in the same settlement.

Following this early colonial conjuncture, the local populace was forcibly resettled into a series of reducción villages during Francisco de Toledo's general tour of the viceroyalty in the 1570s. Rather than a strictly eradicative project, chapter 6 reveals how reducción was instead locally experienced as a complex process of two-way "structural grafting" by which reducciones mapped onto extant centers of Inka power and regional networks of ayllu affiliation and exchange remained intact. In chapter 6, analysis of the over 8,000 agricultural fields registered in the visitas from 1591, 1604, and 1615–17 reconstructs how local households maintained access to diverse agricultural fields and livestock in far-flung locales while local elites in Yanque continued to articulate supra-local networks of ayllu authority and exchange of Inkaic and pre-Inkaic origin.

The naming patterns of the ayllus registered in the visitas also reveal how the Inkas sought to reorganize the Collagua Province. Dualism was expressed by ranked moieties, Hanansaya (upper) and Urinsaya (lower), each of which was composed of several ranked ayllus. However, ayllu naming patterns within each of these moieties reveal that Inka attempts at reorganizing local community organization in the image of imperial ideals was unevenly achieved. While the names of the ayllus of the lower-ranking Urinsaya moiety conform exactly to Inkaic tripartite rank and decimal administrative nomenclature, the names of the ayllus of the upper moiety maintained local Aymara terms that suggest an underlying dualistic organization based on a directional "left/right" logic (a common dualistic principle among Aymara groups; Platt 1986).

In chapter 7, my GIS-based reconstruction of ayllu land-tenure patterns from the visita landholding declarations reveals the actual spatial expression of this dualistic ayllu structure, showing how it articulated with Inkaic and

Spanish attempts at imposing new forms of community organization. In this analysis, I show that the field constellations of the autochthonous "left"- and "right"-side ayllus were concentrated on opposite sides of a prominent hydrological divide that separated local irrigation networks. This ravine also bifurcates the reducción of Coporaque itself. That is, the reducción is located precisely on the dividing line between the two systems of autochthonous land tenure and irrigation, revealing a process of negotiation by which Spanish administrators adapted this bounded construct of community to local dualistic organization. By contrast, the land-tenure patterns of the Inka-engineered ayllus were much more widely dispersed on either side of this divide, signaling a contrasting form of state-directed rationalization aimed at dispersing hydraulic and agricultural interests. Through statistical exploration of spatial relationships between these ayllu land-tenure patterns and the archaeological settlement pattern, I also reconstruct where the majority of the ancestral populations of each ayllu resided prior to reducción resettlement. This analysis indicates that the left- and right-side Collagua ayllus resided at two of the largest settlements with local elite and Inka architecture, while those of the Inka-engineered ayllus of the upper moiety were dispersed throughout settlements on both sides of the local divide.

This reconstruction therefore reveals common processes of negotiation between local ayllus and distinct imperial ideals of community differentially articulated. On the one hand, it illustrates how, in Andean terms, Inka administration both mapped onto extant community organization while simultaneously grafting a state-ordered system aimed at dispersing settlement, agricultural, and hydraulic interests. On the other hand, it shows how the reducciones were not built upon, and could not effect, a tabula rasa in the local landscape but, rather, involved highly localized negotiations between colonial administrators and local interest groups. By placing Inkaic and Spanish attempts at rationalizing ayllu organization toward state ends within a comparative framework, this book provides a unique window into how local communities engaged these contrasting modes of colonialism, advancing toward a unified historical-anthropological paradigm that transcends the boundaries created by the narrative of conquest. This perspective identifies and locates a dialectic of social change in colonial encounters that is significantly different from conventional frameworks based on reactive, oppositional relations of domination and resistance.

Resisting the Dominance of Resistance

Striving for this kind of emplaced account is motivated in part by a conscious effort to confront the logic of the conquest narrative. Indeed, "conquest" is one of those tropes of Western historiography that is so ingrained that even attempts to write against it are structured by its logic (see Lamana 2008; Restall 2003). The narrative of conquest (whether Inkaic or Spanish) assumes the protagonist position of "conqueror"—the historical actor of initiative—while the "conquered" is relegated to acquiescence, accommodation, flight, and resistance. Thus even as resistance frameworks aimed to open up more analytical space to the agency of the colonized, they largely reduced that agency to a dyadic, conflictive, and, at base, *reactive* role (Brown 1996; Hollander and Einwohner 2004; Liebmann and Murphy 2011; Ortner 1995; Wernke 2007b). This is no less true as varieties of resistance frameworks have proliferated to include "everyday forms" (Scott 1985, 1990) and as its counterpoised force, "domination," has been similarly traced out in its "capillary forms" and seems to lurk everywhere in social relations (Foucault 1978). What has resulted, as Sherry Ortner points out (1995:176–77), is a thinning of ethnographic description, as the complexities of daily practice and politics are obscured by the black box of resistance and agents become "resistors":

> If we are to recognize that resistors are doing more than simply opposing domination, more than simply producing a virtually mechanical *re*-action, then we must go the whole way. They have their *own* politics—not just between chiefs and commoners or landlords and peasants but within all the local categories of friction and tension.

Elucidating "all the local categories of friction and tension" is beyond the scope of this study (and is probably a presumptuous claim for any study to make), but the constitution and reproduction of community and landscape are certainly important dimensions of such friction and tension—of the resistance of culture. A thick, emplaced description and systematic analysis of the constitution and transformation of community and landscape under Inka and Spanish colonial rule can thus provide an empirical basis for overcoming the binary oppositions of dominant/subordinate, self/other, superior/inferior that define the contours of much scholarship of colonial encounters. The following chapter discusses my approach to community and landscape, and how these theoretical concepts are mobilized in a spatially integrated archaeological and ethnohistorical framework.

2

SITUATING COMMUNITY AND LANDSCAPE

In the introduction, I advocated a perspective on colonial rule as an improvised order that emerges from the everyday engagements that colonial projects require, and I argued that community and landscape constitute two primary cultural interfaces through which these collusions are negotiated. This chapter situates these concepts in three ways. Each is first defined and developed in dialogue with broader theoretical literatures of community and landscape. This discussion builds toward a practice-oriented approach that focuses on the recursive relationships between what people do on a day-to-day basis and the schema and resources that emerge from and structure those practices. Second, each is situated within the context of the late prehispanic and early colonial Andean highlands and, third, within the specific context of the Colca Valley. Since an emplaced perspective is central to the study, the chapter closes with a discussion of the spatial analytic framework used in the chapters that follow.

Community as Interface

It would seem that such an intuitively important unit of social organization as "community" would have been the object of sustained scrutiny among archaeologists, but perhaps because of its seemingly self-evident status as a social fact, community until recently had remained undertheorized, usually coinciding with the "site" (Kolb and Snead 1997). Recent debate (both within archaeology and the ethnographic literature) has made such unspoken assumptions untenable, opening doors to new modes of analysis. The debate over community has wide implications because in many ways it reflects on broader debates over the ontological and epistemological status of culture as an object and construct of anthropological knowledge. As the culture concept—especially as an orderly, shared, enduring system—was subjected to sustained interrogation through the 1980s and 1990s, culture came to be viewed as ever-emergent and contingent on the continuous negotiation of power. In similar fashion, theories of community as the "natural," taken-for-granted, and harmonious supra-household unit of social reproduction have undergone intense scrutiny.

But behaviorist approaches to community still remain widely influential within archaeology, both on theoretical and methodological grounds. Much as in the case of "chiefdoms" (see Whitehead 1998a), a preoccupation with the supposed limits of archaeological data—particularly with correlates, units, and scales appropriate to "community"—has tended to shape research frameworks. Although those approaches contributed much to rigorous methodologies, they have left the concept of community itself underdeveloped— as simply a behavioral outcome of habituated interaction. That is, the "quality of distinctiveness" (Redfield 1955, as cited in Kolb and Snead 1997:611) of community identity is often considered epiphenomenal to conditioned behavior—to the everyday interactions of living and laboring in a bounded and defined space (for critique, see Isbell 2000; Wolf 1956). Such approaches consider community as the "natural," fundamental unit of supra-household social and biological reproduction, produced by co-residence, proximity, and shared economic/ecological praxis (e.g., Murdock 1949; Redfield 1955, 1956). Some archaeologists have recently advocated this framework as the most pragmatic and testable approach to reconstructing and comparing prehistoric community organization (Kolb and Snead 1997; Peterson and Drennan 2005). But to say that "our focus here is on behavior, not beliefs" in the archaeological study of community organization (Peterson and Drennan 2005:5) is to assume that the two can be examined as separate variables—an assumption hardly warranted in light of five decades of practice theory and its exploration of the recursive relationships between practice, beliefs, subjectivity, and social forces.

My approach builds on practice-oriented frameworks, which posit that communities are socially constructed arrangements that structure and are structured by supra-household interactions (for a review of this and other approaches, see Yaeger and Canuto 2000). A practice-based approach requires an empirically robust foundation of systematically collected data. Like behaviorist approaches, it is fundamentally empirical because its objects of analysis are what people *do* and how they do it (Pauketat 2001). The difference is that practice theory does not assert what people do is only a conditioned response but is, rather, a negotiated outcome between agents and the structures that enable and constrain their actions. I thus conceive of communities as emergent matrices of social interaction that both create and emerge from a sense of common interest and affiliation—a sense of shared identity. In this sense, community can be seen as a primary sociocultural interface, whether at the scale of daily practice of interacting households or the less frequent (but often ideologically freighted) collective actions of larger affiliations. As such, it was a key interface for the improvisation of colonial order. Clearly, proximity and co-residence affect the patterning and frequency of interaction between social actors and groups, and community identity often is expressed in the idiom of settlement, neighborhood, or territory. But even as patterns of daily interaction enmesh social actors in structures that constrain the parameters of imagination and action (Bourdieu 1977), they provide the rudiments with which agents can question, contest, and alter those structures (Giddens 1979).

A discussion of what is meant by "structure" will be useful as a general framing for understanding communities as emergent matrices of interaction and identity. My approach to structures and their relation to practice is significantly influenced by Sewell's revision of Giddens's theory of structuration (Giddens 1979), which begins with the principle of the "duality of structure," that structures are both the medium and outcome of practice. That is, structures shape practice—in both constraining and enabling ways—even as culturally knowledgeable agents recursively instantiate and reproduce structures in social practice. What Sewell contributes is a more explicit theorization of materiality and power in structuration. For Sewell, "structures" themselves are constituted by another recursive relationship—that between "schema" and "resources." Schemas are (following Giddens) "generalizable procedures applied in the enactment/reproduction of social life" (Sewell 2005:131). Such schemas, such as social etiquette, routinized gender relations, aesthetic norms, or more general categorical associations (female and male, light and dark, private and public) are generalizable because they are (at least potentially) transposable across different domains and situations and thus are also potentially generative of new structures and social relations. Resources, on the other hand, critically introduce materiality and more explicit theorization of power in structuration. Sewell divides resources between "human" and "nonhuman" types: "Nonhuman resources are objects, animate or inanimate, naturally occurring or manufactured, that can be used to enhance or maintain power; human resources are physical strength, dexterity, knowledge, and emotional commitments that can be used to enhance or maintain power, including knowledge of the means of gaining, retaining, controlling, and propagating either human or nonhuman resources" (Sewell 2005:133). To this, I would add that the categories and boundaries (and their porosities) of human/nonhuman and subject/object vary relative to culturally specific ontologies (whether unspoken or as "semiotic ideologies"; see Keane 2003, 2007) and should not be assumed to be self-evident. Conversely, the sheer physical properties of material things (and the distinctive qualities of different material things) set certain parameters on their uses and potential as resources (Ingold 1993).

The division between schema and resources brings analytical precision, then, but it bears emphasis that *in practice*, each is an effect of the other; they are not related in linear fashion but recursively, as structure is to practice. Even so, the schema/resources formulation of structure runs the risk of reproducing the ancient division between "spirit" and "matter" or the "idealist" and "materialist" approaches that it seeks to resolve. The emergent, recursively constitutive aspect of the schema/resources of structures therefore must remain at the center of attention (Keane 2003, 2007). As Sewell notes, "Nonhuman resources have a material existence that is not reducible to rules or schemas, but the activation of material things as resources, the determination of their value and social power, is dependent on the cultural schemas that inform their social use" (Sewell 2005:135). Whether portable artifacts (Appadurai 1986; Kopytoff 1986), buildings (Gieryn 2002), or features in a landscape (Ingold 1993), material things at once stabilize and provide the potential for novel schema to emerge. This is because for a sign to function socially, it must be instantiated (whether linguistically or materially) and provided with instructions (Keane 2003, 2007). Thus a platform with a cross placed in the center of a plaza materializes doctrinal teachings. In practice, however, such an embodied sign can never only have one meaning or quality, especially in a colonial context, where outwardly similar material arrangements (plazas and central platforms in plazas were also key features in Inka settlement planning) can be apprehended through schema not of the colonizer's making. So words and things—the meanings and qualities of materialized signs—inevitably take on different valences and become bound to other qualities, a process Keane (2003:410) terms "bundling." Embodied signs thus necessarily become subjected to and implicated in historical dynamics. Moreover, when signs are materialized, their very materiality ensures their embeddedness "in subsequent presents" (to paraphrase Olivier 2004:206)—presents in which they are variously salient, meaningful, and effective. Thus rather than a process by which power is orchestrated by elites, as some models of materialization have emphasized (DeMarrais et al. 1996), materialization as conceived here is the process by which schemas are constrained, maintained, and potentially destabilized.

"Community," then, is a structural interface—between schema and resources and between structure and practice. Communities are symbolically constructed and "imagined" (sensu Anderson 1991). Communities can be composed of individuals who do not frequently interact or even know one another but nonetheless share a deep sense of affiliation and common interest (Anderson 1991). As in other dimensions of identity, community is a two-sided coin, entailing solidarity and exclusivity (Cohen 1985). The sense of solidarity in communities emerges from discourses and "practices of affiliation" (Yaeger 2000), which reify and manifest within-group commonalities and interests. Different practices of affiliation can be seen to predominate at (but are not exclusive to) different scales of community affiliation. Daily practices of domestic life at the scale of neighborhood or settlement forge common quotidian interests and constitute a powerful, yet often unspoken and taken-for-granted, sense of commonality. Multisettlement communities predominantly emerge from collective projects, discourses, and rituals of affiliation. Each is integral to the other, but even as local-scale communities also actively construct a sense of belonging (and thus also have important "imagined" dimensions; see Isbell 2000), the practices of affiliation of supra-local communities can become hegemonic and therefore less open to reflexive monitoring (as in the habitus of the local community). Indeed, the romance of community can be seen as a potentially powerful ideological currency in polity formation and in the emergence and maintenance of ethnic identities (Joseph 2002; Pauketat 2000). That said, the cohesive, "public face" of community always masks conflicting interests and discourses (Cohen 1985:70–75).

The other side of the identity coin—exclusivity, or what might be called the "marks of distinction"—is also at least implicit (and often explicit or predominant) in practices of affiliation (Barth 1969; Cohen 1985). Marks of distinction demarcate where "we" end and "they" begin. Instances such as intercommunity boundary marking, litigation, and violent conflict are obvious such examples, but boundaries are integral to affiliative practices and markers as well, such as dress (Femenias 2005), bodily adornment and modification (Blom 2005; Knudson and Stojanowski 2009; Sofaer 2006), cuisine (Bray 2003; Fischler 1988), and domestic architecture (Aldenderfer 1993; Bawden 1982; Bourdieu 1973; Gillespie 2000; Goldstein 1993; Joyce and Gillespie 2000; Stanish 1989a, 1989b; Whitridge 2004). In sum, as a dynamic process of social identity, "community" need not be associated with any particular socio-spatial scale or unit; communities are just as likely to cut across spatial boundaries as to adhere to them (Goldstein 2000).

The Andean Ayllu

Such a flexible, dynamic conception of community is entirely befitting of the

Andean context. Ever since the early years following the European invasion (Polo de Ondegardo 1917 [1571]), students of Andean communities have recognized their supra-local, "archipelagic" patterns of residence, production, and exchange (Murra 1964, 1968, 1972). The ayllu was central to the social, political, and economic articulation of territorially discontinuous communities in the Andes (Abercrombie 1986; Cock Carrasco 1981; Isbell 1997; Platt 1982; Salomon 1991; Spalding 1984). *Ayllu,* commonly translated as "clan," was emically defined as a multiscalar concept that could reference any segment along a continuum of socially or biologically related collectivities, from the consanguines of a patrilineage, to clan-like groupings of patrilineages, moieties, and even an entire ethnic group. For example, Platt (1986) has illustrated how the modern-day Macha of Bolivia conceive of ayllus in a nested fashion, from "minimal" ayllus of small patrilocal groups of neighboring households to "minor" and "major" ayllus made up of groups of related ayllus and a "maximal" ayllu encompassing the ethnic group as a whole. The scalar plasticity of the concept has led to a plethora of definitions that emphasize different aspects of ayllu membership and organization (for reviews of definitions, see Goldstein 2000:184–86; Isbell 1997:101–35; Salomon 1991:21–23; Spalding 1984:28–29). Common to all, however, are two attributes: Ayllus are resource-holding corporate collectivities and ayllu membership is reckoned by reference to an actual or fictive focal ancestor.

As resource-holding collectivities, ayllus mediated households' access to agricultural land and other immovable assets (Patterson and Gailey 1987; Rowe 1946a; Salomon 1991:22). While ayllus held these resources as corporate entities, ayllu members gained access to land and other resources in reciprocity for their labor in collective work projects (e.g., canal cleaning, terrace construction and maintenance) and their participation in rituals of affiliation, including ancestor veneration (see below). However, ayllu landholdings were not always spatially discrete, and in this sense they were not necessarily conceived of as bounded units (Murra 1980:30–31). Ayllus of different scales of inclusiveness organized agro-pastoral infrastructural systems and the labor to construct and maintain them, from the daily interactions of cultivation, terrace maintenance, and the distribution of irrigation water to larger-scale mobilizations such as canal construction and cleaning (Gelles 1993, 1995, 2000; Guillet 1978, 1981, 1992; Mitchell 1976; Sherbondy 1982; Treacy 1989b). Like their land-tenure patterns, ayllus were not residentially discrete; ayllus could not only occupy several vertically and horizontally dispersed settlements, but members of several ayllus could also share single settlements. For example, early colonial native testimony from Huarochirí Province indicates that prehispanic settlements were composed of multiple ayllus (Salomon

1991:23–24). Also, the protohistoric Andean concept of settlement, or *llacta*, did not necessarily coincide with a nucleated settlement but appears instead to have encapsulated a huaca (an ancestrally related shrine or landscape feature), its territory, and the people within it (Salomon 1991:23–24). Thus even the concept of "settlement" in the late prehispanic Andes was not necessarily considered a territorially discrete cluster of houses.

As ancestor-focused kindreds, ayllu affiliation was reckoned by reference to a pointillist landscape of ancestral huacas that were hierarchically related in space and time. As Goldstein (2000:185) notes,

> Even those aspects of ayllu identity that explicitly refer to place refer not to spatial boundaries, but to the huacas that link an ayllu to its ancestors. . . . This association of ancestor worship to group identity suggests that as a community form, the ayllu is more genealogical than territorial in nature—it is bounded by history rather than borders.

Members of minimal ayllus traced their affiliation by reference to a focal, chartering ancestor, usually embodied in the actual mummified corpse of that individual. The criteria used in the actual reckoning of inclusion is a perennial topic of debate in Andean anthropology, but in practice, the precise genealogical relationship appears to have been of less importance in the reckoning of ayllu membership than a person's social conduct and political standing as a genealogically connected individual (Salomon 1991:22; Spalding 1984:28–29). Ayllu members reaffirmed and reified their community affiliations by consulting and feting their ancestral mummies, who occupied "cities of the dead"—clusters of above-ground, multiple-interment mortuary monuments ("houses of the dead," or *chullpas* in modern archaeological parlance), often situated on prominent hilltops or under cliffs near settlements (see Dillehay 1995; Isbell 1997). Such ancestral mummies were also considered huacas (Salomon 1995). As such, they were reckoned as proximal descendants in a hierarchy of superhuman huacas—each the guardian of fertility in its domain, and each increasingly remote, both spatially and in terms of kinship reckoning—terminating at its apex in the origin place ("place of dawning," or *paqarina*) of an entire ethnic group, usually a prominent mountain peak (Salomon 1991; Spalding 1984).

As political entities, I argue that the ayllu represents an example of heterarchical organization, in which "each element possesses the potential of being unranked (relative to other elements) or ranked in a number of different ways" (Crumley 1979:144). Heterarchical organization is based on lateral connections between elements in an organization, each of which can take a more dominant role depending on the circumstances. By contrast, hierarchical organization is based on the vertical integration of elements of fixed rank. Examples of complex, orderly, heterarchical systems abound in nature, including the neural network of the human brain and the "patchiness" of plant and animal communities such as in the case of the ecological tiers of the Andes. Hierarchy represents only a specific kind or state of heterarchical organization and in this sense is a more restricted concept (Crumley 1979:145). Crumley (1975, 1979, 1987; Ehrenreich et al. 1995) has proposed that heterarchy provides an important alternative metaphor and model for the comparative and diachronic study of social complexity, which has long been conflated with hierarchy. Thus, rather than charting the presence, absence, or degree of complexity of a social system by reference only to its degree and strength of vertical integration, the concept of heterarchy provides a more three-dimensional perspective that also accounts for flexible, horizontal integration between social groups that can be variously ranked according to historical circumstances.

Testimony in early colonial texts indicates that the ethnic polities subsumed by Inka administration were self-defined as bundles of rival ayllus of fluid prestige, rank, and wealth (see, e.g., Duviols 1973; Rostworowski de Diez Canseco 1983). The political organization of protohistoric ayllus, as well as inter-ayllu power relations, were governed according to both ascribed and achieved criteria of rank. The huacas of clan-level ayllus generally were conceived of as siblings born of a paqarina. For example, as we know from the Huarochirí testimony, the origin huacas of clan-like ayllu sets often were ranked according to their birth order from the apical huaca in the ethnic charter myth. According to this ideology, the "firstborn or leading member of a set (e.g., noble heads of a village's component ayllus) functions within the set as first among equals, but outside the set as the totalizing representative of it" (Salomon 1991:20). In this way, native lords (kurakas), as ayllu representatives, could also be ranked according to an ideal social structure derived from the relative birth-order position of their respective huacas. However, crosscutting these ideal-typical criteria of genealogical rank, individuals and ayllus could also achieve higher status through supremacy in warfare. The thousands of Late Intermediate period hilltop fortifications (*pukaras*) throughout the central and south-central Andes strongly indicate that both intra- and inter-ethnic conflict was endemic prior to Inka consolidation. For example, the distribution of pukaras in the northwestern Lake Titicaca basin indicates that the Qolla and Lupaqa—two major ethnic polities with populations of nearly 100,000 people—were much more politically decentralized (i.e., heterarchical) prior to Inka incorporation than their leaders' early colonial memorial accounts depicted (Arkush 2010; Stanish 1997a, 2003:209–20). Indeed, their coherence as political entities may have been most salient primarily when they were faced with a common external threat such as the Inka army (Arkush 2010; Stanish 2003:209–20). Such macro-scale hierarchical political organization appears to have been rather exceptional and ephemeral in the Andean highlands during the LIP.

Elite manipulation of ayllu ideology—most elaborated by the Inka—involved the representation of asymmetrical, hierarchical relationships within and between clan-like and maximal ayllus in the same terms as the lateral, symmetrical links between consanguines of lineage-like micro-ayllus (Murra 1956, 1980). Following in the substantivist tradition of Murra (see La Lone 1982), archaeologists and ethnohistorians have demonstrated how Inka strategies of expansion and consolidation were so successful in part because they manipulated key cultural principles and practices familiar to their subjects, such as vertical complementarity as a logistical system for articulating populations and resources (see Masuda et al. 1985), conspicuous public feasting as a primary forum for displaying state largesse (e.g., Morris and Thompson 1985), and ancestor veneration as a primary idiom of political discourse (e.g., Rostworowski de Diez Canseco 1983).

Clearly, ayllus constituted the primary building blocks of imperial administration, and Inka statecraft relied heavily on the representation of state/subject relations as an extension of ayllu relations. However, in effect, Inka policies also significantly altered intra- and inter-ayllu relations, and fomented the formation of new imagined communities of the state. The Inkas sought to build stable, hierarchical structures of governance out of heterarchically organized ayllus by amplifying and codifying latent or extant rank differences and its means of attainment while preserving the corporate character of the ayllu itself. In Cuzco, the royal ayllus (panacas) sealed off achieved status as a criterion of rank, and membership rank was narrowly defined according to bilateral reckoning (Julien 2000; Zuidema 1977). In the provinces, imperial administration submerged local differences as some ethnic groups and elites were promoted in status. As a result of Inkaic consolidation and centralization, the authority and domains of pliant ethnic elites expanded greatly under Inka rule. The process of consolidating competing ethnic polities into vertically integrated provincial units has been demonstrated in many cases, from the northern provinces of Pichincha and Imbabura in modern Ecuador (Salomon 1986) to Cajamarca Province of northern Peru (Julien 1993), the Wankas and Xauxas of the Mantaro Valley in the central Peruvian Andes (Costin and Earle 1989; D'Altroy 1987, 1992), and the Qolla and Lupaqa of the Titicaca basin (Hyslop 1976; Julien 1983; Lumbreras 1974a; Stanish 1997b), to name a few.

In chapter 4, I illustrate in detail how the autonomous, heterarchical communities of the Collagua ethnic polity of the LIP were partially reordered under Inka imperial occupation according to a formal hierarchy structured in the image of Inka ideals. As we will see through spatial analysis of the visitas to the valley, the improvised order that resulted left partially intact autochthonous structures of community organization, which were subsumed under an encompassing moiety organization. As subsequent chapters explore, even after Toledan reducción resettlement, autochthonous ayllus within the Hanansaya moiety maintained distinct patterns of land use from the ayllus of Urinsaya, findings that take on more significance when considering the spatial relationships between these distinct patterns and the late prehispanic settlement pattern in the same area. Both the Inkas and the Spanish attempted to institute rationalized models of ayllu-based community organization, though, as will be demonstrated, according to ideals of settlement and land use which were radically different.

Landscape as Interface

Understanding diachronic relationships between communities and landscapes requires analytical frameworks that can account for both constrictive, limiting processes and constructive, generative ones. Recent approaches are working in this direction, as the reactive, one-way causality implicit in the concept of "adaptation" has been challenged by models of "interpenetrating," "dialectic," and "recursive" relationships between humans and their environment. Under various rubrics, such as political ecology (e.g., Bryant 1992; Zimmerer 2000), historical ecology (e.g., Balée 1998; Balée and Erickson 2006; Crumley 1994a; Kirch and Hunt 1997; Patterson 1994), and landscape archaeology (e.g., Bender 1992; Crumley 1999; Erickson 2000; Knapp and Ashmore 1999; David Lewis Lentz 2000; McGlade 1995; Rossignol and Wandsnider 1992; Treacy 1994; Wagstaff 1987), recent formulations are collectively changing underlying assumptions regarding human/habitat relationships as dynamic disequilibrium has come into favor as a guiding principal over homeostatic balance (Botkin 1990). Simultaneously, a shift toward understanding landscapes as historically contingent and anthropogenic has highlighted the shortcomings of the nature:culture dyad still prevalent in the literature, which reduces explanations of landscape dynamics to a comparison of the causal forces of natural versus cultural systems of activity. The inadequacy of this ecology:economy opposition, however expressed, becomes especially apparent when considering that both terms derive from the Greek term for "household/habitat" οικοσ (oikos), a fact that points toward an alternative approach that considers human *synergy* with the environment as the dynamic process at the interface between nature and culture (Whitehead 1998b).

The paradoxes that arise from this economic/ecological ambiguity are especially apparent in the Andean region. Discussion of human/environment relationships in the Andes has been dominated by the ecological complementarity model of Murra (1964, 1968, 1972), which posits that the altitudinally compressed ecological zonation of the Andes required societies of varying scale and complexity to adopt mechanisms of access to a sufficiently diverse resource base. Rather than relying on trade with outside groups or centralized markets, the uniquely Andean solution, according to Murra, was the direct colonization of multiple ecological tiers by a single ethnic group, forming a "vertical archipelago" of settlements linked through intra-ethnic reciprocal and redistributive exchange (Murra 1972). Thus the "maximum control of ecological tiers" came to be viewed by many as a pan-Andean cultural ideal of balancing resources and demography, differentially achieved through space and time. The development of asymmetrical systems of redistribution was treated as epiphenomenal to the adaptive process of securing ecologically diverse resources (see Van Buren 1993; Van Buren 1996).

However, both the ecological and political-economic aspects of the verticality model have come under increasingly critical scrutiny. Ecological anthropologists and geographers have noted that the construction of stable and secure production systems in the Andes is predicated on a simplification of highly localized ecological variability by humans (Brush 1977:9). Humans transform ecological gradients into "ecological tiers" (Erickson 2000; Zimmerer 1999), themselves composed of smaller anthropogenic "production zones" (Mayer 1985) created through human interventions such as irrigation, augmentation of soils, and alteration of microclimates. These observations require that a more dynamic view be developed that is mindful of the ways in which the landscape itself is altered by humans so as to lessen ecological strictures. As Mayer (1985:47) observes,

> When we think of production zones as man-made things, rather than as "adaptations" to the natural environment, our attention is directed to how they are created, managed, and maintained. Then the importance of the political aspects of control by human beings over each other in relation to how they are to use a portion of their natural environment will again come to the fore.

Recent researchers have indeed emphasized the "political aspects of control" inherent in vertical complementarity. Archaeological investigations of the prototypical case study of a vertical archipelago system—that of the Lupaqas of the Titicaca basin—have found that the outlier Lupaqa settlements in the lowland valleys of Moquegua were not of the great antiquity hypothesized (Stanish 1985, 1989a, 1989b, 1992) and probably never functioned to provision whole populations (Van Buren 1993, 1996, 1997). Building on these findings, Van Buren has presented a general critique of the verticality model as overly functionalist and essentialist, suggesting instead that vertical complementarity is better viewed as a dimension of social power, that is, as a mobilization of labor and material by ethnic lords toward specific political ends (Van Buren 1993, 1996).

I propose a bridging position that approaches the dynamics of land use and sociopolitical change as complex, multicausal processes both constructed culturally and constricted ecologically. I explore human/environment synergistic processes through a theoretical framework that posits a recursive relationship between a particular, Andean oikos—that of the late prehispanic and early colonial Colca Valley and surrounding region—and the ecological and economic practices of the members of local Collagua communities. Rather than documenting the formal attributes of a vertical complementarity system as a social "formation" or "structure," the processual variability of land-use practices is of primary interest. Within this formulation, ecological and economic practices are structured by, while also constituting through their aggregate effects, the household/habitat of oikos. This approach therefore conceptualizes complementarity as a particular kind of *agency*, related recursively to the *structures* of landscape and community organization.

Analysis at several temporal and spatial scales is required to understand the historical and spatial relationships between built landscapes and the communities that alter and adapt to them. Diachronically, the construction of built features, such as canals, terrace complexes, anthropogenic soil regimes, and so on, is an aggregative process that alters the physical and energetic parameters of production at varying rates and scales, depending on historical circumstances. Synchronically, anthropogenic landscape features constitute the "congealed labor" (Lansing 1991:12) or "landesque capital" (Blaikie and Brookfield 1987:9–10) that structure production. While political change—as in the case of the Inka and Spanish conquests of the Andean region—can occur over short ("event-" and "conjuncture-" level) time spans, landscape-scale infrastructures are generally designed to be durable and stable (Braudel 1972). Systems of production *qua* systems are organized to produce reliable returns on given inputs of labor and material and in this sense are inherently conservative in nature. These contrasting temporal rhythms of political and economic-ecological change therefore produce a dialectic from which new social formations emerge. Thus built landscapes have tangible effects that both constrain and present opportunities for economic and ecological praxis. In order to understand these varied scales of spatial and temporal interaction, this book combines analysis of long-term changes in the built landscape of the Colca Valley, with a shorter-term view of regional and local-scale patterns of production and exchange during early colonial times.

Space, Place, and Spatialized Imaginaries

In a more general sense, the dichotomy between economy and ecology runs parallel with the well-established anthropological and cultural-geographical literature of "place" founded on a distinction between *space* as abstract, quantifiable, measured aspects of spatial dimension and form and *place* as "meaningful space," a subjective (and intersubjective), qualitative, and ever-emergent effect of perceiving, interacting, and dwelling that imbues space with significance (e.g., Bender 1993; Ingold 2000; Low and Lawrence-Zúñiga 2003; Pred 1984a, 1984b; Soja 1989; Tilley 1994; Tuan 1977). The distinction has been beneficial to spatial thinking: Place-based research, often under the rubric of landscape, has highlighted how discourses and practices involved in the inscription and gathering of meaning, historicity, and power in locations inhere to social practice in complex ways that escape spatial measures of distance, volume, topography, and so on.

But as pointed out by Peter Whitridge (2004), the stark space/place theoretical dichotomy that has hardened in the literature is insensitive to how spatial objectification is only meaningful within specific discursive frames and how such objectification itself can be an integral aspect of place making—the inscription and gathering of meaning in location. Dichotomizing space and place, where "space" is associated with European thinking and "place" with indigenous ideals, therefore risks reproducing the same categories that motivated colonial policy, reifying cultural difference between "the west and the rest." Whitridge suggests that place is instead best conceived as a "spatialized imaginary," a "nexus of imaginary significations at the site of its intersection with the real" (Whitridge 2004:214). The resonance between this approach and that of community as an emergent interface between virtual and tangible schema/resources is evident and consistent with this approach to place and landscape.

Places in this sense, following Whitridge, are also embedded in broader, regional networks of interaction to produce multiple spatialized imaginaries with overlapping and porous boundaries. I would add that in colonial contexts—such as those explored in this book—where often radically different spatial imaginaries come into contact, the *same space* can be the product and object of multiple modes of signification and practice, of multiple spatial imaginaries in varied relations (conflict, competition, accommodation). The discursive and practical processes by which such overlapping spatialized imaginaries resolve their contradictions, become entangled, or remain in tension, produce new kinds of places. This is another dimension of the constitution of colonial community and landscapes that has not been systematically analyzed in situ. Chapters 5–7 explore these negotiations at different spatial and temporal scales.

Bridging Empirical and Interpretive Approaches through Spatial Analysis

If the theoretical virtues of current anthropological conceptions to community, landscape, and place are evident, methodologies for investigating them are less developed. To put it bluntly, rigorous, empirically driven archaeological studies of emplaced landscape approaches are still scarce. As Llobera has observed some time ago (1996), one of the problems associated with practice-based approaches to landscape is the lack of a formal methodology. Commenting on the phenomenological approach to landscape of Tilley, Llobera (1996:614) notes:

> Tilley (1994), makes several references to the local topography surrounding the sites and the relation of the sites to landscape features; he includes comments about the movement of people through the landscape. Most of his conclusions follow field observations and no attempt is made to ascertain whether these comments would also apply to other locales in the landscape, rather than only to the sites studied.

The analytical tools available now, GIS chief among them, can remedy such impressionistic shortcomings and enable a synthesis of empirical and interpretive approaches. It may seem odd to propose GIS as a tool for this job since it has come under heavy critique—for its supposed treatment of space as a universal, objective, uniform, and neutral canvas or container, empty of human significance, for its supposed privileging of environmental variables, and ultimately for its behavioral and environmental reductionism or determinism (see contributions in Pickles 1995). But I agree entirely with Wheatley and Gillings, who "see formal spatial analysis not as a means of producing complete archaeological interpretations but as an extension of our observational equipment" (Wheatley and Gillings 2002). Seen this way, spatial analysis is useful regardless of theoretical proclivities about space or place. But to again traverse that false dichotomy, GIS—a technology seemingly most inherently wedded to "space"—can actually enable thick description of place and is an instrument in place making itself. To turn again to Whitridge:

> A cartographer employing the most elaborate technoscientific approaches to precisely quantify spatial relationships (e.g., analyzing satellite images) is not less engaged with the locations she manipulates than the native elder who presences a mythic time in telling a story about some of the same locations. Rather, the two are differently engaged in *imaginative projects* of practically and discursively realizing a complexly textured reality. (Whitridge 2004:217; emphasis added)

Archaeologists of all stripes are familiar with this kind of place making; visualizing and interpreting spatial distributions and putting them into broader cultural context is the stock in trade of archaeology. That is to say, archaeologists are intimate knowers of the places they study. The knowledge that results is a form of place making. GIS enables and enhances this activity in a number of ways: by providing measures of distributions, by enabling the integration, query, and analysis of spatial display of data of many types, and by enabling simulation of perspective and movement, among other means. Below I discuss how I employ these aspects to work toward an emplaced spatial analytic perspective.

A Spatially Integrated Archaeological and Ethnohistorical Approach

Patricia Seed has observed, "Spanish officials in highland Peru and Mexico counted people, the English in India surveyed the land. Spanish colonialism produced the census, British colonialism the map" (Seed 1992:206–7). This would seem to dim the prospects for a spatially integrated understanding Andean community and landscape during the Spanish colonial era. But if Spanish colonialism left us comparably paltry cartographic registries of how Andean communities and landscapes were organized, spatial information is still textually registered in such censuses (visitas) and other classes of documentation. The pioneering work of Murra, Pease, Rostworowski, and others in what might be called the "golden age" of Andean ethnohistory was essentially spatial in nature in that it reconstructed the latent spatial patterns registered in visitas and a range of other previously underutilized documents (see Murra and Morris 1976). In retrospect, the contributions of that generation are even more impressive when considering the tools available at the time. But largely due to technological limitations, models of ecological complementarity were

necessarily coarse in nature and most often rendered in narrative, not cartographic, form.

Given the advances in spatial and computing technologies, then, it is surprising how little GIS and related spatial analytic tools have been used to
further this line of research today. In part, this owes to the narrative-driven
and humanities-oriented nature of ethnohistory as it has developed as a sub-
discipline. Spatial history and the spatial humanities are still nascent fields
but are growing rapidly (Bodenhamer et al. 2010a, 2010b; Gregory and Ell
2007; Knowles 2000, 2002; Knowles and Hillier 2008). Within the context
of Andean studies, the lack of formal spatial analysis probably also owes to
a hardening of thinking around the seemingly hoary old topic of ecological
complementarity in the Andes. But Murra himself considered the model
provisional (Murra 1985), and its "dynamic potential" (Salomon 1985) has
not been fully explored (but see Goldstein 2005). Indeed, GIS and related
technologies enable precisely the kinds of analyses wished for but virtually
impossible through manual cross-tabulation and summary of data or with
only static cartographic representation. Through creative use of GIS, spatial
patterns otherwise obscure in documentary sources can be represented car-
tographically, flexibly queried, and systematically analyzed at varied spatial
scales. Moreover, as noted above, perspective and movement can be modeled, permitting more experience-near rendering of place (see also Ayers
2010; Lock 2010). A reinvigorated spatial ethnohistory of the Andes can open
new lines of inquiry for the region and contribute in a grounded manner to
the burgeoning literatures on place and landscape.

The emplaced perspective I strive for in this book is thus undergirded by
spatially integrated archaeological and documentary analysis. In outline, it
builds from a foundation of archaeological basemaps, adds spatially coinci-
dent data from documentary sources, and builds a range of derived models and simulations. The study first tacks back and forth between analysis of
settlement and land-use patterns based on data from a full-coverage archaeological survey of the area best-documented in the colonial visitas of the valley, which also coincides with the political nucleus of the Collagua Province,
around the villages of Yanque and Coporaque. Chapter 4 presents the findings of this survey, focusing on settlement patterning under autonomous and
Inka rule and the attendant change and continuity in the surrounding agro-
pastoral landscape over this 400-year span. Chapter 5 follows this analysis of
settlement patterning through the early years following the Spanish invasion,
tracking the establishment of a series of Franciscan doctrinas at former nodes
of Inka administration in the valley. Complementing this settlement pattern
perspective, the focus then tightens to the scale of a single doctrina, Malata,

using GIS-based walking simulation and spatial network analyses to model how foot traffic was deliberately routed away from the former Inka ceremonial complex at the site to instead form processionals through its colonial plaza and into the chapel beyond. Finally, a variant of social network analysis is adapted to this spatial context to model patterns of surveillance as the site's inhabitants moved through the doctrina.

With this trans-conquest perspective, chapters 6 and 7 reconstruct how ayllu affiliation structured regional- and local-scale land-use patterns through analysis of the visita declarations from the same area as the survey. Using what I call a "reverse site catchment" approach, I use GIS to reconstruct the land-tenure patterns of ayllus resettled to the reducción of Coporaque by matching toponyms from agricultural field declarations in the visitas with their counterparts on the modern landscape. This method allows mapping of a large sample of the individual agricultural fields declared in the visitas. As alluded to earlier, these findings show that the ayllus of apparent pre-Inkaic origin in the Hanansaya moiety had significantly different distributions than the ayllus of the Urinsaya moiety, which show more evidence for Inka social enginerring. Using point-pattern measures of dispersion and centrality, I then compare these contrasting land-use patterns to the terminal prehispanic settlement pattern to infer the pre-reducción residential patterns of particular ayllus (chapter 7). This spatial synthesis therefore enriches understanding of how community and land use were negotiated both before and after the Spanish invasion, since, on the one hand, it shows how local, pre-Inkaic schema and resources of community organization and land use continued to be used and practiced through both imperial occupations, even as they were fitted to distinct colonial ideals of settlement and land use.

Building from this rendering of prehispanic and colonial land-use patterns, I then explore the long-term downstream or legacy effects of colonial reducción resettlement on the abandonment of large tracts of agricultural terraces and their supporting irrigation systems. This analysis first employs a least-cost path (LCP) walking simulation from the reducción village (Coporaque) to abandoned and unabandoned fields as a measure of how colonial resettlement affected the specific spatial patterning of terrace and canal abandonment. While most models of historic-era agricultural deintensification tend to focus on prime movers (for example, colonial-era demographic collapse, colonial resettlement, drought, etc.), this analysis employs a multivariate approach to discriminate how community (in this case, ayllu) affiliation acted as a mediating factor to the effects of population decline, ecological risk, and colonial resettlement in the decision-making calculus to abandon agricultural infrastructure.

3

THE LAND AND PEOPLES OF THE COLCA VALLEY

From space (Figure 3.1) the Colca Valley appears as a large and rich resource patch in a region otherwise dominated by expanses of high-elevation grassland steppe (*puna*). The valley forms the heart of the largest drainage system in southern Peru. After curving northwest from its source near Laguna Lagunillas (close to the city of Puno), the Colca River turns south before trending westerly toward the Pacific. Below the confluence of the Capiza River near the village of Andamayo, the river changes names to the Majes, and eventually to the Camaná, where the valley widens again before discharging into the Pacific on the arid coast. The valley is also a spectacular example of a human-engineered landscape: Virtually all slopes below about 3,800 m are covered with contour bench terraces tied into a complex irrigation system that transports meltwater from the surrounding glaciated peaks. It is the synergy of its natural features and human ingenuity—how the people of the Colca Valley capitalized on its endowments, adapted to its risks, and turned some of its potential liabilities into assets—that account for this remarkable landscape. This chapter explores those endowments and risks—the great palimpsest of built features in the valley landscape—and the peoples who built them.

Valley Physiography

The Colca River forms the heart of the modern Caylloma Province of the Department of Arequipa (Figure 3.2). The river cuts through the plateau that dominates this region of the Andes—fully 89 percent of the 12,046-km^2 area of the province (an area slightly smaller than the state of Connecticut) lies above 3,800 m. In this vast, semiarid plateau, punctuated by the high peaks of the western cordillera, the valley can be seen as an oasis of relatively moderate climate and considerable agricultural and pastoral productive potential. The main 50-km stretch of the Colca Valley proper can be divided into lower, central, and upper sections according to physiographic changes over the course of

Figure 3.1. LANDSAT ETM+ image of the Colca Valley (*top*) in relation to the city of Arequipa, showing intervening high puna grasslands.

the river (Figure 3.2). The lower section of the valley, encompassing the area around the village of Cabanaconde, is set apart from the central and upper valley areas by a deep section of canyon. It is steeper, deeper, and warmer than the middle and upper sections of the valley, and arable land there is situated

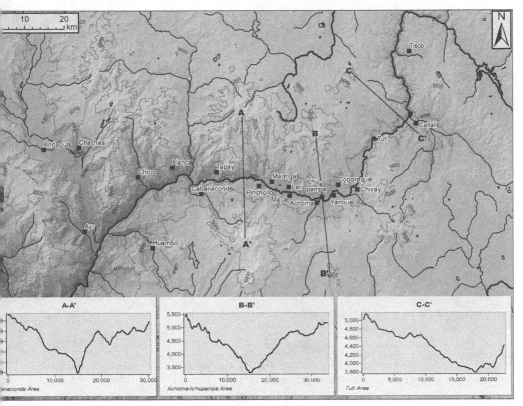

Figure 3.2. Topographic map of the Colca Valley, showing transects in lower, middle, and upper valley sections.

in the lower *kichwa* and upper *yungas* ecological zones (between about 2,800 and 3,400 m), where frosts are less common and maize agriculture predominates. Cabanaconde is still renowned today for its high-quality maize (known as *maíz cabanita*) which commands a premium in markets in the valley and in the city of Arequipa. Villages here also cultivate fruit orchards in the lowest reaches of the river gorge (Gelles 2000:115–18).

The central valley extends upstream from the Colca Canyon to just upstream of the village of Chivay and constitutes the core agriculturalist area of the Laricollaguas (in the lower part of the central valley) and the Yanquecollaguas (in the upper part of the central valley). Massive complexes of stone-faced, irrigated bench terraces cover virtually all of the lower slopes of the central valley, creating a visually striking human-engineered landscape (Figure 3.3). In general terms, the central valley encompasses the kichwa (ca. 2,800–3,600 m) and *suni* zones (ca. 3,600–3,800 m) and is surrounded by the grasslands of the puna (ca. 3,800–4,400 m) in the surrounding uplands and valley rim. The upper valley begins above an area of serpentine hills formed

Figure. 3.3. Panorama of terracing near Lari.

by Quaternary volcanic flows that border of a long, arcing corner of the river between the villages of Chivay and Tuti.

The upper valley takes on a different aspect, being shallower and more open than the central and lower sections of the valley. Agriculture is untenable in the uppermost reaches of the valley due to near-nightly freezing temperatures, so there are no agricultural terraces, and the scrub and cactus vegetation of the central and lower valleys give way to bunch grasses and high-altitude, high-insolation plants such as yareta (*Azorella compacta*), a slow-growing, resinous evergreen perennial highly valued as firewood.

The valley was formed by the counteracting forces of tectonic uplift and fluvial incision during the Pleistocene, and over the course of its entrenchment, the river has exposed a 2,000 m cross section of geologic strata spanning the Jurassic (205–135 m.y.a. [million years ago]) to Quaternary (1.8 m.y.a. to 10,000 BP) periods. The geomorphology of the valley is characterized by a series of seven alluvial terraces of volcanic parent material divided by higher-angle escarpments from the puna lands above 4,000 m to the inner river gorge around 3,300 m (Sandor 1987a, 1992). These surfaces of these terraces, denominated Qal 1–7 (Quaternary alluvium 1–7), increase in age with elevation, with the

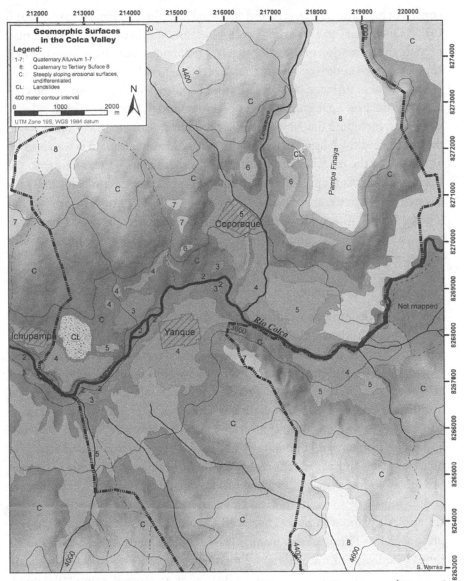

Figure 3.4. Map of geomorphic surfaces around Yanque and Coporaque. (Digitized from Sandor 1986.)

most recent surface (Qal 1) at the entrenched river channel and surrounding floodplain (Figure 3.4). Above this lowest surface, three previous alluvial terraces (Qal 2–4) consist of gravels, fine alluvium, and volcanic ash. These are obscured in places by intrusive alluvium from tributaries. Next, Qal 5 is constituted by volcanic flows (Sandor 1987a, 1992). The Qal 1–5 terraces and intervening slopes encompass most of the agricultural zone in the valley (Denevan et al. 1986). The remaining two Quaternary alluvium surfaces, Qal 6–7, consist of high alluvial terraces and stranded interfluves (Sandor 1987a, 1992). QT 8 (Quaternary to Tertiary 8), the highest and oldest of these surfaces, may predate the formation of the valley itself (and hence would have been the first subjected to river downcutting) (Sandor 1987a, 1992).

Above these surfaces, glaciated stratovolcanoes, which continue to be venerated as the principal *apus* (mountain deities) today, tower over both sides of the valley, including the Nevados Hualca Hualca, Ampato, and Sabancaya to the south, and the Misme massif to the north. Mount Ampato is well known as the site of the recovery of a frozen female sacrificial victim, likely from an Inka *capac huccha* ("opulent prestation"—empire-wide sacrificial rituals) excavated by Johan Reinhard (see Reinhard 1998). On the north side of the valley, the Misme massif forms the continental divide. Glacial melt from these peaks, either through runoff or springs, supplies the water for the extensive irrigation systems of the valley.

Geological Endowments

The high peaks provided another key resource beginning in remote prehispanic times: obsidian for lithic tools. Geologically recent volcanism deposited beds of obsidian around two rhyolitic domes (Cerro Ancachita and Cerro Hornillo) in the uplands to the east of Chivay (Burger et al. 1998; Burger et al. 2000). Research by Brooks and colleagues report a large quarry to the immediate east of Cerro Cotallalli (or Cotallaulli) in similar stratigraphic context (Brooks 1998; Brooks et al. 1997). More recently, intensive survey and excavations around the source by Nicholas Tripcevich revealed extensive quarrying and initial reduction at the source (Tripcevich 2007). Exchange of Chivay source obsidian stretched as far north as Machu Picchu (Burger et al. 2000:289), and it dominates the assemblages of the Lake Titicaca basin and Altiplano. Obsidian chemically sourced to the Chivay source was present in the Titicaca basin from at least Late Archaic (AD 4500–3500 BP) times (Stanish et al. 2002:451), and it constitutes some 75–80 percent of the sourced obsidian at Tiwanaku sites (Brooks et al. 1997; Burger et al. 2000). By all indications, extraction and processing at the source was done by local peoples, indicating ancient exchange relationships between the inhabitants of the Colca Valley and those of the Titicaca basin and Altiplano, stretching back even before the advent of agriculture (see Brooks 1998; Burger et al. 2000; Stanish et al. 2002; Tripcevich 2007).

The valley is also endowed with very fertile soil, both as a consequence of its geology and the soil management practices of its inhabitants. Soils in the Colca Valley are among the best documented in the Andes as a result of research by Jon Sandor and Neal Eash as part of the Río Colca Abandoned

Terrace Project, as well as David Guillet's multidisciplinary project on modern soil ethnoclassification (Denevan et al. 1986; Dick et al. 1994; Eash and Sandor 1995; Guillet et al. 1995; Sandor 1986, 1987a, 1987b, 1988, 1992; Sandor and Eash 1991, 1995; Sandor and Furbee 1996). These studies have shown that the soils of the valley are Mollisols of volcanic alluvium and colluvium parent material with high humic content and are of comparable organic content, tilth, and water-holding capacity as the Mollisols of the midwestern United States (Eash and Sandor 1995; Sandor 1987a, 1992; Staff 1975; for soil taxonomy, see Staff 1990). Topsoils of bench terrace complexes that line the valley slopes exhibit various anthropogenic characteristics. Bench terrace topsoils tend to be loamy, exhibiting plaggen[1] and anthropic (high phosphorous content) epipedons (Sandor 1992). Bench terrace topsoils are also unusually thick (0.3–1.3 m). In sum, the thick, fertile topsoils of Colca Valley bench terraces are the product of long-term accretions of fertilization and indigenous soil management (Sandor 1992).

Risk Factors: Climate

If the anthropogenically enhanced soils of the valley provide a reliable foundation for agricultural production, the climate of the valley is best characterized as a limiting or risk factor, being cool, semiarid, and unpredictable. Climatic patterning at the latitude of the Colca is most proximately determined by the orographic effects of the cordillera but is also the product of continental- and planetary-scale circulations (Johnson 1976). As opposed to the central and northern Andes (north of about 11° latitude), where moisture transport is influenced primarily by oscillations in the Intertropical Convergence Zone (ITCZ) (a planetary-scale circulation that determines the location and orientation of the trade winds), precipitation in the south-central Andes is produced primarily by convection of warm, humid air from the eastern slopes of the Amazon basin in combination with local low-pressure systems that develop during the austral summer. From the latitude of the Colca Valley and farther south (that is, below about 15° south latitude), precipitation decreases markedly and is more unpredictable than in the central and northern Andean regions (Johnson 1976). Precipitation is markedly seasonal and unpredictable because of high inter-annual variability. Due to the high elevation and tropical latitude of the valley, mean annual temperatures are low (about 10°C for the central portion of the valley; see below), and diurnal temperature fluctuations are greater than seasonal ones.

Differences between the minimum and maximum temperatures within each month are greater than seasonal changes, reflecting strong diurnal fluctuations in temperature (ONERN 1973; Denevan et al. 1986). Warm daytime temperatures result from overall sunny conditions throughout the year. However, at night, frost is a common hazard to crop viability, especially during the months of May through October, although frosts can occur during any month of the year. Frost is most problematic on the plains above the valley bottom, due to the settling of cool air over the terraced valley sides. Hail is also a significant risk factor for crops and occurs most commonly between December and March, the months of greatest precipitation.

Elevation greatly influences temperature in this highland setting, and marked temperature gradients are present even within the agricultural core of the survey area. Denevan and colleagues report an 8°C difference in minimum temperatures along a 500-m transect from the valley floor (3,272 m) over complexes of irrigated bench terraces along the lower valley slopes to a high group of abandoned fields at Chilacota (3,752 m) (Treacy and Denevan 1986).

Frost and hail pose significant risks to farmers, but water scarcity is the primary constraint to agricultural production in the valley (Gelles 2000; Guillet 1992; Treacy 1989b; Winterhalder 1993). High evaporation rates result in absolute water deficits for as many as eight months of the year (Treacy 1989b:54, 56). The annual precipitation of around 400 mm in the central and lower valley villages is below the minimal requirements for rain-fed potato or maize production, which require at least 500 mm of rain (Knapp 1991).[2] Precipitation generally increases with elevation in the valley, but this benefit of greater precipitation is offset by higher frost and hail risks. Quinoa (Chenopodium quinoa), when broadly spaced, can be successfully cultivated with as little as 300 mm of precipitation a year, but only a tiny minority of fields are dry farmed in the valley today.

The timing of precipitation is equally important as the amount. Throughout the valley, precipitation is highly seasonal, with an average of 65 percent of the annual total occurring between the austral summer months of January and March. The wet and dry seasons are, at least grosso modo, predictable, but inter-annual variation is great. Some years bring adequate rainfall even for dry farming, but others are exceedingly dry and make unirrigated agriculture impossible.

Compounding inter-annual climatic unpredictability are the effects of El Niño/Southern Oscillation (ENSO) events. These effects vary depending on the intensity of ENSO events, but moderate to severe ones, which bring torrential rains and flooding to the coastal regions of southern Ecuador and northern Peru, most often affect the southern Peruvian highlands in the opposite manner, causing drought. ENSO-related droughts are often doubly damaging because they can occur even after heavy September and October rains, which modern farmers use to forecast the nature of the coming rainy season (Treacy 1989b). Thus belying local indices of abundant rainfall, the sudden onset of an ENSO drought can lead to especially heavy agricultural losses, as in the severe ENSO events of 1971–72, 1982–83, and 1997–98 (Brooks 1998:212–13; Caviedes 1975, 1984; Treacy 1989b:57). It is possible, however, that modern Colca farmers have not retained ENSO forecast knowledge documented elsewhere in the central and south-central Andes, such as observance of the clarity of the Pleiades during the winter solstice (Orlove et al. 2000). Prehispanic farmers may have been better able to forecast the weather than their modern counterparts. Nonetheless, the scarcity, seasonality, and unpredictability of precipitation within the current climatic regime make cultivation virtually impossible without some kind of water augmentation regime.

Because the absolute temperature and precipitation requirements of Andean cultigens are exceeded in the higher elevations of the valley, small changes in either would significantly alter the mix of risks and opportunities for agricultural production in the past by moving the line of cultivation up or down slope or by changing irrigation requirements. As pointed out by Erickson for the Titicaca basin (2000), present climatic conditions should not be assumed to be a baseline or even representative state. As is becoming increasingly clear through paleoclimatic research from neighboring areas, the chaotic (but not random) inter-annual variability in temperature and precipitation observed in the recent past occurs within longer-term climatic oscillations. During wetter periods in the prehispanic past, rain-fed agriculture was possible and widely practiced in the Colca Valley. Conversely, prolonged dry periods may have created an impetus for the elaboration of irrigation systems (Brooks 1998; Treacy 1989b:106, 136).

Paleoclimatic data from glacial cores from the ice cap of Mount Quelccaya (Thompson 1992, 1995; Thompson et al. 1986; Thompson et al. 1988; Thompson and Mosley-Thompson 1989; Thompson et al. 1985; Thompson 1993; Thompson et al. 1994), located to the southeast of Cuzco, and from sediment cores from Titicaca and nearby lakes (Abbott, Binford et al. 1997; Abbott, Seltzer, et al. 1997) are key data for reconstructing long-term Holocene climate change in the region. Within the 1,500-year overlap between the two (ca. AD 540–1985) there are points of both congruence and incongruence (Table 3.1). Only the most severe and prolonged dry period, from AD 1040 to 1490, corresponds with low water levels on Lake Titicaca (Abbott, Binford, et al. 1997).

This drought, which roughly corresponds with the Late Intermediate period (AD 1100–1450), has been cited as a prime factor in major social

Table 3.1. Dry and wet periods derived from glacial and lake sediment cores

Quelccaya Ice Cores		Lake Cores
Wet Periods	Dry Periods	Dry Periods
AD 1870–1984	AD 1720–1860	AD 1050–1450
AD 1500–1720	AD 1040–1490	50 BC–AD 250
AD 760–1040	AD 650–730	450–250 BC
	AD 540–610	950–850 BC
		1550–1400 BC

transformations in the Andean culture-historical sequence, including the collapse of Tiwanaku (e.g., Kolata 1993) and the onset of widespread warfare during the LIP (e.g., Arkush 2008). While models positing resource stress as a prime mover in social transformation may underestimate endogenous factors and the flexibility of Andean social organization in general, closer analysis of the two data sets suggests that a more detailed chronology is also possible and can potentially clarify chronological relationships between periods of drought and social transformation. The lake core evidence, dated via radiocarbon samples, indicates the lowest lake levels between AD 1030 and 1280 and the return of shallow water to the area of the lake core by AD 1350, followed by deep water during a subsequent wet period between AD 1500 and 1720. Precise dating of the onset of dry conditions is not possible with the lake core data because the sediments of the core were eroded during the drought. The Quelccaya core data, on the other hand, provide annual-scale resolution. Oxygen isotope ratio data from the cores indicate that most of the LIP was indeed dry, but the most severe droughts were during the second half of the period, 1305 to 1380 (Arkush 2008). As discussed below and in chapter 5, this more refined chronology has a significant impact on models of landscape modification and social processes, including the shift from extensive, unirrigated field systems to intensive, irrigated ones, the collapse of the Middle Horizon states, and the proliferation of violent conflict during the LIP.

Anthropogenic Landscape Features

The above review of the valley physiography presents the broad (and ever-shifting) material and energetic parameters of the Colca Valley as a human habitat. But the Colca Valley landscape is also a product of—not just a setting for—human inhabitance, and it is a prime example of how "ecological zones" themselves are anthropogenically constructed so as to lessen ecological strictures. The Colca Valley presents a striking example of monumental-scale ancient geo-engineering. It is one of the most intensively terraced valleys in the New World (Donkin 1979). Approximately 14,000 ha of agricultural terraces and fields cover both sides of the valley, from the inner river gorge to abandoned terraces between approximately 3,600 and 4,000 m (Denevan 1987; 1988b:Table 1; Denevan and Hartwig 1986).

Because the river course is deeply entrenched, water from the river is impossible to harness for irrigation using nonmechanized methods. Thus irrigation water originates from glacial meltwater, springs, and associated drainages (*quebradas,* or "ravines") around the high peaks on both sides of the valley. The glaciated peaks of Misme, Huillcaya, and Quehuisha supply the meltwater for the irrigation systems of the north side of the river. The peaks of Huarancate, Sabancaya, Ampato, and Hualca Hualca fulfill the same function on the south side of the river. Canal systems vary in length according to local hydrology and topography, ranging from less than 1 km to more than 30 km in length. In addition to serving as insurance against drought, irrigation offsets the effects of marked seasonality of rainfall in the region, enabling farmers to regulate the timing and quantity of water. Irrigation makes it possible to stretch the growing season by planting well before the onset of summer rains, as well as watering crops after seasonal rains stop, allowing harvest before the frosts of May (Treacy 1989b:276–79).

Given massive anthropogenic alterations to natural landforms in the valley, the agricultural landscape of Colca Valley is best understood as composed of many intensively managed "production zones" (Mayer 1985). Of the total field area in the Colca Valley, 62 percent (8,962 of 14,356 ha) is terraced (Denevan 1988b:22, Table 1). Terraces provide several productivity-enhancing properties, including the facilitation of water management, soil thickening and enhancement, and beneficial microclimatic changes. Primary among these, however, is the hydrological function (Treacy 1994). Now-abandoned unirrigated terraces once augmented precipitation and runoff by pooling water with diversion walls and were concentrated around natural ravines (see below). The form of irrigated bench terraces was determined primarily by the concern to regulate the flow of irrigation water over their surfaces and between terraces (Denevan 1987; Donkin 1979; Treacy 1989b:348). This allows for the management of water flow over terrace surfaces and minimizes soil erosion. As discussed above, terracing results in much thicker soils, and through soil management practices such as manuring, fallowing, crop rotation, and tilling techniques, fertile topsoils have resulted. Also, terraces mitigate frost risk by shedding cold air better than unterraced slopes and, because of their high surface area to mass ratio, accumulate heat from insolation and radiate it at night (Brooks 1998:126; Denevan 1980; Treacy 1989b:81–82,

349–50). These combined frost-shedding and heat-sinking functions extend the effective altitudinal limits of frost-sensitive crops such as maize, allowing for an expanded area of their cultivation.

Building on comparative research by Spencer and Hale (1961) and Donkin (1979), Denevan and colleagues have developed a local typology of field and terrace forms based on morphological and functional characteristics (Brooks 1998:126–37; Denevan 1980, 1987; Treacy 1989b:74–100). While terminology differs slightly between investigators (Brooks 1998:127), four general categories terrace forms can be differentiated.

Bench Terraces

Bench terraces have vertical or slightly inclined fieldstone facings and subtly front-sloping (but nearly level) surfaces. They form large "staircases" on valley slopes, presenting visually distinctive fractal patterns, and are concentrated on the lower valley slopes. Bench terrace walls range from under 1 m to over 3 m, depending on slope (the steeper the slope, the higher the terrace wall and narrower the field surface). Bench terrace retaining walls were constructed by excavating through duripans and B horizons to provide a firm structural foundation. They are often divided by rock sidewalls. While the vast majority of bench terraces are irrigated, small pockets of unirrigated bench terraces have been reported around Coporaque (Treacy 1989b:93) and the Japo basin in Chivay (Brooks 1998). Denevan (1987:22) subdivides irrigated bench terraces into three subtypes: contour terraces, "long, relatively narrow terraces curved to match slope"; linear terraces, "short, relatively narrow segments running laterally across slope"; and broadfield terraces, "irregular in shape or rectangular but not as wide as valley bottom terraces, with low stone retaining walls."

Sloping Field Terraces

Found primarily along the upper slopes of the valley, above contour terrace complexes, sloping field terraces are fieldstone enclosed with a thick, downslope retaining wall, behind which soil buildup (probably the result of both intentional slope modification and erosion processes) creates a more level planting surface. The lower portion of most sloping field terraces probably served as the most densely planted area, as well as a collection area for runoff water. Since precipitation tends to occur in short bursts, the thickened soils and basin form of the fields would have functioned to store moisture between storms. This property would have been accentuated in areas underlain by duripan soils, which would serve as a natural barrier to water filtration (Treacy 1989b:131). Thus the construction and use of sloping fields were not dry farmed in the strict sense but instead represent a "hydraulic half-way house between complete dry farming and canal irrigation" (Treacy 1989b:127).

Segmented Terraces

Segmented terraces fall within the category of "isolated, short, sloping dry field terrace" (Spencer and Hale 1961:9, as cited in Treacy 1989b:97), and while sharing the basic hydrological characteristics with sloping field terraces, they are distinct enough to be considered a separate type. A segmented terrace consists of a low (0.5–2 m), arcing retaining wall (composed of surrounding colluvium), behind which a small, nearly level water catchment and planting area (as in the case of sloping fields) is followed by a steeper grade. The total area behind retaining walls is usually 6–17 m long and 2–6 m wide. As the name implies, segmented terraces are not aligned, as in the case of bench terraces, but form discontinuous clusters on a slope. In general, segmented terraces are most visible along upper, steep colluvial slopes (but were probably also prevalent in areas now covered by bench terracing; see below). In the Yanque-Coporaque survey area, the largest concentrations are found along the high-angle scarps of the southern and eastern flanks of the Pampa Finaya massif. In these areas, especially dense clusters are found around natural quebradas, which were modified through the use of diversion walls to channel runoff to these fields. Treacy identified five areas in Coporaque where such runoff-control features and associated sloping field and segmented terraces are found (Treacy 1989b:127–33), and others have been identified in the Japo basin to the south of Chivay by Brooks (Brooks 1998). Terraces which straddle the ravines themselves have also been called "cross-channel" terraces and can be considered a subtype of segmented terraces (Brooks 1998:127–29).

Rock-Walled Fields

Rock-walled fields generally occur on the flattest terrain of the valley bottom and are essentially unterraced fields enclosed by fieldstone walls. In some cases, the enclosure walls are informal accumulations that result from clearing the enclosed fields of colluvium. Many of these are very recent in origin, serving as enclosures for cattle and other livestock, as many valley bottom fields are dedicated to alfalfa cultivation (González 1995). In other cases, especially among the broad expanses of the Qal 4 pampas on which the modern reducción villages are situated, large areas of rock-walled fields are enclosed by complexes of "agro-mortuary" wall complexes—massive, thick (up to 3 m) walls that reach up to 3 m in height, with ovoid, cyst-like features on top.

Terrace and Field Chronology: Origins, Use, and Abandonment

The diversity of field and terrace forms outlined above is a reflection of not only functional differences but also change over time. Much archaeological research in the valley has focused on terrace origins and abandonment, and considerable progress has been made in determining the relative sequence and absolute dates for the origins, use, and abandonment of the valley's different terrace and field systems. Given the inherent difficulties of dating terraces through absolute means (due to their often intractably turbid fills and indeterminacy of carbon sample associations), relative dating of terrace and field complexes has produced more definitive results. Therefore, the sequencing of terrace forms is better known than the specific timing of these changes.

There is consensus that irrigated bench terracing superseded earlier unirrigated field systems (Brooks 1998; Denevan 1980, 1987, 2001; Treacy 1989b). But even here, it should be noted that there were periods when a spectrum of dry-farmed, runoff-augmented, and irrigated field systems was in use. Such could have been the case during wetter than average periods, such as those between AD 610–50 and 760–1040 (Thompson et al. 1985:973). Dry-farmed and runoff-augmented systems can even function in today's climate for certain crops. For example, quinoa can be successfully cultivated with as little as 300 mm of rain when broadly spaced (Treacy 1994:107). Runoff augmentation via check dams or cross-channel terraces could further mitigate crop failure risk. The fact that so little is actually cultivated in either of these ways today reflects on the distinction between what Daniel Gade (1967:153) has termed the *effective* and the *absolute* limits of crops, where the effective limits are emically defined as the range beyond which optimal or satisfactory levels of risk and yield are possible and the absolute limits are the most extreme conditions under which a crop can survive. The calculus of such distinctions was doubtless bound not only to ecological conditions but also political and economic ones. In times of increasing population density and/or mandates for surplus production, more land could be expected to be converted to higher-intensity irrigated systems, enabling greater yield per unit area and the potential for significant surplus production. Nonetheless, the two should not be considered mutually exclusive in a systemic fashion, since cultivation in unirrigated, low-intensity systems may continue in parallel as part of a suite of household agricultural practices, depending again on perceived risk, and culturally bound conceptions of satisficing production outcomes (see also Covey 2006b:46–53).

In general, what we see today in the landscape of the valley is one in which irrigated terracing dominates in all but the most marginal areas below about 3,800 m, while the earlier, abandoned unirrigated sloping fields and segmented

terraces extend higher up the valley slopes. Thus the general pattern is characterized by an irrigated "core" of bench terraces and valley bottom fields surrounded by a "corona" of (generally) earlier, unirrigated sloping fields and segmented terraces along the valley's upper slopes (figure 3.5). Using stratigraphic
evidence, Treacy has demonstrated in detail how irrigated bench terrace complexes intrude upon extant segmented slopes on the southern and eastern
slopes of Pampa Finaya (Treacy 1989b:122–27). The landscape-scale evidence
used to support the sequence is presented in Figure 3.6, a three-dimensional

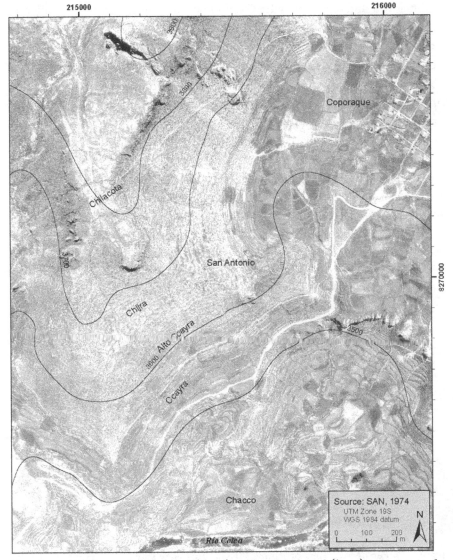

Figure 3.5. Air photo of abandoned (*upper*) and unabandoned (*lower*) terracing in the
Chijra/San Antonio/Chilacota area, Coporaque.

perspective view of Pampa Finaya from the south. Along the southern slopes of Pampa Finaya, the "Inca" canal (the canal's local, modern name) descends diagonally, demarcating a sharp boundary between unirrigated segmented terracing above and irrigated bench terracing below. As pointed out by Treacy (1989b:122–27), the segmented terraces must have originally covered the entire slope face and predate the canal and bench terracing, otherwise one would have to imagine that the segmented terrace construction abruptly stopped at the canal, forming a wedge-shaped border along the descending line of the canal. Also, on the eastern side of Finaya, segmented fields are found both above and below a different canal (the Qachulle canal, now abandoned), which irrigated valley bottom fields to the south of Pampa Finaya. The segmented fields surrounding the canal must predate it, since there would be no point in constructing unirrigable fields below a canal (Treacy 1989b:122–27). Also, the eastern slopes of Pampa Finaya illustrate how the southern slopes most likely appeared before being modified with irrigated bench terraces below the "Inca" canal. As shown in Figure 3.6, segmented terracing extends to the bottom of the slope and onto the valley bottom on the eastern side (Treacy 1989b:122–27).

Although radiocarbon dates and artifact associations provide some clues, the timing and causes of the terrace origins, and the shift from unirrigated to irrigated agriculture, is a more disputatious topic. The evidence is derived from reconnaissance and trench excavations at a series of bench terraces along an altitudinal transect near the site of Chijra in Coporaque by the Río Colca Abandoned Terrace Project (Figure 3.6) (Denevan 1986, 1988a; Malpass 1988;

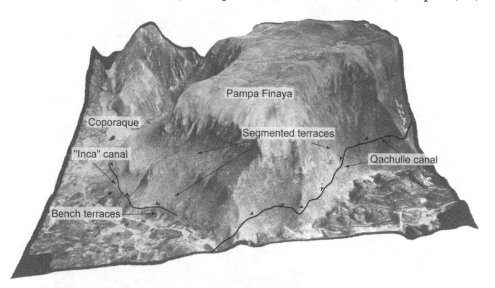

Figure 3.6. Perspective view of Pampa Finaya. This view shows stratigraphic relationships between early segmented terracing and later canals and bench terracing.

Malpass and de la Vera Cruz Chávez 1990; Treacy 1989b) as well as reconnaissance and excavations by Brooks in the Japo drainage to the south of Chivay (Brooks 1998).

Dating early terracing in the valley is complicated by the difficulty of differentiating terrace construction, use, and reconstruction episodes, as well as the methods used for absolute dating. Brooks presents a hypothesized succession scenario of terrace types and argues that unirrigated terracing began in the Colca Valley sometime prior to 2400 BC (Brooks 1998:400–401, 405). However, such an early date would place the construction of the first terracing in the valley in the Late Archaic period (4000–2000 BC), an unlikely scenario, since this time period is characterized by pre-ceramic, pre-agricultural hunting and foraging lifeways throughout the southern highlands. Also, the dating methods used to support this argument are problematic because they are based on radiocarbon dates (uncalibrated) from bulk soil samples in terrace fill.[3] However, the rest of the succession scenario presented by Brooks—in which unirrigated sloping fields, segmented terraces, and bench terraces were replaced by irrigated bench terracing during the Middle Horizon (Brooks 1998:409)—is more plausible. Based on evidence from reconnaissance around Coporaque, Treacy argued that local Middle Horizon ceramics are most associated with sloping fields and segmented terracing, while Late Intermediate to Late Horizon period ceramics are much less prevalent in these contexts but are found in heavy concentrations amid irrigated bench terrace complexes (Treacy 1989b:106–17). These associations, combined with radiocarbon dates from excavations in bench terraces (using discrete charcoal samples), led Treacy to hypothesize that dry farming predominated from Middle Horizon and earlier times (that is, prior to the eleventh century AD) and was subsequently replaced by irrigated bench terrace agriculture around AD 1000–1100 with the onset of the Late Intermediate period (Treacy 1989b:122). Sandor and Eash reach similar conclusions based on bench terrace trench excavations (Sandor 1986, 1987a, 1992). Malpass presents an alternative scenario, citing an apparent lapse in the ceramic chronology during the LIP (Malpass 1988). Malpass (1988) suggests that the construction of irrigated bench terrace complexes along the slopes surrounding Chijra may pertain to the Late Horizon but does not exclude the possibility that they could have been constructed earlier. In sum, while the history of unirrigated terrace origins in the Colca Valley remains debated, there is some consensus that the initial construction and use of irrigated bench terracing and associated canal systems, as well as the abandonment of previous unirrigated field and terrace systems, took place sometime between the eleventh and twelfth centuries AD.

Previous researchers have favored climatic stress as the primary causal factor behind the development of irrigated terraced agriculture in the valley, noting that the timing of the conversion to irrigated bench terracing generally correlates with the dry conditions recorded in the glacial and lake core data (discussed above) between the eleventh and fifteenth centuries AD. As summarized most recently by Denevan (2001:200):

> This scenario, drawing on Brooks and Treacy, is an argument that the development of complex labor-intensive irrigated terraces resulted, in part at least, from climatic stress. This is contrary to some popular and academic thinking that climatic deterioration (dryer, colder) was the cause of agricultural and social collapse at various places in the world. In the Colca Valley, climatic stress instead seems to have motivated the development of a more efficient, more productive, and less risky method of food production.

Thus rather than playing a casual role in collapse (Binford and Kolata 1996; Binford, et al. 1997; Kolata 1996; Ortloff and Kolata 1993), climate change in this scenario is instead the prime mover impelling an intensification of agricultural production through the elaboration of irrigated terrace and canal systems. Although all have been cautious not to discount demographic, economic, and political factors, previous research designs, with their focus on terrace and field systems rather than on settlements, have made evaluation of the role of social processes as causes for these changes difficult to assess. By considering political processes, particularly those which manifest as "community," as mediating factors in the relationship between humans and the environment, this study approaches the dynamics of land use and sociopolitical change as recursive, multicausal processes both constricted ecologically *and* constructed culturally.

The Peoples of the Colca Valley

Though the province and its peoples were only briefly mentioned in the chronicles,[4] the *corregidor* (provincial magistrate), Juan de Ulloa Mogollón, provides a description of the valley and its peoples based on responses gathered from the survey he administered for the *Relaciones geográficas de Indias* (Ulloa Mogollón 1965 [1586]). This brief account was extracted from the testimony of the native lords and elders of the province in one day (20 January 1586) through the interpreter and scribe Diego Coro Inga (of Coporaque) in the plaza of Yanque. It has served as the starting point for ethnohistorical analyses of the social organization of the peoples of the province during late prehispanic and early colonial times. As a compendium of self-representations by the elites of two ethnic groups refracted through the lens of a Spanish magistrate, it is, rather than a transparent registry, an idealized and palimpsest rendering. Accordingly, it must be analyzed with caution so it does not tyrannize the interpretation of other written sources or the archaeological record. Nonetheless, it does provide unique insights into how the Collaguas and Cabanas conceived of their origins and organization.

Ulloa describes how the Collaguas and Cabanas occupied separate areas of the province, spoke different languages, professed different mythical origins, and maintained distinct traditions of agricultural production, dress, and body modifications—all hallmarks of ethnicity that were strictly reinforced under Inka administration (Blom 2005; Cook 1997; Femenias 2005; Murra 1962a; Zorn 2004). These were among the largest ethnic polities of Condesuyu, the southwestern quarter of Tawantinsuyu (see Julien 1991), with a population numbering 33,000 during the Toledan census of the early 1570s. The best available demographic retrodictions (based on projection of the trajectory of demographic decline back in time to 1530) suggest that the population of the two groups combined on the eve of conquest was roughly double that— in the range of 62,000–71,000 (Cook 1982:84–88). The colonial province of the Collaguas constituted about a third of the population under the purview of the city of Arequipa and generated about 35 percent of the tax revenue collected there, making it the largest source of revenue outside city and surrounding environs (Manrique 1985). As a point of regional comparison, the Lupaqas and Collas of the western Titicaca basin—the largest of the southern Andean late prehispanic ethnic polities—have been estimated to have numbered in the range of 100,000 people (Stanish 2003:209–20).

As was common among highland ethnic polities, the Collaguas and Cabanas traced their origins to deified founding ancestors embodied in specific high Andean peaks. The very distinct locations of their respective origin places (paqarina) reinforced perceived differences between the Collaguas and Cabanas. The Cabanas (also called the Condes or Kuntis of Cabana) claimed descent from Mount Hualca Hualca, the glaciated peak that towers over the lower valley directly above Cabanaconde. The Collaguas, on the other hand, did not claim descent from a local peak but traced their descent from conquering hero-ancestor siblings, who descended from Mount Collaguata, an otherwise-unremarkable peak located near the village of Vellille in Espinar Province, Cuzco, some 100 aerial km north of the valley. The narrative of descent from a conquering people from the heights is a trope in many central Andean ethnic charter myths (Duviols 1973; Gose 1996; Salomon 1991). Typically, two groups are represented: the original inhabitants of a valley locale—called *huaris*—credited with having built the agricultural infrastructure of valley landscapes, and invasive, aggressive pastoralists from the heights—the *llacuazes*—who conquered the huaris but were assimilated to their sedentary agricultural lifeway (Duviols 1973, 1986; Gose 1996, 2008:19–20). The huari-llacuaz dyad is often metonymical of the upper-lower status relation of Hanansaya-Urinsaya moieties, representing the former as invading pastoralists and the latter as conquered agriculturalists, but it could also operate at lower orders of intra- or inter-ayllu relations or up to the largest segments of an ethnic polity (Gose 1996). As a community ideology, it created a durable hierarchical structure between complementary but oppositional groups, enacted in both periodic fertility rituals and ritual battles. This arrangement both naturalized the idea of intrusive conquest (an ideology that facilitated the incorporation of external invaders as ancestors) and emphasized the outsider status of ancestry rather than an ideal of primordial autochthony as ancestry. Ancestors were intimately linked to fertility and were seen as mediators with outside forces, particularly productive forces such as distant water sources (e.g., snowcapped peaks, lakes, the Pacific Ocean). Such distant ancestor huacas—often beyond local boundaries—were also the focus of ancestor cult of other groups, and thus political alliances could form through shared ritual allegiances in a shifting constellation of ancestors. Built into the ideology of late prehispanic Andean communities, then, was a flexible system for incorporating "new ancestors" and thus new alliance relations with external groups (Gose 2008:19–20).

A literal reading of an ancestral proto-Collagua population descending from the high-elevation southern provinces of Cuzco would have to withstand critical scrutiny and independently evaluated archaeological evidence. As discussed in the following chapter, it likely reflects an ossified version of oral tradition recounting a period of frequent violent conflict during the Late Intermediate period. It is probable that the higher-ranking Yanquecollaguas, who occupied the central to upper reaches of the valley, were considered the "llacuazes" relative to the "huaris" of Laricollaguas. It is also plausible that the Aymara-speaking, agro-pastoralist Collaguas collectively were considered llacuazes relative to the valley-dwelling, agriculturalist huaris of Cabanaconde in the lower, warmer reaches of the valley: The Collaguas, residing in the mid- to upper reaches of the valley, cultivated maize up to its effective upper altitudinal limits, as well as the high-altitude crops of quinoa (*Chenopodium quinoa*) and potatoes (*Solanum* spp.) and other Andean tubers, along with small amounts of kañiwa (*Chenopodium pallidicaule*) and the Andean legume tarwi (*Lupinus mutabilis*). But the Collaguas were especially renowned for their large herds of Andean camelids (primarily alpacas, *Lama pacos*) maintained by an extensive network of pastoralist communities in the high grasslands of the puna (Málaga Medina 1977; Pease 1977a). Through the early colonial era, the villages of Caylloma and Tisco were the primary pastoralist centers of Laricollaguas and Yanquecollaguas, respectively. Yanquecollaguas, located the farthest up valley and seat of governance in Inkaic and colonial times, had the largest pastoral holdings. The overall size of the Collaguas herds during colonial times are unknown, but a witness from a judicial inquiry from 1585 to 1586 estimated that the flocks of Callalli and Tisco alone totaled over 25,000 head (AGI Justicia 480, fol. 1196v, published in Crespo 1977:71–72). The total herd in the province almost certainly numbered well over 100,000. As discussed in chapter 6, the pastoralists who tended them were under the direct or indirect purview of their respective ayllu paramounts in the agriculturalist villages of Yanquecollaguas and Laricollaguas.

The Cabanas were settled in the lower part of the valley, from the village of Pinchollo downstream on the south side of the valley and in the lands downstream from Madrigal on the north side of the valley. As discussed in the previous chapter, the valley is steepest in these lower reaches, and it includes a stretch of canyon that ranks among the deepest in the world and separates the Collaguas and Cabanas areas. The generally steeper lower valley landscape affords household-level access to a great diversity of ecological zones within a day's round trip walk, including subtropical fruit orchards in the warmth of the valley bottom and high-altitude pasturage in the puna above. But more than anything, the Cabanaconde area is a prime area for maize production, and the prized variety produced there, maíz cabanita, is prized for its quality and taste (Gelles 2000:13).

Both Collagua and Cabana settlements were distributed throughout different ecological and altitudinal zones of the valley, herding settlements in the surrounding puna, and specialized agricultural colonies in lower-lying valleys to the south and west, forming large-scale vertical archipelago systems similar in scale to those of the Qollas and Lupaqas of the western Titicaca basin (Murra 1964, 1968, 1972). In these outlying locales—for example, in the maize production enclaves around the villages of Huanca, Lluta, and Huambo, and in several settlements in the valley of Arequipa—colonies of both groups lived cheek-by-jowl, most likely in separate but neighboring villages (Galdos Rodríguez 1984; Pease 1977a; Wernke 2006a), forming multiethnic mosaic landscapes much as predicted by Murra's vertical archipelago model (Murra 1972).[5]

The two groups also testified to having marked their ethnic identity permanently on their bodies through distinct forms of cranial modification. The Collaguas were said to have heightened, elongated heads, likely due to the constriction and posterior extension of the parietal and occipital bones using the annular-style head-binding technique (Blom 2005). Ulloa relates that this elongated and pointed head shape was said to be iconic of the volcano from which the Collaguas descended, and they further accentuated this shape by wearing a distinctive hat called a *chuco* (a tall, brimless hat). The Cabanas, as a result of a different binding technique (most likely a variant of the fronto-occipital method; see Blom 2005), had squat, widened heads, also said to be iconic of their paqarina (Ulloa Mogollón 1965 [1586]:327). Whether such neat distinctions in head and headdress forms were adhered to in practice remains an open question and is the subject of ongoing dissertation research by Matthew Velasco (Velasco, pers. comm. 2011).

Ulloa presents the linguistic boundaries between the Collaguas and Cabanas in terms as stark as those regarding their territories—almost certainly a reflection of the testimony he recorded from the kurakas and elders of the two groups. The Collaguas were described by Ulloa as Aymara speakers who lived in the central and upper portions of the Colca Valley, while the Cabanas were described as Quechua speakers settled in the lower part of the valley. But this pat description papers over what was almost certainly a much more complex and fluid linguistic landscape in the valley. First, Ulloa himself mentions the presence of a small population who spoke another unspecified language in the lower part of the valley. But the homogeneity of Aymara among the Collaguas is also doubtful, since with Inka administration, a trend toward increasing Quechuaization—at least among their kurakas—would be expected. There is evidence for intermarriage among the daughters of Collagua lords and Cuzco nobility, and Collagua *yanaconas* (a prestigious retainer class who serviced the Cuzqueño nobility) are documented in the Cuzco area (specifically, on the estate of Tupa Inka). Given these ties, it is likely that the children of Collagua kurakas were among the provincial elites educated in Cuzco and would have learned Quechua there. As I discuss in chapter 7, there is also some evidence for the Quechuaization of local toponym mosaics in the Collagua heartland. Though most toponyms are Aymara or Aymara/Quechua cognates, there are also some Quechua toponyms that seem to reflect patterns of agricultural expansion and intensification under Inka administration. Finally, the descendent populations of the Collaguas today speak a dialectical variant of Quechua that appears to have combined elements of the Cuzco-Collao and Ayacucho-Chanka variants of Southern Peruvian Quechua (Valderrama Fernández and Escalante Gutierrez 1988:26). Thus, over some period after Ulloa's relación, Aymara was superseded by Quechua. Of course, the Spanish quickly recognized the potential of Quechua to function as a lingua franca. Viceroy Francisco de Toledo officially promoted it for administrative purposes, and the Lima councils (especially the second [1567–68] and third [1581–83]; see Durston 2007; Mannheim 1991:64–67) employed it as a language of proselytization. The territory of the Collaguas was one of the earliest centers in the southern highlands of evangelization by the Franciscans, who came to include among their ranks the notable friar Luis Jerónimo de Oré, a bilingual Spanish/Quechua speaker from a prominent family of Huamanga, who was reputedly present during the writing the official Quechua catechism of the Third Lima Council (see Tibesar 1953:77–78, note 20). The Collaguas doctrinas were ceded to secular priests of the Diocese of Cuzco by the commissary general of the order, Fray Jerónimo de Villacarrillo, in 1581, but in response to repeated petitions from the Collagua kurakas, the Franciscans were reinstated—first to Yanquecollaguas in 1585, then to Laricollaguas in 1591 (Cook 2002; Tibesar 1953:66–68). Oré was among this second group. Oré, and presumably at least some of the other friars and diocesan priests, knew Quechua, either through their family background (as in the case of Oré, who likely learned Quechua from his wet nurse; see Cook 1992) or through the Quechua courses of the Cathedral in Lima (Castro Pineda 1963; Mannheim 1991:65–67). So there is little doubt that evangelization contributed to the local extinction of Aymara and its replacement with Quechua, but the transition was likely well underway under Inka rule.

Political Organization

Below the ethnic division between the Collaguas and Cabanas, a nested hierarchy of bipartite and tripartite subdivisions structured the political and economic organization of the province. As Ulloa reports in his relación, the Collaguas were internally divided between the lower-ranking Laricollaguas (or Lari Collaguas) to the adjacent east of the Cabanas in the lower-central valley and the higher-ranking Yanquecollaguas (or Yanque Collaguas) in the central and upper stretches of the valley. These respective subethnic group names expressed kin-based rank distinctions: *Yanque* (or *Yanqui*), according to Ulloa, was a locally venerated name that was used as an honorific in the address of the paramount kurakas of the province and was the name of the provincial capital, where the principal kurakas "used to and continue to reside" (Ulloa Mogollón 1965 [1586]:329). *Lari* (or *Lare*) was likewise used as an honorific of the lords of Laricollaguas and means "uncle" or "relative" (specifically, mother's brother; see Zuidema 1964:115–18). This avuncular terminology connotes that the Laricollaguas reckoned their status relative to an apical female ancestor, marriage partner of the apical male progenitor of the

Yanquis. Indeed, Ulloa (Ulloa Mogollón 1965 [1586]:329) goes on to affirm this logic:

> And because the *lares* and *yanquis* consider themselves as brothers who both emerged from *Collaguata*, the mountain mentioned previously, they say that they founded these two principal towns, the one called *Yanqui*, where the greater Lords [*Señores*] were and the other *Lare*, where the Lords are that follow them and are uncles and nephews.[6]

Each of the three provincial subdivisions—Yanquecollaguas, Laricollaguas, and Cabanaconde—was administered through its eponymous capital settlement (Cabanaconde, Lari, Yanque) during colonial times. Yanque, as the capital of the high-ranking Yanquecollaguas repartimiento, served as the capital of the province as a whole. As I discuss in chapter 4, this top-tier administrative and settlement arrangement appears built on Inkaic precedents.

Moving down the scale to the interior organization of each of the provincial subdivisions, an ideal structure is apparent, as indicated in the quote from the relación above. First, as is ubiquitous in Andean social organization, each was subdivided by ranked moieties (called *parcialidades* by the Spanish), Hanansaya (upper moiety) and Urinsaya (lower moiety). In colonial times, the moieties of Laricollaguas and Cabanaconde were the units of encomienda grants, while Yanquecollaguas, the largest of the three, was granted singly, making it among the most sought-after encomiendas in the viceroyalty. Within each of the three provincial subdivisions, each of the moieties was in turn composed of a series of named, ranked ayllus.

It is at this scale, within each of the moieties of the three provincial subdivisions, where the tripartition and decimal administrative categories is evident. The striking characteristic of the system is its direct parallel with the reckoning of prestige among the royal ayllus, or panacas, of Cuzco. In the case of Inka kinship classification, the prestige and rank of each of these categories—Collana, Pahana, and Cayao—was determined by reference to the calculation of kinship distance from an apical ancestor. Members of the Collana group, an Aymara word meaning "of excellent quality, of primary origin" (Bertonio 1956 [1612]), would be most closely related to the focal ancestor, those of Pahana less so, and those of Cayao only distantly related. Zuidema has illustrated how in Inka kinship, Collana denotes bilateral descent from the ruling sibling-spouses, those of Pahana unilaterally, and those of Cayao were not directly related (Zuidema 1964:115–18; 1973, 1977). These kin affiliations in turn governed the spatial organization and ritual calendar of the *ceque* network of shrines in Cuzco. Several researchers have noted the close parallels between this tripartite hierarchical structure and the political organization of the province of the Collaguas and Cabanas (Bauer 1998:35–38; Cock Carrasco 1976–77; Pärssinen 1992:362–71; Rostworowski de Diez Canseco 1983:121–23; Wachtel 1977:77). An elegant ideal tripartite decimal Inkaic administrative structure for the province as a whole can be deduced from the organization implicit in Ulloa's description. Each of the three ayllus within each moiety was said to be composed of 300 tributaries, for an ideal total of 900 tributaries in each moiety, or 1,800 tributaries in each of Yanquecollaguas, Laricollaguas, and Cabanaconde, for a total of 5,400 tributary households in the province as a whole (Table 3.2).

The process of articulating such imperial forms with local counterparts had produced an emergent improvised order by the time the Spanish stepped into the scene. A closer look at the visitas to the valley shows that many ayllus, especially those of Hanansaya, did not actually follow the tripartite or decimal nomenclature. Analysis of the "deviations" from the ideal Inkaic structure can thus provide important inroads into these processes and help to move beyond static or generic characterizations of the organization of these ethnic polities and the form of Inka administration in the province.

Table 3.2. Schematic of the ideal ayllu organization of the Collagua Province as reconstructed in prior research

I. Yanquecollaguas

A. Hanansaya		B. Urinsaya
1. Collana	1.1 Collana	Structure repeats
	1.2 Collana Taypi Pataca	
	1.3 Collana Cayao Pataca	
2. Pahana (Payan, Taypi)	2.1 Pahana Collana Pataca	
	2.2 Pahana Taypi Pataca	
	2.3 Pahana Cayao Pataca	
3. Cayao	3.1 Cayao Collana Pataca	
	3.2 Cayao Taypi Pataca	
	3.3 Cayao Pataca	

II. Laricollaguas

A. Hanansaya	B. Urinsaya
Structure repeats	Structure repeats

III. Cabanaconde

A. Hanansaya	B. Urinsaya
Structure repeats	Structure repeats

In chapter 6, I look more closely at the traces of this ideal structure and deviations from it, and chapter 7 reconstructs the land-tenure patterns of the constituent households of each ayllu based on their landholding declarations in the visitas. This GIS-based spatial analysis shows distinct distributions of the field holdings of the ayllus that do not conform to the Inka tripartite and decimal nomenclature, permitting reconstruction of finely attuned negotiations between local communities and Inka imperial administration.

Across the "Divide" of Conquest: Early Spanish Administration and Evangelization

By the same token, then, it is equally critical to reconstruct such (already hybrid) state-local articulations in the Inka empire to understand the contingencies through which early agents and institutions of Spanish colonial administration and evangelization were inserted in the early years following the conquest. The importance of the Collaguas and Cabanas to the Inkas, and subsequently to the Spanish, is also evident in the recipients of their grants of encomienda.[7] As early as August, 1, 1535, the Cabanas were granted in Cuzco by Francisco Pizarro to Cristóbal Pérez—an important member of the group of reinforcements that arrived from Hispaniola shortly after the initial invasion of Tawantinsuyu—and his son Juan de Arbes. Two Cabana lords, Yaquinicho and Ampire, were resident in Cuzco, suggesting close ties between the Cabanas and the ruling dynasty. The terms of the grant reflect the hazy state of Spanish knowledge of the lands to the south, as they relied on the vague testimony of the Cabana lords regarding the size and locations of their subject populations: about 1,500 people "in the province of Condesuyo" scattered in the hamlets of Ayomarca, Tirpa, Pascya, and Api to the east and Guanca, Marco, Guambo, and Yura to the west. There are no indications that Pérez ever visited his Cabanaconde encomienda personally; the Cabanas' catechist or majordomo was probably the main contact between the Cabanas and their encomendero (Cook 2007:31–32).

The Collaguas were not included in this grant, but not for lack of connection with the Inka nobility, as has been suggested (cf. Cook 2007:32). Instead, they appear to have been initially retained in encomienda by Manco Inka himself, along with other valued estates and provinces with intimate ties to the Inka dynasty, such as Ollantaytambo, Yucay, Calca, and Andahuaylas (Julien 1998). Aside from the estate holdings, this encomienda bloc, referred to obliquely in the repartimiento documents as the "encomiendas del Inka," extends over much of the southern highlands—a vast area the extent of which

Pizarro had only a vague notion prior to the return of Almagro's southern expedition in 1537. Contrary to the norm, these encomiendas del Inca were not granted to conquistadores in the *repartimientos generales* (general distributions) of 1534, 1535, or 1540—perhaps in exchange for other concessions from Manco Inca to Pizarro (Julien 1998:490–502). In any case, the Collaguas were prized as one of the largest and most lucrative encomiendas in Peru and were granted to individuals of the highest echelons of the Spanish elite. Francisco Pizarro granted Yanquecollaguas first to Gonzalo Pizarro on January 10, 1540 (Málaga Medina 1977), and subsequently to the prominent *vecino* (gentryman) of Arequipa Francisco Noguerol de Ulloa, in recognition for his role in defeating the rebellion of Gonzalo, before it reverted to Phillip II himself in 1559 (Cook and Cook 1991:29–32, 127–29).[8]

After the initial encomienda to Pérez, the encomiendas of the Cabanas, as well as the Laricollaguas, were split by moiety. Noble David Cook has reconstructed the most detailed history of the early encomiendas of the Collaguas and Cabanas, and the following draws on his discussion (Cook 2007:31–33, 51–64). Following the quelling of the sieges of Cuzco and Lima led by Manco Inka, and the defeat of the Almagrists in the Battle of Salinas in April 1538, Pizarro was for the first time in a position to consolidate control, and he orchestrated the first repartimiento general of encomiendas. Cristóbal Pérez died in the Battle of Salinas, and his Cabana encomienda was passed to his son, Juan de Arbes. Pizarro also granted a group of about 300 Cabanas, apparently *mitmaqkuna* (ethnic colonists) cultivating maize and coca in the lower Majes and Camaná stretches of the river, to Juan Ramírez, and another group to Lope de Idiáquez. Ramirez and Arbes became embroiled in a protracted legal battle because of confusion over the jurisdictions of their respective encomiendas—a common occurrence in these early years, since the Spanish assumed coterminous and contiguous jurisdictional and territorial boundaries but Andean political jurisdictions were discontinuous by nature as ethnic colonists in often distant lands maintained ties of reciprocity to their homeland kin and lords. Another bout of litigation threatened to flare up again over the Cabanaconde encomiendas when Idiáquez, in closing his affairs in Peru to return to Spain following the renewed conflict between the Pizarrists and Almagro the Younger, passed his Cabana encomienda to his fellow Basque associate Juan de Vergara. Though normally not a legal transfer (since Vergara was not next of kin), Vaca de Castro approved it. Arbes issued a legal challenge, claiming that the encomienda Indians in the Idiáquez encomienda actually pertained to the original encomienda granted by Francisco Pizarro to Arbes's father, Cristobal Pérez. With the suit threatening to consume a wealth of legal fees, a settlement was reached to partition Cabanaconde by moiety, with Arbes retaining Urinsaya and Vergara granted Hanansaya (about 600 tributaries each).

During the first four decades of Spanish rule, permanent Spanish presence in the valley was restricted virtually exclusively to priests and friars. Franciscan friars, with the order of La Gasca to reinvigorate religious instruction in the provinces, made early inroads in the Colca Valley during the 1540s by establishing a series of rustic chapels at the principal settlements in the valley (Tibesar 1953:46, 65). These villages probably grew gradually as they became officially recognized as doctrinas in 1557 by Viceroy Marqués de Cañete (Tibesar 1953:47, 65–66). As discussed in chapter 5, I have identified several of these doctrinas, which are still readily identified at local late prehispanic settlements with early colonial occupations and the standing remains of chapels.

These provisional doctrinas were short lived, however, as they were abandoned or overbuilt when the Toledan regime—headed by the corregidor and acting visitador Lope de Suazo—forcibly resettled the population of the Corregimiento of Collaguas into 24 nucleated reducción villages during the visita general in the early 1570s (Málaga Medina 1974, 1977). Despite this reorganization of settlement, colonial administration continued to siphon tribute through vestiges of the Inkaic order, leaving the collection of tribute to local kurakas (see chapters 7 and 8). Because tribute was assessed by population, tribute quotas based on the original Toledan censuses became proportionately greater burdens on households in the face of demographic decline brought about by successive waves of European-introduced epidemics and out-migration (Cook 1982). Undoubtedly faced with growing protests from their subjects, the Collagua lords were vocal advocates for lowering their tribute levies and petitioned several times for population recounts.[9] The resulting post-Toledan censuses, or *revisitas*, represent one of the largest series for any single locale in the New World (Table 3.3). They are also among the most meticulous visitas known, rivaling modern censuses and cadastral surveys in their level of detail in recording household-level demographic and economic information (see Pease 1977b; Robinson 2003a, 2006, 2009).

The original document photocopies and paleographic transcriptions done for the Río Colca Abandoned Terrace Project were graciously entrusted to me by Maria Benavides, and the analyses presented in this book are based on the original transcriptions by Laura Gutiérrez Arbulú, with extensive cross-checking against the photocopied originals. The listing of the visitas in this series is found in Table 3.3.

As in many Andean locales, the late colonial and early republican periods in the province of Collaguas are not as well documented or understood as

Table 3.3. Visitas to the Colca Valley

Repartimiento (Provincial division)	Moiety	Year	Completeness/Provenience
Yanquecollaguas	Hanansaya	1591	Fragment, published in Pease 1977b; APY
Yanquecollaguas	Urinsaya	1591	Large fragment, published in Pease 1977b; MNH
Cabanaconde	Hanansaya	1596	Near complete, transcribed,[b] published in Robinson 2009; APY
Yanquecollaguas	Urinsaya	1604	Large fragment, transcribed,[b] published in Robinson 2006; APY
Laricollaguas	Hanansaya	1604	Large fragment, transcribed,[b] published in Robinson 2003a; APY
Laricollaguas	Urinsaya	1604	Complete, published in Robinson 2003a; APY
Yanquecollaguas	Hanansaya	1615–17	Large fragment, transcribed,[a] published in Robinson 2006; APY
Cabanaconde	Urinsaya	1645	Fragment, transcribed,[b] published in Robinson 2009; APY
Yanquecollaguas	Hanansaya	1667	Callalli only, published in Galdos Rodríguez 1984; ADA

Notes: APY: Archivo Parroquial de Yanque, housed in the Archivo Arzobispal de Arequipa (Benavides 1990, 1992); MNH: Museo Nacional de la Historia; ADA: Archivo Departamental de Arequipa.
a. Transcription by Laura Gutiérrez Arbulú. Transcription funding provided primarily by William Denevan, with additional funding from Maria Benavides and Mauricio de Romaña (see Benavides 1990).
b. Transcription by David Robinson.

the early post-Toledan period. The best records for the period between the late seventeenth and early nineteenth centuries are from local parish archives, including the *libros de fábrica,* which register the economic transactions of the local churches, some of the activities of the priests, nuns, and sacristans, as well as the physical upkeep of the church and church lands. The parish archives also include (somewhat patchy) birth, baptismal, marriage, and funeral registries of parishes, all housed in the Yanque Parish Archive within the archdiocese archives of Arequipa (Benavides 1988b, 1991, 1992).

While documentation is relatively sparse, the seventeenth and eighteenth centuries were apparently difficult years of decline and hardship in the province. Using the parish registries, Cook estimated that the population of the valley reached its nadir in the mid-eighteenth century at about 8000–10,000 inhabitants—a drop of 87 percent from the projected 1530 (pre-Conquest) population—before slowly recovering and eventually reaching 32,000 in 1972, approximately the same size as four centuries earlier (Cook 1982:84–88). During this period, the *parcialidad*-level authority of kurakas diminished as ecclesiastical authorities sought to reign in their power. Such rivalry between church and cacique claims to authority is recorded in the 1689–1731 libro de fábrica of the parish of Yanque, which reveals that during this time period, the church obliged kurakas to provide extensive resources and labor to the parish and its priests (Benavides 1986a:519; 1986e:387; 1991). As in other regions of the Andes (Saignes 1995), a system of parish confraternities had been introduced that deflected the reciprocal obligations of the villagers from the kurakas to the church (Benavides 1986a:519). These changes had a curdling effect on kuraka political power and local constructs of community, as the parish within each village became linked to political authority. It is also during this time period that kurakas are first seen referring to ayllus as "pueblos" (Benavides 1997). Thus, two centuries after reducción, Andean and Spanish constructs of community were thoroughly fused. The collapse of native kuraka authority continued in the wake of the reforms after the great Tupac Amaru rebellion of 1780–82, when it was determined that governing officials of the pueblos would be named by Spanish provincial authorities (Benavides 1986a:519).

Today, village identity is more salient than a sense of ethnic Collagua or Cabana identity per se, although the villagers of the former areas of the Collaguas and Cabanas mobilize their identities in other ways and maintain different styles of elaborately embroidered dresses and hats (Femenias 1997, 2005; Femenias 1998). The primary irrigation canals originally built during the LIP and Late Horizon continue to carry water to fields from the snow-capped peaks surrounding the valley, and their trajectories cut across modern community boundaries. As a result, conflict, at times violent, between villages over rights to water sources for their canals have been frequent over the last century (Benavides 1997; Gelles 1990, 2000). In this way, the built landscape of the prehispanic past continues to assert itself in opposition to the nucleated pattern of villages imposed by Toledo over four centuries ago.

Notes

1. Plaggen: "An artificially made surface layer produced by long-continued manuring" (Soil Survey Staff 1975, 1990).

2. Quinoa, when planted with wide spacing (70 to 120 cm apart), can be cultivated successfully with as little as 300 mm of rain annually (Tapia et al. 1979:92, as cited in Treacy 1989b:132). In theory, then, some rain-fed agriculture of quinoa is possible under the current climatic regime but is not practiced when much higher yields are possible with irrigation.

3. Aside from problems of discreteness and a lack of association with features, bulk soil samples constitute an average value of the pooled charcoal in the sample. Contamination by old carbon in the soil results in skewing toward old values. This becomes especially

apparent when comparing well-provenienced, discrete charcoal samples with bulk soil sample dates.

4. The Collaguas are mentioned in the chronicles only by reference to their purported period of Inka imperial incorporation. Garcilaso (1966 [1609]:153) and Cobo (1979 [1653]:119–20) relate that the Collaguas as having been incorporated by the Inka Mayta Capac, the fourth ruler in the dynastic succession, through his marriage to a daughter (Mama Yacchi) of the principal kuraka of the Collaguas. Both probably derive their accounts from that of the Franciscan friar Luis Jerónimo de Oré (1992 [1598]:41), who worked and lived in Coporaque during the last two decades of the sixteenth century. Oré derives his account from the ex-oral testimony of this marriage alliance—a common Inka stratagem for establishing hierarchical affinal ties to subject peoples (see Covey 2003:352–53). The reference likely refers to a marriage alliance with Mayta Capac's panaca rather than with Mayta Capac himself, since his rule precedes the expansionist imperial period by at least four generations (Pease 1977a:140–41). But it does point to important and potentially longstanding links between Collagua elites and the Cuzco dynasty.

5. The antiquity and functions of those outlier colonies remains unresolved, however, and may, like the Lupaqa colonies of the upper Moquegua drainage, prove to be later than predicted by the Murra model (Van Buren 1996, 1997) or to have functioned to serve Inkaic imperial designs in the region rather than an ancient adaptive system to Andean ecological zonation.

6. "Y como entre los lares y yanquis se tienen por hermanos y salidos de Collaguata, cerro ya dicho, dicen que fundaron estos dos pueblos principales, el uno llamado Yanqui, donde estuvieron los mayores Señores y el otro Lare, donde están los Señores que le siguen e son tíos e sobrinos."

7. For general discussion of the institution of encomienda, see Lockhart 1968:11–33.

8. La Gasca issued the encomienda grant of Yanquecollaguas to Noguerol on September 10, 1548, five months after the defeat of Gonzalo Pizarro at Jaquijahuana. Awarded in recognition of his military service against the Pizarrist rebellion, it was apparently unknown to the Crown that Noguerol had supported the insurgency before switching allegiances (see Cook and Cook 1991:21–32). Laricollaguas was divided into two encomiendas along moiety lines. Francisco Pizarro granted Hanansaya to Marcos Retamoso and Urinsaya to his personal secretary, Alonso Rodríguez Picado, both on the same day as the grant of Yanquecollaguas to Gonzalo (January 10, 1540) (see Málaga Medina 1977).

9. There is also specific evidence within the visitas that suggests that they resulted from the dogged protests of their leaders. For example, the 1604 revisitas were undertaken in response to a petition to the viceroy by the *protector de los naturales* (protector of natives; almost certainly at the urging of the Collagua kurakas) because the population could not produce their tribute levies in the face of widespread hunger and poor harvests, in part due to heavy ashfall from the Huaynaputina eruption of 1600 (Cook 2003:xxiv). A crisis may have precipitated calls for the previous visitas of 1591 as well, since epidemics of smallpox (*sarampion*) are mentioned in the 1591 Yanquecollaguas Urinsaya visita, and the head Franciscan priest of the province, Luis Gerónimo de Oré, was present to register and confirm deaths declared by the villagers (Verdugo and Colmenares 1977 [1591], fol. 97r [343]).

4

NEGOTIATING COMMUNITY AND LANDSCAPE
UNDER AUTONOMOUS AND INKA RULE

Drawing on a variety of archaeological and ethnohistorical data, this chapter explores the emergence of the autonomous ethnic polities of the Colca Valley during the Late Intermediate period and their subsequent incorporation into Tawantinsuyu. Major transformations in the scale and organization of local communities occurred during the five centuries spanning the LIP (AD 1000–1450) and Late Horizon (AD 1450–1532). In this chapter, I present the survey data that document a shift from heterarchical, segmentary community relations during the LIP to the emergence of a more centralized but locally mediated political arrangement under Inka rule. The chapter evaluates the often contrasting views that emerge from documentary and archaeological perspectives on the LIP and Late Horizon in the valley. On one hand, ex-oral depictions of the origin myths of the Collaguas and Cabanas, their representation as powerful chieftaincies in conflict over resources prior to Inka rule, and their seemingly comprehensive reorganization under Inka imperial aegis according to an intricate administrative hierarchy suggests a high degree of coherency and centralization as ethnic "señoríos" during the LIP and a direct form of centralized, hierarchical administration—along with a variety of kin-based alliance strategies—under Inka rule. The archaeological evidence, on the other hand, signals a more fluid social landscape during the LIP, in which different scales of community identity and practices were salient in different contexts. Relations between these corresponding scales of community organization likely oscillated between cooperation and conflict. The material traces of Inka administration indicate an improvised order in which extant patterns of settlement and land use were left intact, while local-imperial relations were mediated by local elites and through the idiom of commensalism.

After briefly discussing the survey methodology, I first present an overview of the long-term history of human occupation and land-use patterning in the valley to provide the context in which the emergence of the LIP polities of the valley occurred. The settlement pattern data for the LIP, which signal a marked expansion of settlement in all three areas of the valley—Yanquecollaguas, Laricollaguas, and Cabanaconde—are then presented. Distinctive ceramic and architectural styles emerge throughout the valley during this period, suggesting some sense of shared identity, though there is also strong evidence for internecine violence, especially in Yanquecollaguas, in the pattern of hilltop fortifications typical of this period. I weigh textual and archaeological evidence for the form and timing of violent conflict, comparing local patterns to those found in neighboring locales. After a discussion of local textual representations of Inka rule, the chapter turns to a discussion of the settlement pattern during the Inka occupation of the Late Horizon, when imperial structures were built at each of the large settlements with local elite architecture and primary administrative centers established in each of the three areas of the valley. I then discuss the distinctive features of local Collagua domestic architecture, as well as the significance of intra- and intersite disparities in the size and elaboration of houses, the distribution and types of Inka imperial structures, and the elaboration of large complexes of mortuary monuments associated with ancestor veneration near the principal settlements in the survey. The infrastructure of agricultural and pastoral production expanded markedly with settlement during the LIP and Late Horizon, and I describe how systems of hydraulic and agricultural landscape engineering that developed during these times reflect a coordinated regime of multisettlement communal water and land allocation. Most of the canals and bench terraces in the survey area were apparently built and used during the LIP, while Inka efforts at increasing (surplus) agro-pastoral production were focused on intensifying camelid production in the puna and improving extant agricultural infrastructure while regimenting agricultural inputs and building terraces in a few previously uncultivated areas.

Archaeological Surveying Techniques in a High Andean Landscape

The natural and built features of the Colca Valley landscape present many opportunities and challenges for systematic archaeological survey. The semiarid climate of the valley affords very good ground visibility, especially during the dry season (May to October), when we conducted the survey. Valley topography and various built landscape features, however, sometimes hindered strict adherence to survey transects. We adapted a number of techniques to deal with the obstacles presented by the valley's high topographic relief, extensive terracing, and field walls.

Such obstacles were especially dense inside the valley rim. We generally surveyed this core zone of the survey area using transects spaced between 5 and 20 m. The specific distance varied according to local conditions and considerations. On the relatively flat, alluvial terraces of the valley floor, where agricultural field sizes are generally large, the crew was distributed at 10-m transect intervals in unharvested fields because of reduced ground visibility, and at 20-m transect intervals in harvested fields where surveyors could readily see the ground surface. Surveyors would advance from field to field, crossing over the stone walls that divided them. However, the bench and contour terraces of the steep lower slopes of the valley made strict transect surveying virtually impossible. To ensure full coverage in these areas, each crew member surveyed a terrace group, walking a single transect across each terrace unless a terrace exceeded approximately 10 m in width. Canals and dividing walls formed natural endpoints for each transect, and the crew descended and ascended terraces in a zigzag fashion, using canals or dividing walls as boundaries between terrace groups. Given the intensity of the survey, the density of sites, and the difficulties of the terrain, average daily survey coverage in the agricultural core of the valley was usually 0.3–0.5 km^2 per day.

In contrast, the open expanses of the suni and puna zones allowed for more regularized use of transects. Because of its distance from modern settlements, we surveyed most of the puna during several four- to five-day expeditions, using backpacks and camping equipment. Good ground visibility and the scarcity of built features allowed for wider transect intervals, ranging from 25 to 30 m, depending on local topography. The slow pedogenic processes and good ground visibility in the puna permit more ready observation of features, even relatively ephemeral soil stains and artifact scatters. For example, we recorded discrete concentrations of lithic debitage of less than 10 m^2. It is probable that we did not register some scatters of this small size using transect intervals of 25 to 30 m. Given the objectives of the project, I considered these potential oversights acceptable, since all sites greater than about 10 × 10 m would be observable and the wider transect intervals allowed for much greater total coverage. In the puna, daily survey coverage averaged approximately 3 km^2, an acceptable compromise for balancing the overall scale and resolution of the survey and comparable to other survey projects in the nearby lacustrine and Altiplano zones (Bandy 2001; Seddon 1998; Stanish 1997a).

In all areas, crew members were encouraged to leave their transects if they came upon potential features or artifact concentrations between transects, returning to the transect after investigating and recording the sites. Sites were defined as significant concentrations of ceramic, lithic, or other cultural features in a discrete area. In the case of sherd and lithic scatters, we did not employ formal artifact density thresholds as site definition criteria but based our decision on our shared judgment that there was a distinct increase in density of distinguishable extent in contrast to the "background noise" of low-density artifact scattering. Although this approach is judgmental, with coordination between members of the field crew, our site-inclusion criteria remained consistent throughout the project. In the field, I also used a "100 meter rule" in order to maintain a standard for including features in a site. That is, I registered features or clusters of features more than 100 m from any other features as different sites and those within 100 m as part of the same site. While arbitrary, this rule helped standardize the definition of sites and prevented overly impressionistic site definition in the field.

Site Nomenclature

Site names were assigned using the first two letters of the modern district (YA for Yanque and CO for Coporaque) followed by the site number (001–169). Thus, for example, YA-032 is in the District of Yanque and was the thirty-second site recorded in the survey. In cases where I divided sites into more than one sector (whether based on functional, temporal, or arbitrary criteria), we assigned a capital letter (A, B, C, etc.) to each sector. Once we identified a site, the crew would rejoin to record observations of the site and its constituent features on standardized forms, photograph any features of interest, map the site's perimeter and features, and collect a representative sample of diagnostic artifacts from the surface. I describe each of these operations in further detail below.

Site Sizes

Determining the sizes of most LIP and Late Horizon sites with standing architecture was relatively straightforward. At these sites, we recorded GPS points around the maximal area with cultural features. In a few cases (e.g., CO-100, CO-164), this total site area, which could include mortuary features or artifact concentrations, significantly exceeded the area occupied by standing domestic architecture, and in these cases, I plotted a second, smaller polygon for "residential area," defined by the outermost domestic structures. The reducción villages of Coporaque and Yanque presented special problems because even the late prehispanic features of these sites have been virtually obliterated. Furthermore, because it was not feasible to gain access to most house patios, we restricted our survey in the villages to the unpaved streets. However, the formal grid pattern facilitated division of the villages into arbitrary collection sectors, which provide a degree of provenience resolution. Site abandonment and construction processes have displaced artifacts from their original depositional contexts, so strict presence/absence criteria were not rigidly applied for inclusion of a given sector within a prehispanic occupation. In both cases, a few isolated structures made with Collagua and Inka-style cut-stone masonry also aided in estimating the site area. Size estimates for these sites is more subjective, relying on the distribution of structures made of prehispanic building materials and areas with the highest prehispanic artifact concentrations. Site coordinates and sizes, along with descriptions of the principal settlements in the Yanque-Coporaque survey area, are presented in the appendix.

Survey Area Coverage and Total Sites Recorded

Using the methods described above, between May and December 1999, our crew in the Colca Valley Regional Survey Project surveyed a contiguous area of 90.4 km^2 between 3,400 and 4,800 m across the valley to the surrounding puna on either side. We recorded 169 archaeological sites with 300 temporal components during the survey (Figure 4.1). The sites cover virtually the entire sequence of human occupation in the valley, from Early Archaic period lithic scatters through late prehispanic and colonial habitational sites with well-preserved architectural remains. As discussed in chapter 1, the survey was not designed to maximize the total area covered, as in a regional survey, but was guided by the goal of maximizing meso-resolution data by collecting detailed metric and stylistic data on the well-preserved late prehispanic architecture present at many sites. The discussion below supplements our findings in the Yanque-Coporaque area with those of Miriam Doutriaux in the Lari and Cabanaconde areas (Doutriaux 2004), which were collected using methods derived from this project to ensure comparability of results. Readers are encouraged to reference Doutriaux's dissertation directly for more detailed discussion of those findings.

Chronological Controls: Late Prehispanic Ceramics of the Colca Valley

The ceramic sequence that I developed divides local Collagua ceramics into four stylistic categories—Collagua I, II, III, and Collagua Inka—which I group into two chronological components: LIP (Collagua I and II) and Late Horizon (Collagua III and Collagua Inka). The sequence builds on the preliminary chronology developed by Malpass and de la Vera in the 1980s (de la Vera Cruz Chávez 1987, 1988, 1989; Malpass and de la Vera Cruz Chávez 1986, 1990) and the work of Brooks (1998:317–56), who differentiated Collagua ceramics from Chuquibamba (Cardona Rosas 1993; Kroeber 1944; Morante 1939; Sciscento 1989), Churajón (Kroeber 1944; Lumbreras 1974b:208), and

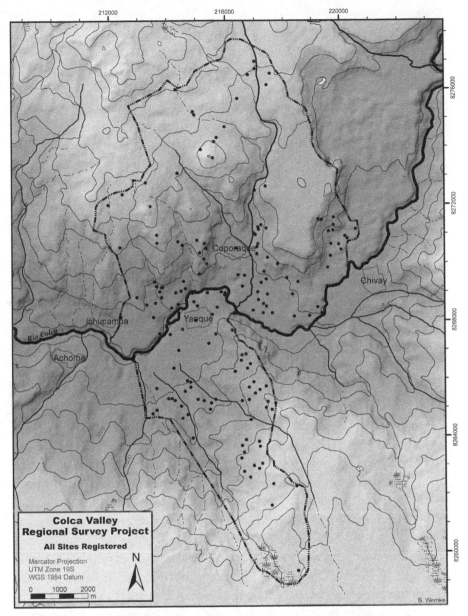

Figure 4.1. The Yanque-Coporaque survey area and all sites registered (N = 169).

other regional styles. Radiocarbon dates associated with local Middle Horizon ceramics excavated by Malpass and de la Vera Cruz provide *ante quem* dates for the beginning of the Collagua sequence (Collagua I). These dates, AD 429–694 and AD 436–779 (calibrated 2 sigma),[1] roughly coincide with the first half of the Middle Horizon. Thus Collagua I ceramics may overlap slightly with the terminal Middle Horizon. The end of the sequence, marked by clear Inka stylistic influence, is positioned according to the generally accepted dates of Inka imperial occupation of the region (AD 1450–1532), which are cross-dated with radiometric dates from the neighboring western Titicaca basin (e.g., Bauer and Stanish 2001:251–55; Stanish 1997a:47–48). Currently, there are no local radiocarbon dates from undisturbed contexts associated with decorated Collagua I or II ceramics, so the LIP portion of the sequence must be considered provisional. Future excavations and chronometric data should allow for evaluation and refinement of the current sequence.

The sequence derives from a similiary seriation approach (Rowe 1961:326–27) based on differences in formal and decorative elements, but it is also bolstered by cross-dating with related styles in surrounding locales. Bowl and plate forms dominate the diagnostics, and the general trend over the sequence in terms of form is a change from the more constricted, globular bowls of Collagua I to the more open, flat-bottomed bowls and shallow plates of Collagua III and Collagua Inka from the Late Horizon (Figure 4.2). Accompanying this morphological change is a shift in the placement of decoration from the external to internal surface between Collagua II and Collagua III. Collagua I decorations, executed in black on red and black and white on red on the vessel exterior, are organized in horizontal design fields and show continuity in design motifs from local Middle Horizon ceramics, such as Q'osqopa and other regional Wari variants. Collagua II bowls are intermediate in form between the constricted forms that dominate Collagua I and the open forms of Collagua III and Collagua Inka. Collagua II decorations are executed in black on red only and are generally not delineated as horizontal design fields. The thick-lined curvilinear motifs of Collagua II are broadly similar to Altiplano period (local LIP) styles of the western Titicaca basin, such as Pucarani Black on Red (Stanish 1997a:47–48, 153 [230.001–3]), Kelluyo (Stanish 1997a:46–47, Figure 22) and Tanka Tanka Black on Orange (Hyslop 1976:431–35). Collagua III and Collagua Inka ceramics exhibit clear indices of Inka influence. Collagua III bowls show greater continuity in slip color, surface treatment, and design motifs with Collagua I and II, but with formal details, such as the rim protuberances typical of Inka bowls (e.g., Stanish 1997a:47, Figure 99).

Collagua Inka vessels are local variants of Cuzco pottery, executed in bichrome and polychrome, and are well crafted in terms of firing, surface treatment, and decoration (see Figure 4.2). As a general observation, Collagua Inka ceramics are finely crafted and highly standardized as provincial Inka wares. We know that these ceramics were produced in the valley, both by their sheer quantity in local assemblages and because three ayllus of official state potters are registered in the visitas of Coporaque (APY Yanquecollaguas

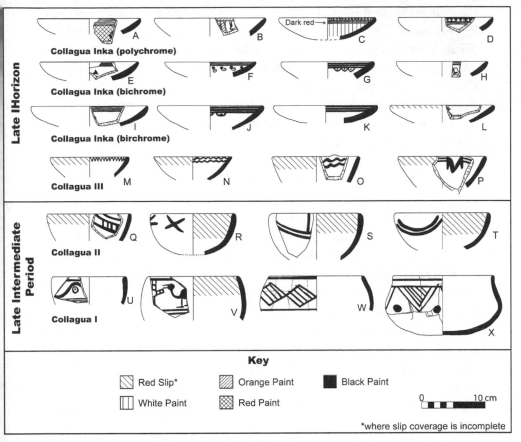

Figure 4.2. Examples of diagnostics from the Collagua ceramic sequence.

Hanansaya 1615–17, fols. 603v–611v; APY Yanquecollaguas Urinsaya 1604, fols. 268v–270r). As discussed in chapter 7, it is likely that the ancestors of these potters resided in the settlement of San Antonio (CO-100; originally named Cupi—see chapter 7). The form inventory of Collagua Inka vessels is dominated by the plates, constricted neck jars (aríbalos), and beakers (k'eros) typical of imperial Inka assemblages (for detailed discussion of local ceramic chronology, see Wernke 2003:Appenix A).

Antecedent Settlement and Land Use

The full breadth of human occupation of the Colca Valley is beyond the scope of this book, but an outline of broad changes in settlement in land use during the Formative period (locally defined as 1500 BC–AD 500) and Middle Horizon (AD 500–1100) is necessary to set the general context for understanding the changes evident in the LIP and Late Horizon (for fuller discussion, see Wernke 2011a). The earliest hunter-gatherers to reach the valley and environs occurred sometime during the Early Archaic period (8800–6800 BC), based on diagnostic projectile points we recovered from several open air and rock-shelter sites in the puna. The largest of these were used repeatedly throughout the epochal expanse of time encompassed by the Middle through Terminal Archaic periods. The shift to a more sedentary lifeway, associated with the first agriculture in the valley, occurred during the transition from the Terminal Archaic (3000–1500 BC) to the Formative period. Much of our knowledge of this early era is derived from obsidian recovered in faraway locales, which was compositionally sourced back to the Chivay source (also referred to as the Cotallalli source), one of the largest obsidian sources in the southern Andes (Brooks et al. 1997; Burger et al. 1998; Burger et al. 2000; Tripcevich 2010; Tripcevich and Yépez Álvarez 2009). The presence of Chivay source obsidian throughout the south-central Andes reveals extensive trade networks, with especially strong ties to populations in the Altiplano, stretching back to at least the Late Archaic (4800–3000 BC) (Brooks et al. 1997; Burger et al. 1998; Burger et al. 2000; Stanish et al. 2002; Tripcevich 2010). These data are generally consistent with Altiplano models of exchange (in the comparatively low relief, expansive landscape of dispersed human occupation), which emphasize the importance of regional networks and camelid-based caravaneering (Browman 1981; Dillehay and Núñez 1988). The Colca was evidently a nodal area in such regional networks since Archaic times.

Formative period chronological controls are still rudimentary, though we did identify ceramics broadly diagnostic of the period (Chiquero ceramics) and registered 30 Formative period sites in the Yanque-Coporaque survey area, distributed throughout all physiographic and ecological zones (Wernke 2011a). Unlike the neighboring Titicaca basin, no major Formative ceremonial centers have been identified, and there are no corporate art styles or decorated ceramics associated with the period locally. The earliest agricultural settlements were probably dispersed hamlets and villages associated with unirrigated sloping fields, valley bottom stone-bordered fields, and segmented terraces. The largest Formative period settlement, Chiquero (YA-032), is 3.88 ha in area, and at an elevation of 3,655 m, it is situated in the suni zone, providing access to both the valley bottom and puna lands above. The majority of diagnostic ceramics for the period was collected from Chiquero (64 percent, or n = 97 of 152 diagnostics), and the largest sample of basalt hoes (n = 69) was collected from this site as well, signaling agricultural cultivation by the site's inhabitants. The prevalence of hoes at the site may in part reflect opportunistic exploitation of the abundant basalt clasts found over the site surface. However, obvious evidence for use-wear—distal-end polishing and striations—indicates that the implements were used, not just manufactured locally. These basalt hoes are very similar in size and form to those recovered from Formative period contexts throughout the southern Peruvian Pacific drainages and circum–Titicaca basin (Seddon in Bandy 2001; Stanish 1997a; Stanish et al. 1994:65–71). The occurrence of stone hoes drops off dramatically in post-Formative contexts throughout the south-central Andes, as other (presumably perishable) materials replace this lithic technology, and such appears to be the case in the Colca as well.

Though the settlement pattern was evidently decentralized, some of the field complexes of the period collectively reached monumental proportions (though their construction was likely a gradual process). The stone-bordered fields of the valley bottom formed large "agro-mortuary" wall complexes composed of high and wide stone walls, varying from 2 m to as much as 10 m in thickness, which enclosed small field areas (most less than .25 ha in size). In plan view, these wall and field complexes formed a cellular pattern (suggesting a gradual agglutination process, rather than centralized planning of field layout), covering large areas of the relatively level valley bottom. Given their great thickness, the walls could easily be traversed on foot and used as elevated paths between fields (Wernke 2011a). Their flat tops were perforated from above by large cist tombs, forming larger mortuary complexes at their especially wide intersections. Human remains and Chiquero ceramics were observed in association with looted cist tombs at five sites composed of these wall complexes in the Yanque-Coporaque survey area. The largest complexes are located on the pampas to the adjacent west of Yanque. Doutriaux reports similar complexes in Lari (Doutriaux 2004:175–79).

As discussed in the previous chapter, the early field systems of the valley sides relied on a variety of water harvesting techniques rather than canal systems—some clustered around quebradas to capture the natural runoff accumulation, while others relied on check dams to guide runoff to sloping fields and terraces. The dating of these early field systems and associated settlements is imprecise, but landscape-scale superposition of later field systems provides a relative sequence. As Treacy has demonstrated (1994:102–3), unirrigated segmentary terraces are directly overlain by irrigated bench terrace complexes in several areas. The valley bottom was probably once more or less covered by unirrigated stone-bordered fields, but have since been similarly overbuilt by irrigated terraces. The basal levels of trench excavations through irrigated bench terraces at the site of Chijra (registered as San Antonio/Chijra in the Yanque-Coporaque survey) produced radiocarbon dates within the range of the Middle Horizon (see note 1; Malpass 1987; Malpass and de la

Vera Cruz Chávez 1990). The transition to irrigated field systems therefore likely began in earnest during the Middle Horizon, a period when the lower parts of the valley, in the areas around Cabanaconde and Lari, were under considerable influence or direct imperial presence of the Wari state. The construction of irrigation systems associated with Wari imperial installations has been documented in other valleys of the region, particularly in the Moquegua Valley to the south (Williams 1997, 2002). Whether Wari imperial influence or administration in parts of the Colca Valley, especially in the lower reaches of the valley, were similarly an impulse in the expansion of irrigated terracing remains a hypothesis to be tested, and one that merits further investigation.

The strongest evidence for a direct Wari imperial presence comes from the large sites of Charasuta near Lari (Doutriaux 2004:212–20) and Achachiwa near Cabanaconde (de la Vera Cruz Chávez 1988:40–55; 1989:56–70; Doutriaux 2004:202–7). Charasuta in particular exhibits an orthogonal core area that is reminiscent of other Wari provincial centers (Doutriaux 2004:202–7). But the Wari presence declines moving up valley; in the Yanque-Coporaque survey, no sites of identifiable Wari architectural attributes were registered and the local ceramic style of the period appears only indirectly influenced by Wari styles. The number of sites in the Yanque-Coporaque area increases slightly from the formative period (from 30 to 37), but 57 percent of these sites represent new occupations, marking a marked shift in settlement. Habitational sites were more concentrated in the lower elevations of the survey area than during the Formative, and evidence for valley bottom agriculture in the form of agro-mortuary wall complexes also expanded. Most of this expansion occurred on the pampas and rolling volcanic hills on the north side of the river, to the southeast of modern Coporaque, in association with a group of small settlements. While site areas for these settlements could not be determined, they later become large villages and towns during the LIP and Late Horizon. Overlying occupations at most settlements hinders inference of social organization during the Middle Horizon, but the diversity of mortuary features dating to this period provides the first tentative indices for power asymmetries in the local prehispanic sequence. There is no evidence for direct imperial administration by either Wari or Tiwanaku in the Yanque-Coporaque area, although evidence for Wari influence, as reflected in local ceramics, is generally stronger.

On the other hand, not a single Tiwanaku-affiliated sherd has been recovered anywhere in the valley, despite clear trade ties with Tiwanaku and other Altiplano sites through the Middle Horizon as evidenced by the dominance of Chivay source obsidian in their assemblages. Thus it appears that the upper Colca constituted a buffer zone between two spheres of influence, on the one hand being a terminus of Wari political influence, and on the other an important exchange node area in a longstanding orbit of trade with Altiplano groups (see Tripcevich 2007, 2010). Interestingly, Chivay source obsidian is exceedingly rare at Wari-affiliated sites (particularly, Cerro Baúl and Cerro Mejía) in Moquegua (Nash and Williams 2009). Instead, the bulk of the obsidian assemblage from those sites was from the Alca source in the Cotahuasi Valley, to the *north* of the Colca (i.e., farther away from Moquegua), indicating separate exchange networks in which the Chivay/Colca source was tied into the Altiplano/Tiwanaku network and the Alca/Cotahuasi source was tied into the Wari network.

In sum, there appear to have been markedly different modes of influence and interaction with Middle Horizon states in different areas of the valley, with more direct Wari imperial presence down valley and only minimal evidence for Wari influence up valley, where economic ties to the Altiplano are strongly in evidence. As discussed below, these differences in the Middle Horizon political and economic landscape of the valley surely account for some of the differences in settlement patterning and land use in these respective areas during the Late Intermediate period.

The Late Intermediate Period Settlement Pattern

Throughout all areas of the valley, major changes in settlement, architecture, land use, and material culture occurred after the Middle Horizon and during the 450 years of the LIP (Figure 4.3). Overall, settlement expanded dramatically during the LIP. It was during this period that the hamlets, villages, and towns of distinctive Collagua architecture and ceramics still readily visible on the landscape today proliferated throughout the valley, most located on defensible promontories and hillsides or the near-concentric-walled hilltop fortresses (*pukaras*) so characteristic of this period of strife throughout the central and south-central Andean highlands. Terracing and irrigation systems also expanded considerably during the LIP to cover all but the most marginal steep slopes below about 3,800 m. By all indications, then, the population grew and the valley landscape was transformed dramatically. There is strong architectural and mortuary evidence for growing social inequalities and sociopolitical complexity, but there is no indication of an overarching, centralized political organization for the valley as a whole, or even within any locale of the valley. Instead, political relations were apparently decentralized and fluid, probably oscillating between conflict and cooperation at different societal scales.

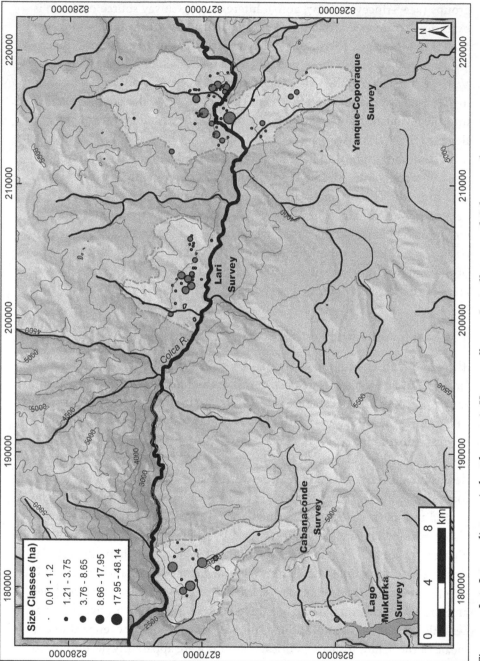

Figure 4.3. Late Intermediate period settlements in Yanquecollaguas, Laricollaguas, and Cabanaconde.

Late Intermediate Period Settlement in Yanquecollaguas

In the Yanquecollaguas survey area, where settlements were limited to the scale of hamlets and villages during the Middle Horizon and evidence for Wari imperial influence was minimal, the shift from the Middle Horizon to the LIP is marked by a great expansion of settlement and the appearance of the first large, town-sized settlements. We registered 53 sites with LIP components: 28 settlements, 10 cemeteries, nine agro-mortuary wall complexes, and three hilltop pukara fortifications (Figure 4.4). The great majority of

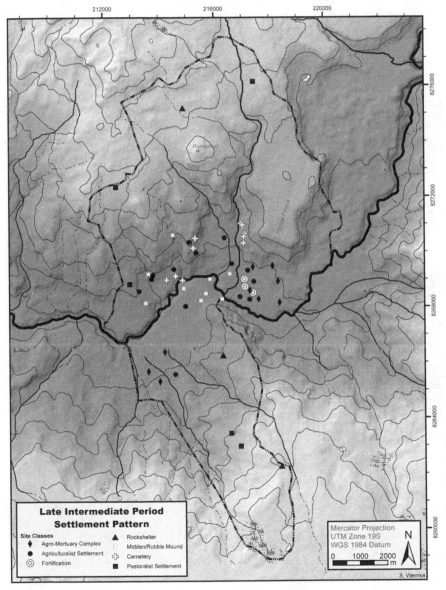

Figure 4.4. Late intermediate period sites in the Yanque-Coporaque survey area.

the settlements in this area are concentrated on the north side of the river in promontory and hillside contexts amid agricultural terracing, including the two largest towns of the period, San Antonio/Chijra (CO-100) and Uyu Uyu (YA-050). A cluster of settlements, including the large sites of Tunsa/Llacta-pampa (CO-150/163), Llanka (CO-127), and Kitaplaza (CO-164), are on the pampa and low, rolling hills to the south of modern Coporaque (Figure 4.5).

Overall, the settlement pattern in Yanquecollaguas is decentralized—no site dominates in terms of size, centrality, or elaboration of architecture. The site of San Antonio/Chijra is nearly twice the size as Uyu Uyu by aereal measure (8.65 vs. 4.26 ha, respectively), but it is a much more dispersed

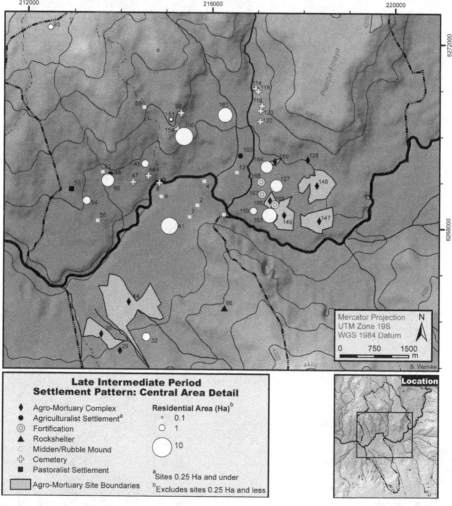

Figure 4.5. Detail of Late Intermediate period sites in the central part of the Yanque-Coporaque survey.

settlement. The dating of domestic structures is imprecise, but judging by the total number of LIP/LH houses (n = 136 at San Antonio/Chijra, n = 139 at Uyu Uyu), they were likely more or less equivalent in terms of population. Both are located in defensible promontory settings overlooking the alluvial plains above the river gorge and are surrounded by extensive contour and linear bench terraces in warm microclimates. We registered the sites of Tunsa and Llactapampa as separate sites during the survey because they are located slightly over 100 m apart, but they probably functioned as a single, dispersed settlement. Considered together, Tunsa/Llactapampa is of comparable size to Uyu Uyu and San Antonio, both in terms of area and number of houses. The largest LIP settlements in the surrounding areas beyond the survey zone, Juscallacta near Chivay to the east (Brooks 1998; Guerra Santander and Aquize Cáceres 1996) and Malata and Achomaniy near Achoma to the west (Oquiche Hernani 1991; Shea 1997), are in the same size range or smaller than the largest settlements in the survey, so the decentralized pattern almost certainly holds for the entire Yanquecollaguas area.

Below this top tier of town-sized settlements, a number of smaller villages were distributed throughout all ecological zones. In the kichwa and suni zones, Lama (CO-103) and Kitaplaza (CO-164) were established near Tunsa/Llactapampa on the pampas and rolling hills to the southeast of Coporaque. On the south side of the river, the site of Chiquero, former location of a sizable Formative settlement, was resettled after being virtually abandoned during the Middle Horizon and continued to grow through the Late Horizon. In the puna, two pastoralist villages were registered with LIP occupations, one on the north side of the river (YA-093) and one on the south side (YA-034). Architectural remains were preserved only at one of these (YA-093), where we recorded 12 circular houses and associated corrals, while at YA-034, occupation continued from Early Archaic, Formative, and Middle Horizon times.

The remaining 20 small hamlets and ceramic concentrations make up the bulk of the site count for the LIP, and are distributed throughout all ecozones. Three agriculturalist hamlets with domestic architectural remains are found amid agricultural fields near larger villages and towns. For example, the site of Llactarana (YA-054), a hamlet of seven preserved small houses surrounded by terracing, is located about 500 m to the southwest of Uyu Uyu, and the two sites were clearly intervisible. The hamlet of Lama (CO-103), composed of 12 poorly preserved domestic structures, is situated on the pampa to the south of Coporaque and is part of a larger site cluster that includes the larger settlements of Kitaplaza, Tunsa/Llactapampa, and Llanka. In the puna, one hamlet-sized open-air ceramic scatter was recorded at CO-105. Three small sites in the puna are rockshelters, which were probably used as refuges or encampments for pastoralists.

The trend of overall growth and decentralization during the LIP is readily apparent in the Laricollaguas and Cabanaconde areas as well. In these areas, where the evidence for Wari imperial influence (or possibly occupation) is stronger, the change in settlement to the LIP is marked by the abandonment or depopulation of the major, large Wari sites of Achachiwa (CA-33) and Charasuta (LA-99). As Doutriaux notes, "With the disappearance of Wari influence in the valley, the population exploded out of the two main 'Wari influenced' centers into dispersed settlements and homesteads scattered throughout the quichua and suni ecological zones" (Doutriaux 2004:225). But even as the settlement pattern became more dispersed among more moderately sized settlements in Lari and Cabanaconde, internal disparities in wealth and status increased during the LIP, as in the Yanquecollaguas.

Late Intermediate Period Settlement in Cabanaconde

In Cabanaconde, just over half of the Middle Horizon sites (8 of 13) continued to be occupied during the LIP, but in much diminished form, with the exception of the sites of Umawasi (CA-37) and Liway Kocho (CA-13) (Doutriaux 2004:225). The dominant Middle Horizon site of Achachiwa is all but abandoned during the LIP (Doutriaux 2004:225). So the changes in settlement patterning were quite dramatic, especially when considering that half (9 of 17) of the LIP occupations were new sites in previously unoccupied locations (Doutriaux 2004:225–29).

As in Yanquecollaguas, no settlement appears dominant, and the largest town-sized settlements—Kallimarka (CA-18/CA-19; 10.0 ha), Umawasi (CA-37; 7.9 ha), and Antisana (CA-32; 6.3 ha), are similar in scale to those of Yanquecollaguas and situated in promontory or hilltop contexts (Figure 4.6). Architectural preservation is much poorer than in Yanquecollaguas, but several hundred domestic structures,[2] along with later Inka public architecture, are preserved at the largest and best-preserved LIP settlement in the Cabanaconde area, Huch'uy Kallimarka (CA-18; 9.1 ha). The LIP occupation of this site covered the top of a 550-m-long ridge and was probably functionally integrated as a single settlement with the site of Hatun Kallimarka (CA-19; 0.9 ha), situated a few hundred meters higher on the same ridge. As in the central valley, the Late Horizon and LIP occupations are commingled, precluding relative dating of particular domestic structures at the site. But the domestic architecture at Kallimarka shows a broad range of size and elaboration—internal social differentiation within settlements thus probably begins during the LIP similar to Yanquecollaguas.

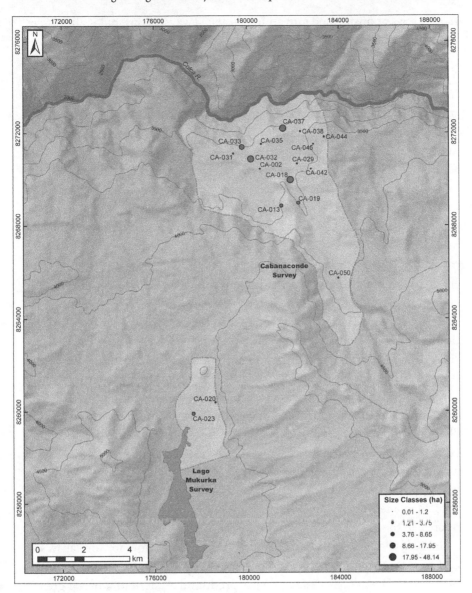

Figure 4.6. Late Intermediate period settlements in Cabanaconde. (Data from Doutri-aux 2004.)

The remaining settlements are composed of small ceramic scatters—some with poorly preserved domestic structures (such as Liway Kocho, CA-13)—that are distributed throughout the kichwa through puna zones. The site of Tambo de Mukurka (CA-23), situated on the north shore of Lake Mukurka in the high puna, was established during the LIP. The original site layout is obscured by subsequent Late Horizon occupation, when (as implied by the name) it was transformed into an Inka *tambo* (waystation), but it almost certainly functioned as a small herding hamlet during LIP times.

The LIP settlement pattern of Cabanaconde is therefore best characterized as a pattern of a few coequal, large agriculturalist towns and smaller villages in the kichwa and suni zones, as well as herding hamlets in the puna, that is overall less extensive and intensive than that of Yanquecollaguas. If anything, settlement is more concentrated in a few town-sized settlements, but these are more or less evenly distributed among the terrace systems of the area. Unlike the Yanquecollaguas area, however, there is no clear evidence for fortifications in the Cabanaconde area, suggesting that there was less internal conflict and/or perceived outside threat than in the central and upper reaches of the valley—a point I will explore in further detail later in this chapter.

Late Intermediate Period Settlement in Laricollaguas

In Lari, settlement similarly expanded and dispersed from 17 Middle Horizon sites to 28 LIP sites (Figure 4.7). But the changes are even more striking than in Cabanaconde: The large Wari-influenced center of Charasuta (LA-99) that dominated the Middle Horizon settlement pattern in the Lari area is essentially deserted during the LIP, and all but three of 20 LIP settlements were in unoccupied locations during the Middle Horizon. Moreover, at two of the three LIP settlements with prior Middle Horizon occupations, the LIP component is exceedingly ephemeral, suggesting near-abandonment and marked change in their function. In general, settlement shifted away from the few large Middle Horizon sites to the west and east of the village of Lari to form a concentration of settlements on and around the pampa that surrounds the village (Doutriaux 2004:243–48). Doutriaux suggests this shift in settlement "points to a temporary upheaval of Lari society upon the demise of Wari influence in the area" (2004:247).

In Lari, the principal agriculturalist sites of the period are similar in size and in close proximity, suggestive of coordinated, multisited communities of farmers. Overall, small settlements predominate here to a much greater degree than in either Yanquecollaguas or Cabanaconde—the largest sites are only hamlet to village in scale and do not approach those of either of the other two areas of the valley. This is especially noteworthy given the strongly centralized settlement pattern during the Middle Horizon, which was dominated by Charasuta. But at the same time, these small LIP settlements are confined to a relatively small area, all but one within a few hundred meters of each other. The settlements with the highest density LIP ceramics—Kantupampa (LA-21; 3.6 ha), Ch'apimoqo (LA-27; 5.0 ha), and Loclla/Kantupampa (LA-16; 0.5 ha)—are clustered on low hilltops around a bofedal called

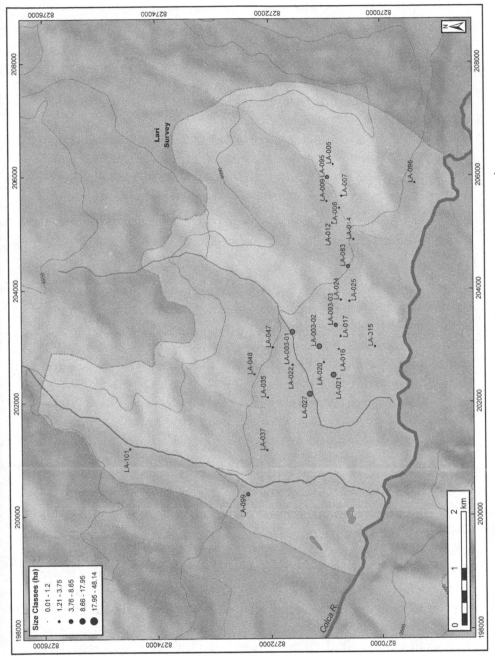

Figure 4.7. Late Intermediate period settlements in Laricollaguas. (Data from Doutriaux 2004.)

Kantupampa, situated on a plateau above the main agricultural terrace complexes of Lari. These settlements, together with smaller hamlets in the same area around the plateau, collectively make up the population center of the Lari area.

In aggregate, then, this cluster of small settlements results in a settlement pattern that is less widely dispersed than in other locales in the valley: As Doutriaux (2004:253) notes, "In the absence of another such 'central place,' the inhabitants of Lari's many homesteads and small settlements seem to have been *more*—not less—centralized than the inhabitants of Cabanaconde's several towns." Though settlement patterns and political structures need not be isomorphic, the most parsimonious interpretation here is that in Lari, a system of small, cooperative peer communities were established following the collapse of Wari and the abandonment of the large Wari-era site of Charasuta.

Violent Conflict during the Late Intermediate Period

A picture of widespread violent conflict and political fragmentation after the collapse of the Middle Horizon states has dominated frameworks for understanding the LIP (Arkush 2005, 2008; Covey 2008; Hyslop 1976; Julien 1993; Parsons and Hastings 1988; Parsons et al. 2001). All over the central and southern Andean highlands, settlement patterns shifted as communities relocated to defensible locations and built pukaras, readily identifiable by their concentrically arranged fortification walls. The period is traditionally depicted as one of a balkanized political landscape of (generally large) ethnic *señoríos* (chiefdoms) at war with one another and vying for power in the power vacuum left by the Middle Horizon states (Hyslop 1976; Kolata 1993; Parsons and Hastings 1988). This picture draws heavily from the chronicles (see especially Cieza de León 1985 [1553]:6; Cobo 1964 [1653]:bk. XII, chap. 1) and testimonials of ethnic lords in the early years following the Spanish invasion.

The sources and interests of each of these sources must be considered in evaluating their representation of the pre-Inkaic past in this way. It is a double hermeneutic process involving ex-oral translation and transcription that is refracted again through the author's perspective and genre conventions, which can vary widely—from a member of Cuzco nobility recounting dynastic history (in which Inka imperialism is depicted as a civilizing mission among otherwise barbaric peoples), from a provincial elite perspective as a means of undergirding ethnic elites' claims to centralized authority over large ethnic polities, or, as in the case of official Toledan historiography, from a colonial official arguing that the Inkas were tyrants and usurpers of the natural lords of the land.

Locally, ex-oral testimony of Collagua elites taken down by Corregidor Juan de Ulloa Mogollón for the *Relaciones Geográficas de Indias* survey (Ulloa Mogollón 1965 [1586]), and by the noted Franciscan friar for his doctrinal manual *Symbolo Cathólico Indiano* (Oré 1992 [1598]), though sketchy, presents just such a vision of the pre-Inkaic past. As discussed in chapter 3, Ulloa provides the only recorded summary account of the charter myths of the Cabanas and Collaguas. To recount, the Cabanas claimed descent from Mount Hualca Hualca, the glaciated peak that towers over Cabanaconde on the south side of the lower valley, while the Collaguas are depicted not as autochthons but as an invading people who originally descended from their paqarina, Mount Collaguata, located 100 aerial km north of the valley, in the high-elevation herding region near the border between the provinces of Chumbivilcas and Velille in the Department of Cuzco:

> Some are called Collaguas; they call themselves this since ancient times; they have passed the name on by inheritance from parents to children,[3] which came from a *guaca* or ancient shrine in the far reaches of the Province of *Velilli*, domain of this province, that is a snowcapped mountain [shaped] like a volcano, distinguished from the other peaks around there, which is called *Collaguata*; they say that from around or inside that mountain many people came out and descended to this province and its valley, of this river that they populated, and conquered those that were natives and threw them out by force, while they remained; they prove this with forts, which they call *pucaras* in their language, which are built on some of the high peaks of the valley, from which they descended to make war; and because that is how the volcano from which they issued, called *Collaguata*, they call themselves Collaguas. (Ulloa Mogollón 1965 [1586]:327)[4]

This account maps out a plausible narrative, and a literalist reading would implicate that LIP warfare was instigated by conquest and the territorial expansion of a proto-Collagua polity—a reading that would hue closely to many chroniclers' representations of the pre-Inkaic era.

Of course, such a face-value interpretation would have to withstand (well-founded) critical scrutiny—given the highly contested uses of the representations of the past in ayllu and ethnic politics during late prehispanic and colonial times—as well as comparison with archaeological evidence. Such representations of dominant local ethnics group as descendants of primordial conquering out-groups is a ubiquitous trope in central Andean charter myths (Duviols 1973; Gose 2008; Parsons, et al. 1997; Salomon 1991), and of the Inkas themselves (Bauer 1992, 1996; Julien 2000; Rowe 1946b; Urton

1990). These claims legitimated an aggressive conquest ideology and reinforced ethno-political boundaries between neighboring groups (see especially Bauer 1996; Julien 2000). In this case, one can imagine how the more
pastorally oriented, Aymara-speaking Collaguas (occupying the "llacuaz"
position common to central Andean charter myths; see chapter 3) mobilized
a version of the past to reify boundary distinctions vis-à-vis the more agriculturally focused, Quechua-speaking Cabanas of the lower valley (occupying
the "huari" position). But the Collagua origin myth could plausibly allegorize
an extended series of incursions from northerly, puna-dwelling peoples in
the centuries between the collapse of the Middle Horizon states and the Inka
conquest. Such a scenario has parallels in other locales, such as in Huarochirí Province, where María Rostworowski de Diez Canseco (Rostworowski
de Diez Canseco 1978, 1988) has tracked correlations between the mythic
charter of the Yauyos, which depicts the conquering descent of the avatars of
Nevado Paria Caca, paqarina of the Yauyos, down through the warm yungas
valleys of the central Peruvian coast, and a corresponding gradual movement
of pre-Inkaic highlanders through the Lurín and Rimac valleys, displacing
and acculturating to the resident Ychma and Colli peoples (see also Salomon
1991:6–9).

What evidence is there of warfare in the Colca Valley, then, and how does
it compare with these accounts of ethnic origins and conquest? Before discussing the archaeological evidence, a closer look at the documentary evidence is warranted. Ulloa also briefly mentions the presence of hilltop forts
and gives a detailed account of Collagua weaponry, including maces, axes,
slings, and bolas (Ulloa Mogollón 1965 [1586]:330, 332). Oré, writing of his
time in Coporaque during the 1580s, relates collected lore of how the population lived around hilltop bastions that they defended with slings, in a period
of conflict over resources before the Inkas:

> The Viceroy don Francisco de Toledo put diligent effort in uncovering
> the true origin of the Inka Kings of this realm, and found out that in
> truth there was no general lord of all the land, but rather that in each
> province, each kindred and generation was governed in barbarism by
> its most principal curaca or cacique, and their little villages and houses
> without order, separated by kindred, or *ayllo* one from the other on the
> hilltops and escarpments because these served as fortresses, which (as
> they were all at war) they shared among nearest neighbors between
> them above the lands and fields where they planted, and in this way they
> expanded and defended them by force of slings, because Indians of the
> sierra are very skilled slingsman.[5] And in the province of the Collaguas

I knew an Indian that had saved a shirt covered with the [finger]nails of the Indians that his elders [*abuelos*] had killed, and as a heroic memory it was admired for the many lives lost that it represented, and it was in defense of the fields of that province, that they possessed. (Oré 1992 [1598]:155 [39])[6]

Here, while Oré follows the position of reactionary Toledan historiography on the topic of natural lordship prior to Inka rule, he also provides important local details regarding the organization and motivations for warfare, namely, that the peoples of dispersed hamlets and villages would congregate by ayllu in their hilltop redoubts to defend their lands from raids with their slings. A scenario of competition for scarce resources seems most fitting with this depiction. But equally evident is how an ideology of warriorhood persisted—or at least a nostalgia for it—in the form of an heirloom tunic festooned with enemy fingernails. Clearly, such fierce displays of enemy trophies reflected and perpetuated an ideology in which elites benefitted from their role as warlords, as did the built features of the fortresses themselves.

The documentary accounts of warfare during the LIP—both in terms of general representations of the era and the specific local scenario described above—can be readily compared against the archaeological evidence for conflict during the period. The scenarios evident in the accounts of Ulloa and Oré would have left distinctive material correlates. For instance, if warfare were primarily associated with an invasion of a proto-Collagua polity from the north, fortifications would be concentrated in the upper reaches of the valley and would likely date to the early part of the LIP. If warfare occurred primarily at the level of inter-ethnic conflict between the Collaguas and Cabanas, or if warfare was a factor in the formation of distinct Collagua and Cabana ethnic polities, one would expect an amassment of fortifications along the boundaries between them, or, at a minimum, a distribution of fortifications throughout the lands of both. The same would be expected if there was internecine conflict within the Collaguas: a concentration of pukaras along the boundary between Yanquecollaguas and Laricollaguas or a distribution of forts throughout the two areas.

As we have already seen, there is little evidence for strong differentiation of material culture or architecture between the Collagua and Cabana zones, and the settlement patterns of each of the areas of the valley are consistent with heterarchical communities, not with large, unified, or politically centralized señoríos. As will be shown, the distributions and types of pukara fortifications documented in the valley are also inconsistent with large, unified ethnic polities in sustained conflict with one another. In general, it is striking how different the evidence for violent conflict during the LIP is among the three areas of the valley. Pukaras are markedly concentrated in the central and upper reaches of the valley, and none have been documented in the areas surrounding Lari and Cabanaconde (Doutriaux 2004:243). The furthest downvalley pukara currently documented is near Maca, where Neira reported fortification features at the site of Pachamarca during a brief site visit (Neira Avendaño 1961:181). But aside from that preliminary identification, only a few pukaras are located below the Yanque-Coporaque area. Two pukaras have been reported in Achoma: a small fort (identified as Koricancha by Oquiche Hernani 1991:143–49) and the large fort of Aukuinikita, located on a prominent ridgeline descending from the valley rim (Shea 1987, 1997). Another small hilltop pukara and an associated LIP/LH settlement of is found across the river from Achoma, to the west of Ichupampa.

A full inventory of pukaras has not been completed, but the existing survey and reconnaissance clearly shows that the highest concentrations of pukaras are in the core of Yanquecollaguas—in the Yanque-Coporaque survey area— where there are five forts in a relatively small area, all within sight of each other on the north side of the river. Three of these are very closely situated on hilltops adjacent to a cluster of settlements on the broad alluvial terrace and rolling hills above the river gorge (Figure 4.8). A fourth is located upslope of the residential sector of San Antonio/Chijra (CO-100). This hilltop is naturally protected on its downslope side by high cliffs, while a series of ditches span its exposed approach from the north. These four forts are typical small pukaras with concentric walls encircling hilltops next to settlements (Figure 4.9). They take advantage of natural topographic features, like cliff faces and steep scarps, where fortification walls are not needed. Full doorways are still preserved at CO-165 and CO-168, and the doorways of outer and inner walls are not aligned, but offset, requiring intruders to risk an exposed traverse (well within range of slings) to gain access through the inner wall. Such "killing alleys" are common features of pukaras in the region (Arkush 2008:347). The hilltops inside these topmost walls did not house domestic structures, so they were clearly not intended as permanent places of residence but as temporary refuges for the surrounding settlements. The three closely situated pukaras near the valley bottom are equidistant from the five surrounding settlements, each within 600 m of a settlement. No single settlement would have held a tactical advantage in accessing the forts. So they were not at war with each other; the perceived threat was almost certainly external to all of these settlements collectively.

The fifth pukara in the Yanque-Coporaque survey area, however, is of a qualitatively different nature in both scale and location. This fortification

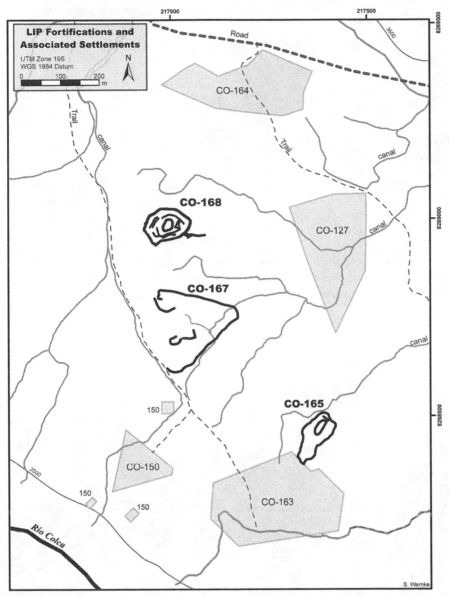

Figure 4.8. Group of pukara hilltop forts (CO-165, CO-167, CO-168) and associated settlements (CO-127, CO-150, CO-163, CO-164) to the southeast of Coporaque.

(CO-158) is located on Cerro Pumachiri, which dominates the northern horizon of Coporaque and remains today the principal apu (mountain deity) of the village (see Figure 4.10). Reaching a height of 4,557 m, Pumachiri is protected by three fortification walls: an outer perimeter wall and two internal concentric walls enclosing the peak itself. The outer perimeter wall is massive

Figure 4.9. Pukara fortification of site CO-165, from the northwest. A doorway, partly blocked for modern corral use, is partially visible in the outer concentric wall (*center-left foreground*).

Figure 4.10. The peak of Pumachiri (CO-158) overlooking Coporaque (*center*). The top of the peak is ringed by two fortification walls (not visible from this distance).

in volume and length for such a high and remote peak, skirting about 350 m across its eastern flank, thus bridging a relatively exposed section between a steep ridge and a cliff (Figure 4.11). Like the other pukaras, there are no formal domestic structures at Pumachiri. But there is a dense group of small (6–10 m²), ovoid fieldstone windbreaks situated inside the perimeter wall on the northeast side of the peak. The ephemeral nature of the occupation is also evident in low artifact densities at the site: We recovered only five diagnostic sherds, all from the Late Horizon. Befitting its high-elevation, remote setting, the pukara would have thus served as a temporary encampment suitable for relatively brief engagements but not prolonged sieges.

Figure 4.11. Cerro Pumachiri (CO-158) from the northeast. Arrows denote outer stone wall around eastern flank.

Two distinct classes of pukaras are thus apparent—small refuges suitable for the residents of a few nearby hamlets and villages and large hilltop bastions probably used for larger engagements involving personnel from several settlements. Large pukaras such as Pumachiri are intervisible, forming a network of defense sites that could have allowed visual relay—perhaps by means of smoke signals or other visual cues—of an invading force. In the upper reaches of the valley, the (aptly named) site of Cerro Pukara occupies a high hilltop jutting above the plains over the river gorge. Strategically situated at a topographic bottleneck in the upper valley where quaternary volcanic flows create a rugged, hilly landscape, it provides a clear view up not only to the highest reaches of the valley but also across to the southwest over the high plains of the puna to the back side of Pumachiri, which juts out prominently in the skyline (Figure 4.12). Together, the large viewsheds of Cerro Pukara and Pumachiri would have provided surveillance for the populations of the upper and central portions of Yanquecollaguas for raiding or invading forces entering the valley from the puna heights to the north.

This concentration of fortifications in the central and upper sections of the valley clearly signals that warfare was more common in Yanquecollaguas and probably involved different scales of conflict: relatively small raids and skirmishes affecting small groups of settlements and large-scale conflicts involving the amassment of sizable forces against an external threat, most likely coming from the puna heights beyond the valley's upper reaches.

Figure 4.12. Panorama of Cerro Pukara (*foreground*) and Cerro Pumachiri (*background, right*), showing intervisibility between these two major pukara fortifications.

Several intriguing disjunctions and parallels between the ethnohistorical depictions of warfare and ethnic origins during the LIP and the archaeological evidence are therefore evident. The range of possible scenarios can be reduced by first noting the disjunctions. Clearly, amassed, inter-ethnic conflict between Collaguas and Cabanas is not supported, given the apparent absence of fortifications in Laricollaguas and Cabanaconde. Warfare in the LIP was not predominantly structured around inter-ethnic conflict between two already-formed ethnic groups. There is a similar lack of correspondence between archaeological and documentary evidence for inter-ethnic warfare in the western Lake Titicaca basin, where the Lupaqa and Qolla ethnic polities have long stood as case studies in the kinds of large warring señoríos iconic of the LIP and are similar in scale to the Collaguas and Cabanas. The western and northern Titicaca basin landscape is studded with scores of pukaras, ranging from small bastions on low-slung hillocks next to hamlets to massive fortresses housing hundreds of domestic structures on the higher hilltops jutting above the basin floor (Hyslop 1976). But as the survey of pukara sites by Arkush has demonstrated, the distribution of the forts is inconsistent with warring, centralized polities (Arkush 2008, 2010). As in the Colca, there is no amassment of fortifications around the Qolla/Lupaqa boundary zone, or along the ethnohistorically documented Hanansaya/Urinsaya boundaries within them. Nor is there evidence for hierarchically organized or centrally controlled señoríos, but a much more fluid and segmentary political structure.

Moreover, the dating and organization of pukaras in the Titicaca basin have recently come into focus (see Arkush 2005, 2008) and point to a different scenario than one involving warfare provoked by political fragmentation in the wake of Middle Horizon state collapse. Though a few forts date to the early LIP, the big uptick in pukara construction and use (and thus warfare) in the Titicaca basin does not follow on the heels of Tiwanaku collapse but instead correlates with a period of severe regional drought two centuries later—during the fourteenth century (Arkush 2008). Pukara use and warfare did not end with the abatement of the drought, however, but continued through the fifteenth century (Arkush 2008). Arkush argues that the perpetuation of warfare resulted from three interlocking factors: (1) the benefits that warfare conferred to elites through the spoils of war and in the centripetal effects of unification against common enemies; (2) the continued strategic advantages that the built landscape of fortifications conferred by thwarting conquest (for example, by invading Inka forces) and acting as "landscape capital" (sensu Blaikie and Brookfield 1987; Erickson 2000), that is, durable labor investments that discouraged novel forms of settlement; and (3) the cyclical nature of blood vengeance in which individual killings were seen as offenses against the collectivity in the corporate, segmentary organization of LIP polities (Arkush 2008:364–65).

What can be said affirmatively of the evidence for warfare during the LIP in the Colca Valley is still relatively limited. First, violent conflict was clearly a sustained preoccupation among the populations of Yanquecollaguas. Major investments of labor and material were dedicated to the construction and maintenance of large, multiwalled fortifications on difficult terrain, including high-elevation peaks well above the valley floor. The concentration of fortifications in the territory of Yanquecollaguas is not inconsistent with a scenario of invasive population incursions from the high-elevation puna regions to the north of the valley, akin to the one depicted in the Collagua origin myth recorded by Ulloa. A hypothesis of llacuaz-like Collagua ethno-territorial expansion cannot be rejected. But the presence of multiple small forts adjacent to habitational sites could also reflect a situation of frequent small-scale skirmishes among neighboring communities. A possible scenario is one of frequent local-level conflict punctuated by less-frequent larger-scale warfare. Conflict likely varied between these two scales, resulting in the activation of distinct scales of community affiliation and identity. In general, the distribution of pukaras is consistent with a more decentralized, segmentary form of political organization than is suggested by colonial texts. It is likely the case, similar to the situation in the Titicaca basin, that unification of higher-order political organization and identity became more salient in the face of common external threats, such as an invading Inka imperial force. Tentative indices suggest that the largest fortifications in the Titicaca basin date later than minor forts, and intriguingly, the only diagnostic ceramics we recovered from the major pukara of Pumachiri were from the Late Horizon. Clearly, more robust lines of evidence are required to support an affirmative case for such a scenario, including data regarding possible in-migration, the timing of the construction and use of the pukaras, and ancient mtDNA or nuclear DNA studies to investigate the long-term genetic history of the valley's population. Each of these are the subject of ongoing research. But this sketch provides a set of working hypotheses.

Inka Administration of the Province as Represented in Colonial Texts

Points of correspondence and disjunction between the textual and archaeological record are also evident when considering the articulation of Inka administration with local communities. The sometimes stark differences between them confound a simple characterization of local Inka administration as direct or indirect in form. In general, the documentary sources would seem to reflect a situation of centrally administered imperial rule through the reorganization of local communities into an elegant, nested administrative hierarchy based on bipartite, tripartite, and decimal administrative structures. As discussed in chapter 3, Ulloa's summary account of the organization of Collagua ayllus according into the same tripartite ranking as the ceque system of Cuzco would seem a clear indication of such reorganization. That each of the three ayllus of Collana, Pahana, and Cayao were apparently subdivided recursively by the same tripartite scheme into three smaller ayllus of 100 households furthers this impression. The logic and obligations of kinship were apparently central to local-imperial relations in other ways as well. Inka rulers commonly took noblewomen from subject peoples as secondary wives to form affinal bonds while subordinating non-Inka ethnic groups to Cuzco dynastic lineages (see D'Altroy 2002:86–108). Evidence of this kind of marriage alliance between the Inkas and the Collaguas is found in Oré's *Symbolo*, in an often cited (e.g., Cook 1982, 2002; Guillet 1992; Neira Avendaño 1961, 1990) passage that also makes reference to the construction of a copper palace in the Collagua princess's honor (Oré 1992 [1598]:159 [41]; my translation):

> In the service of Mayta Capac Inka, who had as his wife Mama Yacchi, a native of the Collaguas, the Indians made in that province a great house all of copper to accommodate the Inka and his wife, as if coming to their homeland they came to visit, and I have experience in that province, and I diligently searched for the copper and found a quantity in the possession of an old Indian in his depository, and four large bells were made and still copper remained left over, and asking where the remainder was, they said that they gave it to Gonzalo Pizarro and his militia to make horseshoes, for fear that they would suffer the fate of a principal cacique who the tyrant had burned for not revealing its whereabouts.[7]

Because Oré was based in Coporaque, it has been assumed that the palace honoring Mama Yacchi was in Coporaque (presumably in a prehispanic settlement near the reducción) and that Coporaque must have been the primary center of Inka administration in the valley. The reference to the marriage between "Mayta Capac" and the Collagua princess most likely refers to a high-ranking member of his panaca, or to a war captain of the Inka Pachacuti, rather than to Mayta Capac himself, since he is only the fourth Inka in the dynastic sequence and his reign predates the expansionist imperial period by at least four generations (Pease 1977a:140–41).[8] As Cook, Pease, and Julien all note, the tradition that links Mayta Capac in marriage to the Collagua princess cannot be traced back earlier than Oré. Garcilaso (in typically florid, summary style; 1966 [1609]:153) mentions the advance of Mayta Capac through the lands of the Collaguas, and Cobo (1979 [1653]:119–20), drawing directly on Oré, mentions the marriage of Mayta Capac to "Mama Tancaray Yacchi." An earlier, independent genealogy originating in Cieza de León is at odds with this later tradition, holding that Mayta Capac did not conquer areas beyond the vicinity of Cuzco and married the daughter (named Mamaca Guapata) of a lord from the village of Oma, just two leagues from Cuzco (Cieza de León 1967 [1553]:100). Cieza's chronology of Inka imperial expansion is much more consistent with the archaeological evidence, and by all indications the region did not come under Inka rule until the reign of Pachacuti, the ninth Inka, in the mid-fifteenth century.

As Cook notes, Oré's account should be taken as a distillation of local oral tradition remembering a marriage alliance between the Collagua elite and the Inkas (perhaps a member of Mayta Capac's panaca, or an emissary of Pachacuti named Mayta Capac), not literally the marriage of the Inka ruler Mayta Capac (Cook 2007:17). Such marriage alliances between the panacas and provincial aristocracies were a key strategy in Inka expansionism, as well as a primary currency of the internal politics of the Cuzco elite (Covey 2006a). As discussed below, my archaeological findings suggest there was a significant Inka imperial presence in the Coporaque area, but subordinate to the primary center established at Yanque.[9]

Other documentary evidence provide clues to other kinds of inter-elite alliances between the Inkas and the peoples of the Colca. For example, in the 1604 visita of Yanquecollaguas Urinsaya, a few individuals are exempted from colonial tribute because they were avowed descendents of the Inka Huayna Capac (APY Yanquecollaguas Urinsaya 1604, fols. 219v, 220v). Collagua elites were also moved to the Cuzco heartland to serve as yanacona retainers on the royal estates of Topa Inka and Huayna Capac (the tenth and eleventh Inka rulers). One Goméz Condori, a Collagua native residing in Chinchaypuquio near Cuzco, testified to officials of Viceroy Toledo in 1571 that his father had been taken from his homeland to serve Amaro Topa Inga, brother of Topa Inka, and later Huayna Capac. Condori inherited his father's yanacona status and was exempt from tribute (Levillier 1940:113–14). Other Collagua households (an unspecified number) were relocated by the state to serve as mitmaq colonists in the Province of the Wankas in the Upper Mantaro Valley (Levillier 1940).

A sizable and diversified craft specialist sector under Inka rule in the province is also evident in the visitas. These included ayllus of official state potters, silversmiths, and cumbicamayocs (weavers of sumptuary cumbi cloth). As mentioned in the previous chapter, three groups of official state potters were listed, all resident in Coporaque. They are listed as separate segments within the ayllus that conform to the Collana-Pahana-Cayao nomenclature, not as retainers of particular kurakas—a pattern consistent with "embedded specialization" (Janusek 1999). This kind of embedded arrangement is contrasted by ayllus of prestige good specialists who are listed as retainers of the paramount kurakas of province, resident in Yanque. Specifically, cumbicamayoc ayllus and silversmiths are listed as pertaining to the paramount kurakas of each moiety in Yanque (APY Yanquecollaguas Urinsaya 1604, fols. 383v–385v; Verdugo 1977 [1591]:414–20; Verdugo and Colmenares 1977 [1591]:fols. 42r–44r). Interestingly, the silversmiths were reduced to the village of Maca, technically within the territorial bounds of Laricollaguas, and were the only households registered from that village in the Yanquecollaguas Hanansaya visita of 1615–17, suggesting that they were once (and perhaps continued to be) a key holding of the paramounts (APY Yanquecollaguas Hanansaya 1615–17, fols. 326v–338r). These same kurakas also held rights to groups of pastoralist yanacona retainers (Verdugo 1977 [1591]:420–22). While chapter 6 focuses on the political economy of the province, suffice it to say here that there is strong documentary evidence of significant investments and oversight by the state in both staple and prestige sectors of a well-developed provincial economy.

But for all of these apparent state interventions, the usual archaeological indices for direct imperial rule were not at all apparent in the findings of prior archaeological research. No administrative center had been identified, nor were any complexes of storehouses (*qolqas*) for the storage of the staple produce from tributary labor that accompany imperial centers identified. Only minimal evidence for Inka imperial architecture—in the form of a few isolated structures of Inka-style cut-stone masonry—had been recorded by prior reconnaissance projects (de la Vera Cruz Chávez 1987, 1988, 1989; Neira Avendaño 1961). As discussed below, through systematic survey with particular focus on the well-preserved architecture of Late Horizon sites, other indices of considerable imperial investments are evident, but in a manner which suggests centralized but locally coordinated rule: a locally improvised order.

The Late Horizon Settlement Pattern

The settlement system of the valley's three zones reached its apogee during the Inka occupation. A number of indices point to expansion and intensification of settlement, as well as increased political centralization and hierarchization during the Late Horizon. Parallel developments in Yanquecollaguas, Laricollaguas, and Cabanaconde point to an overarching imperial strategy. In Yanquecollaguas, Laricollaguas, and Cabanaconde, the largest number of settlements and greatest occupational area from any time period date to the Late Horizon (Figure 4.13). Not only the extent but also the intensity of occupation increases throughout the valley, suggesting a growing and increasingly dense population. Ceramic quantities at sites provide a relative measure of intensity of settlement, and this indicator clearly points to increasing intensity compared to the LIP. In Laricollaguas and Cabanaconde, Doutriaux reports that Inka-style ceramics dominate assemblages at sites with both LIP and LH occupations, often on a 5:1 factor (Doutriaux 2004:254). In Yanquecollaguas, that ratio is also marked, though not quite as high—a 3:1 factor (1,468 LH to 433 LIP ceramics among settlements)—probably a rough reflection of the larger LIP population in the core of the valley. Other determinants could account for these dramatic rises in Inka-style ceramics. The proportion of decorated to undecorated wares may have increased—perhaps, as discussed previously, as part of a state policy of conspicuous generosity of fine (if mass-produced) crafts. There could also be sampling error, as the later LH materials overlie those of the LIP and would therefore be found in greater abundance through surface survey. But as Doutriaux (2004:254) also points out, these potentially confounding factors are offset by the fact that the duration of the LIP (AD 1000–1450) is fully four times as long as the LH (AD 1450–1532). So there was apparently a large increase in the presence of ceramics during the Inka occupation.

Unlike many of the directly administered provinces in the core of the empire, there does not appear to have been a single, large state installation from which the province as a whole was centrally administered. Instead, Inka administration was apparently coordinated between Yanquecollaguas, Laricollaguas, and Cabanaconde with a similar amount of involvement and investment, and with a center in each, while further coordination with local communities was facilitated through the construction of certain ceremonial-administrative complexes at local settlements, forming a series of secondary centers. The state apparatus thus reached down to the subprovincial level, as it also amplified and stabilized the latent hierarchies within each (see Wernke 2006a, 2006b).

In outline, top-level administration is archaeologically evident in parallel changes in the settlement patterns of the three areas of the valley. Not only did overall settlement grow and intensify throughout the valley during the Inka occupation, but the distribution of settled area became more centralized in each of the three sectors of the valley (Figures 4.14–4.16). Changes in site-size hierarchy between the LIP and LH using site areas alone are not possible, since the LIP and LH occupations are thoroughly commingled at most

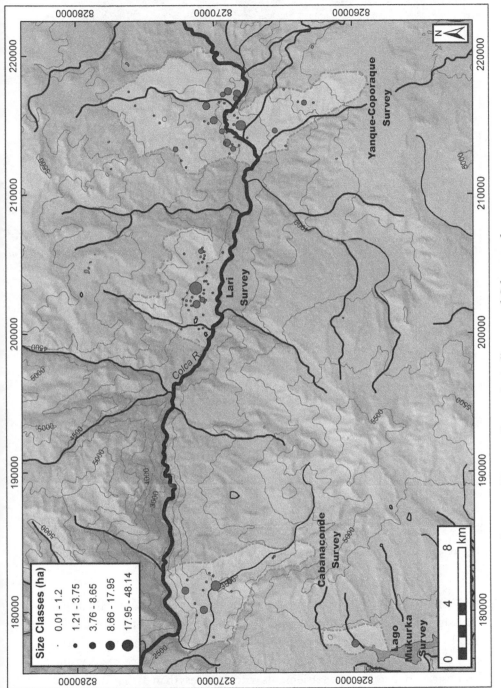

Figure 4.13. Late Horizon settlements in Yanquecollaguas, Laricollaguas, and Cabanaconde.

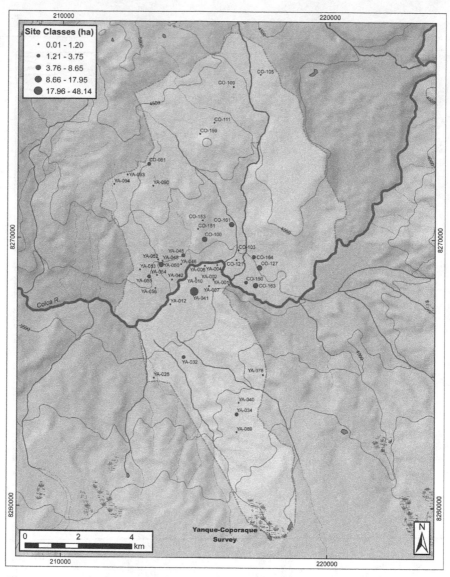

Figure 4.14. Late Horizon settlements in the Yanque-Coporaque survey area.

settlements. Nonetheless, comparison of the two time periods is still important since there is an obvious expansion in the settlement between the LIP
and LH. Settlement-size histograms for each of the three zones shows markedly skewed distributions (Figure 4.17), with a preponderance of very small
homestead- or hamlet-type settlements with areas less than 0.5 ha. There is not
as clear a site-size hierarchy as might be expected in an integrated, centrally
administered imperial system: Above these small hamlets are one, or perhaps

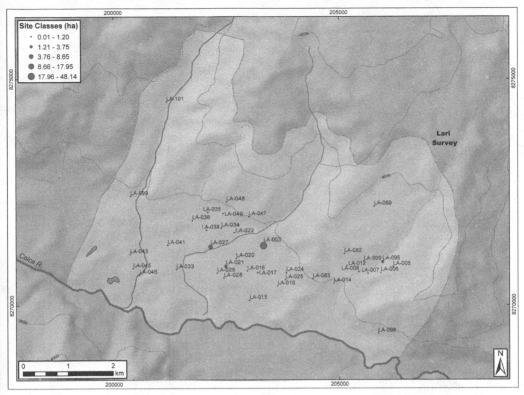

Figure 4.15. Late Horizon settlements in Laricollaguas. (Data from Doutriaux 2004.)

two, distinct classes of village-sized (0.5–3.0 ha) and town-sized (3.0–9.5 ha) settlements. Virtually all of these settlements were previously occupied during the LIP, so this "lack" of order in the site-size hierarchy (which of course in itself assumes an isomorphic relation between site size and hierarchical control—a questionable assumption; see Crumley 1979) is a legacy of fitting an administrative system onto extant settlements (see below).

A site-size hierarchy is more evident, however, when counting domestic structures at LIP/LH settlements in the Yanque-Coporaque survey area, where architectural preservation is better than in Laricollaguas or Cabanaconde. Using house counts as the measure, the sample size decreases (due to lack of architectural preservation at some sites), but a three-tiered hierarchy is apparent (Figure 4.18). This excludes the primary center of Yanque (YA-041), however, because the reducción obliterated the original architecture. Keeping in mind that the LIP component of Yanque is extremely light and dispersed (only 27 sherds), it becomes clear that the dramatic growth of Yanque during the Late Horizon constitutes a qualitative shift in scale and centrality in the settlement system. Thus the settlement system in the

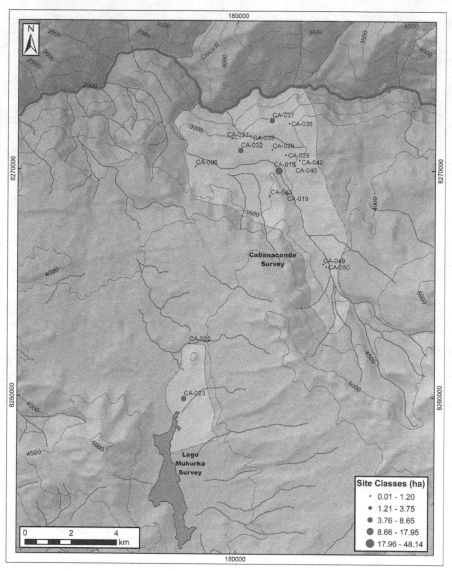

Figure 4.16. Late Horizon settlements in Cabanaconde. (Data from Doutriaux 2004.)

Yanque-Coporaque area became dominated by a primary center at Yanque, with secondary centers at formerly top-tier towns (Uyu Uyu [YA-050], San Antonio/Chijra [CO-100], and Tunsa/Llactapampa [CO-163/150]). The same is true of Lari, where a primary center was constructed in the location of the eponymous reducción. In Cabanaconde, two very large settlements in the immediate vicinity of the reducción were the primary centers. The largest sites of any time period in each of the three zones of the valley thus correspond to what were almost certainly primary imperial administrative

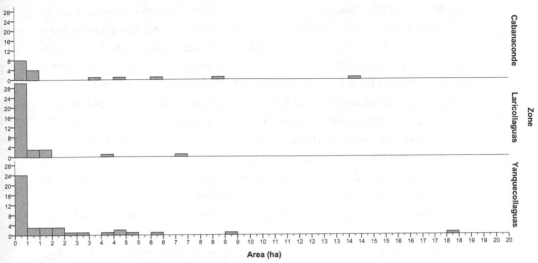

Figure 4.17. Late Horizon site-size histograms.

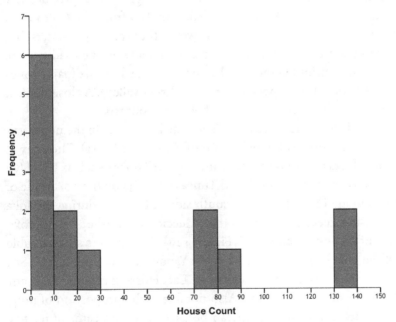

Figure 4.18. Site-size histogram by house count in Yanque-Coporaque survey.

centers of Yanquecollaguas, Laricollaguas, and Cabanaconde. In this way, the pattern of competing peer towns in the LIP was transformed into a settlement hierarchy of primary and secondary administrative centers, followed by villages and hamlets.

Another notable change associated with these administrative centers is that none of them is situated in a defensible locale, nor are there any pukara fortresses in their surrounding areas. All are located in relatively level, open areas on the broad pampas above the inner river gorge. While this was not a marked departure from LIP settlement patterns in Laricollaguas and Cabana-conde, where fortifications were not documented (Doutriaux 2004), within the Yanque-Coporaque survey zone, Yanque is the only settlement in the LIP or LH within the agricultural zone of the valley that is neither defensible nor located within 1 km of a pukara. This clearly signals a shift in priorities—from a situation in which defensive considerations factored heavily in settlement locations during the LIP, to one in which centers were situated in open, flat areas. Logistical considerations—the articulation of a network of roads and centers as well as the facilitation of an orderly urban plan in relatively open, level areas—probably factored more heavily as conflict abated under a Pax Inka. Inka policies regarding the location of regional administrative centers seem to have generally favored the efficient flow of goods and people rather than their placement near zones of highest agricultural productivity (D'Altroy and Hastorf 1984). But here again the data from the Colca does not fit either "direct" or "indirect" models well—there are large centers, but no single dominant one, and they are situated nodally on the road system, but they are also distributed more or less evenly in each of the major zones of agricultural production (upper, central, and lower valley). A closer look at each will explore their functions within their local contexts.

In Yanquecollaguas, the Inkas established the largest site in the upper valley in the same location as the reducción of Yanque (YA-041). The apex of the settlement hierarchy thus shifted from large LIP towns such as Uyu Uyu (YA-050), San Antonio (CO-100), and Tunsa (CO-163) on the north side of the river to Yanque (YA-041) on the south side of the river during the Inka occupation. Our street survey within the reducción established the approximate extent of the Inka occupation (Figure 4.19). At 18 ha, the site is double the size of the next largest settlement in the Yanque-Coporaque survey, San Antonio (CO-100). This site produced more Late Horizon ceramics than any other site in the survey (n = 209). Also notable is the proportion of poly-chrome ceramics at the site, which can be used as an indicator of relative status. This dense scatter that defines the extent of the site is composed of a significantly higher percentage of polychromes than at other settlements (17 percent [31/210] vs. 8 percent [68/895] at other LH settlements; p < .01). Also notable is the near total absence of LIP ceramics at the site. Only 26 LIP sherds (seven Collagua I, 19 Collagua II) were recovered from Yanque—too few and too dispersed to reliably estimate a site area or, for that matter, define

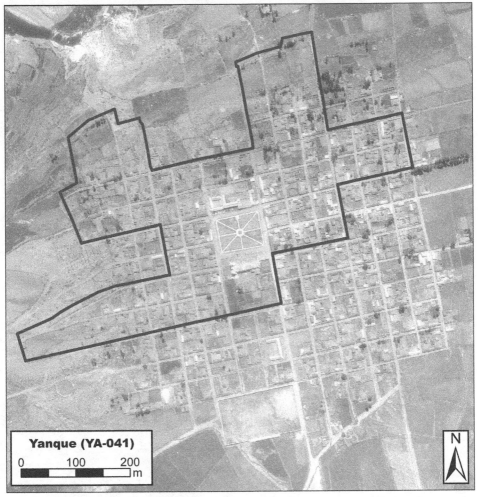

Figure 4.19. Late Horizon occupational extent of the reducción of Yanque (YA-041).

an LIP occupation per se. The Inkas thus established the largest settlement in Yanquecollaguas in a virtually unoccupied location.

The original layout of the site was obliterated by the construction of the reducción village in the early 1570s, but the only Inka cut-stone masonry in the survey is found in Yanque. Although the masonry is not in its original structural context (Figure 4.20), its unique presence, together with the site size and ceramic evidence, suggest that Yanque was an important administrative center. The fact that Yanque was also the provincial capital during colonial times suggests continuity in its administrative function.

Adjacent to this wall, colonial structures locally known as the Casa Choquehuanca (the house of the kuraka Choquehuanca) are built with

Figure 4.20. Structure in Yanque composed of Inka-style cut-stone blocks.

well-worked cornerstones that were probably mined from prehispanic structures (Figure 4.21-A). Bas-relief animal motifs, perhaps representations of vizcachas,[10] are also carved in stones adorning the exterior north wall of the easternmost structure of the Choquehuanca house (Figure 4.21-B). The mixture of LIP/LH masonry types in these structures reveal their colonial period of construction.

The reducción of Coporaque (CO-161), by contrast, appears to have been a much smaller settlement than Yanque during late prehispanic times, leaving a much more ephemeral scatter of ceramics. These findings are contrary to expectations, since as discussed above, Coporaque is widely cited in the literature as the Inkaic capital of Collaguas (Cook 1982, 2002, 2007; Málaga Medina 1977; Neira Avendaño 1990). Our ceramic collections from street survey in the village were very scant: only 15 diagnostic LIP or LH sherds. Architectural evidence of a terminal prehispanic occupation in Coporaque is also limited and ambiguous. No Cuzco Inka stonemasonry is present, and we

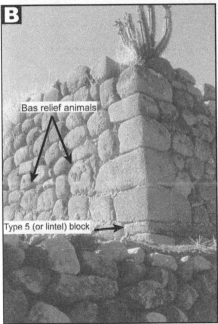

Figure 4.21. A: The Casa Choquehuanca (*foreground, top*) from the east. B: Bas-relief zoomorphic motifs and mixed masonry types in corner of Casa Choquehuanca, from the northwest.

identified only one house of probable prehispanic origin. This large house of tabular (Type 6) masonry is positioned diagonally relative to the street grid in the southeast corner of the village, breaking with the otherwise regular orientation of houses in relation to the streets (Figure 4.22). It was modified after its original construction with an internal wall that separates the structure

Figure 4.22. A: Probable LIP/LH house at the southern edge of Coporaque (CO-161), from the north. Note type 5 masonry. An internal dividing wall was added during colonial or republican times. B: Same house from the southeast, showing doorway (with some headers and stretchers looted).

into two separate rooms—a colonial feature, since no prehispanic rectangular domestic structures were divided. A handful of other houses, concentrated in the southern half of the village, incorporate tabular (Type 6) and rectangular (Type 7) worked blocks of probable prehispanic origin but were clearly constructed and used during colonial or even republican times. Also, the church of Coporaque, one of the only original reducción churches still standing in Peru (Tord 1983:82–89), is built of tabular (Type 6) and rectangular (Type 7) masonry. Given the paucity of ceramic collections in Coporaque and the widespread evidence of cornerstone mining at the nearby sites of San Antonio/Chijra (CO-100), Tunsa (CO-163), and Llactapampa (CO-150), the vast majority of the blocks used to construct these buildings appear to have been transported from these sites.

Down valley in Laricollaguas, the eponymous reducción of Lari (LA-03) is the location of a primary administrative center that dominates the local settlement pattern. Street survey by Doutriaux documented dense ceramic scatter concentrated in the western side of the reducción, with northern and southern concentrations that extend beyond the street grid of the village itself. Doutriaux reports a total occupied area of 48 ha—over 2.5 times the size of Yanque. It is unclear if this very large area is due in part to a different collection strategy or site-inclusion criteria by the two surveys, but in any case, the dominant Late Horizon site in the Lari area was clearly in the location of the reducción. This center dominates the local settlement pattern even more than was the case in Yanquecollaguas, home of large preexisting Collagua towns. In Lari, the second largest settlement was only 6.7 ha, forming a highly primate settlement system.

As in Yanque, elements of Inka-era architecture remain discernable within and beyond the limits of the reducción. To the immediate south of the village, wall bases of a probable great hall that faces east to an open space or plaza are visible on the surface. Measuring 22.0 × 11.8 m, the structure is similar in scale and proportion to the great halls at San Antonio, Uyu Uyu, and Tunsa in the Yanque-Coporaque area. Also similar to Yanque, Lari was also the only site in which Inka-style cut-stone masonry was recorded in the Lari survey area. Located only 12 m northeast of the great hall, a well-preserved probable domestic structure with tall gables, measuring 8.3 × 6.9 m, is constructed of double-coursed walls with exterior facings almost entirely made of finely cut blocks. Though it is known locally as the "Casa Inka," this building shows some clearly local traits—most strikingly, its high (approximately 2.7 m) and very narrow (approximately 50 cm) tapering doorway (now destroyed, but visible in earlier photos) typical of Collagua domestic architecture. Also striking is a band of very long (some over 2 m long) cut blocks four courses below the top of the facade wall. As Doutriaux (2004:281) notes, with its mix of local and Inkaic traits, it seems likely that this structure was part of a domestic compound for an important, most likely local, leader of the settlement and locality. About 200 m east of the Casa Inka is another domestic structure with a mix of local and Inka traits. Regular courses of rectangular cut stones compose the gable ends of this building, while the rear of the building was constructed of poorly coursed to uncoursed fieldstone. The facade was rebuilt, but its doorway was made with large, Inka-style cut-stone blocks. Entering the building, two trapezoidal niches of finely cut stone grace the interior of the rear wall.

In Cabanaconde, home of the Quechua-speaking Cabanas, evidence for a single primary administrative center is somewhat ambiguous. Instead of a single center, two very large settlements grew to dominate the settlement pattern in Cabanaconde during the Inka occupation: Antisana (CA-32) and Kallimarka (CA-18/CA-19). Overall, indices for major state investments in new settlements and architecture are if anything even stronger than in Yanquecollaguas or Laricollaguas. Also, a major Inka center does not directly underlie the reducción village as in Yanque and Lari—street survey by Doutriaux produced no diagnostic ceramic collections. Antisana, however, does occupy a promontory hilltop directly adjacent to the reducción. Architectural preservation at this 8.4-ha site is poor, but the presence of structures of Inka-style cut-stone blocks at the edge of town nearest Antisana suggests that there once was imperial-style architecture at Antisana (Doutriaux 2004:264). These buildings are similar to the colonial or republican structures of Inka blocks in Yanque—that is, clearly constructed of material mined from earlier Inka-era structures.

Kallimarka, on the other hand, is the best preserved of the top tier Inka settlements in the valley (de la Vera Cruz Chávez 1987, 1988; Doutriaux 2002, 2004). Located 1.5 km southeast of Antisana, Kallimarka is a very large ridgetop site with a central ceremonial sector and surrounding habitational sectors. Together with Antisana, Kallimarka is clearly a focal point in the local landscape: Four smaller sites established during the Inka occupation are all oriented with a view toward the two sites. Kallimarka was previously occupied during the LIP, but the settlement was much smaller and limited to the top of the ridge itself. The Late Horizon occupation dwarfs that of the LIP, with rectangular domestic structures covering the flanks of the ridgeline, organized around a central ceremonial sector.

The ceremonial sector is situated on a wide natural platform between what is known today as Huch'uy Kallimarka (CA-18) and the neighboring settlement of Hatun Kallimarka (CA-19). Although registered as separate sites, they may have functioned as a single site with the ceremonial core of Sector C functioning as the symbolic center (Doutriaux 2004:265–68). Combined, the Late Horizon occupation of these two areas totals Kallimarka 16.7 ha—on a scale with the Inka center at Yanque. It may even have been in the process of further growth and construction at the time of conquest, since a stone quarry with a large (25-×-12-m) pile of semiworked blocks is found at the southern end of Hatun Kallimarka (Doutriaux 2004:232). The ceremonial sector is organized around two large plazas spanning the width of the ridge. Between the two plazas is a large platform 13 m wide and over 5 m tall with 10 stone steps—almost certainly an *ushnu* (ceremonial platform) (Doutriaux 2004:267). Ushnu platforms occupy the center of plazas at important sites throughout Tawantinsuyu, and in Cuzco itself. They were the focal points of feasts, processions, and other large-scale public events; they were the locus from which state officials presided, acting as stagings for the projection of state largesse through conspicuous and ostentatious giving. Ushnus often incorporate natural features, and that is also the case here: the platform is built around a large natural boulder, the top of which projects beyond the top of the uppermost wall facing. To the adjacent north of the ushnu, a plaza is flanked on the north and south by two long, narrow structures that were almost certainly great halls. As discussed below, great halls are also a hallmark imperial structural form and probably served a variety of functions ranging from temporary housing for travelers to preparation and serving of food and drink for the feasts that were hosted in their associated plazas. Their presence at Kallimarka also fits a repetitive pattern of plaza–and–great hall at large Late Horizon sites throughout the valley. They are not large by imperial standards—the southern structure measures 16.4 × 7.0 m and the northern one measures 13.6 × 7.2. They were not lavish constructions of Inka cut-stone masonry but were constructed of double-coursed, lightly dressed fieldstones set in thick mortar, each with two trapezoidal doors opening to the plaza. Only one structure at Kallimarka was built of cut-stone masonry similar to those of Yanque, Lari, and Antisana.

In Cabanaconde, then, there is strong evidence for major state investments in the construction of administrative sites and new architectural complexes. Rather than a single administrative center as in Yanque and Lari, two major sites (Antisana and Kallimarka) shared the top of the settlement hierarchy. The apparent presence of more cut-stone masonry at Antisana, located just beyond the edge of the modern village of Cabanaconde, may signal its primacy over Kallimarka in a primary-secondary center administrative hierarchy. This would closely resemble the scenario found in Yanque and Lari, where the colonial reducciones were built atop the primary Inka centers and large, long-established Collagua settlements (especially in the case of Yanquecollaguas) were transformed into secondary administrative sites through the construction of great halls and plazas. Alternatively, it may be that the foundational dualistic Hanansaya/Urinsaya complementary opposition so evident in local colonial texts was inscribed or reinscribed in built form on the landscape and administered separately at Antisana and Kallimarka. In Cabanaconde, further ethnohistorical and archaeological research is required to clarify the mode of Inka administration and its relationship to local community organization. As we will see in greater clarity in Yanquecollaguas, dualism was a primary means by which the Inkas attempted to rework local communities in their own ideal self-image.

Community Life under Inka Rule

But how much did Inka administration effect a reworking of local community life to an overarching imperial scheme? Elements of general policy and strategy are evident in the significant changes they introduced to the settlement pattern, but privileging such a top-down, imperialist perspective is insensitive to how the archaeological remains visible today must have been a negotiated outcome between the interests and prerogatives of the state and local communities. How did the everyday world of the built environment in the hamlets, villages, and towns of the valley change under Inka occupation? If there was a violent or abrupt imperial conquest of the valley, one would expect a corresponding abrupt change in the settlement pattern. Such conquest patterns have been documented in other highland locales throughout Tawantinsuyu, such as in the upper Mantaro Valley, where large fortified hilltop sites occupied during the LIP were abruptly abandoned and the valley bottom was densely settled during the Late Horizon (D'Altroy 1987, 1992). A broadly similar pattern has been documented in the northern and western Titicaca basin, where the settlement shifted dramatically from a highly fragmented hilltop pukara pattern during the LIP to much more expansive settlement of the broad plains surrounding the lake margin during the Late Horizon (Stanish 1997a, 1997b, 2003).

In contrast, a number of archaeological indices point to a local scenario of overall continuity for the bulk of the population over the transition from autonomous to Inka rule in the Colca. Many new sites were established during the Late Horizon, but very few sites occupied during the LIP were abandoned after imperial incorporation. Most settlements grew, some dramatically, as total occupational area and occupational density grew under Inka rule. In the Yanque-Coporaque survey area, fully 87 percent of LIP sites of all classes also had Late Horizon components. Among habitational sites (i.e., settlements), the continuity is even more striking: All but one of the LIP settlements (n = 28) remained occupied during the Late Horizon. There was a similarly high degree of continuity of settlement in Lari and Cabanaconde.

In both areas, every LIP settlement continued to be occupied during the Late Horizon, while five new sites were established in Cabanaconde and 12 new sites were established in Lari (Doutriaux 2004:256–87). Clearly, there was not a radical break with LIP patterns of settlement, even among those sites in defensive or promontory contexts.

Instead, the Inka imperial presence in local settlements is most architecturally visible in the presence of a repeating architectural couplet common in Inka provincial centers: the great hall and plaza. These are very long, single-room, rectangular buildings with multiple trapezoidal doorways that occupy the side of large walled plaza spaces. In the Yanque-Coporaque survey, three are located in prominent locations at each of the secondary centers with standing architecture: Uyu Uyu (YA-050), San Antonio/Chijra (CO-100), and Tunsa (CO-163) (see Figures 4.23–4.26). A smaller great hall structure with at least two (and possibly three) trapezoidal doors is located at San Antonio/Chijra, and a structure of similar size and proportions (but poorly preserved) is situated in front of an open plaza at Kitaplaza (CO-164). In the upper valley, great halls and plazas are present at the sites of Malata and Laiqa Laiqa. That of Malata is very small (at 9.7 × 6.0 m in exterior dimensions, it is similar in size to the smaller hall structure at San Antonio Chijra) and has two trapezoidal doorways fronting a terraced plaza. The example at Laiqa Laiqa is similar in size to those of Uyu Uyu and San Antonio and also fronts a terraced plaza along the main path through the site, though it has not been studied in any detail.

Though they vary in size and elaboration, their repeating co-location with prominent plaza spaces suggests similar functions, which is why I lump them together in the category of great hall. Great hall structures of this type are similarly situated along the sides of open plazas at most major Inka settlements (Hyslop 1990; Morris 1966; Niles 1984, 1987). Large central plazas were a key feature of Inka site layout, setting an open, public stage for state rituals that enacted the Inka ideology of state redistributive largesse (Moore 1996). As discussed in chapter 1, plazas in Inka settlements were essential for creating a central, structured ceremonial space for the ostentatious display of state "generosity" through ritual feasting (Hyslop 1990; Morris and Thompson 1985). The long, multidoor structures such as the ones documented during the survey may have functioned as feasting areas for elites, as opposed to the more public space of the plaza itself. The massive kallankas that line the huge plaza at Huánuco Pampa are archetypical in this regard, and excavations there revealed high concentrations of serving wares, especially large amphora (*aríbalos*) for serving *chicha* (maize beer) (Morris and Thompson 1985).

The great halls documented during the survey, all situated adjacent to

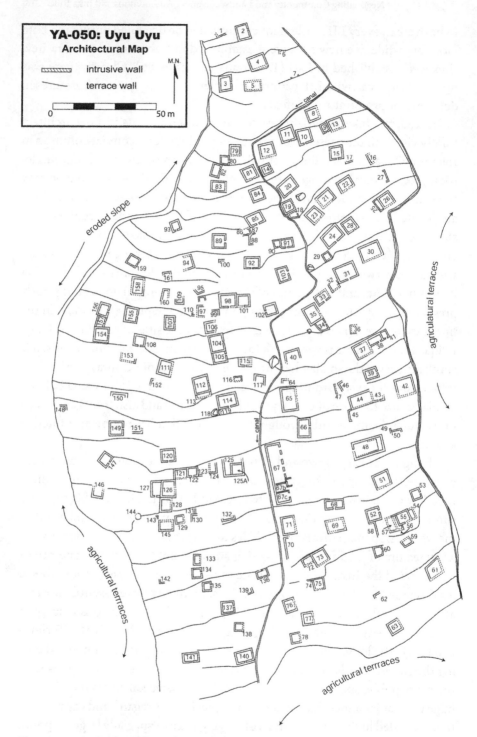

Figure 4.23. Architectural map of Uyu Uyu. The Inka great hall (Structure 67) and plaza are in the south-central portion of the site, adjacent to the main canal.

Figure 4.24. Oblique air photo of Uyu Uyu (YA-050). (Source: 1931 Shippee-Johnson aerial expedition, Image 334676, Special Collections, American Museum of Natural History Library.)

central plaza areas, appear to follow this pattern at a much more diminutive scale. Our excavations of the great hall at Malata (the only one extensively excavated in the valley to date) produced an assemblage that was also dominated by serving wares. Of the Late Horizon ceramics from the structure, Collagua Inka plates, bowls, cups, and jars made up 74 percent (n = 82/111, rim sherds only), aríbalos made up 21 percent (n = 23/111), and only 5 percent of the assemblage (n = 6/111) was made up of cooking vessels.

The dimensions and construction details of the great halls I documented are very distinct from Collagua houses. Those at Uyu Uyu (YA-050) and San Antonio (CO-100), the two well enough preserved to measure building footprints, are much longer and narrower than Collagua houses, measuring 29.3 × 6.8 m and 24.3 × 7.5 m, respectively. The long axis of the great hall at Tunsa has been partially obliterated, but four doorways are visible, and it appears to be of similar dimensions, measuring 7.2 m wide. There are other design similarities common to all three. The great hall at Uyu Uyu, the best

Figure 4.25. Promontory of San Antonio (Sector N) from the southwest.

preserved example, has seven doorways ranging in width between 1.6 and 1.7 m wide at the base—much wider than Collagua doors. Their trapezoidal form is evident, although none is preserved to its full height. This great hall was later modified, probably during the colonial period, dividing the interior into two rooms, with an adjoining, external room built against the facade (Figure 4.27). Abutting wall joins clearly show that these were not part of the original layout of the structure (Figure 4.27-D). The great hall at San Antonio is poorly preserved, but sections of all four walls remain standing. It probably had six trapezoidal doorways, but none of them has both sides preserved. Also, in all cases where walls are well enough preserved, trapezoidal windows are situated between doorways, as is the case at Uyu Uyu and Tunsa. Like-wise, in cases where the gable is preserved (at Uyu Uyu and Tunsa), a trap-ezoidal window was situated along the central axis of the gable, with its base at the height of the roof hip. Trapezoidal niches, another hallmark of Inka architecture, were placed at regular intervals in the interior of the great halls. Two complete niches and one partial niche are present in a preserved section

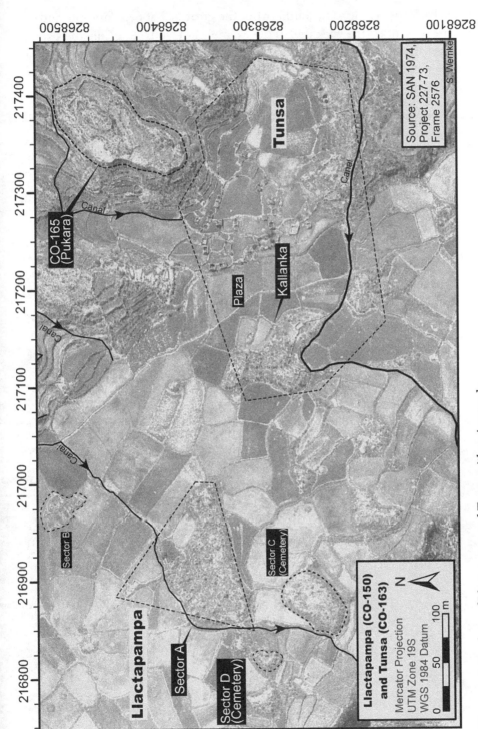

Figure 4.26. Air photo of Llactapampa and Tunsa, with major canals.

of the back wall (long axis, southern) of the great hall at San Antonio, and two are present on the back wall of the example at Uyu Uyu. While the size and morphology of these structures follow Inka architectural canons, their masonry in all cases is of uncoursed, roughed-out fieldstone with dressed stones in the corners, doorways, windows and niches (Type 2 masonry).

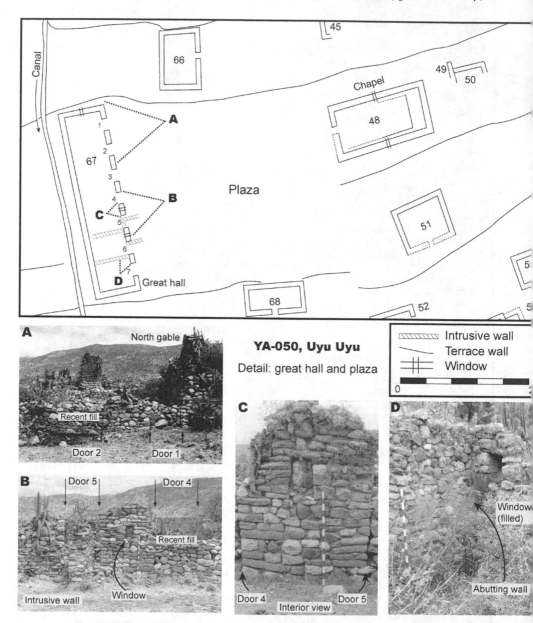

Figure 4.27. Plaza area of Uyu Uyu, showing great hall to the west and chapel to the east. Photo orientations noted in map.

Clearly, these buildings are not the product of specialized state stonemasons. However, fitted cut-stone masonry is very rare in general, even in the imperial capital and amongst the royal estates and major administrative centers in and around the Cuzco heartland (Niles 1993). In short, these buildings were probably constructed using local labor with some form of state oversight. Given their size and locations, they were probably used as public halls, or perhaps as the reserve of elites during state-sponsored feasts.

Another long, multidoor structure (Structure 64), smaller than the great hall described above, lies adjacent to a major path along a prominent ridgeline that divides San Antonio and Chijra (CO-100). Like the other great halls, this building is of markedly different proportions than Collagua houses, measuring 13.5 × 5.4 m. Two wide trapezoidal doors (basal width: 90 cm, superior width: 70 cm, preserved to 1.3 m above present surface) on either side of the eastern-facing long axis are visible, and a third door may have been present in the center, in the position of a void in the front wall. Like the other examples, this structure opens to a terraced plaza space (26.5 × 15.0 m) just off a major path through the site. Another structure of the same dimensions (13.4 × 5.0 m) is located on a terrace in front of a large patio at Kitaplaza (CO-164). Based on its dimensions and location within the site, it appears to be another example of Inka public architecture, but this is a more tentative identification, since the facade of this structure is almost entirely obliterated, and no doorways were definable.

Late Prehispanic Domestic Architecture

Since Neira's pioneering archaeological reconnaissance of the valley in 1959 (Neira Avendaño 1961), researchers working in the Colca Valley have commented on the distinctive features of local domestic architecture, such as the unusually narrow, tall doorways, high gabled rooflines, and finely worked tabular-style masonry of many buildings (Brooks 1998:429–30; Guerra Santander and Aquize Cáceres 1996; Linares Málaga 1993; Malpass 1987; Neira Avendaño 1990; Shea 1986a, 1987). Compared to neighboring locales such as Condesuyos to the west, Chumbivilcas to the north, Soras and Lucanas to the northwest, and the Qolla and Lupaqa areas of the northern Titicaca basin, the domestic architecture of the Colca Valley clearly constitutes a discrete style. Its distribution, however, is not isolated to the Colca Valley. It also appears in lower-lying valleys to the south—particularly around the villages of Huanca, Lluta, and Huambo—which were the locations of ethnohistorically documented Collagua and Cabana colonies of maize agriculturalists (see chapter 6). Domestic architecture has been advocated as a particularly salient index of group affiliation in the south central Andes, especially in cases of colonization of ecological zones remote from the ethnic homeland (Aldenderfer and Stanish 1993; Goldstein 1993, 2000, 2005; Stanish 1989a, 1989b, 1992).

Clearly, processes of more or less self-conscious identification were materialized in Collagua houses. Their conspicuous and distinctive attributes at once reflected and projected a sense of broad affiliation, while more doxic forms of identification inhered in the everyday activities that they structured. To refer to a Collagua "style," then, is both accurate (local late prehispanic architecture shows a coherent and distinctive aesthetic sensibility) and analytically useful (for example, in the identification of Collagua populations beyond the Colca Valley heartland). But a description of the common attributes of this style is also partial, potentially masking a range of variability in form, scale, and function. Using the meso-scale resolution methods of our survey we were able to collect stylistic and metric data on a large sample of domestic architecture, allowing for systematic analysis of both shared attributes and variability.

During our survey in the Yanque-Coporaque area, we collected architectural data from 654 structures (excluding mortuary structures and recently abandoned buildings), including size, layout, orientation, masonry, and other architectural details (such as wall thickness, windows, niches, doors, gables, plaster). The great majority of these, 91 percent (n = 593), were categorized as "houses." I use the term "house" to refer to undivided, single-room architectural spaces that could have served primarily as habitational structures.[11] Of these, 580 were categorized as LIP/Late Horizon in construction date based on relative dating of the site and the absence of colonial architectural attributes. The remainder were clear cases of colonial or republican constructions. Because most Collagua settlements of the LIP continued to be occupied through the Inka occupation, it is not possible to reliably differentiate LIP from Late Horizon periods of construction.[12] One settlement with very well preserved Collagua architecture just north of our survey, Juscallacta, has been the subject of considerable research (Brooks 1998; Guerra Santander and Aquize Cáceres 1996) and represents a more chronologically controlled case, with both ceramic and radiocarbon data pointing to a primary LIP occupation and minimal evidence for continued Late Horizon occupation. Together, the combined data from the Yanque-Coporaque survey and Juscallacta yield a sample of 638 late prehispanic houses. Its size allows systematic exploration of patterned stylistic attributes as well as quantitative analysis of the variability of house size, form, and elaboration.

Figure 4.28. A: Small house of Type 1 masonry with preserved doorway, from the south. CO-163 (Tunsa), Structure 33. B: Detail of doorway, from the east. YA-050 (Uyu Uyu), Structure 84. Basal width of doorway: 50 cm; top width: 40 cm; 220 cm above present surface. C: Detail of doorway/facade, from the east. YA-050 (Uyu Uyu), Structure 103. Type 2 masonry. Basal width of doorway: 60 cm; top width: 50 cm, 220 cm above present surface.

There is clear patterning in the layout and construction of local domestic architecture. These patterned attributes signal shared local conceptions regarding the proper organization of residential space and constitute the Collagua architectural style. The most distinctive and diagnostic trait of Collagua houses are their extremely narrow and tall doorways. All houses have a single doorway, and in the case of rectangular houses, the doorway is always situated on the center of the long axis (Figure 4.28). They are slightly trapezoidal and much narrower than the trapezoidal doorways of Inka architecture—most would require an adult to turn sideways to enter. Basal widths of doorways range between only 40 and 80 cm, with an average of 60.7 cm (standard deviation = 7.6), with top widths tapering by 10–30 cm compared to basal widths (mean = 16 cm). Their height is much greater than required for entry, averaging 1.8 m in height (standard deviation = 0.29) (e.g., Figure 4.28-B/C). Also, the doorways are invariably made of dressed fieldstones laid up in regular headers and stretchers and topped by a long lintel stone; in small, rustic houses, the doorway stones are often the only worked stone in a structure.

Questions immediately arise when seeing these striking doorways. For example, why did they make them so tall and narrow? They may have helped to protect against the elements (wind, rain, hail, and so on), but their proportions seem to go well beyond the strictly functional (if only for protection from the elements, for example, why make them so tall?). Their unusual appearance and well-worked masonry, instead, suggest aesthetics in addition to functionality accounts for the form of Collagua doorways.

House Forms

There are two basic house forms present at late prehispanic sites in the valley: those of rectilinear floor plan and those with circular floor plan. They have distinct spatial distributions: Nearly all of the rectilinear prehispanic houses documented in the valley occur in the kichwa zone in the agricultural core of the valley (below about 3,800 m), while all the prehispanic houses documented at sites in the high pasturelands of the puna (above about 4,000 m) are circular. The two forms also have distinct roof types. Circular houses have hip roofs, and rectilinear houses have gabled roofs; gables are always situated on the short axis of rectangular houses (i.e., are side gabled). In the Yanque-Coporaque area, we also documented a small number (n = 13) of circular houses scattered among agriculturalist sites, but given that the structures of pastoralist puna sites are uniformly circular in form, the pattern is clearly one related to ecozone and economic focus. At the site of Malata, situated in the transitional suni zone, houses of both forms are present (Figure 4.29). For reasons discussed in the following

Figure 4.29. Circular house (Structure 018) with complete doorway at Malata (TU-170).

chapter, this co-occurrence is likely due to distinct periods of construction rather than a mixed agriculturalist/pastoralist population.

But if there are such basic differences in form, how can we speak of a common Collagua domestic architectural style? At a regional scale, the circular house form could reflect longstanding ties with agro-pastoralist and herding peoples to the east, since circular domestic structures are common to the Qollas, Lupaqas, and other Aymara-speaking peoples of the Titicaca basin and Altiplano (Hyslop 1976; Stanish 2003). A key difference, however, between local circular houses and those of neighboring locales is once again the diagnostic high, narrow doorway, which appears in both rectilinear and circular houses in the Colca Valley. As discussed below, there are also similarities among the tabular-style masonry of some of the larger circular houses in the puna and that of the large rectangular houses in agriculturalist sites such as Juscallacta. The circular house form of the pastoralists thus probably represent a local expression of a regional puna/Altiplano domestic architectural tradition during the LIP and Late Horizon.

These data thus suggest distinct scales and modes of identification were materialized in local domestic architecture: from ethnic or pan-ethnic in scale to one at an intra-ethnic scale based on economic specialization. With increasing economic intensification under Inka rule, and the Inka penchant for maintaining markers and practices of distinction between their subject groups, such divisions were likely maintained and probably further accentuated. This kind of dualistic division is also consistent with the agriculturalist "huari" and pastoralist "llacuaz" distinction previously discussed (Duviols 1973). As Duviols notes, this dynamic of complementarity and opposition was not just marked in customary relations between the groups—for instance, in the exchange of complementary produce and in ritual battles (tinku)—but also materially manifested in distinct dress, dialect, and places of worship on the sacred landscape. Parsons and colleagues note similar distinctive architectural and settlement patterns among LIP agriculturalists and pastoralists in the Tarama-Chinchaycocha region of the central highlands and attribute it to this kind of huari-llacuaz division (Parsons, et al. 1997).

By all indications, then, agriculturalists and pastoralists built distinct houses during the LIP and Late Horizon: Agriculturalists built rectilinear houses and pastoralists built circular houses. Shared stylistic attributes in both suggest an overarching level of common affiliation. Such normative characterizations may be correct in broad outline but still incomplete, however, since they imply conformity to a reference "style." But there is a wide range of variation in scale and form among Collagua houses as well. An analysis of this variation can enable inference of inequality and distinctions in status within and between Collagua agriculturalists and pastoralists.

House Size, Status, and Inequality

The corregidor Francisco de Ulloa Mogollón, in his entry for the *Relaciones Geográficas* (1965 [1586]:332), noted the link between house size and social status: "The houses [of the people of the province] are small, covered with thatch; those of the caciques are larger; they are recognized by the large amount of thatch that they put on them."[13] But how great were the differences among Collagua houses? A quantitative analysis of the large house data set we collected provides a systematic means of tracking status and inequality. Of the total of 638 houses in the sample,[14] 423 were sufficiently preserved to measure both axes for size analysis. A histogram of house footprint area shows a very broad range of house sizes, with the largest examples being more than 10 times the size of the smallest (Figure 4.30). The modal size is between 20 and 30 m, and three-quarters (75 percent, n = 317/423) are less than 40 m². These constitute the housing for the bulk of the commoner population. There is a

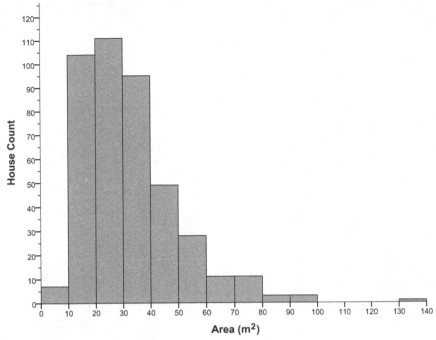

Figure 4.30. House-size histogram, all sites (n = 423).

sharp drop in houses greater than 40 m², suggesting that they are a distinct class of elite houses.

Comparison of house sizes by form shows a clear pattern: The average rectilinear house (34 m²) is double the size of the average circular floor plan house of pastoralists (17 m²), and the range of variance among rectilinear houses is over double that of circular houses, while ovoid houses are in the middle of the range (mean = 20 m²). In part, this probably reflects on different functions of housing between the two groups—agriculturalists probably spend more time in and around their houses than pastoralists, who likely rotated residences occasionally between a few settlements as grazing lands were rotated. However, such a stark difference also derives from the great investments made in the largest agriculturalist houses.

Plotting the distribution of house sizes at these sites shows both greater inequalities and larger houses at large settlements compared to small settlements (Figure 4.31). This is evident in the higher medians, the higher and wider mid-spread values, and extremely large houses that make up the upper quartiles and outliers in the large settlements of San Antonio and Uyu Uyu on the right side of the graph compared to the smaller settlements on the left side of the graph. This suggests that the largest settlements also had the most diverse populations and were home to elite households, while smaller

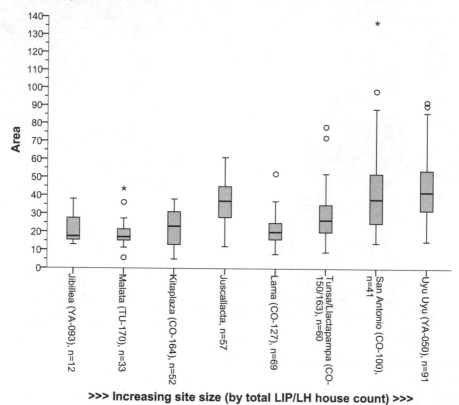

>>> Increasing site size (by total LIP/LH house count) >>>

Figure 4.31. Boxplot of house footprint area by settlement. Excludes sites with fewer than 12 cases.

settlements were populated by a more homogeneous commoner population. Juscallacta, a medium-sized settlement, stands out for its high and broad range of house sizes relative to its size, but as discussed above, it is also distinct in that it apparently was not substantially altered and did not grow appreciably during the Late Horizon. It seems to have been occupied largely by Collagua elites. With even casual observation of the houses at Juscallacta, it is obvious that many were not commoner dwellings (Figure 4.32). Virtually all of the domestic structures at the site are constructed of finely worked tabular masonry, and the median size is just under the 40 m² cut point between commoner and elite houses.

House Elaboration: Masonry

Masonry style and quality range widely among houses, from small, very rustic dwellings to grand two-story constructions of well-worked cut-stone mortared masonry. During the survey, I have categorized the spectrum of masonry styles and qualities into seven types (see Table 4.1). At the low end

Figure 4.32. Large house at Juscallacta.

of the spectrum, Type 1 masonry is composed of uncut fieldstones of various sizes, shapes, and colors set in large amounts of mortar (*Opus incertum*) (Figure 4.33-A). Wall headers and blocky corners were left undressed and lack header and stretcher rows to tie the walls together. Houses of Type 1 masonry are very common; they make up 37 percent of the 454 observable cases (Table 4.2). Type 2 masonry, while uncoursed like Type 1, is composed of fieldstones of more uniform shape and color (*Opus poligonale*) (Figure 4.33-B). Also, the doorways, wall heads, and corners are made with dressed stones that are laid up in alternating header and stretcher rows. Cornerstones can be either blocky or tabular in form. Type 2 masonry is also the most common: 40 percent of houses were built of Type 2 masonry. Type 3 masonry, making up 12 percent of the cases, is similar to Type 2 in the quality of wall heads, doorways, and cornerstones, but stones of more uniform size and shape were laid up together to form roughly coursed wall facings (Figure 4.33-C).

At the high end of the masonry spectrum, fine masonry houses were built of selected fieldstones of uniform size and color that were dressed, carefully chinked and laid up with minimal amounts of mortar. Doorways, wall heads, and corners were constructed of dressed stones of interlocking headers and stretchers, firmly tying the structure together. Types 4–7 are all finely executed in these respects, but each is stylistically distinct.

Houses of Type 4 masonry make up 1.8 percent of the cases, and all but one of them are located in Uyu Uyu (YA-050). Houses of this masonry type

Table 4.1. Masonry typology

Type	Description	Labor Input: Shaping	Labor Input: Construction
1	Unworked fieldstone of varying size, shape, and color, no coursing, rough corners and heads	Low	Low
2	Some worked, selected fieldstone, no coursing, dressed corners and heads	Medium	Medium
3	Worked, coursed fieldstone, dressed corners and heads	Medium	High
4	Coursed split river boulder facade, dressed corners and heads	Medium	High
5	Coursed tabular worked slabs, finely dressed corners and heads	High	High
6	Coursed rectangular worked blocks, finely dressed corners and heads	High	High
7	Worked fieldstone with belt courses of alternating color, finely dressed corners and heads	High	High

Table 4.2. Masonry type percentages, Yanque-Coporaque survey

Site No.	Masonry Type							
	1	2	3	4	5	6	7	N
45	17%	67%			17%			6
48		50%	50%					2
50	34%	34%	20%	5%		4%	3%	138
54	100%							1
93	100%							5
100	8%	53%	16%	1%	22%			87
127	56%	40%	1%		1%	1%		77
150	13%	63%	13%		13%			16
163	25%	52%	13%		10%			60
164	77%	19%				3%		62
Total	37%	40%	12%	2%	6%	2%	1%	454

Note: Excludes 127 cases of insufficient preservation to determine masonry type.

are distinguished by their facades, which are composed primarily of rolled river boulders that were split in half and laid up in courses with their cleavage planes facing out (a variant of *Opus mixtum*) (Figures 4.34-A/B). The other walls of these houses were executed in an uncoursed masonry similar to Type 2. While rolled river boulders are plentiful in the quebradas near the site, the

Figure 4.33. A: Small house of Type 1 masonry, from the east (CO-164, Structure 28). B: House of Type 2 masonry, from the southeast (YA-050, Structure 107). C: House of Type 3 masonry, southwest corner (YA-050, Structure 114).

Figure 4.34. A: Facade of large house of Type 4 masonry, from the east (YA-050, Structure 104). B: Detail of split-river boulders of Type 4 masonry (YA-050, Structure 104). C–D: Large house of Type 5 masonry, from southwest (C) and from the northeast (D). Note tenon supports for second floor (YA-100, Structure 17). E: Large house of Type 5 masonry, from the south (CO-163, Structure 10).

fact that only the facades of houses were dressed and coursed in this careful fashion indicates that this masonry style was not simply employed as an expedient use of local materials but conveyed a uniform aesthetic and projected the prestige of their residents.

Type 5 masonry is very distinctive, presenting a laminar visual effect through the coursing of thin, tabular-shaped slabs (*Opus mixtum*) (Figure 4.34-C/D/E). No Type 5 masonry houses are found at Uyu Uyu. They are all located in sites to the east—all but one within modern Coporaque, and most of these (19 of 29) in San Antonio/Chijra (CO-100) and Juscallacta (see Figure 4.32). Like the other finely worked masonry types (Types 4–7), Type 5 masonry houses are uncommon, making up 6.4 percent of the cases.

Type 6 masonry is composed of coursed rectangular to ovoid blocks that are worked on all sides of the stone facing, giving it a more regular, brick-like external appearance (*Opus quadratum*) (Figure 4.35-A). The worked surfaces resemble those of Inka cut-stone masonry, but the blocks are longer and narrower than the quadrangular blocks of late Inka masonry. Six of the nine houses of this type are found in Uyu Uyu (YA-050). Not surprisingly, most are poorly preserved, probably due to colonial and republican-era mining of their blocks for building material.

Type 7 masonry is similar to Type 3 (worked, coursed fieldstone, dressed corners and heads), but with the addition of belt courses of white stones, creating decorative horizontal bands around the structure (Figure 4.35-B/C). All four cases of this masonry type are found in Uyu Uyu (YA-050).

House masonry and size appear to be reliable indices of the social status and economic position of their inhabitants. As the boxplot in Figure 4.36 illustrates, houses of fine masonry tend to be larger than those at the low end of the spectrum, and those of intermediate masonry quality (Type 2 and Type 3) tend to be intermediate in size. Type 6 masonry is an exception to this rule, since houses of this type are generally smaller than those of the other fine masonry types. Two alternative scenarios could account for this lack of correlation. Their small size may be the result of a compromise between masonry quality and quantity or may represent an expeditious use of worked masonry that was quarried from the corners and doorways of other buildings to create a small house with minimal labor investment. If the latter scenario is true, these Type 6 houses are late additions and may have been constructed during the early colonial period, prior to resettlement in the reducción villages. Future excavations could potentially differentiate these alternative scenarios. Nonetheless, the general pattern holds that houses of worked masonry tend to be larger than houses of unworked masonry: When Types 1–3 and 4–7 are grouped into general "coarse" and "fine" masonry categories, a t-test shows

Figure 4.35. A: Wall fragment of Type 6 masonry, from the east (YA-050, Structure 85). B: House of Type 7 masonry (southwest corner of Structure 31, the second largest house at YA-050). Western gable and southern facade are visible, as well as the interior of the eastern gable. Note white belt courses. C: Southeast corner of Structure 31, YA-050. Note belt courses on gable and facade, and dressed cornerstones at base.

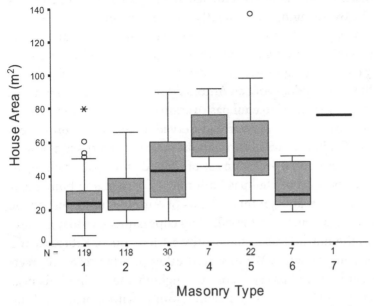

Figure 4.36. Boxplot of house area, grouped by masonry type. Outlier cases marked by circles, extremes marked with asterisks.

that the domestic structures of the fine masonry group, with an average area of 55.0 m^2 are significantly larger than those of the coarse group.[15] The inhabitants of the fine group were apparently able to mobilize more skilled and greater overall labor forces in the construction of their dwellings.

Cemeteries, Tombs, and Mortuary Architecture

During the LIP and Late Horizon, peoples throughout the central and south-central Andes interred their dead in above-ground chullpas, or "houses of the dead," often in large groups of chullpas forming "cities of the dead." As we know from colonial written sources (e.g., Guaman Poma de Ayala et al. 1987), these cities of the dead were conceived of as a kind of parallel settlement system for the deceased members of local ayllus whose living members regularly feted and consulted the mummified remains of their focal ancestors (see Isbell 1997; Salomon 1995). Given the centrality of ancestral mummies as focal points in ayllu membership reckoning, and the importance of ancestor veneration and consultation in ayllu political and economic life, considerable effort was expended in the elaboration of chullpas and the preparation of the dead for interment.

In the survey area, clusters of chullpas are situated in the rocky scarps surrounding each of the major settlements. The largest groups of chullpas are found in the overhanging cliffs directly upslope of San Antonio/Chijra (CO-100) at the sites of CO-154 and CO-098 (Fatinga). The latter site is the largest cemetery in the survey, where we registered 40 elaborate two- to three-story chullpas (Figure 4.37). This impressive site was probably the cemetery of the elite residents of San Antonio/Chijra. Site CO-154 is also a large cemetery composed of 16 chullpas overlooking San Antonio/Chijra, but they are heavily looted and poorly preserved. Eight collection sectors at San Antonio/Chijra, scattered throughout the rocky scarps to the west and south of the residential area, consist of individual or paired chullpas. Another large dispersion of chullpas built under overhanging boulders is located on the western and southern flanks of Pampa Finaya, just above the abandoned "Inca" canal (as it is called by coporaqueños today). These may pertain to the inhabitants of the nearby settlements of Kitaplaza and Llanka on the pampas below. We observed other poorly preserved, rect- angular, freestanding chullpas scattered throughout the rolling hills near Tunsa/Llactapampa (CO-163/150), including some within nearby hilltop fortifications (discussed below) and others within the large agro-mortuary wall sites of CO-148 and CO-149.

Clearly, chullpas were reserved for high-status individuals. Most common- ers probably continued to be interred in the subterranean, rock-lined collared tombs that are scattered throughout settlements. These collared tombs are generally round to slightly ovoid in plan view and cylindrical in profile, rang- ing in size between 50 and 125 cm in diameter and 75–100 cm deep, and were covered with long, flat stone slabs. To the south of Uyu Uyu (YA-050), 12–15 ovoid to rectangular subterranean collar tombs are scattered around the top of a small hill (YA-049). However, these tombs are severely looted and only a few isolated skeletal elements were visible. During initial reconnaissance in 1998, I observed a small group of poorly preserved chullpas on the slopes to the immediate northeast of Uyu Uyu, but these have since been completely obliterated by looting and modern terrace construction.

Chullpa Architectural Characteristics

The freestanding LIP and Late Horizon chullpas we documented are virtu- ally all rectilinear in floor plan. Most are roughly square in proportion and measure 3–5 m on the exterior. Chullpas under boulders and cliffs are set in slightly in from the drip line with flat facades and lateral sides that enclose irregular spaces, depending on the shape of the overhanging area they en- close. The placement of chullpas under the cool recesses of rock overhangs and cliffs was almost certainly explicitly designed as a means of preserving the

Figure 4.37. A: Large group of adjoining chullpas at Fatinga (CO-098). B: Two-storey chullpas at CO-098. Note slab-stone doorways and cornices between stories. C: Side view, showing how chullpas were built against overhang. Note cornice at roofline, addition of second story.

mummified remains. As I discuss below, textile and soft tissue preservation is generally very good despite extensive looting.

The masonry of most chullpas is composed of roughly coursed rubble, primarily of tabular or rectangular slabs with varying amounts of mortar (Figure 4.37). Walls are double coursed and 45–65 cm thick. It appears that most or all exterior wall surfaces were also smoothed over with a mud and pebble plaster of the same consistency as the mortar. This plastered surface may also have been finished with a fine plaster and decorated with paint in a manner similar to the interior walls—patches of red pigment (probably ochre, applied over a second, smooth layer of white plaster) remain on the interior walls of the best-preserved chullpas of Fatinga. Most are of two stories with a semisubterranean first floor, although a few examples with as many as three stories remain (e.g., Figure 4.38). Small doors provided continued access to the dead after interment, as well as a means of interring additional individuals. The doors themselves are generally rectangular to slightly trapezoidal in form, ranging in size from 35 to 60 cm in width and 55 to 75 cm in height, and usually constructed of three long stones—two upright members and a lintel (Figures 4.37-A/B). Second floors (and any subsequent floors, where present) are marked by distinctive belt courses of projecting tabular header stones (Figures 4.37-B/C). Some multistory chullpas originally had only one story, and the original roofs, marked by these belt-courses, then functioned as floors for the story above (Figure 4.37-C). The base of the corbel vaulted roof on most multistory chullpas is marked by a cornice identical to the belt course marking the lower floor(s). Thus additional stories of some chullpas may have been built in a vertically modular fashion during separate construction episodes, perhaps as each level filled with interments and more space was required. Where in groups, chullpas are also horizontally modular, occurring in abutting rows of self-contained structures. The abutments are clearly visible as seams on the exterior (Figure 4.37-C), and their interiors were maintained as wholly separate spaces. As mentioned earlier, some chullpas at Fatinga still have remnants of red paint on the interior walls, which was applied over a smooth layer of white plaster that covered the coarse plaster over the masonry.

Interments

Most interments in rock- and cliff-overhang chullpas are exceptionally well preserved in terms of soft tissue and textile preservation but are often heavily disturbed and disarticulated by looting. The interior of most chullpas are filled with commingled skeletal elements from many individuals. I

Figure 4.38. Large, three-story chullpa with two doors (*right side*) at Fatinga (CO-098). This chullpa was heavily looted, containing only isolated skeletal elements.

have termed this interment style a "cocoon" bundle, since the tightly flexed mummy bundle is bound in a cocoon-like capsule of thick vegetal fiber cable (Figure 4.39). Similar vegetal fiber bundles have been reported by Justin Jennings (2002) in the neighboring Cotahuasi Valley, and in cave cemeteries in the western Titicaca basin (E. de la Vega, pers. comm. 2000). While we only observed one completely intact bundle, it appears that inside the vegetal fiber enclosure, the individual was wrapped in several layers of textiles—both plain and polychrome decorated. Other grave goods we observed in the tomb interiors include both decorated and utilitarian ceramics, including storage and serving vessels.

Figure 4.39. Cocoon-style vegetal fiber mummy bundle salvaged from a looted chullpa at Fatinga. The bundle contained the remains of a three- to four-year-old individual (based on radiographic analysis).

The Built Landscape: Agricultural Terrace and Irrigation Systems

Although none of the prehispanic settlements of the valley can be characterized as monumental in scale, they are set in a landscape of anthropogenic landforms that certainly is. Understanding the construction and reproduction of community and its articulation with imperialism cannot be understood apart from this landscape. Houses and settlements were clearly key arenas of community life, but for the farmers and herders of the Colca and elsewhere in the Andes, most of the daylight hours are spent "in the *chacras* (agricultural fields)" away from the villages. This is doubtless as true in the past as today, as is farmers' constant preoccupation with irrigation water in this semiarid environment—fretting over it, managing it, even fighting with one's neighbors over it (Benavides 1997; Gelles 2000; Treacy 1994). These preoccupations are written out onto the landscape in the vast palimpsest mosaic of terrace systems and irrigation networks that one sees today. They attest not only to massive mobilizations of labor and resources for their construction and maintenance but also to complex systems of water management that bound farmers from multiple villages together in common interest. That is, one's community affiliation during the LIP and Late Horizon would not have been simply a reflection one's village of residence, but could be scaled up and down in part by reference to the primary and secondary canals that irrigated one's fields. The apportionment of scarce water was coordinated at several scales, as can be seen traced through the hydrological relationships between the canal systems of the valley.

Irrigation Communities and the Built Landscape

Upstream-downstream relationships between micro-watersheds and canals map out community water management negotiations. Because the Colca River itself is deeply entrenched, its waters are inaccessible for prehispanic irrigation. So nearly all of the irrigation water in the valley originates in the long feeder canals that divert meltwater from the surrounding glaciated peaks. The main intakes (*boquerones* or *bocatomas*) of most feeder canals are situated at the base of the snowpack and glaciers (many above 5,000 m), but a major portion of their flowage also comes from the many rivulets and quebradas that intersect their courses. Thus, as feeder canals descend and cut across the slopes above the agricultural core of the valley, they cross many micro-watersheds along their courses and capture this water rather than allowing it to continue flowing downstream along their natural courses. This manner of collecting water from several small sources through large traversing feeder canals requires less engineering and labor than constructing multiple small canals from each quebrada while also raising water discharge and velocity and minimizing loss to seepage (Treacy 1989b:147). In systems as complex as those that have developed in the Colca, however, where several feeder canals in proximity provide water for different terrace complexes, this form of water management requires negotiation and coordination regarding which water sources are to supply which feeder canals.

This kind of watershed management is apparent in the hydrological relationships between feeder canal networks. The most detailed data are from the Yanque-Coporaque area, where the longest canals of the valley were built. On the north side of the valley, the 25-km Misme canal irrigates the fields around the LIP/Late Horizon settlements within modern Yanque Urinsaya such as Uyu Uyu (YA-050) and Llactarana (YA-054). A cartographic representation of the canal is found in Figure 4.40, and a schematic of the sources of the Misme and neighboring feeder canals is found in Figure 4.41. The key to understanding how the actual course of the Misme canal bespeaks of negotiation between irrigation communities is to consider how it collects water from several quebradas that would, if left to flow down their natural courses, would otherwise flow into the Sahuara River, which in turn supplies about 80 percent of the irrigation water for the fields around the LIP/Late Horizon settlements in Coporaque (Treacy 1989b:147). The Sahuara itself is a hybrid natural river/anthropogenic *acequia* (canalized stream). Its waters derive primarily from two streams bypassed by the Misme canal, the Waynaqorea and the Aquenta. The courses of the Waynaqorea and the Aquenta also have been altered in order to force their confluences before joining the Sahuara. If left to drain naturally, the

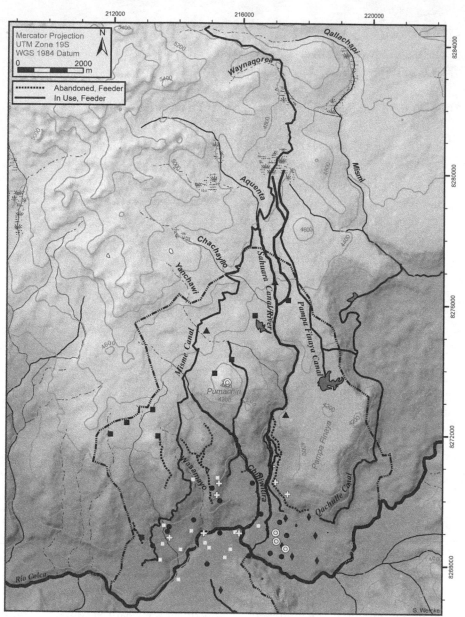

Figure 4.40. Primary feeder canals in the Yanque-Coporaque survey area on the north side of the Colca River watershed.

Waynaqorea stream would flow easterly into the Qallachapi River, toward the fields that surround the reducción of Tuti and the prehispanic settlements of Malata and Laiqa Laiqa in the upper valley. Instead, the Waynaqorea has been channelized to flow more westerly toward the Aquenta, forming the Sahuara River at the point of their confluence (Treacy 1989b:144–47).

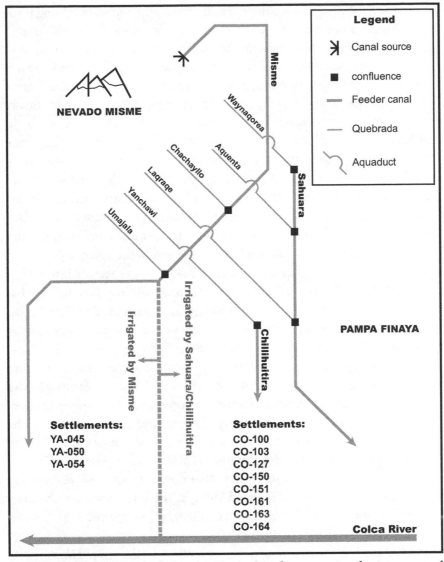

Figure 4.41. Schematic of hydrological relationships between secondary sources and primary feeder canals on the north side of the Colca River watershed.

Moving downstream along the Misme canal, the large stream of the quebrada Chachayllo is shunted into the Misme. Here a brief retelling of the conflict between Yanque Urinsaya and Coporaque is illustrative of the tension that arises when colonial constructions of community are intensely focused on the village amid a prehispanic agricultural landscape of complex, supra-settlement hydrological relations. Chachayllo is the largest secondary source for the Misme canal and continues to be venerated by Yanqueños as an important deity during their annual *yarqa jaspiy* (canal cleaning festival) of Misme from August 1–4 (fieldwork 1999–2000; see also Valderrama Fernández and Escalante Gutierrez 1988). But tensions between Yanque and Coporaque have always ran high over Chachayllo, since it falls within the territorial limits of Coporaque and, if left to run downslope under the Misme canal, would flow into the feeder canals of Coporaque. These tensions finally erupted in a battle between the two communities at the union of Chachayllo and Misme in 1971, which resulted in the death of a yanqueño by slingstone (Benavides 1997). Ultimately, the irrigation councils from each community appealed to the Ministry of Agriculture in Chivay, which found in favor of the yanqueños, who claimed rights to water "since time immemorial" (Benavides 1997). Chachayllo and other secondary sources of Misme remain, however, bones of contention between the communities, and conflict over water sources are common between neighboring villages in the villages.

Moving farther downstream from Chachayllo, it is especially interesting, then, that the next two quebradas, the Yanchawi and the Laqraqe, are bypassed by the Misme and left to flow to the lands surrounding Coporaque. That is, after flowing under the Misme canal (which forms an aqueduct at their intersection), the Laqraqe drains into the Sahuara, while the Yanchawi stream is diverted from its natural drainage with a small crossover canal into the neighboring stream of the Chilliwitira River, which then forms a feeder canal for the western agricultural sectors of Coporaque. After these two quebradas, the Misme canal arcs westerly and captures more water from the springs of Umajala (today still considered to be the primary female deity complementary to the male deity of Mount Misme; see Valderrama Fernández and Escalante Gutierrez 1988) and other minor streams before dropping into the agricultural sector of Yanque Urinsaya. There, it flows in a high waterfall directly above the site of Uyu Uyu and irrigates a large swath of terraced fields surrounding it and Llactarana.

On the south side of the river in Yanquecollaguas, the 15-km Huarancante canal is the primary feeder canal for the fields around modern Yanque Hanansaya (Figure 4.42). This long feeder canal similarly draws water from several quebradas that, if left to flow naturally downslope, would instead irrigate fields around Juscallacta. Similar relations between feeder canals and source waters obtain for most major canal systems in the valley.

Given the constraints of gravity and topography, as well as the large labor investments required for reengineer canals, the current courses of the feeder canals closely approximate their ancient ones. It was not possible to document to what degree these specific hydrological relationships between secondary sources and the Misme canal correspond to those of the prehispanic

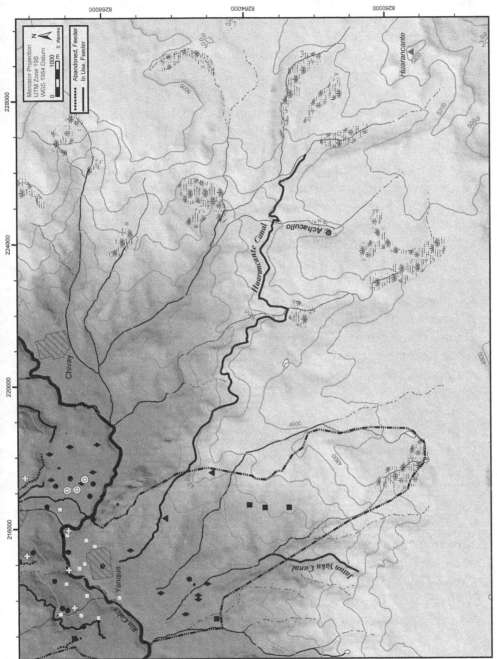

Figure 4.42. Primary feeder canals in the Yanque-Coporaque survey area on the south side of the Colca River watershed.

past, and doubtless they did change through time according to the changing fortunes of different irrigation communities. But these kinds of hydraulic negotiations would have been inescapable. Under autonomous rule, the construction and maintenance of large feeder canals and their connections to primary and secondary sources would have bound multiple settlements of farmers in common interest and affiliation—probably through periodic affiliative rituals related to canal maintenance like those practiced today. Conversely, tributary confluences were probably also flash points of conflict between irrigation communities, as they also are today. Under Inka rule, these hydrological relationships could have been stabilized and rationalized to accommodate the state projects for expanding and intensifying production needs of different irrigation sectors. But simultaneously, the Inkas—as the Spanish after them—must not have ignored extant hydraulic infrastructure and the relationships between them, again given the constraints of gravity and topography, as well as the considerable landscape capital and interests embedded in the extant irrigation infrastructure. It seems likely, then, that the bonds of irrigation communities strengthened and stabilized under Inka rule, and it was not until after the dismantling of the Inka state that underlying grievances between irrigation communities again came to the fore, especially as community identity and interests became increasingly parochialized to the village level following reducción resettlement.

Coordination also would have been required at each subsidiary level in the canal network. As primary canals divide dendritically downstream into secondary and tertiary distribution canals, water must be shunted back and forth between them since there is not enough to supply several at once. The reservoirs often found at nodal locations in the irrigation networks partially mitigate problems of seepage and lack of volume by storing and enabling controlled release of water with greater velocity and discharge. But like today, during late prehispanic times there was probably not enough water to supply more than one secondary canal at once from most primary canals. This means that irrigation sectors had to coordinate scheduling as water was switched between different secondary canals. For example, the fields surrounding the large LIP/LH settlements of Kitaplaza (CO-164), Llanka (CO-127), and Tunsa (CO-163) are irrigated by different secondary canals that share a primary canal, and it would have been necessary to alternate water between them according to some kind of rotational scheduling regime. Residents of those villages therefore probably maintained affiliations with a corresponding hierarchy of irrigation communities—from those of the secondary or tertiary canals nearest their village, where perhaps the majority of their fields were located, to those of the primary feeder canals. These would have corresponded to communities of more or less daily interaction to those more episodic in nature—the annual canal cleaning, or, as discussed below, at rituals at stone sculptures of irrigation and terrace systems that dot the landscape, for example. Likewise, they likely corresponded to distinct scales of ayllu affiliation, from the minimal ayllu of directly related kin, to moiety-scale collectivities that maintained primary canals as a collectivity. In these ways, then, the agricultural landscape constituted a primary interface for the ongoing constitution and contestation of community and state.

Water Management Systems in the Puna

While the settlement and irrigation systems in the agricultural core of the valley indicate overall continuity with increasingly centralized administration rather than an abrupt overall transformation, in the puna there is considerable evidence that the Inkas sought to intensify the production of pasturage for camelids by establishing new settlements and water management systems. Nine new herding settlements were established in the Yanque-Coporaque area under Inka rule, and most of these sites are situated adjacent to large reservoirs, canals, and dam features. Reservoirs in the puna were probably used primarily for controlled inundation of low-relief areas to augment the pasturage growth of natural bofedales.

For example, a large reservoir was constructed about 250 m east of the herding village of Jibillea (YA-093), which consists of 12 circular houses and associated corrals. This reservoir is formed by a large, 86-m earthen berm, 3–4 m high and 5–10 m thick with a stone sluice gate. Upslope of this dam feature is a natural depression. When filled, the reservoir would flood a large area upslope. Two similarly sized reservoirs lie adjacent to the neighboring Late Horizon herding settlement of YA-061 to the west. Two larger artificial lagoon-type features are located at the north end of Pampa Finaya and the slopes to the west. On Pampa Finaya, a stone-lined canal that diverts water from the Waynaqorea stream flows into a large, shallow basin. No settlements are located around this feature, but we did observe diagnostic Collagua Inka plate sherds next to the canal. Today this canal and reservoir are in poor condition but are still used. The reservoir is designed to create an artificial lagoon on the otherwise dry plain of Pampa Finaya, not for regulating downstream flows of irrigation water. There are no apparent outflowing canals from it. However, a secondary canal did divert water from the feeder canal above the reservoir to join the Quachulle canal at the base of the eastern flanks of Pampa Finaya. When full, this lagoon would cover 20 ha, a substantial patch of dense pasturage. To the northwest of Pampa Finaya, another damlike feature (RC-032) encloses a shallow, 50-m-wide draw next to the Sahuara River and appears to have functioned to inundate a few hectares. About 500 m to the east, a canal siphons water from the Sahuara River to irrigate a pasturage patch of 7–10 ha.

Water Ritual Sites: Carved Stone Sculptures of Terracing and Irrigation Systems

The central importance of the agricultural landscape in the cosmology of the farmers of the Colca is also evident in the detailed, large-scale carved stone representations of terracing, canals, and reservoirs on boulders and rock outcrops found throughout the valley. The regional distribution of these sculptures appears to extend throughout most of the Pacific drainages of the northern half of the Department of Arequipa. Similar examples are found in the Chuquibamba Valley to the west, as well as at LIP/LH sites in and around the valley of Arequipa, including Tambo de León in Chiguata (15 km east of the city) and Maucallacta in Pocsi (20 km southwest of the city) (A. Cardona Rosas, pers. comm. 2003).

Although dating these sculptures with precision is virtually impossible, they were presumably made and used coevally with the irrigation and terrace systems with which they are associated. Locally referred to as *maquetas* (models), the sculptures have hydraulically functional miniature reservoirs and canals that may represent specific canal and terrace systems. Whether or not they were literal models of the surrounding landscape features, they were almost certainly important huacas venerated in fertility rituals by irrigation communities. Some carved boulders in the Inka heartland, such as the famous Sayhuite stone (van de Guchte 1999:162) and the Piedra Cansada (see, e.g., Bauer 1998:59), shrines in the ceque system of Cuzco, also show landscape features such as terraces and canals. However, they are stylistically distinct from the examples in the Colca and often incorporate geometric motifs and representations of animals, humans, or supernatural beings. The maquetas found in the Colca appear to represent a separate tradition unique to the Pacific drainages of the Department of Arequipa and surrounding areas.

The maquetas are not associated with or clustered around settlements; in general, they appear to be situated quite distant from them. Many are located near the top of terrace complexes, near the points where canals flow into the viewshed of the terraces they irrigate. For example, a cluster of four maquetas—the only such grouping registered in the valley thus far—is located high on the western slopes of Cerro Pallaclle, just below the Huarancante canal and above the terraces and fields it irrigates to the south of Yanque (Figure 4.43). Three of these are very large and especially elaborate. They range in size from 3 to 4 m on their long axes and mimic their full-scale counterparts

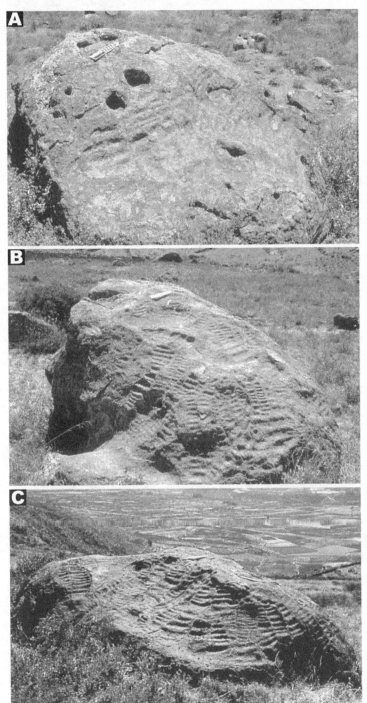

Figure 4.43. A: Maqueta at YA-162. Note reservoirs with distribution canals. B: Another large maqueta at YA-162, showing extensive contour terracing. C: Large maqueta at the site YA-162. Note distribution canals descending between terraces groups.

with long primary canals and subsidiary canals linked to miniature terrace groups. Several miniature reservoirs, which appear to have been created by augmenting natural depressions in the rock, are also present along the tops of the boulders and feed the distribution canals. Another large example is found on the alluvial terrace plain to the west of Yanque among the agro-mortuary walls of site YA-014. This maqueta wraps around all sides of a large boulder and has several reservoirs that feed miniature distribution canals. Another very large maqueta, the largest documented example, covers intermittent areas of a 40-×-30-m section of exposed bedrock on a steep slope directly below the Misme canal. In this case, there are several discrete clusters of terracing that were probably made at several different times, and they are more eroded and not as well executed as the other examples. The other examples (at sites YA-008, YA-032, YA-057, and YA-074) are smaller (less than 2 m on their long axis) but are also hydraulically functional.

Conclusion

This chapter has tacked back and forth between archaeological and documentary data in an attempt to shed light on the processes of autonomous community and polity formation and maintenance during the LIP, associated transformations of the agricultural and pastoral landscape, and the articulation of community, polity, and landscape to an Inka administration of the province. The emphasis has been on the contrasting perspectives that the two classes of information present, but this is not to say that they are contradictory. When considered together, they can be seen as complementary in the sense that written sources permit a view of how specific institutional structures and actors interacted, while archaeological research provides a view of the material setting and media that both emerged from and structured those interactions. A measured set of conclusions can be drawn from these points of contrast and concordance.

First, documentary sources register not only the formation of kin-based alliances and the elevation of local elites to a variety of imperial statuses but also considerable penetration of Inka imperial institutions through the sub-provincial level and the outline of a centrally orchestrated administrative hierarchy. Arguing for an improvisational order in the local articulation of Inka imperialism is not to deny the presence of such an imperial project—to refer back to Dietler's (2005:53) definition of imperialism as "an ideology or discourse that motivates and legitimizes practices of expansionary domination by one society over another." The intent to dominate—an encompassing architecture of administration—is apparent. But the few terse narrative colonial sources that describe Inka administration in the valley conveyed the outlines of an *idealized* order, from the perspective of the native lords of the province (and their Spanish interlocutors). As in the case of the Qollas and Lupaqas, this idealized image likely reflects the elevated, post-imperial position of the descendants of the kuraka-cum-imperial functionaries, as much or more than the actual form of administration or the nature of their ancestors' chieftaincy prior to Inka rule.

The lines of archaeological evidence presented above point instead to a political landscape during the LIP that is more consistent with segmentary, hetarchical form of organization in which community affiliations and relations scaled up and down and shifted between coordination on one hand, and competition or even violent conflict on the other. Throughout the valley, even as clear indices for the emergence of inequalities in wealth and status within and between settlements as the population grew through the LIP, settlement systems remained decentralized. Similarly, even as hydrological management at supra-settlement levels point to higher-order co-ordination (doubtless, a process that was ritually mediated as well, as evidenced by the abundant stone maquetas that dot the agricultural landscape), local-scale conflicts were evidently common. Political relations during the LIP must have been fractious and fluid, even as the potential for the activation of pan-ethnic identity remained throughout. Inkaic expansion into the valley likely even played a role in such tendencies toward centralization, both through their initial incursion and through a colonial project that institutionalized ethnic identity and the positions of the native lords of the Collaguas and Cabanas.

The manner in which the Inkas negotiated the dilemma of analogy and erasure thus begins to come into focus. The push for a new order is apparent as new centers were established in each of the three areas of the valley, and as the Inkas attempted to overwrite a tripartite and decimal ayllu structure in an ideal administrative structure, but they also sought to graft onto extant key settlements by inserting civic-ceremonial spaces, which I have suggested played on the logic and relations of traditional, kin-based community relations through the staging of commensal events. How this kind of locally improvised negotiation was played out in the material context of everyday life is simply not evident in written texts (though it is perhaps indirectly reflected in the institutionalized status of the ethnic lords of the province during colonial times).

So the local experience of Inka imperial expansion and incorporation does not conform to the heuristic categories of "indirect" or "direct" strategies of imperial rule that have dominated much archaeological modeling of Inka provincial politics. Even as such characterizations have clear utility with coarse-grained data or comparative study, they do not adequately describe the fluid state of affairs as they were unfolding on the eve of the Spanish invasion.

Notes

1. The sample numbers and uncalibrated values for the assays as originally reported by Malpass and de la Vera Cruz are WIS-1713 (1440 BP ± 80) and WIS-1714 (1400 BP ± 80) (Malpass and de la Vera Cruz Chávez 1986:163, Table 1; 1990:). I calibrated the dates with Calib 4.3, using the probability distribution curve (Stuiver and Reimer 1993; Stuiver et al. 1998). The 1-sigma values are AD 537–669 and AD 544–757, respectively.

2. A total house count is not available, in part due to heavy cactus growth at Hatun Kallimarka, which prevented detailed architectural analysis there (Doutriaux 2004:232–33).

3. In the phrase "from parents to children" ("de padres a hijos"), the original Spanish is gender ambiguous; it could be intended to mean "from fathers to sons," reflecting patrilineal descent reckoning.

4. "Unos se llaman Collaguas; llámanse desta manera por antigualla; tienen para sí por noticia que se dan heredada de padres a hijos, que proceden de una guaca o adoratorio antiguo questá en los términos de la provincia de Vellilli, comarcana desta, ques un cerro nevado a manera de volcán, señalado de los otros cerros que por allí hay, el cual se llama Collaguata; dicen que por este cerro o de dentro dél salió mucha gente y bajaron a esta provincia y valle della, ques este río en que están poblados, e vencieron los que eran naturales e los echaron por fuerza e se quedaron ellos; aprueban esto con algunos fuertes, que llaman pucara en su lengua, questán hechos en algunos cerros altos del valle, de donde bajaban a hacer guerrañ y porque (así) aquel volcán de donde dicen que proceden, llamado Collaguata, se llaman ellos Collaguas."

5. The term Oré uses is "fundibularios," drawing an analogy with Roman soldiers armed with slings.

6. "El Virrey don Francisco de Toledo puso diligencia en sacar verdadera aueriguacion del origen de los Reyes Yngas deste reyno, halló ser verdad que antiguamente no vuo en el, señor general de toda la tierra, sino en cada prouincia, y en cada parentela y generacion se gouernauan con behetria, por el mas principal curaca o cacique della, y tenian sus poblezuelos y casas sin orden, apartada vna parentela, o ayllo de la otra en los cerros o collados porque les seruian de fortaleza, por tener (como tenian todos ellos guerra) los vnos con los otros entre los vezinos mas cercanos sobre las tierras y chacras donde hazian sus sementeras, y assi las ampliauan y defendian a fuerça de hondas, porque comunmente son los indios serranos muy diestros fundibularios. Y en la prouincia dlos Collahuas conoci vn indio que tenia guardada vna camiseta, sembrada toda ella de vñas de indios que sus abuelos auian muerto y por memoria hazañosa se preciaua tener prendas de tantas vidas como alli se vian que faltauan, y fue por defender las chacras de aquella prouincia, que ellos posseyan."

7. "En feruicio de Mayta capac Inga, que tuuo por muger a Mama Yacchi natural de

los Collaguas, hizieron los indios de aquella prouincia vna grande cafa toda de cobre para apofentar al Inga y a fu muger, que como a patria la vinieron a vifitar, de lo cual tuue relacion en aquella prouincia, y con diligencia que pufe en descubrir el cobre, halle cantidad en poder de vn indio viejo depofitario del, y se hizieron quatro campanas grandes y aun fobro cobre, y preguntando por lo demas que faltaua, dixeron que lo auian dado a Gonçalo Piçarro y a fu exercito para hazer herraduras de cauallos, con temor de que a vn cacique principal que no lo quifo descubrir hizo quemar el tirano" (original orthography).

8. As pointed out by Pease (1977a:141), it is quite possible that the head of the panaca of Mayta Capac would bear his name.

9. By contrast, Brooks (1998:428) has questioned the historicity of the account and attempted to "debunk" the story as a hoax, arguing that the Inkas never established a strong direct imperial presence in the central Colca Valley. My findings are not consistent with Brooks's accompanying assertion, based on brief site walkovers around Coporaque, that "Coporaque and the nearby ruins of prehispanic villages were never more than a cluster of sleepy mountain agricultural hamlets throughout all of prehistory" (Brooks 1998:428).

10. Vizcachas (*Lagidium viscacia*) are large rodents that inhabit rocky areas in the puna.

11. In most cases, houses are freestanding structures, although a few houses are adjoined on their short axis. This judgmental definition probably lumps together buildings that served distinct domestic functions (such as sleeping versus cooking or storage spaces), but given the scant amount of excavation in domestic contexts in the valley, it is not possible to determine these differences from survey data. Not included in this category are small annexes that adjoin some large houses, as well as mortuary structures (chullpas) and obvious examples of public or ceremonial architecture such as Inka great hall buildings and probable colonial chapels. I categorized structures with only one corner or side preserved as unknown.

12. Houses that probably date only to the Late Horizon are limited to 13 circular houses at two pastoralist sites that produced no LIP ceramics (eight at CO-061 and five at CO-159) and one house from Uyu Uyu (YA-050) with a diagnostic Late Horizon sherd in its wall fill.

13. "Las casas son pequeñas, cubiertas de paja; las de los caciques son mayores; conócense en la mucha paja que les echan" (Ulloa Mogollón 1965 [1586]:332). Ulloa goes on to note that the fieldstone and thatch are locally abundant, but because trees were extremely scarce in the central Colca Valley, the timbers for roof supports were brought from far down valley or neighboring valleys, including Arequipa.

14. The sample includes LIP/LH houses from the Yanque-Coporaque survey area, plus those of Juscallacta and Malata.

15. T-test results: Fine group: $M = 55.0 \, m^2$, SD = 24.1; coarse group: $M = 29.7 \, m^2$, SD = 14.2, t (39.551) = 6.261, p = .000.

5

CONVERGENCES IN THE PLACES
OF EARLY EVANGELIZATION

As we saw in the previous chapter, by 1532 the communities and landscape of the Colca Valley were undergoing significant transformations under Inka rule. Ethnic identities and boundaries had hardened, and political hierarchies more fluid under autonomous rule had been amplified and formalized to produce a few key points of articulation between imperial administration and Yanquecollaguas, Laricollaguas, and Cabanaconde. Agricultural and pastoral systems were expanding, with an accompanying regimentation of production logistics. But day-to-day community life was not radically altered, as the great majority of the same hamlets, villages, and towns continued to be occupied. These institutional and physical structures constituted the interfaces through which the peoples of the Colca Valley engaged the Spanish and provided a structure for Spanish colonial administration.

The traditional narrative of the Pizarro-led Spanish invasion of the Andes has been recounted and debated extensively and need not be recited here. Moreover, to recall the discussion of the introductory chapter, dwelling on that narrative risks reifying a sense of historical termination or fatefulness that is at odds with the experiences of the people living in rural places in the highlands like the Colca Valley in the early years following the invasion. "Conquest" was itself a founding mytho-historical framing of the invasion—from the earliest accounts—in the service of the contractual, political, and ideological ends of Pizarro, the Crown, and the church (Seed 1991, 1992). Since at least the Late Intermediate period—and as we saw locally in the previous chapter—the peoples of the ethnic polities of the central Andes had developed their own strategies and frameworks for incorporating invaders: by treating them as ancestors (see also Gose 2008). So it is all too easy to anachronistically ascribe moods and motivations that likely were not prevalent in the lived experiences of Andean communities in the early years of Spanish colonization.

Besides, for vast swaths of the population, the first sustained Spanish presence in Andean community life came not in the form of an armed conquistador bearing sword and harquebus, but in the curious apparition of a sandal-shod, tonsured mendicant friar bearing Bible and cross. Even as epidemics often preceded their presence, it was often the clergy who were the first Spaniards to live in a sustained manner among rural indigenous communities, both in Peru and elsewhere in the Americas. They conceived of their project as an ideological extension of conquest—that is, as a spiritual conquest over forces of demonic deception (MacCormack 1991; Ricard 1966)—but in practice, the pastoral work of evangelization necessitated a concerted engagement with a vast diversity of indigenous religiosities in the Americas (Durston 2007; Estenssoro 2003; Lara 1998; MacCormack 1985). With church institutions weak and the pastoral corps tiny, the early mission field in the Andes was more improvisational and experimental than in the period following the reducción and Third Lima Council (Estenssoro 2003).

But as critical as early evangelical encounters are for understanding the lived experiences of Andean communities during the initial transition from Inka to Spanish colonial rule, precious little is known about them. The ecclesiastical documentary record of the first evangelization—defined by Estenssoro as the 50-year span from the invasion to the promulgation of the first major church reforms of the Third Lima Council (1583)—is dominated by high-level prescriptive texts, which are more illuminating of what church authorities thought they were doing than how initial evangelization was carried out in the field, let alone indigenous responses to it (for an excellent overview of the ecclesiastical documentation that does exist, see Durston 2007). Even less is known about the spatial and material contexts of early evangelization. This is especially regrettable because, as discussed below, the Spanish themselves conceived of the transformation of the built environment and the habits of body and mind that they thought would flow from it as central to turning native Andeans into Christians.

This chapter explores these spatial and material dimensions of the first evangelization through analysis of the built environment and material culture of early mendicant doctrinas in the Colca Valley. The valley was one of the earliest sites of Franciscan evangelization in the Peruvian highlands. A small group of friars first reached the valley in the 1540s, and by the 1560s they had established a series of small, rustic chapels in existing hamlets and villages, which were subsequently abandoned with the establishment of the Toledan reducciones in the early 1570s (Cook 2002; Wernke 2007a). The well-preserved architectural and archaeological remains present in these sites today provide ideal contexts for understanding how material media were both manipulated and played structuring roles in the negotiation of new forms of religious practice and community during peri-invasion times and the first generation thereafter.

The Paradoxes of Analogy and Erasure in Early Evangelization

Ironically, the extent to which Catholic practices were to take hold during the first evangelization depended in rough correspondence to their (at least superficial) correspondence with analogous indigenous forms (MacCormack 1985; Wernke 2007a). The Spanish evangelical ideal of "conversion"—the eradication and replacement of idolatrous practice with Catholicism—thus necessarily ran up against the exigencies of its enactment in pastoral practice. Whether through "guided syncretism" (Lara 1997, 1998, 2004)—explicit attempts by clergy to draw metaphors between root symbols in both traditions—or the indigenous apprehension of Catholic ritual and doctrine through autochthonous or Inkaic forms and spaces, the necessity and outcomes of intercultural communication during initial evangelization made "conversion," at least as conceived in the exclusivist sense by the Spanish clergy, an impossible ideal (Wernke 2007a). As the Inkas wrestled with the paradoxes of analogy and erasure before them, the friars struggled to find ways to translate doctrine into locally intelligible terms without violating doctrinal principles.

Besides, Andean religiosity was not premised on an exclusivist claim to a true faith or compartmentalized as a separate body of doctrine. Acceding to a newly introduced deity and its cult did not entail any necessary renunciation of prior deities or associated devotions (see Gose 2003, 2008; MacCormack 1985, 1991, 2006). Though Inka state religion was predicated on their privileged descent from the solar deity, local and imperial religious practices were generally accommodated by resituating and revalorizing local numina within the Inkaic pantheonic hierarchy. Thus just as Andean peoples had long appropriated invasive peoples and their huacas as ancestors, they could do so with the Spanish (Gose 2008). An ironic effect of this inclusionary stance among Andean communities was its misapprehension as recalcitrance or resistance by ecclesiastical authorities, as early campaigns of mass conversion were typically followed by reports of "backsliding" to idolatry and calls for the institution of more coercive and eradicative measures (MacCormack 1985). The clergy therefore fundamentally misunderstood the openness of Andean communities toward Catholic practices in the early years following the invasion

(Gose 2003; MacCormack 1985, 1991, 1993). As this chapter will show, archaeological evidence for religious "resistance" in early evangelical encounters in the Colca Valley is indeed scant to nonexistent. It is instead consistent with one of the mutual appropriation of religious forms and practices.

Build It and They Will (Be)come: Conversion and Reducción

From the outset, Spanish colonization of the New World was ideologically predicated on the conversion of the native populace to Catholicism. Far from a narrow issue of religious doctrine, however, the church and Crown viewed the inculcation of a Christian lifestyle as a social, spiritual, linguistic, and spatial ordering process—a providential bringing to order of human community. The papal bull *Inter caetera divinae* of 1493 spelled out the evangelical mandate of Spanish colonial rule in the Indies, predicating the legitimacy of colonial rule on the conversion of the native populace to Catholicism. As Tom Cummins (2002:203) notes, the specific term for conversion used in this bull—"*reducere* [to bring them to] the Catholic faith," entails both physical centripetal movement and the sense of bringing about a new state or condition closer to divine unity. Cummins goes on to explore the semantic links between the Spanish verb *reducir* (derived from the Latin root *reduco*), which implied not only movement toward a center but also *ordering* and unifying—the bringing to order and completion of a previously incomplete state of being. Thus, as in the case of the Nebrija's publication of the first grammar of Spanish, to articulate the structure of the language was to "reducir" the vernacular closer to divine unity. Likewise, to reducir settlement—to congregate and articulate the components of the physical layout of settlements—was thought not just to reflect civilized community (civitas) but to actually generate the patterns of social order (policia) of a Christian lifestyle (Cummins 2002:203, 205; Kagan 2000). To recall Sewell's discussion of the dual nature of "structure" (see chapter 2), here was an explicit colonialist theorization of the relationship between schema and resources as structuring forces in social life.

Establishing such new patterns of everyday practice, perhaps as much or even more than rote doctrinal instruction, was considered of paramount importance, especially during the first decades following the invasion, when standardized catechetical texts had not yet been authorized (Durston 2007). The construction of urban settlements was therefore considered necessary to fulfill the spiritual obligations of the Crown (Kagan 2000). In 1549, Charles I first decreed the necessity of settlement consolidation in Peru, largely in response to the prelates of several orders who wrote to him of their difficulties in evangelization among the dispersed hamlets that predominated in much of the rural Andean countryside (Málaga Medina 1974). During the tumultuous times of plunder, Inka revolt, and civil war among the Spanish in the 1550s and 1560s, the church and administrative apparatus in Peru were neither sufficiently developed nor staffed to carry out anything remotely on the scale of a viceroyalty-wide resettlement campaign, but some settlement consolidation had occurred in rural doctrinas (Málaga Medina 1974:150). Given the transformative role ascribed to the built environment by the Spanish, understanding how existing settlements were converted to doctrinas in the decades prior to the reducciones is of critical importance. The first ecclesiastical council of Lima mentions that doctrinas were to be built in the principal settlements where the primary kurakas resided (Vargas Ugarte 1952 [1551–52]), but little beyond that is known about how chapels, friaries, or other buildings were fitted to these settlements, or how they were otherwise modified with incipient settlement consolidation.

Even before the reducción program, policy thinkers had begun proposing specific ways to reconfigure settlements to maximize surveillance by representatives of the church and state. The policy recommendations for overhauling the viceregal state forwarded by jurist Juan de Matienzo in his treatise *Gobierno del Perú* (1910 [1567]) included specific prescriptions and a sketch map for the ideal organization of planned colonial towns. Matienzo's proposals formed the basis of the Toledan reforms, the centerpiece of which was a viceroyalty-wide general tour and inspection, during which a complete census, cadastral survey, and the resettlement program itself were implemented. Toledo's instructions regarding the emplacement of reducciones in local landscapes were rather vague and left considerable leeway to the visitadores, and the processes of resettlement and the actual construction of the reducciones is poorly documented (but see Julien 1991; Urton 1988; Wernke 2007b), but his prescriptions for the internal organization of the reducciones were detailed and explicit in their emphasis on discipline and surveillance:

> Leaving an open space for the plaza and a site for the church . . . and a large space for the council houses and the offices of justice for alcaldes, and jail with different rooms for men and women, and a room for the jailer.
> Item: You shall lay out the Indians houses with doors opening onto the streets, so that no house opens into the house of another Indian, but that each have a separate house. (Toledo et al. 1986:3435)

The spatial structure of the reducciones was to produce an unmediated relationship between households and the monitoring institutions of the church and state—embodied by the priest, *cabildo* (town council), and visiting magistrate (corregidor). Thomas Abercrombie (1998:246–48) likens the panopticism evident in the designs of Toledo (and, by extension, those of Phillip II) to the colonial policies enacted much later in nineteenth-century Egypt, as discussed by Timothy Mitchell (1988). Mitchell was in part concerned with tracing the colonial history and colonizing effects of surveillance and disciplinary mechanisms, a well-founded point not considered in Foucault's analyses (centered as they were in western Europe) (e.g., 1977, 1978). Building on the work of Bourdieu (1977) and Certeau (1984)—particularly on the relationships between habitus, domestic space, and the constitution of subjectivity in the novel spatial and temporal regimentations introduced by colonial powers—Mitchell sees the panoptic technologies of power in modern Europe as colonial in origin. For Abercrombie, the Toledan project represents an independent and much earlier attempt to construct a microscopically attuned monitoring and disciplinary regime: "Nineteenth-century Egypt seems an echo, not of nineteenth-century epistemology, but of sixteenth-century Spanish empire" (Abercrombie 1998:247–48). But Gose (2003:149) cautions against an overly totalizing view of surveillance in the reducciones: "The temptation to invoke Foucault here is understandable, but risks mistaking the will to inspect and correct, which is amply evident in Toledo's writings, for their actual achievement on the ground, which was at best episodic."

I argue that this spotty achievement of reducciones is a result of the negotiation of the paradoxes of analogy and erasure, as reducciones and their precursors that so radically displaced their inhabitants would find little cultural purchase. Indeed, such dislocations threatened the complex logistics that underlie the basic functioning of Andean agricultural and pastoral production systems (see chapters 6 and 7). Those that mitigated such dislocations held greater potential for long-term viability. This is an empirical question, of course, but on-the-ground knowledge of the actual spatial organization and built environments of reducciones and their precursors is extremely limited. Only a handful of archaeological studies at the site level have been conducted at reducciones (Quilter et al. 2010; Van Buren et al. 1993). Elementary questions regarding how they were built remain almost entirely unaddressed (but see Urton 1984). Pre-reducción doctrinas in the highlands have not been archaeologically investigated in any sustained manner at all. This chapter presents the first such study.

The Doctrinas of the Colca Valley in Written Texts

A small group of Franciscan friars arrived in the Colca Valley sometime between 1540 and 1545, most likely at the invitation of the encomenderos,[1] and established a series of doctrinas by building chapels at prominent settlements, making them among the earliest sites of Franciscan intervention in the southern highlands. Franciscan jurisdiction did not extend to Cabanaconde, where instead secular priests were installed, probably also at the invitation of their first encomendero, Cristóbal Pérez, and probably around the same time as the Franciscans in Collagua lands (Cook 1992, 2002; Tibesar 1953; Ulloa Mogollón 1965 [1586]). The first group of friars was headed by Fray Juan de Monzón, who was accompanied by Fray Juan de Chaves and an unknown number of other friars. Monzón reputedly was among the first Franciscans to arrive in Peru, accompanying the noted Marcos de Niza, a member of the original group of twelve Franciscans in Central America (Tibesar 1953:65).

No coeval ecclesiastical documentation on the earliest Franciscan presence in the Colca Valley has been uncovered in the archives. The scant known textual information is derived from Franciscan memorials written forty years later, about 1585 (ASFL registro 15, parte 5). These memorials, written in the context of a protracted conflict between the order and the Diocese of Cuzco over the possession of the Colca Valley doctrinas (discussed below), provide only general statements regarding the timing and organization of the initial years of the first friars in the valley and follow the hagiographic tenor common to the genre.

Bearing these source limitations in mind, the memorial of the first years of Franciscan intervention in the valley describes Monzón and his fellow friars as zealous itinerant preachers. Monzón, in particular, was remembered for his aggressive campaign of mass baptism and extirpation of idolatries, sleuthing out the shrines and mortuary sites of ancestor veneration. He erected crosses at such sites throughout the valley and even attempted to locate and destroy the paramount "idol" (perhaps Mount Collaguata) of the province. He once rounded up so many ancestral mummies and other sacred paraphernalia that 50 to 60 men were said to have been obliged to carry it all back to Lari, where Monzón oversaw their burning and cast their ashes into the river. Some of the spectacular descriptions of Monzón's practices are common to the tropes of the memorial genre, which recall such aggressive early "spiritual conquests" in triumphalist terms (see, e.g., Córdoba y Salinas 1957 [1651]:151–57; Mendoza 1976 [1664]:51–54). But mass baptisms and campaigns to eradicate what the clergy saw as the diabolical presence of Andean deities were also common to the era of the first evangelization.

While such landscape-scale extirpation was considered a necessary pre-condition for a more penetrating conversion (MacCormack 1985:454–55), the actual pastoral practices of Monzón and his fellow friars must not have relied solely on fire-and-brimstone tactics. Though nothing is mentioned of these other practices, the friars evidently established a strong rapport with the people of the valley. In 1547, the Collaguas provided a safe haven for the com-missary general of the order, Jerónimo de Villacarillo, from Gonzalo Pizarro, then the encomendero of Yanquecollaguas. Villacarillo had fled Lima after having been threatened by Pizarro's notorious co-conspirator, de Carvajal, for voicing his opposition to the Pizarrist insurgency, and he found refuge among the Collaguas before escaping to Charcas. The mutual confidence between the friars and the Collaguas hints at their good relations, and that, already by 1547, the Franciscans were well established in the province (Tibesar 1953:65).

As the openness of local communities to the friars is apparent, the situation was also apparently ripe for cultural miscues, as the Spanish here and else-where initially interpreted this openness as an exclusivist "conversion" (Gose 2003; MacCormack 1985). The apprehended meanings of Catholic doctrine and ritual practice that resulted—by and through indigenous schema—were by definition at variance with official doctrine. The colonization of indige-nous religion therefore necessarily brought with it at its roots a rhizomatic heterodoxy. The spread of heterodox practices during the first evangelization quickly became apparent to the church hierarchy, and the phase of early doc-trinal experimentation came to a close when measures for more uniform in-doctrination were mandated, especially by the 1560s, as field reports of apos-tasies such as the Taqui Onqoy movement in the central Andes came to light. This reactionary move to a more repressive regime resonated with trends in Europe, at the height of Counter-Reformation in the 1560s. The decrees of the Council of Trent were received in Lima in 1565, and those of the Second Lima Council three years later.

In the Colca Valley, the Franciscan mission was expanded and formal-ized in the 1560s. Villacarillo assigned four friars under the leadership of Fray Pedro de los Ríos to the valley in 1560. During the following decade, new doctrinas were established and convents were built in the central and up-per reaches of the valley—in Yanque and Callalli, respectively—forming a hub and spoke system of primary and secondary doctrinas. Several of these doctrinas—Chivay, Coporaque, Callalli, Achoma, Tisco, Tute, Lari, Mad-rigal, Sibayo, Yanque, Ichupampa, and Maca—were to become the sites of Toledan reducciones a decade later. But settlement consolidation was already underway in the Franciscan doctrinas, here and elsewhere in the viceroyalty (see Málaga Medina 1977). The ecclesiastical historian Echeverría y Morales, using unspecified archival sources, noted that the friars "were able to bring to-gether the dispersed ayllus or moieties such as *Cupi, Collana-Pataca, Yumasca*, and *Kayaupataca* into one rustic settlement. They built a chapel in Cupi, dedi-cated to San Antonio, and years later raised a formal temple in Coporaque consecrated to Saint James the Greater [Santiago]" (Echeverría y Morales 1952 [1804]:80). As discussed below, San Antonio, the largest (in terms of area) of the Collagua settlements that became a secondary Inka adminis-trative center during the Late Horizon, is indeed also one of the terminal prehispanic settlements with a relict chapel still standing today. Echeverría's identification of the doctrina of San Antonio as "Cupi," an Aymara term that means "right side," also provides an important clue for understanding autoch-thonous patterns of community, settlement, and land-use organization, and their articulation with Inka and Spanish imperial administration, as will be explored in detail in the next two chapters.

The Franciscan doctrinas among the Collaguas were thus well established, growing, and serviced by convents in the central and upper parts of the valley by the 1560s, even as debate stirred within the order about when they would be transferred to secular clergy (Cook 2002:891). Within the church, it was generally accepted that initial evangelization by the mendicant orders was a stopgap measure to cover the acute shortage of secular clergy in the years following the conquest. Mendicant doctrinas were to be eventually replaced by a stable parish system under diocesan administration. When and how this transfer was to take place, however, was a matter of intense debate (Cook 2002:891). Simultaneously, indigenous communities protested and resisted the church's attempts to cede doctrinas to diocesan priests in other areas. In 1569, for example, when Villacarillo relinquished the Franciscan doctrinas in Cajamarca to secular priests, the natives protested to the recently arrived To-ledo, and the church reinstated the friars at his request (Cook 2002:891).

Toledo looked favorably upon the Franciscan mission in the Colca as well, even having granted perpetual jurisdiction to the order before his departure. But this provision was not heeded, as Villacarrillo himself, apparently with-out consulting his advisors, ordered their transfer to diocesan clergy under the authority of Gregorio de Montalvo, bishop of Cuzco, just shortly after Toledo's departure for Spain in 1581 (Cook 2002:895; Tibesar 1953:66). As in Cajamarca, the kurakas of the Colca protested the decision, petitioning the corregidor of the Collaguas, Juan de Ulloa Mogollón, on September 15, 1585, and later presenting grievances first to Lima and then to Spain (Cook 2002:896–97). In a written appeal to an ecclesiastical board in 1586, the kurakas praised the virtues of the friars, who—in contrast to the encomende-ros and secular priests—lived in poverty (Ulloa Mogollón 1965 [1586]:332).[2]

The kurakas' appeal leveled grave accusations that the secular priests engaged in commerce and transported wine (activities prohibited by the Third Council of Lima), and that they charged excessively for the ministration of sacraments (Cook 2002:895–96; Tibesar 1953:66–67).[3]

The appeals of the native lords, with the aid of the noted Franciscan friar Luis Jerónimo de Oré, also reached Toledo's successor, Viceroy Fernando Torres y Portugal, Conde de Villar, who ordered the return of the Franciscans in 1586 (Cook 2002:897). A new group friars led by Oré moved to retake the parishes that year. While they were successful in regaining the parishes of Yanquecollaguas, which was then held in encomienda by the Crown, the secular priests resisted their removal in Laricollaguas, leading to a protracted legal battle. On September 15, 1586, Fray Oré again appealed for the full transfer of the doctrinas to Juan de Ulloa Mogollón, corregidor of the province (Cook 2002:897). The Collagua kurakas also protested the continued presence of the secular priests in the lower valley to the *audiencia* in Lima (Tibesar 1953:67).[4] The corregidor of Arequipa agreed and ordered the return of the Franciscans, but the secular priests again resisted and remained in Laricollaguas four more years. In 1590, the new viceroy, García Hurtado de Mendoza, issued another provision ordering the return of the Franciscans to the valley. Twelve friars headed by Oré, together with the corregidor of Laricollaguas, Gaspar Verdugo, were to orchestrate the actual transfer, arriving with decrees in hand on July 10. The secular priests resisted, especially in Lari, where the resident priest Andrés de Arana actually barricaded himself in the church, and the friars had to remove him and take possession of the church by force. Over the following days the Franciscans similarly evicted the secular priests of Maca, Ichupampa, Tuti, and Sibayo (Cook 2002:896–99).

The bishop of Cuzco, Gregorio de Montalvo, vehemently objected to the forced reinstatement of the Franciscans, and debate regarding the propriety of the friars' continued evangelical work intensified within the order. The provincial, reviewing a complaint sent by the bishop's secretary on November 13, 1590, sought to resolve the debate and settle the conflict. He ostensibly deferred to the bishop's authority and conceded diocesan jurisdiction over not only the recently repossessed doctrinas, but all the doctrinas of the valley. However, the decision was only partially enforced and diocesan priests were reinstated only to the doctrinas that the Franciscans had recently retaken (Cook 2002:898). The friars apparently remained in Yanque and Coporaque, since a year later Oré appears in the visita of 1591 to certify the accounting of births and deaths (Verdugo and Colmenares 1977 [1591]:343).

Only a month after the provincial's decision, the canon lawyer of the order, Fray Mateo de Recalde, summoned all documentation regarding the activities of the Franciscans in the Colca Valley for reconsideration, and he once again argued before the audiencia that the Franciscans' rights to all the doctrinas were legitimate and sanctioned not only by Viceroy Toledo but by the king himself. He noted that some of the secular priests in the valley had become so strident that they had even fortified their positions, setting a bad example for the natives (Cook 2002:901). In April 1591, the authorities in Lima reinstituted jurisdiction of the Franciscans over those doctrinas in the areas held in encomienda by the Crown (i.e., Yanquecollaguas), a ruling reiterated two years later by King Phillip II (Cook 2002:901). Thus ecclesiastical authority in the region was split between the Franciscans in Yanquecollaguas and the secular clergy in Laricollaguas and Cabanaconde. The kurakas continued to denounce the diocesan presence in the lower valley, and their complaints reached Phillip II. His response on January 6, 1594, ruled in favor of the kurakas, citing Recalde's petition and ecclesiastical visitas that documented improprieties and onerous levies by the secular priests. The king ordered that the Franciscans had rightful jurisdiction over not only Yanquecollaguas but also Laricollaguas. Again, the secular priests of Laricollaguas demurred, restating their case that they gained possession of the doctrinas only after they had been vacated by order of Villacarillo, and that they did so by the appointment of the bishop. They also pointed out that the recent accord between the Franciscan prelates and the bishop gave clear jurisdiction to the diocesan priests in Laricollaguas. In the end, the secular priests remained in Laricollaguas and Cabanaconde, and the valley remained divided between the secular priests and the Franciscans until the eighteenth century, when the Franciscans finally withdrew completely from the region (Cook 2002:901–2).

The Built Environment of the Doctrinas

The distribution of the chapels documented archaeologically thus far in the valley clearly indicates that the Franciscans identified nodes of Inka administration as sites for building their doctrinas. In total, six chapels, all of which almost certainly correspond to the pre-Toledan Franciscan doctrinas (Figure 5.1), have been identified in the central and upper reaches of the valley. No chapels have yet been positively identified down valley of the Yanque-Coporaque survey area, but it is there are almost certainly more. Even so, the documented cases provide the best sample of such early doctrinal settlements in any single locale in the Andean highlands.

As discussed below, all are located at Late Horizon settlements. The doctrinas not overbuilt by reducción towns—San Antonio, Uyu Uyu, Malata, and Laiqa Laiqa—are particularly important, since they show how the chapels fit

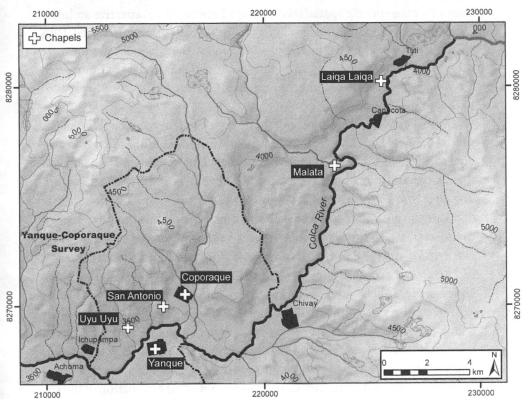

Figure 5.1. Sites in the central and upper valley with early chapels.

within their respective site layouts from Inkaic times. All four of these settlements were locations of Inka administrative architectural complexes—great halls and plazas—set within already established Collagua settlements. When considering that the two reducciones with documented cases of early chapels, Coporaque and Yanque, were also significant Inka-era sites, it is clear that the friars sought out hubs of imperial political, economic, and ritual activity as the most effective centers of evangelization.

The Doctrinas of the Yanque-Coporaque Area

Aside from this general association between sites of Inka administration and sites of Franciscan evangelization, however, the specific manner in which early chapels articulated with Inka architectural spaces and the built environment of the rest of their respective settlements is best described as variations on a theme. There was, as discussed below, a clear tendency to build chapels near the former focal spaces of ceremonial or ritual activities—specifically, Inka great hall structures and their associated plazas. But further scrutiny shows that the specific spatial relationships between the respective architectural couplets of chapel/atrium and Inka great hall/plaza was varied. This variability likely owes to the incipient nature of the evangelical enterprise prior to the establishment of the reducciones, as the massively outnumbered friars were forced to accommodate extant site plans and the built spaces of Inka administration.

The survey of the Yanque-Coporaque area identified four chapels—at the sites of Yanque, Uyu Uyu, San Antonio, and Coporaque. The chapels at Uyu Uyu and San Antonio are prominently situated and closely associated with the Inka great hall structures that line the main plazas of the two settlements. The chapel at Uyu Uyu is located on the eastern side of its plaza, directly opposite the great hall. Its facade, on the short axis of the structure, opened to the west, facing the plaza and the great hall. As discussed in the previous chapter, the great hall at Uyu Uyu was also modified to create three internal rooms, and an external room was constructed against its facade (Figure 5.2). Unfortunately, these modifications were recently demolished as part of an architectural restoration aimed for touristic development of the site. Their dating therefore will probably never be known in absolute terms, but given their ad hoc nature and the fact that such internal divisions are unheard of in great hall structures, they appear to postdate the conquest and therefore most likely date to the four-decade period of continued occupation of the site before reducción resettlement. They probably are related to the construction and use of the chapel across the plaza.

At San Antonio, the chapel is situated on top of a prominent hillock adjacent to the Inka great hall, which occupies the saddle between the promontory and the main elite housing sector on the terraced eastern flanks of Cerro Yurac Ccacca. Its position is visually impressive from the surrounding landscape, and it provides views far up and down the valley. The hill is also encircled by a double coursed wall that likely served as an improvised enclosing wall for the chapel atrium (Figure 5.3).

The size and proportions of the chapels at San Antonio and Uyu Uyu are similar and clearly set them apart from the surrounding prehispanic structures. Only one LIP/Late Horizon house in the survey is larger than the probable chapel at Uyu Uyu, which measures 15.0 × 8.3 m (124.5 m^2), and its 1.8:1 length-to-width ratio is much more elongated than the vast majority of LIP/Late Horizon houses.[5] The long axis of the probable chapel at San Antonio is incomplete and its facade is no longer preserved, but the wall sections that remain measure 11.5 × 7.2 m (82.8 m^2). The walls of both structures are very thick and composed of conglomerate masonry. The walls of the chapel at Uyu Uyu are 80–90 cm thick, and its south and east walls are also reinforced along

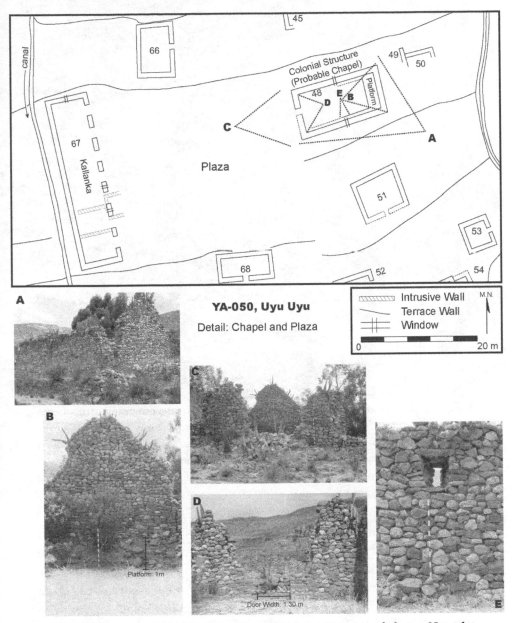

Figure 5.2. Map of the chapel at Uyu Uyu, showing orientation of photos. Note the overall size (A), the probable chancel platform on the interior (B), Front elevation with respect to the plaza (C), the door on short axis and door width (D), and tapering windows (E).

Figure 5.3. Oblique air photo of San Antonio. The chapel is the prominent structure on the hilltop (*center*). The Inka great hall is the long structure fronted by a plaza on the saddle between this promontory and the terraced slope. The abandoned terraces on the upper slope make up the main residential area of the site. (Source: 1931 Shippee-Johnson aerial expedition, Image # 334650, Special Collections, American Museum of Natural History Library.)

their bases, forming a 15-cm-wide horizontal facet in the wall profile at 90 cm above the present surface (a feature that does not occur in any prehispanic structure). The masonry of this chapel is uncoursed, with dressed, tabular corners, door stones, and wall heads similar to Type 2 masonry of LIP/Late Horizon houses (see previous chapter). A mud-and-pebble plaster similar to that used in the LIP/Late Horizon houses was applied to the interior wall surfaces of the chapel, of which 1-cm-thick plaster remnants remained present on the northern wall (prior to its modern restoration). The walls of the chapel at San Antonio are also 80–90 cm thick, but there are no signs of buttressing, and the masonry is of thin, tabular stones similar to elite houses of the Type 5 masonry common to the LIP/Late Horizon houses of this area of the site (Sectors M and N). This similarity may reflect continuity in

Figure 5.4. A: Frontal view of the chapel at San Antonio. B: Interior view of abutting join of narthex wall.

masonry techniques used by local Collagua builders, or the structure may be constructed partly or entirely from masonry mined from prehispanic houses at the site. The San Antonio chapel is badly deteriorated due to looting and greater exposure to the elements in its promontory setting, and no plaster remnants are visible in its interior.

The position of the doors and windows of both structures are also inconsistent with local LIP/Late Horizon domestic architectural conventions. Whereas doors of LIP/Late Horizon structures are always situated on the long axis and windows on the short axis (on the gable ends), the reverse is true of these buildings. Also, the doorway of the chapel at Uyu Uyu is 130 cm wide—much wider than the extremely narrow doors of Collagua houses. Two "windows" (which probably served equally or more for ventilation as for light) of this building are situated just below the roofline opposite one another near the center of the long axis, rather than on the gable ends, as in local LIP/Late Horizon architecture. These windows are also distinct from those of prehispanic structures in that they flare outward toward the interior, such that the exterior window opening is much smaller than the interior opening (Figure 5.2-F).[6] The facade of the chapel at San Antonio is not preserved, so its doorway is not observable (Figure 5.4-A). The chapel's transverse interior walls, however, demarcate a small narthex, creating a transitional entry space before entering the nave, a common attribute of church architecture. The transverse walls of the narthex are poorly preserved, but their joins with the outer walls are clearly abutting, indicating they were built later, perhaps during a remodeling episode after the initial construction of the building (Figure 5.4-B).

The chapel at Uyu Uyu also has internal features typical of churches. The remains of a 1 m high, 2 m wide platform spans its eastern end (see Figure 5.2-B). This feature creates a division in the internal space of the church between the nave and the elevated chancel, reserved for the clergy, where the altar would have been. Also, a 60-cm-wide *patilla* (bench) feature runs along the sides of the chapel, which could have functioned as additional seating for the congregation.[7] The floor of the chapel at San Antonio is extremely pitted and disturbed by intense looting, making observation of the original state of the floor plan impossible without excavation.

Both structures have high gabled roofs. The chapel at Uyu Uyu reached 7 m at the top of its gable, and although the gable of the San Antonio chapel is not fully preserved, it was at least as high. The roof of the chapel at Uyu Uyu was apparently thatched, but scatters of high-fired ceramic roof tiles next to the chapel at San Antonio indicate that its roof was tiled, an unambiguous colonial building technique. The tiles are a surprising find, given that their presence implies the existence of a quite well-developed colonial ceramic industry very early on in the colonial era. Although it may seem unlikely that ceramic kilns capable of mass producing roof tiles would have been in place in the pre-reducción period, the weight and the quantity of tiles required would have made their importation from Arequipa or other centers of tile production very costly. Interestingly, we did register two colonial or republican circular updraft kilns in the survey area: One (site YA-058) is located to the immediate east of the village of Ichupampa,[8] and the other is in the northwest corner of the reducción of Yanque. A roof tile waster recovered from the kiln of YA-058 (located in the quebrada that forms the boundary between modern

Yanque Urinsaya and Ichupampa) confirms that roof tiles were manufactured in the valley, although it is unclear when these particular kilns were used or abandoned.[9]

The structures at San Antonio and Uyu Uyu also share several features with the chapel of San Sebastian in Coporaque. This chapel probably slightly postdates the other two, having been built most likely around 1565, as discussed above. Oré's doctrinal manual *Symbolo Cathólico Indiano* (1992 [1598]) was likely written during his eight-year term of service in Coporaque, and in addition to being one of the most important sources for understanding early post–Third Council doctrinal practice (Durston 2007), it establishes that Coporaque was an important locale for the Franciscan mission in the valley. This chapel reflects that status with its impressive renaissance style facade (Tord 1983:87–88). In fact, it is the earliest standing example of a Renaissance-style church in Peru (Tord 1983:88–89). The front of the chapel has an elaborately decorated facade enclosed by an open vestibule—likely the way the vestibule of the chapel at San Antonio originally appeared. The facade is composed of a portal flanked by doric columns, and the frieze is adorned with a band of rosettes in relief with the faces of cherubs in the center (Figure 5.5). Above the cornice, a pediment encloses an arched niche, now empty. On the inside of the doorway, a baroque mural depicting the sun and moon appears on the top of the arch, while the image of Saint Sebastian tied to a tree and impaled by arrows graces the keystone above the door. Together these images form a hybrid composition (Figure 5.6). Inside the chapel, a rectangular apse sets the chancel apart from the nave, and a rectangular recess that would have held the crucifix occupies the rear wall. Like the chapel at San Antonio, the San Sebastian chapel had a tiled roof. Behind the facade, the remainder of the chapel is constructed of dressed, primarily tabular-shaped blocks similar to Type 6 masonry of LIP/Late Horizon houses interspersed with unworked fieldstones. Almost certainly some, or even most, of these were mined from such houses, many of which were likely abandoned, as populations declined from early waves of epidemics and the friars began congregating ayllus to their doctrinas. The chapel is of similar size and layout as the two structures at Uyu Uyu and San Antonio. Its exterior measures 14 × 7.5 m, while the interior of the nave measures 10.4 × 6 m.

As with the chapel at Uyu Uyu, the chapel of San Sebastian opens to a plaza space, which would have functioned as an atrium. On its opposite side, the southern portal of the main church of the reducción aligns with the facade of the chapel (Figure 5.7). So the chapel appears to have been retrofitted into the overall plan of the reducción church and its atrium, functioning eventually as a miserere chapel.

Figure 5.5. Facade
of the chapel of
San Sebastian,
Coporaque.

Figure 5.6. Interior of doorway, chapel of San Sebastian, Coporaque. Note crescent
moon and sun motif. Image of San Sebastian on keystone is deteriorated but recognizable. (Photo by Matthew Velasco.)

Figure 5.7. Air photo of Coporaque, showing plaza, church, and chapel of San Sebastian.

Doctrinas in the Upper Valley: Laiqa Laiqa and Malata

Standing chapels are also present in the upper reaches of the valley, at the sites of Malata (TU-170) and Laiqa Laiqa (TU-171), two Late Horizon settlements that also house Inka great halls and associated plazas. The chapel of Laiqa Laiqa is much larger and occupies the open plain below the main residential sector of the site, which arcs around the plain in amphitheater-like fashion (Figure 5.8). The doorways of the houses on the surrounding terraced slope uniformly open eastward toward this plain below, making the chapel widely visible. The Inka great hall and its plaza at Laiqa Laiqa is situated at the apex of this curving hillside, providing a commanding view of the residential sector and the chapel below. Nothing beyond this basic description is known of the chapel at Laiqa Laiqa, though it almost certainly pertains to the period of the first evangelization, since this site would have been abandoned with the establishment of the reducción of Santa Cruz de Tuti, located just 1 km upslope to the northwest.

Figure 5.8. The chapel at Laiqa Laiqa from the northwest.

Given the excellent architectural preservation and minimal evidence for looting at Malata, my efforts were focused there. This site, though seemingly rather minor or insignificant, provides an ideal context for the in depth study of change and continuity in daily and ritual practices at an early rural Andean doctrina. I directed three seasons of excavations in a variety of contexts at the site.

A Close in View: Changing Daily and Ritual Practices at the Doctrina of Malata

Malata is a small village of 80 standing fieldstone structures situated in a shallow quebrada above the deeply incised river, 200 m below in the steep inner river gorge (Figures 5.9 and 5.10). The village is composed of a main residential area of 72 domestic structures, which in turn are made up of a mix of circular (n = 25), ovoid (n = 4), and rectilinear (n = 43) domestic structures stretching roughly east to west along the bottom of the quebrada. The public and ritual areas of the site are situated at the higher, western end. Here, a small, rustic Inka hall structure faces west to an irregularly shaped plaza, and to the adjacent west, a chapel of similar scale and elaboration to those of Uyu Uyu and San Antonio faces east, overlooking the main residential sector below.

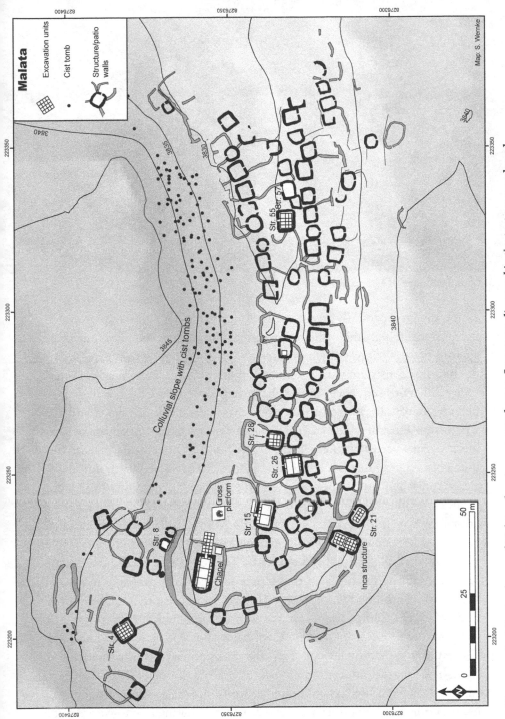

Figure 5.9. Architectural map of Malata, showing excavated areas. Structures discussed in the text are numbered.

Figure 5.10. Panorama of Malata, from the north.

It is the first such early post-conquest doctrina to be extensively excavated in the Andean highlands. The occupational chronology, based on our three seasons of excavations (which exposed 300 m in a variety of contexts) is well defined and consistent with a terminal prehispanic and early post-conquest (pre-reducción) sequence. Of the phase diagnostic ceramics (n = 6,659), 89 percent are of Late Horizon styles, 9 percent are early colonial types, and just 2 percent—most of which are likely derived from the continued use of heirloom vessels—are of the Late Intermediate period. Other artifact classes further isolate the colonial occupation to the first half of the sixteenth century—again, consistent with a pre-reducción, doctrina-era occupation. A small but significant collection (n = 26) of Nueva Cádiz beads was recovered from floor-level contexts at Malata (Figure 5.11). Nueva Cádiz beads are a drawn glass bead of square cross section, of smaller, larger, straight (Nueva Cádiz Plain) and helically twisted (Nueva Cádiz Twisted) variants. They were only produced during the first half of the sixteenth century, probably in coastal Venezuela (Smith and Good 1982). Though the precise temporal distributions of Nueva Cádiz variants are not well documented in the Andes, they likely follow those of the circum-Caribbean and Mesoamerican lowlands. There, the larger variant fell out of style by midcentury, while the smaller one, though no longer produced, continued to circulate through at least the 1570s. At the site of Tipu (Belize), for example, Smith and colleagues consider large Nueva Cádiz beads in primary context as likely predating 1550 to 1560 (Smith

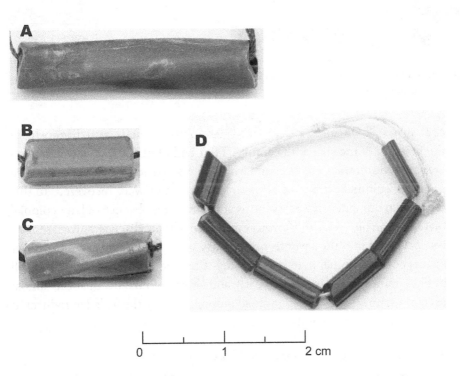

Figure 5.11. Examples of Nueva Cádiz beads from Malata. Large variants (A–C) include twisted examples. Smaller variants (D) are darker in color and more transparent.

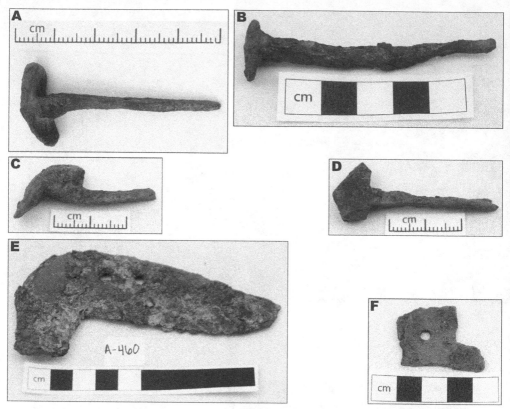

Figure 5.12. Examples of iron artifacts from Malata, including caret head nails (A–D) and possible door hardware (E–F).

et al. 1981:43). Distinctive "caret head" wrought-iron nails, also diagnostic of the first half of the sixteenth century (Flint and Flint 2003:253), were recovered from domestic structures and from the Inka structure at the site (Figure 5.12). No colonial artifacts diagnostic of later times were recovered. In this case, given our extensive excavations at the site, this absence of later colonial materials can be reasonably taken as evidence of their absence, since if the site was occupied into the seventeenth century or beyond, increasing quantities of diagnostic colonial materials through time would be expected. Thus all indices point conclusively to an early and short colonial occupation, almost certainly truncated as the site was abandoned during the Toledan reducción resettlement program of the 1570s.

The Malata Chapel and Associated Plaza

Like the other doctrina chapels, the chapel at Malata is fronted by a plaza space, where much of the actual catechetical instruction likely occurred. Similar to the chapel at San Antonio, the Malata chapel is enclosed in an atrium, but unlike the other examples, this terraced atrium opens down to a larger walled, irregularly shaped plaza space to the adjacent east. The chapel is of similar scale and elaboration to those of Uyu Uyu and San Antonio but has a well-formed, angled apse that appears curved on the exterior (Figure 5.13). With maximum interior dimensions of 10.3 × 4.5 m, the chapel could have housed a congregation of roughly 40–60 participants, depending how densely they were arranged. This is probably in the range of the adult

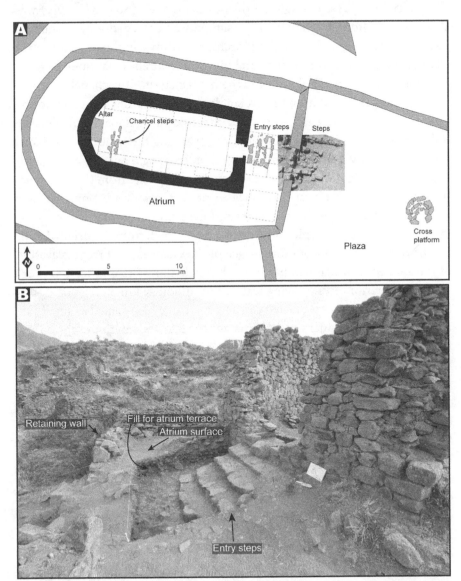

Figure 5.13. A: Plan view map of the chapel, atrium, and plaza area, Malata. B: Photo showing how original entry steps were buried by the fill for the construction of the terraced atrium.

population of the village, but as was the case throughout the Andes during the first evangelization, much catechetical instruction would have been conducted outdoors (Gisbert and Mesa 1985).

Our excavations exposed nearly the entire interior of the chapel, providing a view of its internal spatial organization and construction sequence. Entering the chapel, in the northeast corner inside the doorway (to the right, or Epistle side) is a feature of very compact silty clay that likely was the area of a baptismal font. A tiny fragment of spondylus shell (*Spondylus* spp.) was also recovered from the feature. This is significant because spondylus shells (a sacred sumptuary good throughout prehispanic times in the central Andes) were historically—and in many rural highland churches, continue to be— used for the affusion of holy water in the baptismal rite. The chapel floorplan itself was originally composed of a single floor level from the entry to the foot of an intact altar base, which is centered against the apex of the apse wall in the rear. A platform with two steps spanning the width of the chapel was subsequently added in front of the altar, creating a raised (31-cm-high) chancel extending 1 m in front of the altar base, separate from the congregation (Figure 5.13). The altar base (measuring 1.67 m wide x .80 m deep) was a rustic construction of heavily mortared fieldstone masonry facing coursings with a mud-and-cobble core. It stood 84 cm high from the original floor height and 53 cm high from the surface of the chancel platform. Excavation of the altar base, which was partitioned in half along the east-west axis, revealed no interior or underlying features or offerings. On either side of this fieldstone altar base were packed earth features that likely acted as small side altars, perhaps for statuary or other paraphernalia. The interior of the chapel thus shows evidence for remodeling during its use-life with the installation of a chancel platform in the arched space of the apse, separating the altar from the congregation.

Our excavations in the chapel also exposed 18 burials below the chapel floor. Their description is beyond the scope of this chapter, but their positions, orientations, and associated artifacts clearly point to a mortuary complex that synthesized Catholic and Andean practices.

Looking out from the chapel entry gives a view of the plaza and main residential area of the doctrina below (Figure 5.14). The plaza was clearly laid out according to a preconceived plan. A large rectilinear structure (Structure 15) with a (complete, with fieldstone lintel in situ) wide, low doorway—a diagnostic colonial feature—faces the plaza on the center of its southern side. In its approximate center is a circular, three-tiered fieldstone pedestal feature (2.0 m in diameter), which aligns with all other features in the plaza: the single entry to the plaza to the east, the doorway of Structure 15 to the south, and the stepped entrances to the atrium and chapel to the west. An apparent void in the center of the top tier of the pedestal suggests that it held a post— almost certainly a cross—though the feature was not preserved well enough on the southeasterly quadrant to fully confirm the void as a feature and not simply the absence fieldstones in the center of the top of the platform. But the fact that it aligns with the other prominent colonial features of the plaza points to a colonial rather than Inkaic date of construction and use. Clearing excavations on and around the platform produced no Inka features or in situ artifacts. So it almost certainly functioned as a pedestal for a central cross. The configuration of the chapel and plaza complex at Malata is thus well suited for outdoor catechesis, as the friar could address the catechumenate in the plaza from the elevated position of atrium at the entrance to the chapel, overlooking the plaza below. Groups would have likely entered the plaza as a processional through its single entrance on its eastern end.

As was the case throughout the Andes during the first evangelization (Durston 2007; Estenssoro 2003; Gisbert and Mesa 1985), much catechetical instruction was likely conducted outdoors at Malata.[10] Emphasis on outdoor catechesis likely derived from the humble, provisional nature of the earliest

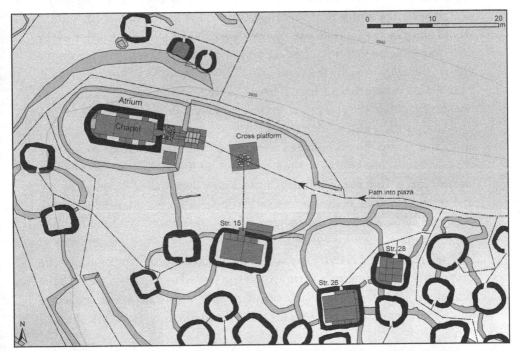

Figure 5.14. The colonial plaza area of Malata, showing how traffic would have passed Structures 26 and 28 before entering the plaza through its single entry from the east. Note rough alignments of accesses and doorways with the cross platform.

ecclesiastical edifices and the fact that the unbaptized—a large portion of the population during the early post-conquest years—were prohibited from entering the sacred space of the church. Moreover, outdoor, communal pageantry resonated with local communities since, much as in Mesoamerica (Burkhart 1998), it was central to public rituals in terminal prehispanic times in the Andes. Inka state commensal rituals in particular, such as those likely enacted in the plaza space in front of the Inka hall structure at Malata itself, incorporated orchestrated processionals and dramatic prestations of consumables and prestige goods (Coben 2006).

Formalization of the Chapel, Atrium, and Plaza at Malata

But this chapel-atrium-plaza complex as currently observed was not the original configuration but was the result of significant remodeling (see Wernke 2011b). As discussed above, the interior of the chapel was reconfigured to include a formal chancel platform, dividing the sanctuary from the congregation. Clearing excavations in front of the chapel show a similar sequence of elaboration and segregation of public and sacred space. The chapel was originally built directly on the natural hill slope and accessed via four fieldstone entry steps up to its doorway. In contrast to the doorway of the chapel at Uyu Uyu, the doorway of this chapel was quite narrow; at 65 cm wide, it would allow only single file entry. Jambs on either side of the interior of the doorway indicate that it once held two narrow doors that opened from the center, swinging inward (see Figure 5.13-A). The terraced atrium around the chapel was constructed during a subsequent remodeling episode, burying all but the top two of the entry steps in the atrium terrace fill (see Figure 5.13-B). The composition of the fill itself suggests that the terrace was built quickly and expediently: It is dominated by cobble- and boulder-sized rocks with very porous (large voids were present) soil infilling. The eastern retaining wall for this atrium terrace fill also forms the western wall of the plaza below. The plaza, therefore, became more formally defined only after the remodeling event associated with the construction of the atrium. With the terraced atrium in place, steps were then built from the newly formed plaza below to the atrium and chapel entry, completing this more formal approach to the chapel. The leveled, terraced atrium and the walled space of the plaza to the east, along with the steps between the plaza and the atrium, were all added to the chapel after it had been in use for some time with its original four-stepped entry.

Structure 15 on the south side of the plaza was also built during the colonial occupation, having been obviously fitted and aligned with the plaza and the central cross. With an interior area of 32.6 m^2, it is larger than any domestic structure at the site, ranking only behind the chapel and Inka hall structure in size. Its doorway, with dressed stone lintel still intact, is diagnostic of its colonial origin, since it is much wider and lower than prehispanic Collagua doorways. Given its position in the plaza, an administrative or public function would be expected, and indeed our excavations are consistent with this hypothesis. Unlike domestic contexts, which uniformly produced abundant artifacts, common production-related features, and refuse from cooking and other production activities (discussed below), the packed-earth floor of this structure was remarkably clean and devoid of any features. It was obviously not used for domestic purposes and was kept clean. Indeed, the only macroscopic artifact of note from its interior was a small fragment of a silver adornment. At 97 percent purity, it was the purest of the silver artifacts from the site that were analyzed by portable XRF. The fragment is small and could be part of a variety of adornments, though among the more likely sources would be the silver adornments that clad the *varas*—the staffs of office—of community leaders throughout colonial times to the present (see Mishkin 1946:443–45; Salomon 2004:78–79). As in other locales in the southern Peruvian Andes, patrimonial varas passed between the authorities of the *comunidades campesinas* (peasant communities established during the agrarian reform of the 1970s) and irrigation commission officials. These varas are typically elaborately decorated with silver filigree and embossed sheeting (Fieldwork 1999–2000; also see Valderrama Fernández and Escalante Gutierrez 1988). In sum, these data are all consistent with the public or administrative functions expected given the location of the structure. It probably served as a building for meetings—likely related to the collection of encomienda tribute and other administrative and community matters.

The basic elements of a Spanish settlement were thus implanted at Malata: church and atrium, plaza and public administrative building, all set within a recognizable, if rustically executed and miniaturized, urban form. Implementation of a foreign normative model even in such a small rural village so early after the invasion might be taken as an embodiment of Spanish colonial domination, an example of the "architecture of conquest." And it certainly does illustrate how even during those early years, friars were able to bring about significant changes in the built environment of even small, seeming marginal rural hamlets like Malata. But to stop there would neglect consideration of the legibility and effectiveness of the plan—how the chapel and plaza complex articulated with the community, both in terms of the built forms of the overall settlement plan and in how its spaces were apprehended and understood by community members. As Thomas Gieryn (2002:35) succinctly observed of the seeming fixity of buildings, "Buildings don't just sit there imposing themselves. They are forever objects of (re)interpretation, narration and representation—and meanings or stores are sometimes more pliable than the walls and floors they depict. We deconstruct buildings materially and semiotically, all the time." The relationship between the built environment and subjectivity ("build it and they will become") is not so fixed or deterministic as the Spanish would have it, as a general principal (if Gieryn, or practice theory in general, are at all correct) and in this case, especially, because new built forms were necessarily brought into a practical dialogue with extant buildings, site layouts, settlement patterns, and so on, as well as the daily rhythms of practice that they structured.

New Kinds of Domestic Spaces: The Friar's Quarters at Malata

So how did the chapel and plaza complex fit within the rest of the settlement plan? Interestingly, it was far from the only colonial modification to the site. As discussed above, documentary evidence indicates that some settlement consolidation was already underway at the doctrinas in the valley, and at Malata, there is clear architectural evidence for the addition of new kinds of colonial domestic spaces, set within newly configured neighborhoods at the eastern and western extremes of the site (Wernke 2011b; Wernke et al. 2011). The older residential core to the adjacent north and east of the Inka hall is dominated by agglutinated domestic compounds, composed of multiple circular-to-ovoid structures situated around common patio areas. By contrast, the eastern and western neighborhoods are composed almost exclusively of rectilinear houses in distinct domestic compound configurations. Domestic compounds behind the chapel, which are located at the high, western end of the site, overlook the rest of the settlement and are situated singly within large patio enclosures (which likely doubled as corrals). The quarters of the visiting friar seemed likely to be located among these prominent structures given their proximity to the chapel and separation from the rest of the settlement. Among them, Structure 4 in particular seemed the most likely to have housed the friar because of its large size relative to other domestic structures (at 18 m² of interior area, it is the fourth largest domestic structure) and the presence of a large arched niche near its northwest corner—a diagnostic colonial feature. Our excavations exposed nearly the entirety of the interior of this structure (leaving 50-cm perimeter buffers to mitigate risk of wall collapse). Its layout proved to be unique among the structures excavated at the site, as it is the only domestic structure with an interior divided space; that is, fieldstone wall foundations were added to the interior to create a small room in the southwest corner. Abutting wall joins indicate that the walls were added after the initial construction of the exterior walls. A narrow doorway for this room faces eastward toward the building entryway. No features were recovered from the interior of this small room, making its function difficult to ascertain, though it appears not to have been used for cooking, as no hearth features or cooking refuse were recovered from it. It could have served for storage, sleeping, or perhaps a changing room. In any case, such internal divisions are not present in any prehispanic domestic structures in the valley, and none of the other excavated structures at Malata had a separate internal room.

The artifact collections from Structure 4 also set it apart from other domestic structures at the site. First, 27 percent, (90 out of 337) of its phase diagnostic ceramics were early colonial wares, a significantly higher proportion of colonial ceramics than any other structure (Table 5.1). Among the most notable ceramics were two joining rim sherds from a green glaze ware—the only colonial ceramics with colored glaze recovered from the site. The vessel, a bowl form, is likely of the Morisco Green style, which was produced during the first half of the sixteenth century. Also, a large (approximately 10-x-5-cm), heavily oxidized, iron artifact with two perforations—perhaps a latch or other piece door hardware—was recovered near the northeast corner, inside the door, where a caret-head nail was also recovered.

Botanical collections from this structure, analyzed by Lizette Muñoz and David Goldstein, also point to patterns of consumption that are unique at the site (Muñoz and Goldstein 2010).[11] In particular, maize made up a significantly greater proportion of the food plant assemblage, and quinoa a significantly lesser proportion, than in other domestic contexts. Specifically, maize from Structure 4 made up 29 percent of the overall site assemblage—by far the largest proportion from any structure—and no appreciable quinoa was recovered. This is especially noteworthy when considering that Malata is situated well above the effective limits of maize production in the valley.

Table 5.1. Counts of early colonial phase diagnostic sherds by domestic structure

Structure	Early Colonial	Other	Total
4	90	245	335
21	6	154	160
26	64	1,209	1,273
28	27	384	411
55	7	221	228
57	28	1,029	1,057

Note: Compared to Structure 4, the other structures have significantly less early colonial ceramics. Fisher's exact P < .0001.

It was therefore either obtained through exchange with lower-lying settlements (likely via ayllu kin ties) or through direct cultivation of remote fields by Malata households. Clearly, the inhabitants enjoyed privileged access to this culturally valued grain. Friars were owed tribute in staple goods under the tribute system of Viceroy Marqués de Cañete (1556–61), including two *fanegas* of maize (Cook 2007:135).[12]

Other aspects of the house were similar to those common to other domestic structures in the main residential area to the east. Semicircular platforms of flat fieldstones were situated in the northeast and northwest corners, which, as discussed below, were used as work areas for a variety of domestic and production activities. The ceramic assemblage overall is consistent with a domestic context. Among rim sherds (n = 90), 57 percent were serving vessels, 30 percent were cooking vessels, and 13 percent were arábalos (a typical Inka imperial jar form, used for fermentation, storage, and serving of *chicha* [maize beer]).

In sum, the significantly greater prevalence of artifacts of European technological or stylistic attributes compared to other domestic contexts at the site, together with the location, layout, and architectural features of the structure, make it the most likely residence for a person of European origin at the site (or, at least, a person with distinctively European-oriented consumption habits). It is close to the chapel, separated from the rest of the settlement, distinctive and large, but not grandiose by any means (certainly still consistent with the Franciscan vow of poverty). All of these aspects combine to make it the most likely quarters for the visiting friar, who likely came to the site only occasionally during pastoral rounds through the valley.

Pre-Reducción Settlement Consolidation: A New Neighborhood at Malata

At the opposite, eastern end of the site there is a distinct change in the organization of domestic structures that coincides with the sudden prevalence of rectilinear structures: They are arranged in rows facing each other, in the manner of streets. Several exhibit diagnostic colonial architectural features, such as low, wide doorways and arched niches. A handful of circular floor-plan houses are intermixed with these rectilinear houses, but they were likely extant when the rectilinear houses were built in rows. Their positions and orientations break with the pattern prevalent among the rectilinear houses (Figure 5.15). As discussed below, excavations also support the interpretation of this end of the site as a discrete neighborhood that was added during the short doctrina occupation, likely as a result of congregation of households from nearby settlements.

We excavated two buildings (Structures 55 and 57) from a single domestic

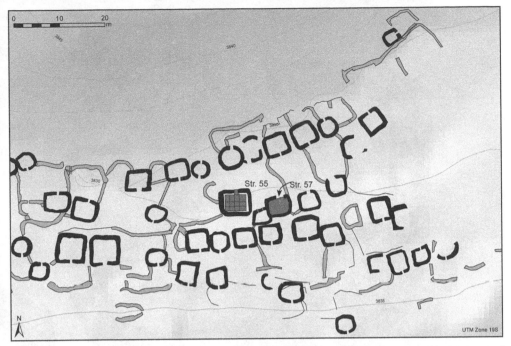

Figure 5.15. The neighborhood of predominantly rectilinear domestic structures at the eastern end of Malata. Note roughly linear arrangement and consistent doorway orientations of each row.

compound in this part of the site. Structure 55, the larger of the two (measuring 5.3 × 4.3 m), is a gabled building that was clearly the main residential structure of the compound. With an interior area of 21.6 m², it is in the top quartile of rectilinear domestic structures at Malata. A walled, ovoid feature—probably a small corral—abuts its western gable end. Our excavations exposed a floor with in situ features and artifacts indicative of a range of domestic and production activities, including cooking, weaving, and metallurgy. The ceramic collections from floor-level loci were typical of a domestic context: Vessel functional categories (rimsherds only, n = 51) were composed of 71 percent serving vessels (plates, bowls, cups), 18 percent arríbalos, and 12 percent cooking vessels (ollas). Phase diagnostics from floor contexts (n = 195) were dominated by Late Horizon wares, making of 95 percent of the sample, with just four early colonial sherds (4 percent) and one LIP sherd. As discussed below, however, several other diagnostic colonial artifacts were recovered from floor-level contexts.

A stone-lined hearth (with abundant ash and carbon deposits) was located in the northeast corner, associated with a mixed midden of domestic refuse (abundant macrobotanicals, faunal bone fragments, utilitarian ceramics, debitage), and semicircular fieldstone platform features similar to those found

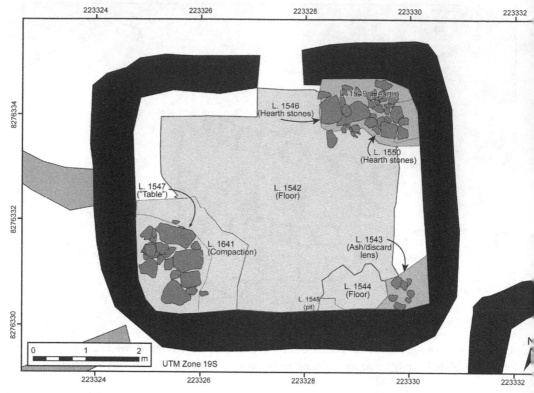

Figure 5.16. Floor-level features of Structure 55, Malata.

in all other domestic structures were fitted into the northeast, southeast, and southwest corners (Figure 5.16). Interestingly, a ceramic mold for casting copper (and possibly silver) ingots was recovered on top of the platform feature in the southwest corner (Figure 5.17). This function is inferred from its form—it is identical in form and size to Late Horizon–era ceramic ingot casters from the Calchaquí Valley, Argentina, reported by Earle and colleagues (e.g., Earle 1994:452)—and from trace amounts of copper and silver residues detected on its surface using portable XRF compositional analysis.[13] Combined with the extensive evidence for craft production in the adjacent structure 057 (discussed below), it is clear that this household was engaged in a variety of production activities related to metallurgy, weaving, and possibly ceramic production. One notable copper-bronze artifact, a small bell with pendant loop, was recovered from the floor of the structure (Figure 5.18-G). It is of the same form as those reported from other Late Horizon sites, including Machu Picchu (Burger and Salazar 2004). As in other cases, then, artifacts of Late Horizon style continued to be used and perhaps produced in this structure through the colonial occupation. But we also recovered the largest collection of colonial glass beads from any building at Malata in Structure

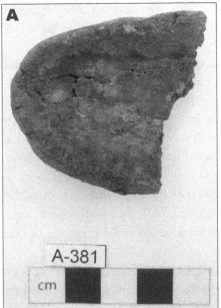

A-381
cm

Figure 5.17. Vessel for casting copper, from floor-level context of Structure 55, Malata.

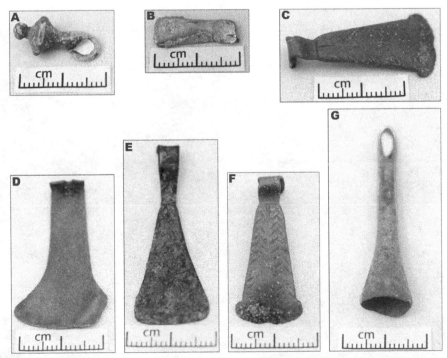

Figure 5.18. Assorted copper-bronze and silver artifacts from Malata. A: Small hooked copper clasp, probably for clothing. B: Folded silver sheeting. C–F: Copper tweezers. G: Small copper bell.

55: 11 Nueva Cádiz beads. Among these were two Nueva Cádiz large variants, which, as discussed above, are the better diagnostic for pre-1550 to 1560 contexts.

Structure 57, located to the adjacent east, is a small (4.4 × 3.3 m) building that is unique in form for its high, flat-topped walls, which presumably supported a hipped roof (a roof type that is not part of the repertoire of late prehispanic domestic architecture in the valley). The structure is also distinguished by its many wall niches: five small wall niches at different levels and a floor-level arched niche (another colonial feature) in the center of its rear (south) wall, opposite the doorway (Figure 5.19). Given its unusual form, diagnostic colonial features, and association with the larger Structure 55, we hypothesized it to be a special function building, perhaps a workshop of some kind. Excavations indeed revealed it to have been used for a range of craft production activities.

The ceramic collections from this structure were of the highest densities of any at the site—the collection, with 2,929 sherds from occupational contexts, exceeds even the much larger Structure 26 (with 2,875 sherds from its occupational contexts; discussed below). This owes largely to an extensive sheet midden of broken ceramics, ash, and animal bone that covers most of the

Figure 5.19. Frontal view of Structure 57, Malata. Note arched niche centered in back wall, opposite the doorway.

floor—almost certainly a secondary refuse feature, as household trash (perhaps from Structure 55) was disposed in this rustic workshop-type building. Of the phase diagnostics from occupational contexts (n = 1433), 97 percent were of Late Horizon styles, 2 percent were early colonial, and 1 percent were of LIP styles. In terms of the functional classes of the ceramic sample from occupational contexts (rim sherds only, n = 261), 48 percent were serving vessels, 32 percent were cooking vessels, and 21 percent were aríbalos. Given that most of the sample is likely of secondary context, these proportions are not to be taken as simple reflections of the activities undertaken in the structure, however. As discussed below, the primary functions of Structure 57 appear to be related to the manufacture of mineral pigments and other production activities.

A large ash lens in front of the arched niche in the rear wall indicates it functioned as a hearth or perhaps a kiln. A large grinding stone was recovered within the niche itself, suggesting it may have been used in the fabrication of pigment (Weaver and DeTore 2009). This seems the most parsimonious interpretation, given other strong evidence for pigment production in the form of discrete lenses of red-yellow, red, white, cream, and brown pigments from small pit features in the floor, as well as a well-sorted, fine clay from discrete lens features in its floor. An especially large, discrete lens of bright orange-yellow pigment was excavated near the western wall (Figure 5.20). A range of rolled river cobbles of varying sizes, perhaps used for burnishing ceramics, was also recovered in association with the pits in the floor. There

Figure 5.20. Orange pigment lens on floor of Structure 57, Malata.

was still fire blackening of the evident on the interior wall stones near the niches in the northeast corner, with a corresponding ash lens on the floor level, indicating fire-related activities in that corner as well. In both the southeast and southwest corners, round platform features of thin fieldstones most likely functioned as tables for production activities. Weaving was also among the production activities of the people of this household, as evidenced by two camelid metatarsal *wichuñas* (weaving tools, similar to those found in Structure 55) found in primary contexts in this structure.

The household that resided in Structures 55 and 57 was thus involved in a variety of production and domestic activities during the colonial occupation of the site. These included diverse craft activities related to metallurgical, pigment, textile, and perhaps ceramic production. All indices also point to a colonial period establishment of these and the other rectilinear houses of this eastern neighborhood. As discussed above, the friars are documented as having congregating ayllus in doctrinas elsewhere in the valley, and it is likely that these households were similarly resettled to Malata from neighboring settlements. Our investigations at Malata thus provide the first archaeological documentation of settlement consolidation and the reordering of settlement and domestic space prior to the establishment of the reducciones themselves.

The Household of the Kuraka at Malata

To the adjacent east of the colonial plaza is a notable exception to the pattern of peripherally situated rectilinear houses at Malata but one that further reveals a deliberate restructuring of space and movement through the doctrina. Here, Structures 26 and 28 form a single elite domestic compound at an important intersection of a transverse path with the main path that routed traffic through the only entrance to the colonial plaza (see Figure 5.14). This is almost certainly the paramount indigenous household compound, emplaced at a key location within the doctrina. They are the last structures before reaching the single entry to the plaza and thus command a view of all traffic entering it. Structure 26 is the largest domestic structure at the site and is notable for its height and mass, with 80-cm-thick walls and 3.5-m-high gables. It is the only house at the site with small, square ventilation holes near the top (on center) of one of its gables (the eastern gable). A distinct angle change at the gable shoulder is also readily apparent—a detail not found among late prehispanic Collagua domestic structures. It is also fronted by the largest patio area of any domestic compound. Access to Structure 26 and its large fronting patio area was controlled by requiring passage through the patio and in front of Structure 28, a much smaller and more rustic structure. Structure 28 and its patio thus could have functioned to monitor visitors before being admitted to the patio area of Structure 26.

Excavations in both structures revealed features and artifacts typical of indigenous houses at the site, but with markedly different densities and distributions. Overall, the floor of Structure 26 was much more regular and compact, with a well-sorted, silty, hard-pack earthen surface with small- to medium-sized gravel inclusions and generally more homogeneous artifact size ranges. This is reflected in sherd weight distributions: In Structure 26, mean sherd weight among floor-level contexts (n = 2875) was 10.3 g with a standard deviation of 20.2, while the mean sherd weight in Structure 28 contexts (n = 872) was 12.2 g with a standard deviation of 43.8. The difference between the mean sherd weights in the two structures is not statistically significant t (985.543) = 1.27, p = .206, but their variance is significantly different (as measured by Levene's Test for Equality of Variance) is (F 9.92, p = .002). This difference likely owes to depositional differences: The sherds in the larger, cleaner, and more formal Structure 26 were generally impressed in the floor (and thus more trodden and uniform in size and weight), while the (more abundant) ceramics of Structure 26 were both impressed in the floor and distributed as sheet middens, including many large fragments of vessels. Phase diagnostic sherds from occupational contexts in Structure 26 (n = 1021) were composed of 95 percent Late Horizon wares, 4 percent early colonial wares, and 1 percent LIP wares. The proportions of vessel functional categories (based on rim sherds from occupational contexts; n = 237) suggest a full range of domestic activities, with occupational-level context collections composed of 42 percent serving vessels, 34 percent aríbalos, and 24 percent cooking vessels.

The floor layout of Structure 26 shared common features found in other domestic structures, including a hearth feature filled with ash, animal bone, carbonized plant remains, and small sherds, bordered by flagstones set on edge (one still standing, the other tipped over) in the northeast corner. This location fits with the placement of a small ventilation hole near the top of the eastern gable above. A circular flagstone platform similar to those found in all other domestic structures was also uncovered in Structure 26, but rather than being located in a corner (as in other cases), it was situated along the center of the back wall, directly opposite the doorway. Some of the largest sherds in the structure were recovered next to this feature, as was a wichuña (again made of a camelid metapodial). As in the other cases, it was apparently used as a working surface, probably for a variety of domestic activities, including weaving. Interestingly, two probable gaming pieces (likely rolled like dice) made of lightweight, soft volcanic tuff were recovered from this structure—the only context from which this type of artifact was recovered (Figure 5.21). One is rhomboid in form with lines ground into the sides, while the other is spheroid with an hourglass-shaped waist (this latter specimen

Figure 5.21. Possible gaming pieces made of volcanic tuff from Structure 26, Malata.

resembles a bola stone, though the light weight tuff material would have been poorly suited for this purpose) (see Figure 5.21). They are very similar in form to those reported from Machu Picchu, though the examples reported there were of ceramic material (Burger and Salazar 2004). A Nueva Cádiz bead was recovered from the lowest depths of the hard-pack floor (which varied in thickness between about 8 and 15 cm) in Structure 26, consistent with a colonial construction date for the structure.

Structure 28, by contrast, was clearly utilitarian in function, with very high concentrations of domestic refuse on an irregular, pitted floor, a hearth, and a table-like circular fieldstone platform feature in its southwest corner. A tool made from a camelid tibia shaft was also recovered next to this feature. The blade-shaped proximal end of this tool was worked to a serrated edge. Given its form and the common occurrence of camelid bone weaving implements in association with these platform features at the site, it was probably a textile-related tool, perhaps a wool-carding tool. Phase diagnostic sherds from Structure 28 (n = 320) were virtually identical in proportion to those of structure 26, composed of 96 percent Late Horizon wares, 4 percent early colonial wares, and one LIP sherd. The vessel functional categories of rim sherds from occupational contexts (rim sherds only, n = 166) were composed of 69 percent serving vessels, 6 percent aríbalos, and 25 percent cooking vessels.

Figure 5.22. Fine Inka pitcher with anthropomorphic motif and feline-modeled handle from Structure 28, Malata.

Among the sheet-midden deposits on the floor were some of the finest poly-chrome Inka ceramics recovered at the site, including the remarkable pitcher in Figure 5.22, with the representation of a person (evidently a male, perhaps a kuraka or ruler) with a staff, wearing a tasseled-brim hat, with a series of rays projecting from his shoulder. Similar motifs have been reported in the collections from Hatunqolla in the northern Titicaca basin (Julien 1983) as well as Torata Alta in the Moquegua Valley (Van Buren 1993).

All indices thus point to this compound as being the residence of a high-status indigenous household. Given its clearly central position relative to the colonial plaza and chapel, indigenous political authority remained quite literally central even after the reordering of the doctrina. The location, form, and spatial organization of this compound must have reinforced the authority of the indigenous elites who resided there, even as their authority became associated with the public and sacred spaces of colonial integration—the plaza and church. Below, a reconstruction of how pathways were routed to converge in front of this compound and into the plaza beyond illustrates how the built environment was manipulated to shape the form of ritual.

Proceeding through the Doctrina: A Spatial Network Approach

Modeling movement through the doctrina originated in our impressions of our own movement through the site while working there over the course of three field seasons. First, it was our impression that the houses of the eastern neighborhood had easiest access to this main path, at least relative to houses of the older core residential area near the Inka great hall and its plaza. Second, it was obvious that there was only one legitimate entrance to the colonial plaza—through a single entry on its eastern side, which is the terminus of a main path running along the north edge of the residential area. Domestic structures along the southern side of the residential area were linked to this main northern path to the colonial plaza via two transverse connecting paths. Thus, when catechetical instruction or mass was called to order, the arrangement of pathways through the site would have literally funneled traffic and created a processional to this single entry into the plaza and chapel beyond. Entering the plaza, one would see directly ahead the central cross platform and the two sets of steps up to the atrium and into the chapel entry.

Spatial network analysis provides a method for moving beyond such impressionistic interpretations, by formally modeling movement from each domestic structure to each of the respective plazas and quantitatively tracking the distinct patterns of access that resulted. Excellent architectural preservation permitted detailed mapping of not only building layouts, but the walls that separated domestic compounds and delineated paths through the settlement, allowing the construction of a network data set in the Network Analyst extension of ESRI ArcGIS (for more complete discussion of methodology, see Wernke 2012b). Most of the walls between buildings and delineating paths are not so high as to physically preclude passage, but presumably their presence demarcated the prescribed routing of foot traffic through the site.

A variety of measures were used to analyze access patterns between domestic structures and the ceremonial and ritual foci of the site: the great hall and its plaza during Inkaic times and the plaza, atrium, and chapel during early colonial times. Spatial network analysis permitted quantitative modeling of walking distances and times from the doorway of each domestic structure to the center of each of the respective plazas via least cost network path simulation. An average walking speed for the model was first determined in the field by timing multiple walks between some of the more distant houses at the eastern end of the site and the center of the colonial plaza and deriving the average (69.8 m per minute). A network data set of polylines and points was then created by digitizing polylines along the pathways through the site and using the doorways as the origin points and the center of the Inka and colonial plazas as terminal points. Separate iterations were then run for each of the two respective plazas. The simulation resolves the least-cost network path—that is, the shortest path (in walking time) between any given domestic structure and the destination (either the Inka or colonial plaza) moving along the network of paths. Isopleth maps displaying time contours relative to each plaza were then generated to show the patterning of walking time relative to the routes through the site.

A first visualization of movement through the site to each of the plazas shows aggregate traffic patterns along the pathways. The patterns represent the shortest routes between each domestic structure and each of the two plazas. The aggregate routes are displayed in Figure 5.23 by varying the line thickness of each path segment in proportion to the number of walkers (modeling one walker per domestic structure). The networks to each of the two plazas are obviously very different, essentially presenting mirror images of each other. Traffic to the plaza in front of the Inka great hall structure converged on the main path running east-west along the southern edge of the main residential area, and entered the plaza through the side entrance (where steps are still preserved today) near the southeastern corner of the plaza. Other traffic was routed through the second entrance to the plaza at the western end of the plaza. Two entrances were thus used to access the Inka plaza. Given clear evidence for the predominance of serving vessels in the great hall itself, the plaza was almost certainly used for the kinds of public commensal ceremonies that enacted and reified state-subject relations, as discussed above.

Figure 5.23-B shows traffic patterns after the colonial plaza was constructed and became the focal point of public assembly, probably most often during calls to mass or catechetical instruction. Here, the path running east-west along the northern edge of the main residential area was the main thoroughfare, all traffic was funneled to it and through the single entrance to the plaza, forming a processional. Two transverse paths, one near the eastern end of the residential area and one near the western end, routed traffic from the southern side of the residential area to the main path along its northern edge. A preoccupation with surveillance is also evident in relation to these two transverse paths. First, the path that cuts north-south across the site to the east literally routes through a small circular structure (Structure 49) with two doorways, thus forcing walkers to pass through this building at the junction of the transverse and main paths. This structure apparently played some kind of monitoring role for traffic approaching the site from the east or walking to the plaza from the eastern neighborhood. Second, the junction of the western transverse path and main northern path into the plaza is equally notable, since it is located to the adjacent east of the elite compound of Structures 26

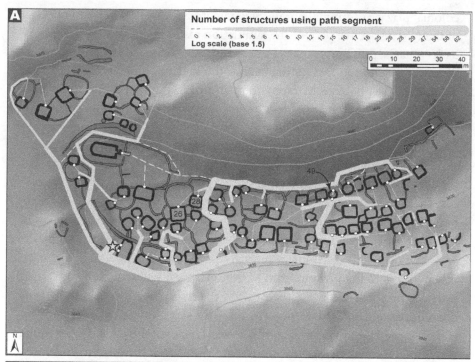

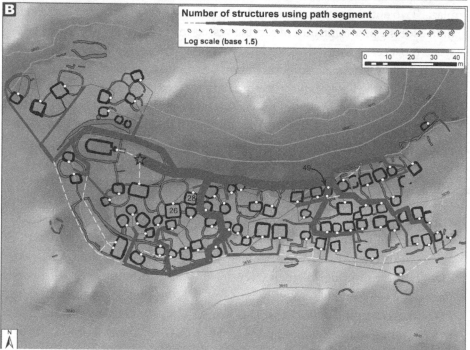

Figure 5.23. Simulated cumulative traffic patterns to Inka plaza (A) and colonial plaza (B), Malata.

and 28, forcing all walkers to file in front of that compound just before they entered the plaza.

The pathways that were *not* used in each of the aggregate path network maps are equally instructive for understanding the spatial reordering of the site. When the Inka plaza is modeled as the destination, the last segment of the main northern path—the most trafficked path segment when the colonial plaza is the focus—was not even used, nor was the double-doored, "monitoring" Structure 49. Conversely, when the colonial plaza is modeled as the destination, the paths around the Inka plaza were not used. Clearly, the two networks were not integrated or complementary but were counterposed and in tension with one another: Going to one plaza from one's house required a very different set of pathways than for the other plaza.

Domestic compounds therefore must have been positioned distinctly in terms of their network centrality relative to each of two plazas. This is readily evident in the maps of Figure 5.24, which show walking time isopleths relative to each of the two plazas. These isopleths were generated through the "service area" function in ArcGIS, simulating the time required to walk the shortest distance through the network at the simulated rate of 68.9 m per minute. The maps of Figure 5.24 show how the compounds of circular structures in the older residential core to the adjacent north of the Inka great hall and plaza were the most central (in relative and absolute terms) during Inkaic times but among the most distal in the network relative to the colonial plaza, despite their proximity in absolute distance. One especially marked change in the walking time contours relative to the Inka plaza (Figure 5.24-A) occurs precisely where the new neighborhood to the east begins. On the southern side of the residential area, a steep cline in time punctuates the beginning of the rows of houses to the east, suggesting that they were poorly integrated into the network of paths leading to the Inka plaza. Conversely, these rows of rectilinear houses were more central (that is, better connected) relative to the colonial plaza than their absolute distance from it would suggest.

Though changes in absolute times are relatively minor—this is a very small village, after all—the key finding is the *relative* difference in access patterns between houses and the two plazas. The pattern of which houses gained and lost centrality is represented in Figure 5.25. Here, each structure is ranked relative to its walking distance to the colonial plaza (the nearest structure in walking time receives a rank of 1, the second nearest, rank of 2, etc.) and relative to the Inka plaza. Structure rank is thus an ordinal scale measure of centrality. Next, the rank of each structure relative to the Inka plaza is subtracted from its rank relative to the colonial plaza. These values can then be used to display the amount of positive (more central) or negative (more distal) rank change

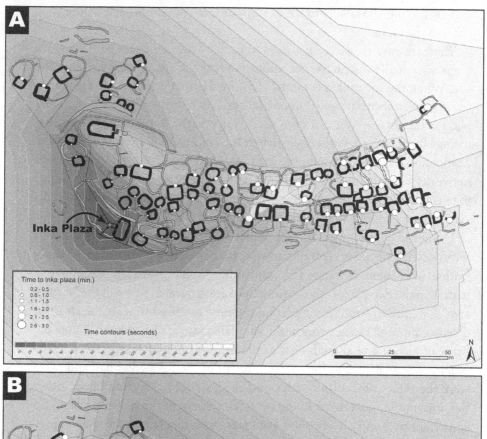

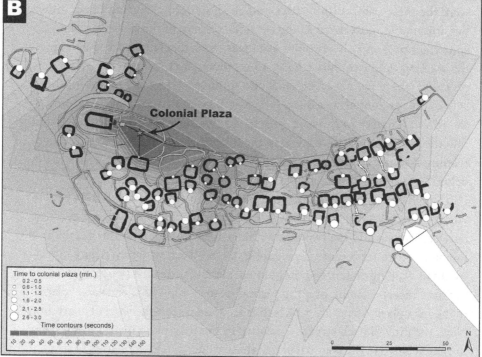

Figure 5.24. Simulated walking-time contours to Inka plaza (A) and colonial plaza (B), using least-cost network paths, Malata.

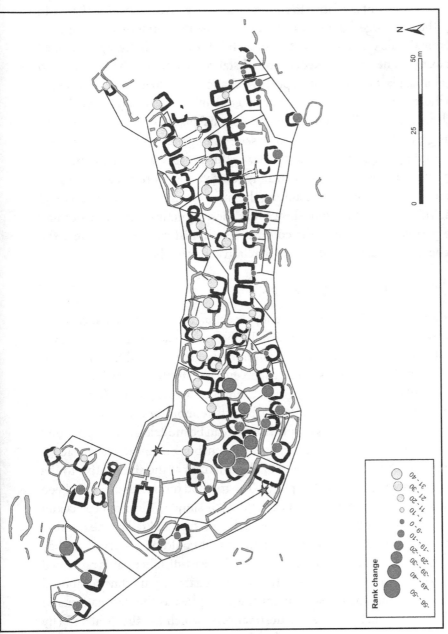

Figure 5.25. Simulated change in centrality rank according to least-cost network paths to Inka and colonial plazas at Malata. For each structure, its centrality rank relative to the Inka plaza is subtracted from its rank relative to the colonial plaza. Dark circles are those that are less central relative to the colonial plaza; light circles are those that are more central relative to the colonial plaza. Difference in size indicates the amount of difference in rank centrality relative to the two plazas.

for each structure as the site layout was reorganized as a doctrina. Houses that became more centrally located relative to the colonial plaza therefore have positive values, while those that became more distal have negative values. The size of each dot is relative to the amount of negative or positive change in rank. Thus the large, light gray dots "gained" the most in terms of their rank (an ordinal scale variable for centrality), while the largest dark gray dots "lost" the most (i.e., became markedly more distal compared to others, relative to the colonial plaza). The greatest positive change was experienced among the households located along the northern edge of the eastern neighborhood, which are clearly well articulated to the colonial plaza via the main path into it. The greatest negative change can be seen among the houses to the adjacent north of the Inka great hall and its plaza. This is especially striking because these were formerly the most centrally located houses relative to the Inka ceremonial space but became among the most distal relative to the colonial plaza. This analysis therefore shows that these structures not only became more peripheral relative to the colonial ceremonial core but also were the most heavily impacted by this change relative to other houses at the site.

Surveillance Patterns and Indirect Rule

I have already mentioned an apparent preoccupation with surveillance in the spatial reordering of the doctrina, as reflected in the placement of the double-door structure on the path at the eastern end of the site and the placement of the probable kuraka's residence at the entrance to the colonial plaza. The funneling of traffic to the only legitimate entrance to the plaza in front of this compound must have enabled its inhabitants to monitor traffic to the plaza and chapel beyond. Patterns of surveillance can be modeled to move beyond this impressionistic interpretation, however, enabling quantitative character-ization of the "surveillance" power of all structures at the site relative to the foot traffic moving to each of its plazas. The method for this analysis has been discussed elsewhere in detail, but in outline it is simple: The model places an imaginary observer in the doorway of each structure and tallies the number of walkers from other domestic structures that could be observed as they made their way to each of the plazas (along the least-distance paths produced in the walking simulation above). The resulting data sets are thus composed of two binary data matrices—one for the Inka plaza as the destination and one for the colonial plaza as the destination—which list the "walker" (by structure number, in ascending order) by row and "observer" (by structure number, in ascending order) by column. A given cell thus encodes whether a walker (for example, from Structure 55) is observable from the doorway of a given structure (for example, Structure 26), encoding "o" for no and "1" for

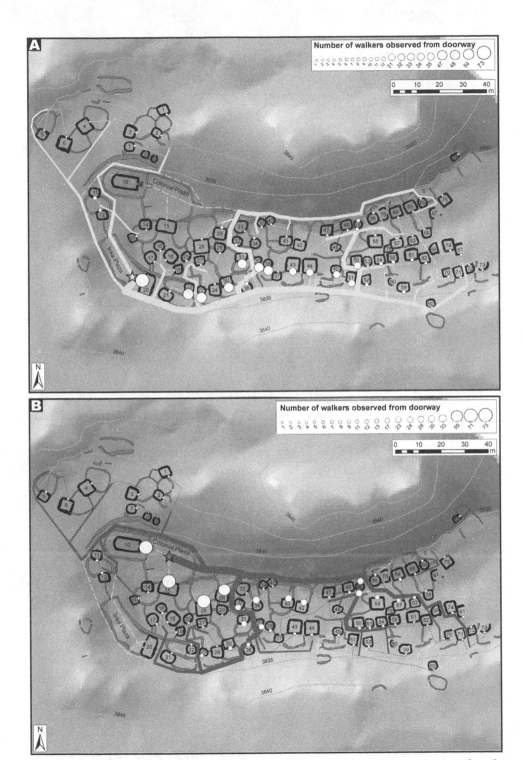

Figure 5.26. Simulated surveillance patterns relative to the cumulative least-cost network paths to the Inka plaza (A) and colonial plaza (B).

yes. By summing the columns, therefore, a simulated "aggregate surveillance power" of each structure can be derived. Derived tables with these aggregate values were then joined to the doorway point theme in the GIS, enabling the visualization of surveillance power at the site by scaling doorway point size to surveillance power values.

The results (displayed in Figure 5.26) show striking differences in surveillance patterns between the two networks. As would be expected, surveillance power shifts from south to north when the destination is changed from the Inka plaza to the colonial plaza. But the surveillance pattern relative to the colonial plaza is more centralized, since the members of the elite compound of Structure 26 would have had a view of literally every other member of the community as they reached the plaza. Only the public building on the plaza and the chapel itself had higher surveillance values. The structure with two doors in the eastern neighborhood is also notable for its high surveillance power. This is also an exceptional case because walkers would have to pass through the building and not just walk past it. It is unclear if this building was purpose-built for this function. It is too small to have served a residential function, though conceivably it could have been used originally as an outbuilding (for example, a kitchen) for a domestic compound and was subsequently repurposed as a monitoring structure. It may also have been ritually important, perhaps marking a transition from domestic to public and sacred spaces of the plaza and chapel. Future excavations may shed light on these possibilities, but it seems clear to have been used as a pass through to gain access to the path to the plaza and chapel when Malata was a doctrina.

As were areas of low traffic, the patterns of structures with low surveillance power relative to the foot traffic to the colonial plaza also shed light on how specific areas of the site were relatively cut off from vistas of movement through the doctrina. For example, the circular structures of the old core residential area next to the Inka plaza and building have generally very low surveillance values. Even in cases of circular structures adjacent to the main path into the colonial plaza, such as Structures 39 and 40, because they are oriented away from the path, they have no surveillance power, while the neighboring rectilinear Structures 41 and 42 are roughly aligned with each other side by side facing the path with high surveillance potentials (surveillance values of 30 and 28, respectively). It is also interesting that the probable friar's quarters, Structure 4, actually has quite low surveillance value relative to the colonial plaza, largely as a result of being separated from the rest of the residential area. Though this compound, located on the higher western end of the site, affords a general view over the nearby chapel and plaza, as well as a portion of the residential area, it was apparently not situated to provide day-to-day monitoring of movement through the site. It seems clear that the friar would have depended on the indigenous elite for day-to-day monitoring of traffic and activities in the plaza, atrium, and chapel.

Finally, in a similar manner to the map of changes in rank centrality above, a map of the *differences* between the surveillance power for each structure relative to the traffic patterns to the Inka plaza and the colonial plaza provides a view of which domestic structures gained and lost potential for monitoring. Figure 5.27, which presents these results, was calculated by subtracting the surveillance power of each structure relative to the Inka plaza from its

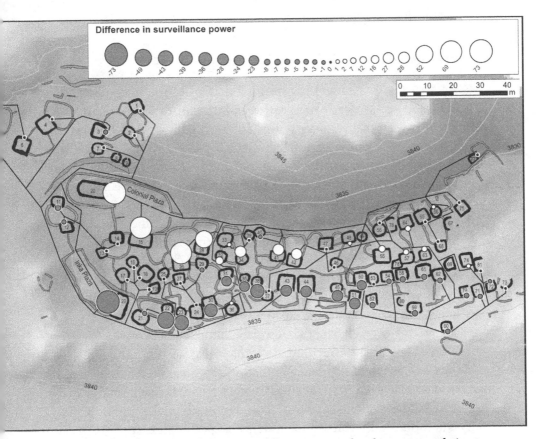

Figure 5.27. Simulated change in the surveillance power of each structure relative to least-cost network paths to the Inka and colonial plazas at Malata. For each structure, its surveillance power relative to a simulation run of traffic walking to the Inka plaza is subtracted from its surveillance power relative to a simulation run of traffic walking to the colonial plaza. Dark circles are those lost surveillance power relative to the colonial plaza; light circles are those that gained surveillance power relative to the colonial plaza. Difference in size indicates the amount of difference in surveillance power relative to the two plazas.

surveillance power relative to the colonial plaza. Gray circles thus represent losses in surveillance power, while white dots indicate gains in surveillance power relative to the colonial plaza. The size of the circle is proportional to the loss or gain. This map shows clearly that the chapel and public structure in the plaza, followed by the structures of the indigenous elite compound (Structures 26 and 28) were the clear "gainers" in the spatial reorientation, while the Inka great hall structure, which saw literally no traffic past it in (again, under the least-distance assumptions of the model), was the biggest "loser" of surveillance power as the site was reoriented to the colonial plaza and chapel. This map clearly shows how the site had isolated and turned its back on the former Inka-era ceremonial focus of the settlement.

A New Kind of Colonial Andean Community

Malata clearly grew and was transformed during its brief time of use as a doctrina, and just as clearly this growth and transformation was structured in particular ways that resonate powerfully with what we know of Spanish colonial schema regarding the relationship between urban forms and the creation of a Christian social order. As the doctrina grew with the addition of new (and new kinds of) domestic compounds, a catechetical complex of chapel, atrium, plaza, and administrative building and a rerouting of movement through the site took shape, effectively funneling traffic away from the old Inka plaza and great hall to converge and form a single processional past the compound of the kuraka and into the plaza and chapel. Members of the households in the old core of the site moved circuitously to join in these processionals, while the newly constructed households at the eastern end of the site found easy access to the main pathway to the plaza.

To a striking degree, then, the postulated production of a new Christian social order (policia) through urban forms (urbs) and communities (civitas)—as well as the maintenance of that order through regimes of surveillance—that is so evident in the documentary record is manifested spatially and materially even in this early and relatively remote, rural setting. Intentionality is notoriously difficult to infer in archaeological contexts, but in this case, the intention seems clear, given pronounced Spanish policy goals of transforming subjects through the restructuring of the built environment ("build it and they will [be]come") and the institution of regimes of surveillance.

But if that was the intention, its *effectiveness* is more ambiguous. As explored in chapter 2, the relationship between schema and resources in the constitution of "structure" is not so simple, linear, or determinative. As Keane emphasizes (2003, 2007), the meaning of embodied signs can never be

unambiguous or stabilized, especially in colonial contexts in which superficially similar forms are derived from and apprehended through often radically distinct schema. Thus the built spaces introduced in this case—chapel/
atrium/plaza—and the rituals carried out there (especially processionals)
must have (if they were to find cultural purchase) resonated with the analogous forms and practices from the Inkaic-era (the great hall–plaza couplet),
even as the friars sought an eradicative strategy that routed traffic away from
them. The legibility of its new spaces for the doctrina's inhabitants (many of
whom were born under Inka rule) depended on such analogies. This negotiation of the dilemma of analogy and erasure therefore must have produced a
new kind of colonial Andean place and community of ambiguous and contested significance and practices.

Conclusion

The findings presented in this chapter show how the Franciscan friars who
first entered the valley clearly identified the key nodal settlements where Inka
administration articulated with local communities and established doctrinas
in them. Within these settlements, the placement of chapels shows glimpses
of how the spatial logic of analogy might have worked as many of the same
spaces used for public ritual under Inka rule were recycled for use in Catholic rites. But close-in analysis of the spatial organization of a particular doctrina—Malata—shows how it grew considerably (most likely as households
from neighboring settlements were congregated to the doctrina) and was reorganized over its short use-life. Simulation of the movement through Malata
shows evidence for the shunting of foot traffic away from the former Inkaic
ceremonial focus of the site to instead form processionals past an elite domestic compound and into the rustically executed colonial plaza and chapel
complex. There is strong evidence for the deliberate reordering of space to
facilitate surveillance and the inculcation of Catholic ritual. But this public, participatory approach to evangelization was necessarily apprehended
through analogous practices, built features, and spatial logics that ordered
this and other settlements like it under Inka rule. Rather than conversion as
the Spanish clergy understood it—the eradication of Andean religious beliefs
and practices and their replacement with Catholic counterparts—the experiences of building, dwelling in, and moving through the spaces of this doctrina
must have produced "convergence" (sensu Lara 2004), a hybrid, improvised
arrangement that was neither conceived nor controlled by either the friars or
their charges. This is not to argue that the people of Malata adopted tactics
of crypto-paganism (the resistant conservation of indigenous beliefs under

the cloak of Catholic practice). There is precious little (if any) evidence for a "culture of resistance" at Malata. Rather, what is at issue in the broadest sense (to return to Sahlins's formulation) is the resistance of culture. This and other Andean communities were quite open to Catholicism in the early years following the invasion. The arrangement that emerged came from a local appropriation of Catholicism as much as a colonization of indigenous practice.

Ironically, it was likely the successful production of these kinds of cultural convergences that contributed to the reactionary and more radically eradicative policies that were to come in the decades that followed, as the sweeping reforms of Viceroy Francisco de Toledo, coupled with post-Tridentine church policies, were instituted in an attempt to remake Andean communities from the ground up.

Notes

1. Gonzalo Pizarro was encomendero of Yanquecollaguas, having been granted both parcialidades (Hanan and Urin) by his brother Francisco in Cuzco on January 22, 1540. Laricollaguas was divided between Marcos Retamoso (Hanansaya) and Alonso Rodríguez Picado (Urinsaya), granted by Francisco Pizarro during the same repartimiento (for details, see Cook 1982:3–4; Julien 1998; Málaga Medina 1977:94, 96).

2. Ulloa Mogollón (1965 [1586]:332; my translation) related their grievance to the board, which included priests who had recently been appointed to serve in the Collagua doctrinas as follows: "The doctrinas of these villages used to be under the charge of the friars of Saint Francis, where eight friars and one guardian lived; they founded the churches which exist in this entire province and adorned them with decorations and other sacred objects of much beauty, made from the silver and gold that they found in the huacas and high mountaintops and old shrines of ancient times, where they went to destroy them with great charity and fervor, and they revealed to them the blindness in which they had lived in former times and taught them the lay of God our Lord through their conversion in these doctrinas, until about two years ago, when they left the doctrinas and returned to their convents at the order of Fray Jerónimo de Villacarillo, their commissary. This saddened the Indians so much that every day they weep for the Franciscan priests and they held such authority to them that they love and respect them tenderly and they have attempted with all their might that they return to take charge of these doctrinas. In place of the friars have come clerics of the Order of St. Peter [the diocesan priests]; these are not as welcome as the friars. They do not have chapels nor is there anything more than confraternities that do little to order the populace."

3. An ecclesiastical visita by the archdiocese of Cuzco confirmed these abuses (Cook 2002:895–96).

4. The Collagua kurakas who signed the power of attorney were Juan Alanoca, Miguel Nina Taype, Francisco Inca Pacta, Diego Hacha of Yanqui-Collaguas, Miguel and Juan

Caqui, Felipe Alpaca, Juan Coaquira, Juan Suyo of Lari-Collaguas, Luis Ala, and Francisco Anti Ala of Cabana-Collaguas (Tibesar 1953:67n115).

5. As discussed in the previous chapter, the length-to-width ratios of 74 percent of LIP/LH houses falls in the nearly square range of 1–1.3:1.

6. The height and width of the north window measures 60 × 40 cm on the interior and 45 × 13 cm on the exterior. The south window measures 70 cm x 40 cm on the interior and 60 × 20 cm on the exterior.

7. This feature runs from the chancel platform westward to just below the windows on both the north and south walls, after which point it is no longer visible. The interior of the structure is currently used as an agricultural field, and cultivation has doubtless disturbed the remainder of these and any other floor features in the nave of the chapel.

8. Specifically, this kiln is situated on the western side of the quebrada Canto Huaycco, which forms the community boundary between Yanque Urinsaya and Ichupampa and the western edge of the survey coverage.

9. Prudence Rice documented 26 colonial kilns at a series of wine bodegas in the Moquegua Valley. Two primary types of kilns were identified, calcination kilns and ceramic manufacture kilns, in which large fermentation vessels (tinajas) and storage/transport bottles (botijas) were made (Rice 1987, 1994; Rice and van Beck 1993). However, both types are much larger than those I documented, and cross-dating in any case is complicated by functional and temporal variability among the Moquegua kilns (Rice 1994:343).

10. The "open chapel" form, composed of an elevated balcony above the church entry overlooking the atrium or plaza, continued to be used even in some Toledan-era churches; in fact, the church of Coporaque is probably the only such surviving original example of this type (Tord 1983).

11. Soil samples of an average of 4L were collected from every discrete provenience context at the site. Each was screened through sieves of 4 mm, 2 mm, 1 mm, and 0.5 mm. Botanical remains were sorted and analyzed using a binocular microscope.

12. Specifically, the church was owed monthly "two fanegas of maize, two fanegas of wheat, and one ewe. Every four months, tributaries were to give one pig and one carga of salt and firewood to the local church. In addition, they were to deliver eight sheep weekly (divided equally, males and females), and each religious holiday a dozen eggs and some fish. They were to refrain from giving *chicha*. Stipends of the doctrineros were paid directly from the local office of the Royal Treasury" (Cook 2007:135). The volumetric equivalent of one fanega is approximately 55.5 liters, or 1.5 bushels.

13. Portable XRF analysis was conducted by Patrick Ryan Williams of the Field Museum.

6

UNEASY COMPROMISES

Colonial Political-Ecological (Dis)Articulations

By the 1570s, the Franciscan mission in the valley was more or less formalized within a system of convents and doctrinas, but the incipient congregation of settlement taking place in the doctrinas was soon to be eclipsed by the massive resettlement program initiated during the visita general of the viceroy Francisco de Toledo. Long favored by the Crown (Abercrombie 1998:223–29) and already partially implemented in New Spain (Gade and Escobar 1982; Málaga Medina 1974), the reducción program became one of the primary policies instituted by Toledo in his efforts to augment faltering tribute collection, foster the civil and religious indoctrination of the native population, and secure a steady labor supply for the massive mining operations of Potosí and Huancavelica (Hemming 1983:392–456; Levillier 1935; Málaga Medina 1974; Spalding 1984:156–68; Stern 1982:76–79; Zimmerman 1938). As discussed in the previous chapter, reducciones were to literally embody the colonialist schema of "reducir" (to order, unify, and make uniform). Drawing again on Sewell's (2005) formulation of the duality of structure, reducción villages constituted a nonhuman resource intended to redefine community and interpellate subjects to a new hierarchical social order. Each village was to be a stage setting for producing a new colonial civitas, with a central plaza surrounded by buildings housing the village's two principal civic and religious institutions—the cabildo (town hall) for orderly administration, surveillance, and tribute collection in the caja de comunidad (community chest) and the church for the religious indoctrination of the native populace (Málaga Medina 1974). It is commonly noted that reducciones were designed around a grid of blocks and streets like European cities, but even considering their variability in execution (see below), they embodied this ideal more perfectly than almost any European city of the time. In this sense, their layout epitomized an urban archetype in miniature.

The resettlement program was an unprecedented experiment in colonial social engineering, and Toledo and his predecessors were aware of the problems that could arise from dislocating native communities. Although the reducción project might seem a straightforward example of top-down state imposition, decision-making processes that determined how and where to establish reducciones in a given locale remains very poorly understood, in large part because local-level protocols detailing the establishment of reducciones are exceedingly rare in the archives (but see Julien 1991). This is a critical lapse in documentation, since in practice, the reducción project had to reckon with existing indigenous schemas and resources. How were they reconciled? It is at this local scale that the negotiation of the conditions of daily life played out.

Research on the layout of reducciones and their domestic spaces are scarce (Cummins 2002; Gutiérrez 1993; Llosa and Benavides 1994; Málaga Medina 1974), and no detailed study exists, but their evident variability, many of which were adapted to local topography (see Gade and Escobar 1982) or built on Inkaic rectilinear and trapezoidal plans (e.g., Julien 1983), belie the prescriptive homogeneity of a standard gridiron plan. Many important aspects of settlement planning must have been negotiated at the local level as the visitadores met with local clerics, communities, and kurakas. For example, while Toledo ordered (echoing Matienzo) that the nucleated villages be established on relatively level terrain "in healthy places of good climate" near abundant water and cultivable land, he also advocated, in the interest of efficiency and minimizing disruption, that reducciones be situated in the locations of previous large prehispanic settlements (Toledo 1924 [1570–75]:163–64). At the same time, the viceroy stipulated that the visitadores establish the new settlements as far as possible from prehispanic cemeteries and huacas—priorities often at odds with one another (Toledo 1924 [1570–75]:163–64). Also, while Toledo set the maximum size of a reducción at 500 tributaries (i.e., men between 18 and 50 years old), many exceeded this size considerably (Cook et al. 1975 [1582]; Gade and Escobar 1982:432). Even the stringent specifications of the settlement configuration were subject to considerable variation. It was left ambiguous whether the church should occupy the same plaza as the buildings of civil authorities or have its own block. But most important, it is unclear how decisions were made regarding who, in terms of Andean community arrangements, was "reduced" where. Given that in many rural contexts, ayllus were spread over several settlements and production zones, resettlement had the potential to fundamentally disarticulate native systems of production, and thus posed a serious threat, both to ayllu organization and to the state's ability to siphon tribute revenue.

How were these conflicting priorities negotiated in situ? The Colca Valley provides an excellent context to investigate this question. In the Corregimiento of the Collaguas, 24 reducciones were established in the early 1570s (Málaga Medina 1977), and the villages of Yanque and Coporaque illustrate distinct outcomes. In the case of Yanque, the capital of the colonial province of Collaguas, colonial authorities placed the reducción village on top of the primary Inka political center in the central valley, a site that also was ideally situated according to the geographic criteria for a reducción (i.e., on the low, broad pampa above the river gorge). A large portion of its population therefore would have come from the same locale and would not have been displaced (see Figure 6.1). Resettlement would have been much more disruptive for the inhabitants of Uyu Uyu (YA-050), Llactarana (YA-054), and YA-045 on the north side of the river. Although their inhabitants apparently retained their agricultural lands surrounding these settlements after reducción, they would have had to cross the river to reach them, as modern Yanque Urinsaya community members still do today.

Figure 6.1. The reducción of Yanque, showing community spatial divisions.

The locational continuity between the capital of the colonial province and its Inkaic counterpart also appears to fit a general pattern amongst the principal villages of the valley. As we saw in chapter 4, both of the capitals of the other repartimientos of the province, Laricollaguas and Cabanaconde, are also situated either atop or adjacent to major Inka settlements.

In the case of Coporaque, its location does not coincide with a major Late Horizon settlement, and it is situated high on the sloping pampa above the river gorge. Thus it is quite distant from the cluster of LIP/LH settlements (CO-103, CO–127, CO-150, CO-163, and CO-164) and their fortifications (CO-165, CO-167, and CO-168) on the valley bottom. The largest LIP/LH settlement in the vicinity of Coporaque is San Antonio/Chijra (CO-100). Although it served as an early doctrina, it is situated on steeply sloping hillsides where it would have been impossible to construct a reducción. Thus Coporaque appears to have reduced the inhabitants of all of these hamlets and villages in a location where scant artifactual traces signal at most a small village had been present.[1] A similar pattern is found in Achoma, just west of Yanque, where the reducción village does not appear to coincide with a major LIP/LH settlement but derives from the nearby hilltop villages of Pilloniy and Achomaniy, as well as the settlements of Escalera, Malata, and Potosina (Oquiche Hernani 1991; Shea 1986b, 1987).

Negotiated Settlements: Reducción, Ayllus, and Kurakas

Even as reducción resettlement attempted to impose an ideal schema of social order on native Andean populations, the built reconfigurations of the program belied uneasy compromises between Andean and Spanish colonial institutions of economic extraction and political administration. At the local level and in most locales throughout the former realm of Tawantinsuyu, the native institutions that post-Toledan administration relied upon were themselves hybrid Inka/local constructs which were increasingly revealed for their "imagined" status after conquest. As discussed in chapter 3, local Inka administration, structured according to clockwork of tripartite and decimal schemas, was only partially instituted on the eve of the Spanish invasion. With the collapse of the Inka state, and in the face of new modes of domestic and community life—even in seemingly far-flung places like a small doctrina such as Malata—in many ways the institutions of the viceroyalty of Peru were being built on a set of institutions that were themselves on unsure footing. Below I briefly contextualize the Toledan reforms, the subsequent crises that produced the flood of post-Toledan censuses such as those I analyze, and identify those hybrid state/local constructs of community that structured both Inkaic and post-conquest administration of the province of the Collaguas.

If the post-Inkaic alliances between kurakas and encomenderos produced a crisis of confidence and legitimacy vis-à-vis their subject communities, the Toledan reforms did little to change this dynamic, since much of its basic architecture still relied on indirect rule. Both streams of revenue in the system— a tributary head tax and a corvée labor draft—were based on homologous institutions in the Inka imperial economy. The corvée labor draft, the colonial *mita* (modeled on its prehispanic precursor, the *mit'a*),[2] was designed primarily as a means of providing low-cost and regular labor to the silver mines of Potosí and the mercury mines of Huancavelica (a new amalgamation process that came online in Potosí in the 1570s required large inputs of mercury). Under Inka rule, the mit'a labor turn owed to the state played upon community-based norms labor exchange, based on an ideal of balanced reciprocity. The mit'a was represented as an extension of these traditional reciprocal arrangements but was actually an extractive measure, as the labor time contributed produced far more than was returned by the state. Under Toledo, the labor turn, the mita, was superficially modeled on the Inkaic mit'a but was in fact a forced labor regime in which one seventh to one sixth of the adult male population was required to perform tasks deemed critical by the state for extended (usually six month) periods (Spalding 1984:164–65; Stern 1982:84–96). Even the pittance wage that was nominally required often went unpaid (Spalding 1984:165). Many *mitayos* died in service; others never returned to their home communities, living as *forasteros* (foreigners) in distant locales after having escaped or served out their mita obligations. Such dynamics further cut into the fabric of community relations because any prestations of labor made by the kin of serving mitayos during their absence—for example, caring for their fields or livestock—were far from assured to be reciprocated (Stern 1982:89–92). In macroeconomic terms over the long run, the colonial mita served to further entrench mining operations in fewer hands, leading to undercapitalization and dependency on unskilled forced labor (see Bakewell 1984; Cole 1985; Garner 1988; Tandeter 1981).

Outside the areas surrounding Huancavelica and Potosí, mita forced labor was used for major constructions (the so-called *mita de plaza*—construction and repair projects for bridges, roads, churches, jails, and other infrastructure) and in the dreaded *obrajes* (workshops) for the production of crafts (e.g., textiles) and consumables (e.g., wine). In Collagua Province, the Potosí behemoth initially loomed large in mita obligations. Toledo's mita distribution of August 1578 mandated that 10 percent of the tributary populations of the Collaguas and Cabanas was to reside temporarily in Potosí, of whom one-third were to act as active mitayos in actual mining operations. But this portion of the mita lasted only about four years in the province, in part because of

the great travel distance and hardships suffered, and because of crises closer
to home in the wake of the 1582 earthquake. Thereafter mitayo service was
varied; some fulfilled their obligation as *trajínes* (long-distance porters, a notoriously difficult service), as workers on the haciendas of the coastal valleys
of Camaná, Siguas, Vitor, and Arequipa, and as laborers in the mita de plaza
in and around Arequipa.

The bulk of mita service reverted back to mining in the decades following
the discovery of silver in nearby Caylloma in 1626. The first draft of 800 mitayos
from the surrounding corregimientos included 324 Collaguas. This heavy burden conflicted with standing obligations of 249 laborers for the mita de plaza in
Arequipa and led to a protracted legal conflict between the elites of Caylloma
and Arequipa that was ultimately won out by the mining interests in the early
eighteenth century (Cook 2007:155–63). As in other regions, then, the consequences of the mita were dire for the native population of Collagua Province
and generated perverse incentives away from innovation, competition, and
capitalization and toward the creation of an entrenched and corrupt provincial
Spanish mercantile elite dependent on forced, unskilled labor. Though initially
conceived and clothed in the analogy of traditional labor reciprocity, the mita
was transparently exploitative to Andean communities. Instead of being a reliable and cost-effective motor for a dynamic colonial economy, it contributed
to a sclerotic and unsustainable arrangement of conflicting elite interests, to
the collapse of the authority of kurakas, and ultimately to the native insurrec-
tions of the late eighteenth century (see Stern 1987).

The tributary head tax, the other pillar of the colonial economy as devised
by Toledo, likewise rested on coercive measures. The head tax applied to able-
bodied men between the ages of 18 and 50 (with the exceptions of kurakas,
the physically disabled, and in-migrants [*forasteros*]) who owed tribute by
dint of their status as vassals to the Crown. Polo de Ondegardo and other
well-informed officials argued against individual-level tributary taxation.
They instead advocated for a community-level levy, which could be more
sensitive to the vagaries of production in the unpredictable climate of the
region and was more akin to traditional norms and the taxation system of
Tawantinsuyu. But Toledo and the Crown insisted on the calculation and
rendering of tax by tributary, putatively to maximize extractive potential.

The critical economizing feature of the system was again its reliance on
indirect measures: viceregal authorities did not intercede in the actual collection of tribute. The state both lacked the wherewithal and personnel for
such a microscopically attuned system, and in any case, since most highland
communities retained land-tenure rights, there was no organic basis for the
rendering of tribute. Instead, the state ultimately depended on the recognized

authority of local native lords: tax assessments were made by census (visita) at the provincial or repartimiento by viceregal authorities (usually the local corregidor), but the actual collection of taxes—much as under the previous La Gascan regime—was left to the kurakas (Spalding 1984:159–65).

This compromise system produced many unintended consequences. Tribute levies became particularly onerous during years of poor agricultural productivity. But more fundamentally, colonial demographic dynamics created a structural problem: Population decline from outmigration and from deaths caused by European-introduced epidemics—a vulnerability aggravated by the close living quarters of the new reducciones—left remaining tributaries with de facto higher tax burdens until a new census could be conducted. This scenario of the living paying for the dead led to a flood of petitions by kurakas, under pressure by their communities, for population recounts, or revisitas (Cook 1975; Saignes 1985; Saignes et al. 1985; Stern 1982:114–37). Pressures from within the colonial administration to raise tribute levies also played a role in calls for revisitas. Claiming that the kurakas hid tributaries from previous counts, corregidores also frequently called for new censuses (Guevara-Gil and Salomon 1994; Stern 1982:114–37).

Special scrutiny would have been warranted in the case of the Collaguas, given that the province of the Collaguas was the most populous under the jurisdiction of Arequipa and produced 35 percent of its tax revenue (Cook 1975; Guillet 1992:23). The numerous revisitas conducted in the valley over the course of the sixteenth and seventeenth centuries thus owes to a combination of factors: the hardships faced by the declining population, the political adeptness of the kurakas, and the regional importance of the province. The publication of these censuses—the largest such collection for any single locale in the Americas—was initiated by Franklin Pease (Pease 1977b) and recently completed by David Robinson (Robinson 2003a, 2006, 2009).

The very existence of such a large corpus of visitas is therefore suggestive of prolonged demographic, economic, and political crises in the wake of the Toledan reforms. Many observers have noted that the contradictions inherent in the new political economy hammered out by Toledo, and its underlying dependence on blunt coercion, ultimately led to its disintegration (see, inter alia, Abercrombie 1998; Gledhill 1988; Larson 1998; Spalding 1982, 1984, 1999; Stern 1982). My focus in this chapter is not on these long-term effects but on identifying points of disarticulation and attempted rearticulation between the Toledan administrative scheme, local community organization, and the remnants of Inkaic administrative structures in order to render a view of the negotiation of power in the conditions of everyday life. Doing so requires tacking back and forth between ethnohistorical reconstruction of Inka-era relations and institutions of power and production and projecting forward to consider the effects of reducción resettlement on those relations and institutions, especially regarding its effects on colonial-era land-use patterns.

Ideal Schemas: Collana, Pahana, and Cayao

As I discussed in chapter 3, we know from the description of the provincial magistrate Juan de Ulloa Mogollón (1965 [1586]) that the colonial and Inkaic Collagua Province was divided spatially and ethnically between the Aymara-speaking Collaguas in the central and upper valley and the Quechua-speaking Cabanas in the lower valley. The Collaguas were internally divided between the lower-ranking Laricollaguas to the adjacent east of the Cabanas in the lower-central valley and the higher-ranking Yanquecollaguas in the central and upper valley. As is evident in their names, and as I discussed in the previous chapters, the Late Horizon and colonial political centers of each of these three provincial subdivisions were Cabanaconde, Lari, and Yanque, respectively. In turn, the populations of each of these three provincial subdivisions—Yanquecollaguas, Laricollaguas, and Cabanaconde—were internally divided between ranked moieties, or *sayas*, called parcialidades, with colonial administration: Hanansaya (upper moiety) and Urinsaya (lower moiety).

While such tripartite and dualistic divisions within Inkaic provinces were common (Pärssinen 1992), Ulloa goes on to explain how the ayllus that composed each moiety within these subdivisions among the Collaguas and Cabanas were again divided according to tripartite categories of rank and prestige. This tripartite system of rank distinction follows a logic of high, middle, and low status designations, called respectively, Collana, Pahana (or Payan), and Cayao. Ulloa explains thus (1965 [1586]:330):

> They governed themselves according to that which the Inka had determined, which was, for their ayllos and parcialidades, he named for each ayllo a cacique, and they were three ayllus, named *Collona* [sic, Collana], *Pasana* [sic, Pahana], *Cayao*. Each of these ayllos had three hundred Indians and a headman whom they obeyed, and these three headmen obeyed the principal cacique, who ruled over all.[3]

Building on Ulloa Mogollón's short account, the ideal ayllu schema of Inka administration can be reconstructed for the province as a whole. This elegant nested hierarchy was ordered by a recursive tripartite and decimal administrative system in which each of the ayllus of 300 households described by Ulloa was composed of three smaller ayllus of 100 households (i.e., *pachaca ayllus*), which in turn were ranked according to the same tripartite logic (Cock Carrasco 1976–77; Pärssinen 1992:362–71; Rostworowski de Diez Canseco

1983:121–23; Zuidema 1964:115–18). Specifically, the 1591 and 1604 visitas of Yanquecollaguas Urinsaya reveal that each of the three ranked groups (Collana, Pahana, and Cayao) noted by Ulloa Mogollón formed "macro" ayllus of an ideal size of 300 households that were each subdivided by the same tripartite ranking system into three smaller ayllus of 100 households each (cf. Cock Carrasco 1976–77; Pärssinen 1992:362–66).[4] The *pataca* designation of these smaller ayllus (cognate to the Quechua *pachaca*), meaning "100" in Aymara, signals that they were considered scalar equivalents of 100 tributary households within Inka decimal administration (see Julien 1982, 1988). The striking feature of this ideal structure is that it precisely reproduces Inkaic categories of descent-based rank. Thus the high-ranking macro-ayllu Collana was subdivided into three 100-household ayllus: (1) Collana (rank 1.1), (2) Collana Pahana Pataca (rank 1.2), and (3) Collana Cayao Pataca (rank 1.3); the middle-ranking macro-ayllu Pahana was subdivided into three 100-household ayllus: (1) Pahana Collana Pataca (rank 2.1), (2) Pahana Taypi Pataca (rank 2.2), and (3) Pahana Cayao Pataca (rank 2.3); and the low-ranking macro-ayllu Cayao was subdivided in the same manner: (1) Cayao Collana Pataca (rank 3.1), (2) Cayao Pahana *(or* Taypi*)* Pataca (rank 3.2), and (3) Cayao Pataca (rank 3.3). In sum, the ideal structure was thus composed of nine pataca ayllus each for Hanansaya and Urinsaya, for a total of 18 pataca-level ayllus within each of Yanquecollaguas, Laricollaguas, and Cabanaconde.

This recursive Collana/Pahana/Cayao ranking directly parallels the ordering of the ceque lines of Cuzco. That is, the ceque lines were organized in a repeating pattern of three groups of three ceques, again named Collana, Pahana, and Cayao.[5] Each of the pataca ayllus was headed by a kuraka, whose title, *pachacuraca*, "lord of one hundred households," also reflected his position within the decimal hierarchy.[6] The corollary of this hierarchical schema in terms of political authority is that the kuraka of the highest ranked ayllu (i.e., the pachacuraca of ayllu Collana) in the upper moiety (Hanansaya) was also the paramount kuraka of the Collaguas as a whole (see Cock Carrasco 1976–77:108–10). His structural equivalent in Lari was head of the repartimiento of Laricollaguas, and likewise for the Collana Hanansaya kuraka of Cabanaconde (Benavides 1987, 1988a; Cock Carrasco 1976–77; Pärssinen 1992:366; Pease 1981; Treacy 1989b).[7]

Articulating Ideal Structures and Collagua Ayllus

This reconstruction of the ideal schema of local Inka administration is only partially correct. A close reading of the full range of visitas to the valley shows uneven conformity to the onomastic schema across the two moieties of the provincial subdivisions. On the one hand, the names of the Urinsaya ayllus conform to the Collana/Pahana/Cayao conventions much more closely than those of Hanansaya, suggesting they were more thoroughly altered under Inka administration. All but two of the nine pataca-level ayllu names appear in the Urinsaya visitas (see Table 6.1).[8] On the other hand, in the visitas of Hanansaya, only the ayllus Collana and Pahana Collana Pataca appear in un-modified form (Table 6.2). Some others are recognizable variations on the tripartite naming conventions, such as Surcollana ([sic], Sur Collana), Pah-ana Caloca, Collana Malco, Ilacachibaicayao Taipi Pataca ([sic], Ilaca Chivay Cayao Taypi Pataca),[9] and Chapoca Collana Cayao Pataca—probably reflect-ing how the Inka fitted extant local ayllus to the ideal administrative hier-archy. But most Hanansaya ayllus did not follow the tripartite and decimal naming conventions at all, having instead names such as Iumasca (Yumasca), Calloca, Cupi, Checa Malco, and Icatunga Malco. The majority of these are Aymara words, the pre-Inkaic language of the Collaguas. This predominance of Aymara names and their lack of conformity with Inka tripartite and deci-mal conventions suggests that Hanansaya ayllus were primarily composed of

Table 6.1. Villages and ayllus of Yanquecollaguas Urinsaya, 1591/1604

Village	Ayllo
Achoma (incomplete)	Collana Pataca [1]
	Collana Pataca [2][a]
	Yndios Cunbicamayos deste ayllo (Collana Pataca [2])
	Yndios Plateros (Silversmiths) deste ayllo (Collana Pataca [2])
	Taypi Pataca [1]
	Taypi Pataca [2][b]
Callalli	Cayao
Canocota	Pahana Taypi Pataca
	Cayao Pataca
Coporaque	Collana
	Pahana Collana Pataca
	Pahana Taypi Pataca
	Pahana Cayao Pataca
	Oficiales Olleros de [Pahana] Cayao Pataca (Official Potters of [Pahana] Cayao Pataca)
Guaraoma (estancia)	Collana Cayao Pataca
	Pahana Taypi Pataca
	Cayao Pataca
	Collana Taypi Pataca
	Unidentified
Mamaniviri (estancia)	Collana
	Taypi Pataca [2]
Sibayo	Collanapaque (Collana Paque)

(continued)

Table 6.1. (*continued*)

Village	Ayllo
	Paragra Pahana Collana Pataca
	Sibayo Pahana Collana Pataca
	Pahana Cayao Pataca
	Cayao
Tisco	Cayao Pataca
	Collana Taypi Pataca
	Collana Cayao Pataca
	Pahana Collana Pataca
	Pahana Taypi Pataca
	Pahana Cayao Pataca
	Collana
Tuti	Taypi Pataca
	Collana Pataca
	Collana Paque
	Pahana Collana Pataca
	Pahana Taypi Pataca
	Pahana Cayao Pataca
	Collana Taypi Pataca
Yanque	Collana
	Taypi Pataca [1]
	Taypi Pataca [2]
	Cumbicamayos [1]
	Cumbicamayos [2]

Notes: Listed in order of appearance in the visitas. From APY Yanquecollaguas Urinsaya 1604, except Yanque, from the 1591 visita (Verdugo and Colmenares 1977 [1591]:191–263, fols. 1r–44r).
a. Collana Pataca is listed as two separate ayllu segments in Achoma, but due to the death of the kuraka of the second segment during the recording of the visita, they were (re)joined under the kuraka of the first segment, Miguel Çapana (APY Yanquecollaguas Urinsaya 1604:fols. 366r, 387v).
b. In Achoma Urinsaya the second ayllu Taypi Pataca data are incomplete. The document fragment ends at folio 413v, in the section recording tributary households from this ayllu.

unmodified autochtonous Collagua ayllus.[10] Here then is an example of the negotiation of community schema, as both imagined by the state and by local peoples, produced a new improvised order.

As I illustrate below, these autochthonous ayllus were originally organized around dualistic principles based on a directional "right-left" orientation, another common feature of late prehispanic Aymara polities (Astvaldsson 2000; Bouysse-Cassagne 1986, 1987). The declarations from Coporaque in the 1615–17 Hanansaya visita provides hints of this directional duality in the names of two groups of ayllus: One was named Cupi, which means (specifically, the

Table 6.2. Villages and ayllus of Yanquecollaguas Hanansaya, 1591/1615–17

Village	Ayllu
Achoma (incomplete)	Surcollana (Sur Collana)
	Unidentified[a]
Chivay	Chapoca Collana Cayao Pataca
	Ilacachibaicayao Taipi Pataca
	(Ilaca Chivay Cayao Taypi Pataca)
Coporaque	Collana Malco
	Icatunga Malco
	Checa Malco
	Iumasca (Yumasca)
	Calloca
	Aipi (Cupi)
	Cupi
	Oficiales Olleros (Official Potters)
Guanca	Collana
	Cupi
Lluta	Collana
Maca	Indios Plateros
Sibayo	Cupi
Tisco	Anaoca
	Collana Malco
	Iumasca (Yumasca)
	Cupi
	Cupi Capa Chapi (Cupi Pachapi)
Tuti	Pahana Collana Pataca
	Pahana Caloca
	Chilpe
Yanque (incomplete)	Unidentified
	Yndios Oficiales Cumbicamayos[b]
	Yndios Yanaconas de don Joan Halanoca
	(Retainers of don Joan Halanoca)

Notes: Listed in order of appearance in the visitas. From APY Yanquecollaguas Hanansaya 1615–17, except Yanque, from Yanquecollaguas Hanansaya 1591 (Verdugo 1977 [1591]). Both visitas are incomplete; only the second half (fols. 303r–611v) of the 1615–17 visita is preserved, and the 1591 Hanansaya visita is a small fragment, lacking foliation. The 1591 fragment begins near the end of the accounting of Yanque.

[a] The 1615–17 visita fragment begins in the middle of this ayllu. Marginalia indicate that the ayllu is in Achoma, followed by ayllu Surcollana, also in Achoma. However, there is no summary ledger following the individual listing of households to identify this ayllu.

[b] Listed as subjects of don Juan Halanoca (Verdugo and Colmenares 1977 [1591]:415 [no folio number]). Although Halanoca is not included in this visita fragment, Ulloa lists him as principal kuraka of the province—that is, kuraka of ayllu Collana of Yanque (Ulloa Mogollón 1965 [1586]:326).

compound *cupitoque*) "right side" (Bertonio 1956 [1612]:60), while another was named Checa Malco (*checa* means "left side") (Bertonio 1956 [1612]:79).[11] My reconstruction of ayllu-level land-tenure patterns in the next chapter illustrates that the names of these ayllus also refer to the locations of their agricultural fields and, by extension, their patterns of residence before reducción.[12]

These observations suggest that the Inkas sought to subsume an autochthonous left-right dualism within a higher-order Hanansaya-Urinsaya moiety division and to reconfigure ayllu organization according to a specific structural model drawn from the imperial capital. But Inka administration did not erase local ayllu organization; rather, local ayllus of the higher-ranking Hanansaya moiety remained largely intact while a greater degree of transformation is evident in the names of the ayllus of the lower-ranking Urinsaya moiety. Thus reorganization of the Collagua province by the Inkas was an improvised order and not as sweeping across both moieties as suggested by prior ethnohistorical reconstructions.

Structural Grafting: Ayllus and Reducciones

As I discussed in the previous chapter, the reducciones themselves grafted onto the physical manifestations of Inka rule in the valley, as the Toledan villages (Yanque, Lari, and Cabanaconde) that served as capitals of the three provincial repartimientos were each located on the site of a major Inka political center. Similarly, post-Toledan administration of the province was linked to vestiges of the Collagua-Inka political structure I outlined above. The reducción villages of the central valley (Yanque, Coporaque, Achoma, and Chivay) were composed exclusively of ayllus from the two higher-ranking macro-ayllus of Collana and Pahana. By contrast, the herding villages (Callalli, Sibayo, and Tisco) in the upper valley were home to the lower-ranking ayllus of Cayao, as well as outlier segments of the higher-ranking ayllus subject to their respective kurakas in Yanque and Coporaque. Thus, as illustrated below, the reducciones and post-Toledan political and economic administration were clearly based on preceding Inka-era networks of ayllu affiliation and authority.

Supra-Local Networks of Ayllu Authority

Even after reducción resettlement, kurakas in Yanque and Coporaque continued to hold authority over a constellation of ayllu satellite populations located in both lower-elevation, prime-maize-producing valleys to the south and the puna grasslands surrounding the upper reaches of the Colca Valley. Settlements in these outlying locales were therefore composed of disparate ayllu segments that were subject to their respective kurakas in the agricultural core of the valley. The herding village of Tisco was the primary settlement in which outlier segments of Yanquecollaguas ayllus based in the central valley were settled.[13] This is why the population of Tisco was divided between so many small ayllu segments: Groups from all six patacas of the high- and middle-ranking macro-ayllus Collana and Pahana (Payan) were settled there, as well as an ayllu from the lowest-ranking macro-ayllu Cayao, whose kuraka was resident there (Verdugo and Colmenares 1977 [1591]:264–92, fols. 44v–64r) (see Table 6.1).[14] Listed with most of the outlier ayllus from Collana and Pahana were local *mandones,* or seconds-in-charge, who would have acted as proxies for their kurakas in the mobilization of labor and collection of tribute. The village of Caylloma served this role for herding branches of ayllus based in Laricollaguas.

The links between kurakas in the central valley and herding populations in the upper valley and surrounding puna can be reconstructed by tracking the names of ayllus and kurakas in each of the villages recorded in the visitas. Figure 6.2 illustrates how the kurakas of ayllus based in Yanque and Coporaque were also listed as the heads of ayllu segments in pastoralist and maize-production enclaves. Within Urinsaya, the kurakas of Yanque and Coporaque were responsible for collecting tribute from ayllu segments in five villages (Canocota, Tuti, Sibayo, Callalli, and Tisco) and three pastoralist hamlets, (*estancias*) (Mamaniviri, Villaya/Hivillaya, and Guaraoma) (Figure 6.2). All of the kurakas of Coporaque Urinsaya were listed as the heads of outlier ayllu populations in three to four herding villages (Figure 6.2). In Yanque Urinsaya, the head of the ayllu Taypi Pataca, one Diego Chacha, collected tribute from outlier ayllu segments in the estancias of Mamaniviri and Villaya (APY Yanquecollaguas Urinsaya 1604, fols. 329v–330r).[15] The paramount kuraka of Urinsaya (and head of ayllu Collana of Yanque) was also listed as head of satellite ayllu Collana populations in Tisco and the estancia of Mamaniviri.[16] In addition to the revenue from these herding populations, he would also have been responsible for collecting the tax levies from each of the pachacuracas of the moiety (via the apical kurakas of their respective macro-ayllus), and tribute would have been funneled through him to the paramount kuraka of the province.

A corresponding schematic for Hanansaya cannot be constructed because most of the Yanque data is missing from the incomplete 1591 and 1616 visitas. However, included within the fragment that remains of Yanque Hanansaya is an important section that registers a group of personal retainers (yanacona) of the paramount kuraka of the province, Joan Halanoca (or Alanoca). As discussed in further detail below, these yanacona were pastoralists that claimed

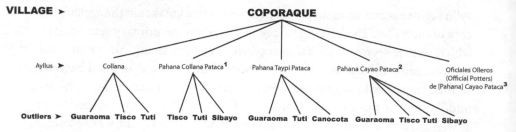

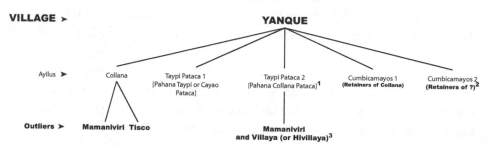

[1]Includes a group of potters (six households) recorded as a separate section within *ayllu Pahana Collana Pataca*.
[2]This *ayllu* was called *Pahana Cayao Pataca* in the section header, but *Cayao Pataca* in the section summary.
[3]Listed as *Cayao Pataca*, but as a subset of the preceding *ayllu*, which was *Pahana Cayao Pataca* (see Note 2). These official potters were listed as subordinate to don Diego Chacha, *kuraka* of the *ayllu Taypi Pataca* 2 in Yanque.

[1]In Yanque, two *ayllus* listed as *Taypi Pataca*, but with different *kurakas*, suggesting that they were separate micro *ayllus* within the middle-ranking macro *ayllu Pahana [Payan]*. The second of these is probably *Pahana Collana Pataca* (i.e. the highest ranked micro *ayllu* of the *Pahana [Payan]* macro *ayllu*) because the *kuraka* is also listed as the head of outlier *ayllu* in the herding settlements of Mamaniviri and Hivillaya, as well as the head of a group of official potters from the *ayllu Pahana Cayao Pataca* of Coporaque. If this is the case, then the first *Taypi Pataca* must have been either the low or middle ranked *ayllu* within the *Pahana* macro *ayllu* (i.e. *Pahana Taypi Pataca* or *Pahana Cayao Pataca*).
[2]Original document is damaged, leaving name of *kuraka* illegible.
[3]For *ayllu Taypi Pataca* 2, the two *estancias* are listed together. The second is spelled "Vllaya" in the section header, but as "Hivillaya in the section summary.

Figure 6.2. Schematic of ayllu outliers in herding villages subject to kurakas in Yanque and Coporaque. Yanquecollaguas Urinsaya.

between 10 and 50 alpacas each, for a total of 510 head. As paramount kuraka of the province, Halanoca was also unique in that he held authority over pro-duction enclaves in prime maize-growing lands of Huanca and Lluta, located 55 aerial km to the south of Yanque near the headwaters of the Siguas River.

The populations of these maize-producing enclaves were even more het-erogeneous than those of the herding settlements. Huanca and Lluta were composed of ayllu outliers not only from Yaquecollaguas but also from Ca-banaconde and Laricollaguas (Gelles 2000; Robinson 2003b). Additionally, large groups of colonists from all three repartimientos were settled in the valley of Arequipa, 90 km to the south (cf. Galdos Rodríguez 1984; Guillet 1992). Although these colonies were not recorded in the visitas, they were registered in the summary ledger (*tasa*) from the Toledan visita general of 1570–75 (Table 6.3) (Cook et al. 1975 [1582]). In the tasa, they were explicitly accounted as part of the Collaguas population and remained subjects of the kurakas in the Colca Valley (ibid: 217–23). Specifically, 481 Collagua and Ca-bana tributary households were recorded as residents of the right bank of the

Table 6.3. Collagua colonists (*mitmaqkuna*) living in La Chimba of Arequipa, 1582

Repartimiento	Tributaries (Adult Males)	Elderly/ Infirm	Males (< 18 years)	Females (All Ages)	Totals
Yanquecollaguas	141	14	122	288	565
Laricollaguas	159	9	159	312	639
Cabanaconde	181	11	192	421	805
Totals	481	34	473	1,021	2,009

Source: From the *Tasa de la visita general de Francisco de Toledo* (Cook et al. 1975 [1582]:217–18, 220–23). Categories are from the original.

Chili River ("La Chimba") in Arequipa—141 from Yanquecollaguas, 159 from Laricollaguas, and 181 from Cabanaconde—a major presence totaling 2,009 individuals (see Table 6.3) (Cook et al. 1975 [1582]:217–18, 220–23).[17]

It is unclear whether these outlying colonies in Arequipa, Huanca, and Lluta were established under Inka aegis or if they had roots in the LIP or earlier times. Recent survey work around Huanca by Erika Simborth reports settlements with architecture and ceramic assemblages indistinguishable from that of settlements in Yanquecollaguas.[18] Neither does the tasa specify if the colonists in Arequipa were exclusively subjects of the paramount kurakas or if they were from several macro- or pataca-level ayllus. In any case, the valley of Arequipa under Inka rule was a complex, multiethnic mosaic of the sort that Murra predicted would exist in the outlier regions of vertical archipelagos (Galdos Rodríguez 1987; Murra 1972).[19]

In other important respects, however, ecological complementarity practices of the Collaguas did not work in the ways predicted by the Murra model. As Van Buren has shown (1996), the far-flung vertical archipelago systems typical of the large highland polities of the south-central Andes did not to function to provision whole populations but underwrote a more limited range of commensal exchanges, the production of prestige goods, and other elite prerogatives. As I illustrate below, this appears to be the case for certain aspects of long-distance colony-homeland relations among the Collaguas as well. More than this, however, the visita declarations from the Collaguas provide insights into how *multiple modes and scales* of ecological complementarity were practiced simultaneously among different segments of Collagua society. These run the gamut of most documented forms of ecological complementarity: household level "microverticality" (direct access to multiple ecological zones at the household scale; see Brush 1977), seasonal transhumance of households (or some household members), intra-ayllu exchange of complementary goods, and strategic mobilization of staple and wealth goods by elites. Clearly these practices were not mutually exclusive but coexisted, probably within a nested set of complementary logistics (see Wernke 2006a). Rather than as part of system of generalized redistribution, then, outlier colonies in vertical archipelagos were linked to their home communities through a variety of measures. But as shown below, produce from these outlier enclaves was not used to provision the high-elevation population as a whole but was mobilized to underwrite the production of prestige goods and other activities related to elite prerogatives.

Reducción, Segmentation, and Succession

These supra-local political and economic ties were increasingly tenuous by the end of the sixteenth century, as resettlement and the structure of Toledan administration cleaved the lower strata of the extant sociopolitical hierarchy between different reducciones. The disarticulation of pataca-level Collagua-Inka structures of authority is evident in the listing of separate kurakas for the same ayllu in adjacent reducciones. In several cases, the same pataca ayllu appears in more than one village, and each group is listed with a separate kuraka, suggesting that they were split into segments that were administered as separate units in each reducción. This kind of disarticulation was probably negotiated between local elites and the Toledan visitadores during the visita general.

The apical ayllu Collana illustrates how pataca-level political leadership was partitioned between villages while higher-order structures of political authority were preserved. In the case of ayllu Collana of Hanansaya, most of the data from Yanque are missing, but the majority of the ayllu probably lived there, given that only a small segment (registered as ayllu Collana Malco) of 25 tributary households resided in Coporaque (APY Yanquecollaguas Hanansaya 1615–17, fols. 480v–493r).[20] In any case, the kuraka of the ayllu Collana segment in Yanque, Joan Halanoca, was also the paramount kuraka of the entire province.

Of course, colonial authorities, doubtless much like their Inkaic counterparts, could and did intervene in the replacement and succession of specific ayllu leaders. The visitas register several instances in which the visitador replaced kurakas who hid tributaries from the census or otherwise neglected tribute collection.[21] However, given the intense pressure from the Crown to increase tribute extraction (and thus to minimize social upheaval), they also had to take indigenous traditions and expectations regarding succession and legitimacy of rule into consideration. For example, similar to its counterpart in the upper moiety, the apical ayllu Collana of Urinsaya also was divided between Yanque and Coporaque, and its kuraka in Yanque, one Jusepe Guaasuri, was registered as the paramount kuraka of the moiety (Verdugo and

Colmenares 1977 [1591]:192 [fol. 1r]).[22] Consistent with Ulloa's description of
the ascribed status of the apical kurakas in the province, Guaasuri, son of the
previous paramount, had recently inherited the office and was only nine years
old at the time of the 1591 visita (Verdugo and Colmenares 1977 [1591]:192 [fol.
1r]). However, Guaasuri was the legitimate successor only according to the
European tradition of primogenitor, and not according to indigenous rules of
succession. As Ulloa (1965 [1586]:330) explained in detail, indigenous tradition prescribed priority of succession to the brother of the former (deceased)
principal kuraka over the son, even the son of his primary wife.[23] Therefore,
according to these rules, Guaasuri, as son of the former kuraka, should have
been passed over in preference to his paternal uncle. However, because of his
young age, a proxy was needed to fulfill Guaasuri's obligations as moiety paramount, and, as noted earlier by Guillermo Cock (1976–77:102–3), the choice
of this proxy is illustrative. Acting in his stead, under the title of gobernador
(second in charge), was Guaasuri's paternal uncle, don Francisco Yncapacta
(Verdugo and Colmenares 1977 [1591]:192, 343 [fols. 1r–2r, 97r]). So it appears
that the legitimate successor from the point of view of the community (the
brother of the former kuraka) remained the de facto authority of Yanquecollaguas Urinsaya despite the alteration of the rules of succession. The tenure of
Yncapacta as gobernador was temporary, however, and 26 years later, in 1617,
this second-in-charge position had reverted to the wealthy lord of the ayllu
Pahana Collana Pataca of Coporaque—that is, the highest ranked pataca of
the middle-ranked macro-ayllu Pahana.[24] This is significant in showing that
the tripartite ranking scheme was in fact instituted (at least among Urinsaya
ayllus), since it is the structurally "correct" individual to fill this second-high-
est post in the moiety. Presumably he was appointed in place of Yncapacta
after Guaasuri reached adulthood and was deemed capable of fulfilling his
role as paramount.

A Regional View of Collagua Community Complementarity Patterns

The visitas provide detailed evidence for reconstructing how this widely dispersed constellation of ayllus structured complementarity relationships between agriculturalists and pastoralists. In the discussion that follows, the declarations of three visitas—from 1591, 1604, and 1615–17—have been combined
to provide the most complete "composite cross-sectional" view of the agricultural and pastoral economies of Yanquecollaguas. Though not synchronic as
in a true cross-sectional study, combining the visitas in this way was necessary
because no complete data for both moieties from any given census year are
lacking. Therefore, for the Hanansaya moiety declarations, the 1615–17 visita

is used for all villages except for Yanque, which is missing. In its place, the portion of the Yanque section that remains in the 1591 Hanansaya visita fragment is used. For the Urinsaya moiety, the 1604 visita is used for all villages again except for Yanque, which is derived from the 1591 Urinsaya visita.

Village-Scale Agricultural Declarations

The total field areas and crops declared by each village in the visitas provide a first index of the organization of agro-pastoral production in Yanquecollaguas (see also Wernke and Whitmore 2009).[25] Figure 6.3 represents the cross-sectional 1591–1617 field declarations from the visitas. The data presented graphically on the map are also summarized in Table 6.4. On the map, pie chart size is proportional to total agricultural field area declared (in topos). As one would expect, agricultural landholding declarations per village generally decrease moving up the valley toward the pastoralist zones, with the greatest areas declared by villages in the valley's agricultural core—Achoma, Yanque, and Coporaque—followed by the mid-elevation suni zone villages of Chivay, Canocota and Tuti, and the much smaller areas declared in the high-elevation herding villages of Callalli, Sibayo, Tisco, Guaraoma, and Mamaniviri. Also, the percentage of maize is greater in the lower-elevation village of Achoma (67 percent) than in Coporaque (59 percent) or Yanque (42

Table 6.4. Crop declarations by village, Yanquecollaguas, 1591/1604/1615–17

Village	Moiety	Maize	Quinoa	Potatoes	Kañiwa	Other	Unknown	Total (topos)
Huanca	Hanan	96%	0%	0%	0%	0%	4%	30
Lluta	Hanan	93%	0%	2%	0%	0%	5%	51
Maca	Hanan	83%	17%	0%	0%	0%	0%	45
Achoma	Both	67%	32%	0%	0%	0%	0%	373
Yanque	Both	42%	27%	1%	0%	0%	30%	804
Coporaque	Both	59%	39%	1%	1%	0%	1%	1,066
Chivay	Hanan	58%	40%	0%	1%	0%	1%	251
Canocota	Urin	18%	71%	6%	0%	0%	4%	125
Tuti	Both	16%	46%	22%	14%	0%	2%	524
Callalli	Urin	74%	24%	1%	0%	0%	1%	47
Sibayo	Both	17%	4%	70%	0%	0%	8%	241
Tisco	Both	15%	8%	47%	1%	0%	28%	376
Mamaniviri	Urin	30%	57%	12%	0%	0%	1%	45
Guaraoma	Urin	70%	26%	2%	0%	2%	0%	12

Note: Due to the fragmentary nature of the original documents, the data for Yanque Hanansaya, Achoma Hanansaya, and Achoma Urinsaya are incomplete. Villages listed in order of increasing elevation. See Figure 6.3 for spatial representation.

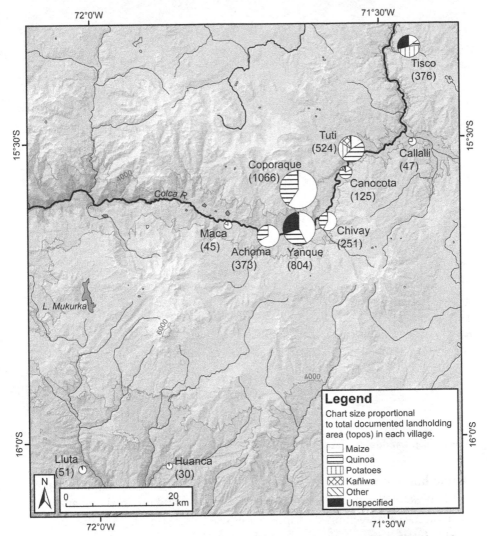

Figure 6.3. Crop declarations by village, Yanquecollaguas, 1591, 1604, and 1615–17. See Table 6.4 for data summary.

percent),[26] and maize dominated the cultivar regime of the lower-elevation villages of Huanca and Lluta (96 and 93 percent, respectively). Clearly, maize was cultivated preferentially to other crops where it could produce reliable yields. By contrast, the proportion of more frost-tolerant quinoa, cañagua, and potatoes increases with elevation.

The total agricultural landholding area claimed per household also generally decreases moving up the valley. Households among villages in the kichwa zone (Huanca, Lluta, Maca, Achoma, Yanque, Coporaque, and Chivay) tend to have more agricultural land, with an average of 1.7 topos per household,

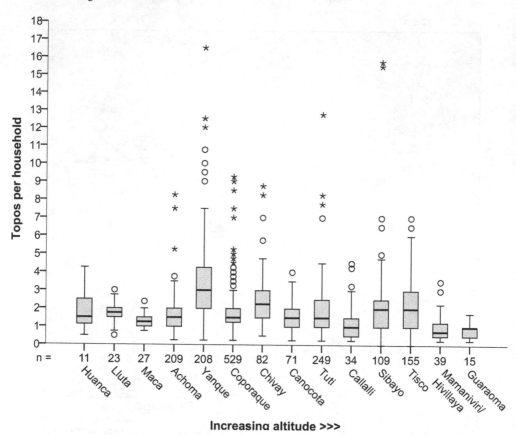

Figure 6.4. Landholding area per household. Outliers and extremes not displayed.

while households in the suni zone (Canocota and Tuti) average 1.4 topos, and those in the puna (Callalli, Sibayo, Tisco, Mamaniviri/Hivillaya, and Guaraoma) average only 0.8 topos per household.[27] But there is also considerable intervillage variability within the central valley in terms of the distribution of landholdings per household. Yanque especially stands out for its high median household landholdings: 3.0 topos (Figure 6.4).

The boxplots in Figure 6.4 illustrate inter- and intravillage inequalities in land wealth. Clearly, residents of the provincial capital tended to have more land overall than the other villages as a group, but there were also greater inequalities in land wealth within Yanque than in other villages. The wealth of Yanque's households as a group is apparent in the high lower hinge and median values for the village: The median household in Yanque claimed more agricultural field area than even the wealthiest house in the third quartile (the upper hinge) of the next richest villages. The greater stratification of wealth among Yanque households is reflected in its broad midspread and the great disparity between the first and fourth quartiles (2–4.25 topos per household). By contrast, the midspread of households in Maca, Achoma, and Coporaque possessed a much smaller range of field areas, illustrating a more homogeneous middle class of landholders.[28]

The outlier and extreme cases in the boxplot represent the kurakas and other elite households which are far wealthier relative to the general population of tributary households (*indios tributarios*). As would be expected, those of Yanque were among the wealthiest, but the kurakas (denoted by the circles and asterisks) of the other villages also clearly stand apart from their respective tributary populations. Interestingly, in Yanque, the person with the most land was not the paramount kuraka of Urinsaya (i.e., the kuraka of Collana ayllu), the nine-year-old Jusepe Guaasuri, but rather his uncle, Francisco Yncapacta, who, as I discussed earlier, was the "legitimate" heir to the position according to the indigenous rules of succession but was serving instead as gobernador. Thus it appears that although the Spanish interceded in the matter of succession, Yncapacta, although not the de jure paramount, did not lose access to land wealth.

Political rank and ayllu affiliation affected not only the total landholdings of a given household but also their access to supra-local fields. The proportions of crops displayed in the map of Figure 6.3 also reveal that herding households in the puna had access to supra-local fields. This is most obviously evident in maize declarations in the suni and puna zone villages, because maize agriculture is impossible at these elevations (see also Table 6.4). Among the high-elevation herding settlements (Callalli, Sibayo, Tisco, and the estancias of Mamaniviri/Hivillaya and Guaraoma), over a quarter (29 percent, or 72 of 249 households) claimed maize fields. Access to maize fields was skewed to wealthier households; as is evident in Figure 6.5, households in the suni and puna zone villages with maize fields tend to have more total agricultural landholdings than those without maize fields. Most of these fields were located in the central valley around Coporaque and Yanque, and the patterning of their locations illuminates how households gained access to these fields through their ayllu membership. For example, the mixed agro-pastoral village of Tuti appears to have been connected via ancestral ayllu ties to Coporaque. Virtually all (27.25 of the 28 topos) of the fields located in Coporaque that were claimed by households from other villages were from Tuti (9.25 topos), Sibayo (8.25 topos), and Tisco (10.25 topos).[29] As I illustrated graphically in Figure 6.2, these villages all have outlier ayllu segments headed by kurakas in Coporaque, so their access to these fields in Coporaque was clearly mediated by their ayllu affiliation.

Households in the herding villages with large fieldholdings also declared

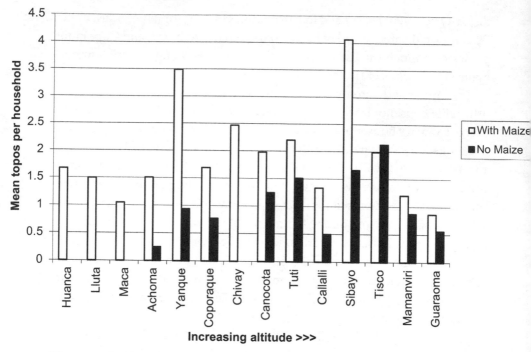

Figure 6.5. Comparison of average landholdings per household among households with maize fields and households without maize fields.

fields in the outlying maize production enclaves of Huanca, Lluta, and Arequipa. Fields in these three maize-production enclaves claimed by households in Callalli, Sibayo, Tisco, and the estancias total 45.75 topos. Thus rather than (or, at least, in addition to) obtaining kichwa zone agricultural produce through redistribution by kurakas or direct trade, these (generally well off) puna households gained direct access to the means of its production, probably through their respective kurakas, and cultivated agricultural fields in lower elevations themselves. This kind of direct access to supra-local maize fields would have required households to either send family members or proxies to tend their fields or to take up part-time residence in the villages near their maize fields. An example is found in the fragmentary section from Yanque in 1604, where the visitador Juan de Rivero noted that the ayllu segment of Collana of Tisco were not censused in their home village "because they were absent and therefore registered in this village of Yanque because their leader had time to assemble them" (translation by Treacy 1989: 220; APY Yanquecollaguas Urinsaya 1604, fol. 317v–318r). This section of the visita was recorded during the planting month of October, so this ayllu Collana segment from Tisco may have been in Yanque to cultivate their fields (see also Treacy 1989b:219–20).

Table 6.5. Nonlocal household fields, Yanquecollaguas 1591/1604/1615–17

Village of Location of Outlier Fields (topos)
Residence

	Arequipa	Huanca	Lluta	Achoma	Yanque	Coporaque	Canocota	Tuti	Callalli	Total
Achoma[a]	9.25	0	0	n/a	0	0	0	0	1	10.25
Yanque[b]	26.75	2	3.5	0.25	n/a	0	0	5.75	0	38.25
Coporaque	33.25	0.25	2.5	0.5	2.75	n/a	0.75	1.25	0	41.25
Chivay	3.25	0	0	2.25	1	0	0	3	0	9.50
Canocota	1.75	0	0.5	0	0	0.25	n/a	0.75	0	3.25
Tuti	6.5	0	0	7.25	3	9.25	0	n/a	0	26.00
Callalli	5	0	0	7	0	0	0	0	n/a	12.00
Sibayo	13.5	0	2	0	0	8.25	0	1	1	25.75
Tisco	19	0	2	0	3	10.25	0	11.25	0	45.50
Mamanviri	0	0	0	0	0	0	0	1.75	0	1.75
Guaraoma	4.25	0	0	0	0	0	0.5	0	0	4.75
Totals:	122.5	2.25	10.5	17.25	9.75	28.00	1.25	24.75	2.00	218.25

Notes: Villages listed in order of increasing altitude. Hanansaya data from Yanquecollaguas Hanansaya 1615–17, except Yanque, from APY Yanquecollaguas Hanansaya 1591 (incomplete; see Table 3.3). Achoma section of 1615–17 Hanansaya data are incomplete; see Table 3.3. Urinsaya data from APY Yanquecollaguas Urinsaya 1604, except Yanque, from Yanquecollaguas Urinsaya 1591 (Verdugo and Colmenares 1977 [1591]). Achoma section of 1604 Urinsaya data incomplete; see Table 3.3.
a. Incomplete data for both Hanansaya and Urinsaya; see Table 3.3.
b. Incomplete data for Hanansaya; see Table 3.3.

Moreover, this kind of household-level access to nonlocal fields was also quite common in the villages of the central valley. Agriculturally well-endowed households in Yanque, Coporaque, Achoma, and Chivay claimed far-flung maize fields along the western bank of the Chili River adjacent to the city of Arequipa and near the villages of Huanca and Lluta (Figure 6.3). These fields constitute significant quantities of Collagua household outlier landholdings, totaling 135 topos (Table 6.5). These fields were almost certainly associated with large colonies of Collagua households settled around the city of Arequipa.

Village-Scale Livestock Declarations

The Collaguas were renowned for their massive camelid herds, and wool was their primary source of wealth—in fact, none of the colonial tribute of Yanquecollaguas and Laricollaguas was levied in agricultural goods. Instead, 60 percent of their tax burden was levied in camelids and textiles made from alpaca wool, and the remaining 40 percent was levied in cash (Cook et al. 1975 [1582]:217–21). In particular, Collagua textile tribute was levied in coarse homespun, or *ropa de abasca* (from the Quechua *ahuasca*), an important commodity because it was one of the provisions that Spanish patrons were legally required to furnish for their native laborers (Guillet 1992:23). But the predominance of pastoralist products in the Collagua tax assessment was almost certainly built on Inka-era precedents (although, of course, tribute was levied in labor, not in specie or kind). As I discuss below, the presence of cumbicamayocs—weavers of fine cumbi cloth, among the most prestigious crafted goods in the Inka empire—in Yanque and Achoma also indicates that the production of fine textiles was also an important component of the Collagua provincial political economy under Inka rule.

Livestock declarations in the visitas fall far short of the actual total herd size of the Collaguas because they only record livestock that was the personal property of individual households. There is no reliable account of the total size of the herds of the Collaguas during early colonial times, but a witness in a judicial inquiry from 1585–86 estimated that the flocks of Callalli and Tisco alone totaled over 25,000 head (AGI Justicia 480, fol. 1196v, published in Crespo 1977:71–72). The combined declarations of these two villages in the visitas—2,354 head—is less than one-tenth of this estimate. Also, even in the herding villages of Callalli, Sibayo, and Tisco, only about one-third of households claimed livestock in the visitas (Figure 6.6). Apparently there

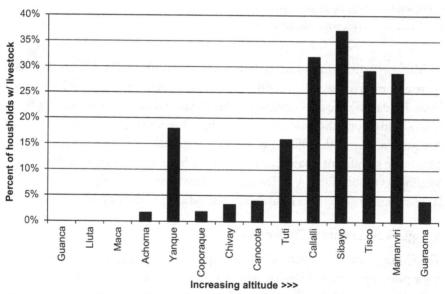

Figure 6.6. Proportion of households with livestock, by village. Hanansaya data from Yanquecollaguas Hanansaya 1615–17, except Yanque, from APY Yanquecollaguas Hanansaya 1591 (incomplete; see Table 8.1). Achoma section of 1615–17 Hanansaya data are incomplete; see Table 6.1. Urinsaya data from APY Yanquecollaguas Urinsaya 1604, except Yanque, from Yanquecollaguas Urinsaya 1591 (Verdugo and Colmenares 1977 [1591]). Achoma section of 1604 Urinsaya data incomplete.

were much larger herds held collectively, and many of the remaining two-thirds of households without personal livestock were probably dedicated to tending these communal flocks.

In contrast to village-level landholdings, the quantity of livestock claimed per village and the percentage of households that claim livestock generally increases with elevation (Figure 6.6). With the exception of Yanque Hanansaya, only 1–3 percent of households in kichwa zone villages declared any livestock. The percentage of households with livestock increases to between 29 and 37 percent in Callalli, Sibayo, and Tisco. Of the 249 households with livestock in these three villages, 69 percent also claimed agricultural fields, and as I discussed above, 29 percent claim at least one maize field. By contrast, only 25 percent of households in these villages claimed fields but no livestock. Kurakas and other elite households with many agricultural landholdings claimed especially large numbers of livestock. For example, in Sibayo, the kuraka of ayllu Paragra Pahana Collana Pataca, don Luis Chacha, claimed 280 head of livestock. Along with 200 alpacas and llamas (ganado de la tierra), Chacha was one of only a handful of kurakas that claimed Old World live-stock in the visitas—40 cattle and 40 goats. He was also wealthy in landhold-ings, claiming the third largest amount of land in the visitas—a total of 15.5 topos—over half of which (8.5 topos) were declared as maize fields.

Overall, the livestock declared in the visitas reflects the wool production orientation of camelid pastoralism among the Collaguas. The great predomi-nance of specified camelids were alpacas, and only a handful of European domesticas (cattle, sheep, goats) were declared (Figure 6.7).

In the central valley, the owners of livestock claimed in Yanque and Copor-aque were almost exclusively kurakas and other elite households with large landholdings. Clearly, livestock ownership was both a marker and motor of wealth and status. For example, 208 of the 212 head of livestock declared in Coporaque Urinsaya pertained to Martin Chuquilanco, kuraka of the ayllu Pahana Collana Pataca (APY Yanquecollaguas Urinsaya 1604, fol. 236r). All 30 head (alpacas) of Yanque Urinsaya were claimed by the second in charge of ayllu Collana, Garcia Checa (Verdugo and Colmenares 1977 [1591]:193 [fol. 2r]). Most significantly, as I mentioned above, the yanaconas of the paramount lord of the province, Joan Halanoca of Yanque Hanansaya (ayllu Collana), claimed a total of 510 head of livestock. However, these retainers claimed virtually no agricultural fields—only two topos among all of them. As I discuss below, it appears that they obtained agricultural produce through the paramount kuraka Halanoca in exchange for wool, which he then used to supply an enclave of weavers of fine cumbi cloth who were also his personal retainers (a point also raised by Cock Carrasco 1976–77:104–5).

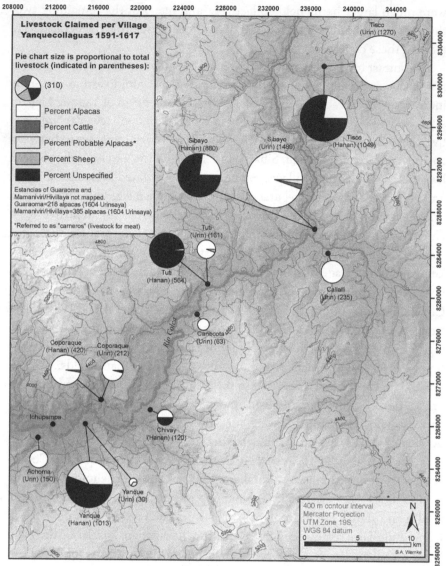

Figure 6.7. Livestock declarations by village, Yanquecollaguas 1591, 1604, and 1615–17.

Kurakas, Craft Specialists, and the Provincial Political Economy

Embedded within the ayllu structure of the Collaguas were groups of official Inka state-craft specialists. They manufactured each of the primary classes of prestige goods that circulated in the imperial political economy—fine cumbi cloth, pottery, and metal (specifically, silver) items. All of these artisans were residents of the central valley in the villages of Yanque, Coporaque, and Achoma, with an outlier group of silversmiths in Maca. As mediators of land-tenure rights, kurakas almost certainly provisioned these groups with their agricultural fields.

Cumbi cloth was among the most valued prestige goods in the Inka imperial economy (Murra 1962b). As was the case throughout Tawantinsuyu, the four groups of cumbicamayoc registered in the Yanquecollaguas visitas (three in Yanque and one in Achoma) were attached specialists held in retainer by their respective kurakas. In the fragment that remains of the Yanque section of the 1591 Hanansaya visita, a group of cumbicamayoc who pertained to the paramount kuraka Halanoca precedes the listing of his yanacona.[30] There were 14 tributary households (as well as four elderly households) listed among these weavers. Based on their field declarations, they were clearly self-sufficient in terms of agricultural produce, claiming a total of 47.25 topos and averaging 2.8 topos of land per household, twice the average per household landholdings of Coporaque or Achoma. However, they declared no livestock or other access to wool, and so they would not have been able to provision themselves with the material for their weavings. The most parsimonious answer to the question of where they obtained their wool is through their kuraka, who, as I discussed above, also held authority over pastoralist yanacona and other ayllu segments of herders. Thus it appears that the paramount kuraka underwrote prestige goods production by strategically mobilizing staple goods. He most likely converted maize from his extensive landholdings and outlier ayllu segments into wool through exchange with his pastoralist yanacona, and then used that wool to supply his cumbicamayoc.[31]

Other kurakas appear to have similarly mobilized their diverse agro-pastoral resources to provide wool for their cumbicamayoc groups. While they did not have pastoralist yanacona like the provincial paramount, many had large personal herds and also held authority over outlier ayllu segments in the puna. There were two separate cumbicamayoc groups among the ayllus of Urinsaya in Yanque. One (a group of six tributary households and one elderly household) pertained to the kuraka Joan Guaasuri of the apical ayllu Collana, who also held authority over ayllu segments in the herding village of Tisco and the estancia of Mamaniviri (see Figure 6.2).[32] These weavers also had plenty of agricultural fields, with an average of 2.5 topos per household (Table 6.6). The other cumbicamayoc group of Yanque Urinsaya were the subjects of the kuraka of the ayllu Taypi Pataca of Yanque, Diego Chacha, who also held authority over herders in the estancias of Mamaniviri and Hivillaya.[33] This group of weavers claimed on average 1.6 topos per household (Table 6.6). In Achoma Urinsaya, a small group of cumbicamayoc households (three tributary households, two widows, and one elderly household) were subjects of the local kuraka of the ayllu Collana Pataca (APY Yanquecollaguas Urinsaya

1604, fols. 383v–385v). They were also agriculturally self-sufficient, with an average of 1.2 topos per household. However, this kuraka is not listed as head of any outlying ayllu segments in the puna and did not claim any personal livestock, so it is unclear how these weavers were supplied; he may have obtained wool through the paramount kuraka or some other means.

Two ayllu segments of silversmiths were also registered in the visitas, one of Hanansaya in the village of Maca and one of Urinsaya in Achoma. The silversmiths of Achoma, like the cumbicamayos there, were part of the ayllu Collana Pataca, and subject to its local kuraka.[34] In addition to his cumbicamayos and yanaconas, the apical kuraka Halanoca held authority over a large ayllu segment of silversmiths reduced to Maca, located within the repartimiento of Laricollaguas.[35] No such outlier ayllus from Laricollaguas are found within the territory of Yanquecollaguas, illustrating the one-way porosity of the

Table 6.6. Landholdings and livestock of craft specialists, Yanquecollaguas 1591/1604/1615–17

Village	Moiety	Year	Ayllu	N	Landholdings/ Household (topos)		Livestock per Household	
					Mean	Sum	Mean	Sum
Achoma	Urin	1604	Cumbicamayocs (of kuraka of Collana Pataca)	4	1.19	4.75	0	0
			Silversmiths of Collana Pataca	5	1.75	8.75	0	0
Coporaque	Hanan	1616	Official potters	40	1.02	40.75	0	0
	Urin	1604	Potters of Pahana Collana Pataca	6	1.13	6.75	0	0
			Official potters of [Pahana] Collana Pataca	8	0.88	7.00	0	0
Maca	Hanan	1616	Silversmiths (subjects of paramount kuraka)	33	0.97	32.00	0	0
Yanque	Hanan	1591	Cumbicamayocs (of paramount kuraka)	19	2.49	47.25	0	0
			Yanaconas (of paramount kuraka)	20	0.10	2.00	26	510
	Urin	1591	Cumbicamayocs (of kuraka of Collana)	7	2.43	17.00	0	0
			Cumbicamayocs (of kuraka of Taypi Pataca)	8	1.56	12.50	0	0

Note: N = Number of households.

boundary and the power asymmetry between the repartimientos: The authority of the paramounts of Yanquecollaguas extended into Laricollaguas, but not vice versa.[36]

Ayllus of pottery specialists are also listed in the visitas, providing important insights into the organization of pottery production under Inka administration. As discussed in chapter 4, the ubiquity, quality, and standardization of Collagua Inka ceramics clearly point to local, specialized ceramic manufacture. But the question as to whether that production was centralized or dispersed over several production loci throughout the valley remains open. The visitas provide evidence that the situation was probably closer to the former than the latter, since all of the recorded ayllus of potters resided in Coporaque. Compared to the cumbicamayoc weavers, and, to a lesser extent, the silversmiths, the ayllus of potters appear to have had a higher degree of autonomy and do not seem to fit a model of attached specialists. While a full discussion of the organization of pottery production awaits more context-specific and compositional research, the visita data are generally consistent with Janusek's (1999) model of "embedded specialization." Neither wholly independent nor directly attached to elite interests, ayllus of potters appear to have been embedded within the ayllu structure of Yanquecollaguas: two pertained to Urinsaya and one to Hanansaya. In all cases, these ayllus are small and almost certainly remnants of larger ancestral populations. The two groups of Coporaque Urinsaya potters were registered as subsections within the ayllu Pahana Collana Pataca and Pahana Cayao Pataca.[37] The first of these (those of Pahana Collana Pataca) was a small group of six tributary households headed by their local kuraka in Coporaque. The second group, also composed of six tributary households,[38] was registered as the official potters of the ayllu Pahana Cayao Pataca. Although this second group had also been resettled to Coporaque, they were listed as subject to don Diego Chacha, kuraka of the ayllu Taypi Pataca (and lord of a group of cumbicamayoc) in Yanque.[39] Again, the process of reducción appears to have split an ayllu apart, but the original structure of authority was preserved. The ayllu of Hanansaya potters in Coporaque was larger than either of the Urinsaya groups, with 19 tributary households, 11 single men of tributary age, 12 households headed by elderly men and 16 widows and unmarried women. This group was also listed as an ayllu of "official potters" but was not attributed as being a segment of a larger ayllu but was registered with its own kuraka.[40]

A range of craft specialists (cumbi weavers, silversmiths, and potters) and a range of modes of production—from attached to embedded specialization—under Inka administration are thus evident and were in varied states of disarticulation under Toledan administration by the turn of the seventeenth century. Groups of official potters were small but their identities and perhaps their continued crafting activities were distinct enough to be registered as separate ayllu segments. Though the long-term stories of these particular groups are unknown, they were likely absorbed into extant ayllus as the lower-order segments of the ayllu hierarchy shrank and as production, exchange, and consumption patterns changed in the regional colonial economy.

Conclusions

This chapter traced out the improvised order that emerged from the grafting of post-Toledan Spanish colonial administration to extant structures of community organization in Collagua Province, which in turn also sheds light on Inkaic administration of the province. Even as the archaeological indices of colonial rule point to an increasingly coercive and eradicative policy, as local communities were displaced by reducción, a close analysis and spatialized rendering of the visitas reveals how the basic structure of Toledan administration still siphoned tribute through indigenous community institutions, which were themselves hybrid state/local constructs. The effect of Inka administration was to augment and harden inequalities within and between indigenous Collagua ayllus by initiating a program for reordering them according to tripartite, bipartite, and decimal ranking concepts. This arrangement would have limited imperial administrative burdens—both for the Inkas and the Spanish—by minimizing points of contact with local intermediaries while also providing a means for gauging productivity and engendering competition between a nested hierarchy of structurally equivalent tribute units.

Second, complex, supra-local networks of ayllu affiliation and authority continued to structure relations of production, exchange, and consumption between agriculturalists and pastoralists a generation after resettlement. Despite segmentation of some high-ranking ayllus in the central valley after reducción, their leaders continued to hold authority over and collect tribute from members of their ayllus in outlier pastoralist production enclaves in the puna as well as maize-production enclaves in low-lying valleys to the south. At the level of domestic economy, commoner agriculturalist and pastoralist households probably participated in direct exchange with their ayllu cohorts in other production zones to gain access to each other's respective produce. By contrast, elite households maintained direct access to the means of production in all production zones: Wealthy pastoralist households declared maize fields in the central valley and beyond and wealthy agriculturalists in the central valley claimed personal livestock held in the puna. These distinct ecological complementarity practices therefore developed not only as adaptations to ecological imperatives but also as a result of community affiliation and social status.

In terms of its contribution to the regional political economy, the province of Collaguas produced the largest single source of revenue collected in Arequipa during colonial times and was an important source of regional revenue for the Inkas. Collagua kurakas not only extracted surplus of staple goods from their variegated ayllu resources but also (re)distributed staple goods, and the means of their production, to finance the production of prestige goods. Some of the kurakas of the high-ranking ayllus in Yanque and Coporaque also held authority over ayllu segments of official state potters, silversmiths, and cumbicamayoc. The kurakas almost certainly provided each of these groups of artisans with access to agricultural fields, and they were generally self-sufficient in terms of subsistence. It also appears that kurakas financed prestige-goods production by exchanging agricultural produce for wool to provide the materia prima for the cumbi weavers.

In complement to the regional-scale view of this chapter, the analysis of ayllu-level land-tenure patterns in the next chapter illustrates how household access to agricultural fields was mediated by community organization at the local scale and provides a means for reconstructing where those ayllus lived before reducción.

Notes

1. Málaga (1977:101) lists the names of the prehispanic villages reduced to Coporaque but does not provide an archival source. The list appears to be derived from an ethnographic account, since the protocol of reducción by Lope de Suazo has not been identified in the archives. In any case, Málaga states, "Upon conducting the Visita General of Toledo, Lope de Suazo, visitador of the Collaguas, reduced the villages of Tunsa, Llanka, Qcuita, Jamallaya y Suripampa, as well as Chiptapampa, Ccanaque, Mosocchacra, Muraypata, Chucpallu, Marquisahui, Machingaya, Huaynalama, Coporama, Cantupampa, Umañasu and Ccayra, in the current village of Coporaque."

2. I follow Stern's (1982:82) orthographic distinction of mit'a versus mita to refer to the prehispanic and colonial-era institutions, respectively.

3. "Gobernábanse conforme a lo quel inga tenía puesto, que era, por sus ayllos e parcialidades nombraba de cada ayllo un cacique, y eran tres ayllos, llamados Collona, Pasana, Cayao; cada ayllo destos tenía trescientos indios y un principal a quien obedecían, y estos tres principales obedecían al cacique principal, que era sobre todos."

4. These micro-ayllus are imperfectly reproduced in the visitas, probably due to postconquest consolidation and fragmentation. For example, in the 1591 visita of Yanquecollaguas Urinsaya, each of the three micro ayllus are present for the macro-ayllus Collana and Pahana; of the third, Cayao, only the ayllu "Cayao" is listed (in the village of Tuti). However, given Ulloa's description, and the close adherence to this stated ideal in the

cases of Collana and Pahana, there is little reason to doubt that the overall tripartite structure was present. See also Cock Carrasco (1976–77) and Pärssinen (1992:366).

5. This is the pattern within three of the four quarters (or *suyus*: Chinchaysuyu, Antisuyu, and Collasuyu) that divide Cuzco's ritual space. The fourth, Cuntisuyu, may also follow this pattern, but with certain irregularities in the naming of the ceques themselves.

6. Pachacuraca is a compound word combining the Quechua term for "100," *pachaca* (a cognate of the Aymara *pataca*), and the word *kuraka* (*curaca*). The term appears in the preambles for the villages of Tisco and Sibayo in the 1615–17 visita, where the visitador called forth quipucamayos and pachacuracas together with the principal lords and gobernadores (seconds in charge) to ensure that all households were present for accounting (APY Yanquecollaguas Hanansaya 1615–17, fols. 338v–339r, 380v–381v). These declarations not only confirm the existence of pachacuracas but also document that *quipucamayoc* (keepers of quipu-knot records; see Ascher and Ascher 1988, 1997; Quilter and Urton 2002) were still active and consulted by the pachacuracas and colonial authorities in 1617. Quipucamayoc are also mentioned in the 1604 Laricollaguas Urinsaya visita. In that case, they were called forth at the end of the census as a means of checking for accuracy of the census counts (see Cook 2003).

7. There is some ambiguity regarding the rank of the head of Cabanaconde in relation to the paramounts of Yanquecollaguas and Laricollaguas. Cock Carrasco (1976–77) has suggested that the kuraka of Cabanaconde could have been ranked in a third position relative to Yanquecollaguas and Laricollaguas in an analogous fashion to the Collana/Pahana/Cayao triad—that is, Yanque represented Collana, Lari represented Pahana, and Cabanaconde represented Cayao. However, there is no explicit discussion of this in any of the colonial documentation, and given the fact that the Cabanas were considered a separate ethnic group, it seems unlikely. I favor an alternative hypothesis, suggested initially by Pease (1977a:141) and later by Pärssinen (1992:365–66), which posits that the Cabanas were considered a discrete group in contrast to the Collaguas as a whole, and the two were administered as separate ethnic groups within a single province. Málaga Medina (1977:119) suggests a third potential scheme in which Cabanaconde and Laricollaguas together form a lower-ranking, Urin group in relation to the higher-ranking Yanquecollaguas as the Hanan group. But as pointed out by both Pärssinen (1992:364) and Pease (Pease 1977a), this is highly unlikely given the fact that the colonial documentation is unanimous in describing, on the one hand, the unity of the Collaguas as a dyadic pairing of the Laricollaguas and Yanquecollaguas groups, and on the other, the Cabanas, who were a separate ethnic group of distinct origin, language, dress, body modification, and economic focus.

8. The only two of the nine pataca-level logical variants of the Collana/Pahana/Cayao triad that do not appear in Urinsaya are Cayao Collana Pataca and Cayao Taypi Pataca. The names of three other ayllus appear as local variations on these tripartite conventions: Collana Paque, Paragra Pahana Collana Pataca, and Sibayo Pahana Collana Pataca. See Tables 6.1 and 6.2.

9. *Ilaca* (or *hilacata*) is the Aymara term for the headman of an ayllu (Bertonio 1956 [1612]:133).

10. The ayllu Yumasca represents an exception to this pattern, since *yumasca* is a Quechua, not Aymara, word, suggesting that it was not of indigenous Collagua origin. In any case, yumasca, from the root *yumay,* "sperm" or "semen" (González Holguín and Porras Barrenechea 1989 [1608]:371), is the conjugated participial form, meaning "inseminated," suggesting "patrilineage." However, the participial form in Quechua does not orient passive influence interpretation, so it could mean either "the one who inseminated" (some entity, for example, its moiety) or "the one inseminated by" (some entity, perhaps the Inka) (F. Salomon, pers. comm. 2003). Given the seemingly nonlocal linguistic origin of this ayllu, I suspect the latter rather than the former, although scrutiny of naming patterns of individuals within the ayllu and comparison with the other ayllus could potentially clarify whether it was composed of local or nonlocal people.

11. *Malco* (as in the ayllus Checa Malco and Malco) means "lord of vassals" ("señor de vasallos") and is the equivalent of the Quechua term *kuraka,* meaning "lord" or "chieftain" (Bertonio 1956 [1612]:212).

12. Also, in the Andes, the right-hand side is generally ranked higher than the left-hand side and associated with Hanan; thus the analogy "Cupi (right) : Hanan :: Checa (left) : Urin." So the Cupi ayllus may have been higher ranked than the Checa (Malco) ayllus, although this must be considered speculative, especially given the fact that the Checa ayllus are listed before the Cupi ayllus in the visita, and ayllus were generally listed in descending order of rank.

13. Similarly, the village of Caylloma was the primary herding settlement for Laricollaguas. An outlier segment of the ayllu Collana resided there that were subject to its kuraka in Lari (Guillet 1992:22).

14. Of these, three (Collana Cayao Pataca, Pahana Collana Pataca, and Pahana Cayao Pataca) were listed as being under the direct authority of their respective kurakas in Coporaque.

15. The estancia of Villaya is also spelled as Hivillaya (APY Yanquecollaguas Urinsaya 1604, fol. 336r). If this second spelling is correct, it probably corresponds to the large terminal prehispanic herding settlement of "Jibillea" or "Jivillea" (my phonetic spellings based on local informants), which I recorded as site YA-093 in the Yanque-Coporaque survey (see chapter 4).

16. Mamaniviri is also spelled Mamanviri (APY Yanquecollaguas Urinsaya 1604, fol. 336r). I have not located this estancia.

17. According to Málaga Medina, they were all reduced to the village of San Juan Bautista de la Chimba (Málaga Medina 1981:49).

18. As in the case of the Moquegua drainage (Stanish 1985, 1989a, 1989b; Van Buren 1993, 1996; Van Buren et al. 1993), future survey and excavations in these outlying areas could shed light on the question of the antiquity of Collagua outlier colonies in Huanca, Lluta, and elsewhere. Stanish (1985, 1989a, 1989b) has cogently argued for explicit correlates of colonist occupations, and advocated the key role of domestic architecture as a marker of ethnic colonization. It is clear that the Collagua materials in Huanca and Lluta are not limited to mortuary contexts or odd trade pieces, but represent a much more substantial presence, including architecture and probably entire ceramic assemblages. The antiquity of these site-unit intrusions remains an open question, though they seem

to predominate from the Late Horizon—a pattern also consistent with the findings in Moquegua.

19. In addition to the Collaguas and Cabanas, colonists from other ethnic groups resident in the valley at the time reducción included the Chumbivilcas, the Canas and Canchis, and the Yuminas (Galdos Rodríguez 1987; Julien 1985).

20. The headman of the Coporaque segment of ayllu Collana was not exempt from tribute (presumably because of the small size of the ayllu segment and/or its colonial origin), but nonetheless, as headman of the highest ranking ayllu segment in the village, he was listed as the mayor (alcalde) of Coporaque (APY Yanquecollaguas Hanansaya 1615–17, fol. 480v).

21. Such was the case in 1604 for the kuraka of ayllu Collana (Urinsaya) of the herding village of Tisco, one Felipe Guapucho, who was not present during the visita to that village, but instead was in Yanque (APY Yanquecollaguas Urinsaya 1604, fols. 106v–107r). When the visitador later arrived in Yanque to conduct the census, Guapucho, along with a large group of households from his ayllu was still there. Upon registering this ayllu while in Yanque, the visitador reprimanded Guapucho and appointed don Francisco Guaasuri to be the kuraka of the ayllu (ibid., fols. 317v–318r). "Visita of Tuesday, October nineteenth of said year [1604], of the Indians of the ayllo Collana, who are reduced in the village of Tisco, were not registered there because they were absent and are instead registered here in this village of Yanque because time was given to the headman to gather them up. Ayllo Collana of the village of Tisco, of whom don Francisco Guaasuri is placed as headman because don Felipe Guapucho, who was the headman, is a fugitive and does not fulfill the collection of taxes" (APY Yanquecollaguas Urinsaya 1604, fols. 106v–107r; my translation). ("Vissita de Martes diez y nueve de Otubre de el dicho año de los yndios de el aillo Collana, que estan reduçidos en el pueblo de Tisco, que no se vissitaron alli por estar aussentes y vissitansse en este pueblo de Ianque porque se le dio tiempo a el prinçipal para juntarlos. Ayllo Collana de el pueblo de Tisco, de que se pone por prinçipal don Françisco Guaasuri, porque don Felipe Guapucho, que lo era, es çimarron y no acude a cobrar la tassa.")

22. This pattern is true of Laricollaguas as well. See Guillet 1992:21–25.

23. "The principal cacique [i.e., kuraka] had command over all of the other headmen, who were very [extremely] obedient in everything that he commanded, as in matters of war or justice or the punishment of offenses. This principal cacique was [had been] placed by the Inka and was succeeded by his sons, and lacking them [sons] by his brothers, although the cacique's legitimate brother was preferred as heir rather than the son, even if legitimate." ("Tenía el cacique principal mando y poder sobre todos los demás principales, los cuales le eran obedientísimos en todo lo que mandaba, así en las cosas de la guerra como en las cosas de justicia y castigo de delitos. Era este cacique puesto por el inga y subcedían sus hijos y a falta dellos sus hermanos, aunque era preferidos en la herencia el hermano legítimo del cacique a su hijo, aunque fuese legítimo.")

24. This kuraka, don Martin Hanco, is listed in the preamble to the visita of Tuti as gobernador of Urinsaya (APY Yanquecollaguas Hanansaya 1615–17, fol. 391r). He is listed as kuraka of the ayllu Pahana Collana Pataca of Coporaque in the 1604 Urinsaya visita.

25. The sample is composed of landholding households that with a male heads of household between 18 and 50 years of age (tributary age), including those (e.g., kurakas) exempted from tribute.

26. Due to damage to the original document, the crops grown in many fields were illegible in the 1591 Urinsaya visita; hence, the high percentage of fields of "unknown" crop type. So this figure almost certainly underrepresents the percentage of maize in Yanque.

27. For these and the following figures regarding land tenure and livestock holdings, I have structured my database queries such that "households" includes those headed by men 18 years of age and older, including elderly households, kurakas, single adult men. These figures also include landless households (as defined by the criteria just mentioned). They exclude orphans younger than 18 years old (except for one special case: the paramount kuraka of Yanquecollaguas Urinsaya, Jusepe Guaasuri of ayllu Collana of Yanque), male heads of household of unspecified or illegible age, widows, and single women.

28. The seemingly high median and midspread values for Tuti, Sibayo, and Tisco—all in the upper reaches of the valley—can be explained in part by the high proportion of potato fields claimed in these villages. As I discussed above, potato fields make up a much higher percentage of the land claimed in these villages (26 percent of the field area claimed in Tuti, 68 percent in Sibayo, and 47 percent in Tisco) than in the villages in the central valley, where virtually no potato fields were declared. As a high-altitude crop, potatoes are generally grown in larger fields that require frequent fallowing, so households need more fields overall in order to manage rotational fallowing.

29. These are conservative figures because they only include those outlier fields that were specifically located by both toponym and village. Many maize fields claimed in the puna were located by toponym only, so they cannot be located by village.

30. Specifically, the oficiales cumbicayos are listed with a headman (one Juan Aromoto), but "subject to" don Joan Halanoca. Thus it appears that Aromoto was the mandón but the group as a whole pertained to Halanoca. The yanaconas are listed as "Yndios Yanaconas de don Joan Halanoca que estan rreduzidos en este pueblo." While yanacona were normally exempt from tribute, in this case the households headed by tributary age men were listed as tributaries. There were 10 tributary households, two households headed by elderly men, and one orphan.

31. Undoubtedly, some of the cumbi produced in the Colca was also made from the wool of the vicuña (*Vicugna vicugna*), a wild Andean camelid abundant in the high puna surrounding the valley. During Inkaic times, the kurakas or other state administrators probably sponsored festivals to wrangle and sheer the chest fur of the vicuñas that they then supplied to the cumbicamayoc.

32. In the 1591 visita, the first cumbicamayoc ayllu is listed as "Yndios Officiales Cumbicamayos del Aillo Co [damaged] [burned]" (Verdugo and Colmenares 1977 [1591]:260 [fol. 42r]). Fortunately, this section is included within the fragmentary section of Yanque preserved in the 1604 visita, and it can be confirmed that this was referring to Collana ayllu: "Yndios Cunbicamayos del ayllo Collana de la parçialidad de Urinsaya, de que es prinçipal don Jusepe Guaasuri, caçique prinçipal de toda la dicha parçialidad" (APY Yanquecollaguas Urinsaya 1604, fol. 66r).

33. In the 1591 visita, the second group of cumbicamayocs is listed as "Yndios Cumbica-mayos [damaged] de Don [damaged] de que es principal dicho Martin Taco." In the 1604 visita, this section header is undamaged: "Yndios Cunbicamayos deste ayllo Taypi Pataca, de don Diego Chacha, de que es prinçipal Martin Taca [sic]."

34. There were four tributary households, one widow, and one elderly man recorded under the heading of yndios plateros of Collana Pataca ayllu in Achoma (APY Yanquecollaguas Urinsaya 1604, fols. 385v–387v). As I noted in Table 8.2, the ayllu Collana Pataca of Achoma had been split in two, but the two were rejoined by the visitador at the death of one of the kurakas and placed under the authority of surviving kuraka, don Miguel Sapana (Çapana) (APY Yanquecollaguas Urinsaya 1604, fol. 387v).

35. A page (two folios) is missing from the section that records the silversmiths of Maca, but among the folios present, there were 29 tributary households, five households headed by elderly men, 18 widows and unmarried women, two orphan boys, and one orphan girl.

36. I thank Maria Benavides for this observation (M. Benavides, pers. comm. 2003).

37. The second of these two are recorded as the "official potters of Cayao Pataca;" how-ever, Cayao Pataca here almost certainly represents a truncated name for the ayllu Pahana Cayao Pataca—that is, the lowest ranked ayllu of the Pahana (Payan) macro ayllu. I arrive at this conclusion because the potters are listed immediately after an ayllu that was re-corded as ayllu Pahana Cayao Pataca in its header (APY Yanquecollaguas Urinsaya 1604, fol. 290r), but similarly truncated as Cayao Pataca in the summary (APY Yanquecollaguas Urinsaya 1604, fol. 309r). Also, these potters are subject to the kuraka of ayllu Taypi Pataca of Yanque (don Diego Chacha), not to any kuraka of the Cayao macro ayllu (ibid., fol. 309v; compare with Verdugo and Colmenares 1977 [1591]:238 [fol. 29v]).

38. Two unmarried women and two households in the elderly and infirm category (APY Yanquecollaguas Urinsaya 1604, fols. 309v–311v).

39. In the 1591 visita to Yanquecollaguas Urinsaya, there are two ayllus with the name Taypi Pataca listed in the Yanque, each with a separate kuraka. The second of these Taypi Pataca ayllus was headed by don Diego Chacha, who, as I discussed above, also held in retainer a group of cumbicamayoc and a group of potters in Coporaque. As I discuss below, he also held authority over ayllu segments of herders in the herding hamlets of Mamaniviri and Villaya (or Hivillaya).

40. Because the previous kuraka had been absent for over two years, a provisional ayllu headman was appointed by the visitador, until the original headman returned. The ayllu header reads, "Ayllo of the official potters of this parcialidad Hanansaya, registered in this village of Santiago de Coporaque, of which the headman was don Juan Suri, but because he has been absent for more than two years, Francisco Limaya is placed in his stead until the aforementioned returns." ("Ayllo de los ofiçiales olleros desta parçialidad Hanansaya, visitados en este pueblo de Santiago de Coporaque, de que estava por prinçipal don Juan Suri, y por estar ausente más a de dos años, se pone en su lugar a Françisco Limaia, asta tanto que venga el susodicho") (APY Yanquecollaguas Hanansaya 1615–17, fol. 603v).

7

THE AYLLU INTERFACE

By taking a trans-conquest perspective, the previous two chapters allowed us to see the common processes involved in how local communities engaged successive Inkaic and Spanish colonial projects aimed at refashioning Collagua society according to ideal images of order and hierarchy. In both cases, new kinds of communities emerged as colonial projects were met by the material and practical dimensions of local landscapes and communities: Even as they were subsumed by colonial projects, they transformed them. The previous chapter explored how hybrid Collagua/Inka community structures continued to articulate regional-scale patterns of agricultural and pastoral production, exchange, and consumption during Inkaic and early colonial times.

This chapter brings a complementary, local view of ayllu- and moiety-level land-use patterns through time, first by presenting a detailed reconstruction of early colonial-era land-tenure patterns of local ayllus and then by using that reconstruction to retrodict the residence patterns of ayllus under Inka rule. Focusing on the reducción of Coporaque and its surrounding landscapes, this analysis will show specifically how it was that Inka administration at once grafted onto the dualistic structures of local land use and community organization and attempted to overwrite them by introducing and distributing the fields and residences of state-ordered ayllus across the autochthonous dualistic divide. It will also put the emplacement of the reducción of Coporaque in a new light. Though situated in a location that was virtually unoccupied, Coporaque can be seen not as an erasure of prehispanic patterns of land use and residence but as quite literally a "negotiated settlement" whose emplacement balanced the interests of its ranked dualistic communities and their vested interests in the surrounding landscape. Even so, the legacy of reducción—the incongruous arrangement of a nucleated colonial town in the midst of a vast dispersion of small terraces and their supporting irrigation infrastructures— was not without significant deleterious effects for its constituent households, ayllus, and their supporting agricultural systems. The last section explores the factors that account for the degradation of the Coporaque landscape—in part a legacy of colonial settlement consolidation—through a GIS-based walking model comparing the patterning of fields that continue to be cultivated today compared to those that were abandoned during historic times.

Reconstructing Ayllu Land-Use and Residential Patterns: A Reverse Site-Catchment Approach

The analysis in this chapter is based on locating landholding declarations in the Colca Valley visitas by matching the toponyms used to locate agricultural fields in the visita declarations with their modern toponymic counterparts. Household landholding declarations in the visitas included the size of each field, the predominant crop grown in it, and the location of the field by reference to a toponym. Coporaque is the best locale to carry out this analysis because it overlaps with the archaeological survey area, it is among the best documented villages in the visitas, and its modern toponyms are the most intensively studied in the valley. The social and spatial resolution of the reconstruction is also important: Visita declarations can be scaled down to the household level or aggregated up in scale through the ayllu, moiety, and village levels. To my knowledge, this is the most detailed reconstruction of colonial land-use patterns to be achieved in the Andes. I use two visitas to provide a complete view of both moieties in Coporaque: the 1604 visita of Yanquecollaguas Urinsaya and the 1615–17 visita of Yanquecollaguas Hanansaya.[1]

To reconstruct pre-reducción ayllu residence patterns from their land-tenure patterns, I employ what I call a "reverse site-catchment" approach. While traditional site-catchment analysis simulates land-use catchment areas around known site locations (Roper 1979; Vita-Finzi and Higgs 1970), this methodology does the reverse: It retrodicts prehistoric residence patterns from historically documented land-use data by comparing the land-tenure patterns of local ayllus with the settlement locations registered in the archaeological survey. Though prehistoric Andean land-use patterns are dispersed, this method assumes that there was still a generally inverse relationship between extent and/or intensity of cultivation and distance from settlement. Thus point-pattern analysis showing clustering of agricultural field distributions in relation to prehispanic settlements are taken to reflect echoes of residential patterns prior to resettlement. This inference is reasonable when considering that the visitas in question were recorded just one to two generations after resettlement and thus, through inheritance, historically documented land-tenure patterns ought to reflect echoes of prehispanic antecedents. This approach can therefore show how the dispersed landholding constellations of the ayllus resettled to Coporaque continued to reflect their pre-reducción land-tenure and residence patterns. By extension, as will be shown below, it also enables reconstruction of how autochthonous community structures filtered land-use practices and articulated with successive Inka and Spanish colonial administration and settlement planning.

The visitas provide the essential data needed for reconstructing the land-tenure patterns of local post-reducción households. As previously discussed, these periodic censuses were conducted by moiety (Hanansaya/Urinsaya) within each repartimiento. Since almost all villages were composed of two moieties, the data for only one "side" or half of each village is registered in a single visita. Complete cross-sectional data for a given village therefore requires two visitas, but no complete synchronic pairing survives in the known documentary corpus. I therefore use visitas from different years to provide a view of both moieties: the 1604 visita of Yanquecollaguas Urinsaya and the 1615–17 visita of Yanquecollaguas Hanansaya.[2]

Household declarations listed all of a household's agro-pastoral holdings, including the location and size of each agricultural landholding and the predominant crop grown there, as well as any livestock. The key to reconstructing household and ayllu land-tenure patterns lies in the fact that the visitas locate fields using place names. In the Colca Valley, as in many other regions within the Andes, toponyms tend to be historically durable, and consequently, landholdings registered in the visitas can be located with considerable precision by mapping them with modern toponyms. Local toponyms are also generally quite small and discrete; they usually refer to a small cluster of fields that share a distribution canal at the distal end of an irrigation network. These names continue to be used today for coordinating water apportionment at irrigation distribution meetings.

To map modern toponyms, I consulted with local farmers, mapping toponym perimeters with GPS receivers.[3] Using GIS, the toponym sectors could then be represented as polygon themes with unique identifying codes linking the map to a database with the visita landholding declarations. The basemap (Figure 7.1) consists of 76 modern toponyms in Coporaque that also appear in the visitas, 51 of which lie within the modern district boundaries of Coporaque (Table 7.1). These toponyms locate 703 agricultural fields in the visitas, accounting for 23 percent of 3,054 fields declared. In terms of surface area, the mapped fields represent a 24 percent sample, 249 out of 1,047 *topos* (Table 7.2). The topo is an Andean unit of measure used to quantify fields in the visita declarations. During Inka and early colonial times, the actual surface area of a topo was not a fixed figure but varied relative to soil quality, elevation, topography, and other factors that affected agricultural productivity (see

D'Altroy 2002:246–47; Rowe 1946:324).[4] For the purpose of visualization, however, a colonial topo can be roughly compared to its modern standardized equivalent of 3,496 m². Thus the total area of 249 topos of mapped fields corresponds to approximately 87 ha.

To implement the reverse site-catchment methodology, I compare the distribution of ayllu landholdings to the archaeological settlement pattern using the standard deviational ellipse (SDE). As a measure of point dispersion in coordinate space, an SDE describes the area within one standard deviation of the spatial mean (center) of a given point distribution. Here, weighted SDEs were generated using the size of each fieldholding as the weighting variable.[5] Within my reverse site-catchment framework, the weighted spatial mean of a

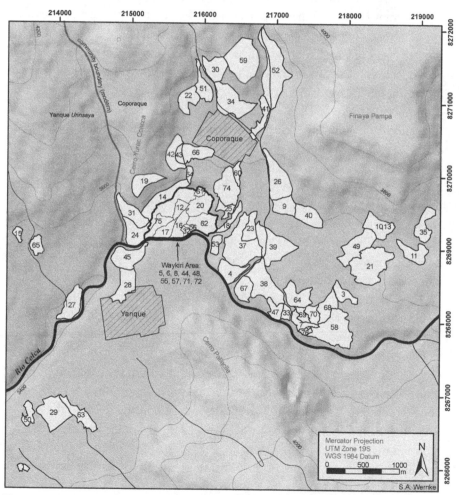

Figure 7.1. Basemap of toponyms with matches in the visitas. The toponyms are listed in Table 7.1.

Table 7.1. Modern toponyms in Coporaque that also appear in the visitas

Code	Name	Code	Name	Code	Name
1	Alcalli	26	Cocawire	52	Sahuara
2	Anchocllo	27	Collpa	53	Sallihua
3	Ancollaya	28	Compuyo	54	Saymana
4	Antacala	29	Cusqui	55	Sumo[a, c]
5	Apo[a, c]	30	Cuyo	56	Supowiri[a]
6	Apopampa[a, c]	31	Fallero	57	Suqilla[a, c]
7	Aquerana	32	Kello[a]	58	Suripampa
8	Avantira[a, c]	33	Kellolucri	59	Tañapaque
9	Bombomcilla	34	Korinapampa	60	Taqllapukio
10	Cachulle[b]	35	Kundurparara	61	Taqowire
11	Canaque	36	Kusipampa		(Toccohuire)[a]
12	Canteria[a]	37	Lama	62	Tocco[a]
13	Caque[b]	38	Llactapampa	63	Tocolle
14	Cayra	39	Llanka	64	Tunsa
15	Ccaya	40	Machingaya	65	Ullullu
16	Chacco[a]	41	Malcapi	66	Umañoso
17	Chacopata[a]	42	Malco	67	Umaro
18	Chaquire	43	Malcopampa	68	Ururani
19	Chijra (Chishra, Chirsha)	44	Nasama[a, c]	69	Utarana
20	Chilcarani[a]	45	Ocolle	70	Vilcarana
21	Chocpayo	46	Pasnaya	71	Waykiri[a, c]
22	Chuñankaya	47	Pataha	72	Waykirilucri[a, c]
23	Churani	48	Patarana[a, c]	73	Waykiripata
24	Churqui	49	Pisnolla	74	Wichokata
25	Chururani	50	Pucjio	75	Yawiso (Llahuiso)[a]
		51	Quelqata	76	Ycani

Sources: Benavides 1986d; Córdova Aguilar et al. 1986; Izaguirre Urbano n.d.; Treacy 1989; Fieldwork 1999–2000.

Notes: a. In the Waykiri basin, a low-lying, bowl-shaped basin of contour bench terraces and valley bottom fields (the dark line outlines the extent of the toponyms within the Waykiri area).

b. Ministry of Agriculture cadastral maps indicate that this sector is called Cachulle. However, Treacy (1989:257) maps a toponym called Caque that is in the same area, but Treacy's maps represent toponym locations as points, so its specific outline could not be mapped. I have thus included Caque within the toponym outline of Cachulle according to the ministry of agriculture maps, since it probably represents a subdivision within that large toponym sector.

c. Treacy (1989:257) is the only source locating these toponyms. They are small toponym sectors in the Waykiri basin, but their specific location could not be determined from Treacy's maps.

Table 7.2. Descriptive statistics for land-tenure reconstruction, by ayllu

Moiety	Ayllu	Population	Total No. of Fields	No. of Mapped Fields	Total Fields Mapped	Total Field Area (Topos)	Mapped Field Area (Topos)	Total Field Area Mapped	Source
Hanansaya	Collana Malco	178	146	15	10%	67.50	7.00	10%	fols. 480v–493r
Hanansaya	Ila Tunga Malco[a]	318	233	37	16%	89.50	14.75	16%	fols. 493v–513r
Hanansaya	Checa Malco	157	128	29	23%	45.38	11.25	25%	fols. 513r–525r
Hanansaya	Yumasca	251	313	97	31%	91.75	28.25	31%	fols. 526r–550v
Hanansaya	Calloca [sic; Caloca][b]	188	158	34	22%	58.75	15.25	26%	fols. 550v–565r
Hanansaya	Cupi 1	177	249	56	22%	85.13	20.25	24%	fols. 565v–585r
Hanansaya	Aipi (Cupi 2) [c]	191	211	61	29%	66.00	19.75	30%	fols. 585r–603v
Hanansaya	Official potters (Oficiales Olleros)	135	155	25	16%	47.50	7.25	15%	fols. 603v–611v
	Subtotal	1595	1593	354	22%	551.50	123.75	22%	
Urinsaya	Collana	388	387	107	28%	137.25	40.25	29%	fols. 208v–236r
Urinsaya	Pahana Collana Pataca	406	495	110	22%	167.25	39.50	24%	fols. 236r–270r
Urinsaya	Pahana Taypi Pataca	294	265	54	20%	89.50	21.25	24%	fols. 270v–290r
Urinsaya	Pahana Cayao Pataca	300	314	78	25%	101.75	24.25	24%	fols. 290r–309r
	Subtotal	1388	1461	349	24%	495.75	125.25	25%	
	Total	2983	3054	703	23%	1047.25	249.00	24%	

Sources: Hanansaya: APY, Visita de Yanquecollaguas Hanansaya 1615–17, fols. 480v–611v; Urinsaya: APY, Visita de Yanquecollaguas Urinsaya 1604, fols. 208v–309r.

Notes: Ayllus listed in order of registry in the visitas.

a. Called "Ila Tunga Masco" in the ayllu summary (fol. 513r).

b. Called "Caloca" in the ayllu summary (fol. 565r).

c. Called "Cupi" in the ayllu summary (fol. 585r).

given ayllu's field distribution is important, because the method assumes that the pre-reducción ancestors of that ayllu likely lived in close proximity to the fields they owned, fields that their descendants continued to cultivate after their resettlement. The analysis presented here excludes nonlocal fields since toponym coverage is not systematic beyond the modern District of Coporaque and these fields are spatial outliers that would unduly distort the SDE measures.

Since toponyms were the minimum unit of provenience provided in the visita declarations, the exact location of individual fields cannot be specified. Also, toponym boundaries almost certainly shifted to some extent over time, most likely in an agglutinative fashion as some small toponyms were absorbed into larger ones. However, point level–provenience of field locations can be simulated by generating a randomized point location for each field within a given toponym polygon in the GIS.[6] To measure the between-sample variance introduced by this randomization, five point-location randomization iterations were performed. The between-sample coefficient of variation of the resulting SDE areas ranges between 1.78 and 12.39 percent, and all but two ayllus have coefficients of less than 6 percent (Table 7.3). The difference between the simulated and the actual field distributions is likely similarly small, since the size of individual toponyms are small relative to the overall distribution of fields over several toponyms for a given ayllu. Thus, despite the limitation of toponyms as a minimal unit of provenience in the visitas, and probable

Table 7.3. Descriptive statistics for field location simulation iterations, by ayllu

Moiety	Ayllu	n	Mean SDE (ha)	Minimum SDE (ha)	Maximum SDE (ha)	Standard Deviation	Coefficient of Variance
Hanansaya	Collana Malco	15	306.42	253.75	339.76	37.96	12.39
Hanansaya	Ila Tunga Malco	37	393.72	367.36	426.14	23.11	5.87
Hanansaya	Checa Malco	29	444.70	413.72	466.09	19.27	4.33
Hanansaya	Yumasca	97	353.45	346.77	362.58	6.30	1.78
Hanansaya	Calloca	34	546.23	534.30	563.73	10.90	2.00
Hanansaya	Cupi 1	56	245.08	235.58	258.16	8.56	3.49
Hanansaya	Cupi 2	61	318.63	312.94	327.76	6.06	1.90
Hanansaya	Oficiales Olleros	25	239.83	209.61	264.24	20.91	8.72
Urinsaya	Collana	107	377.54	366.64	389.12	9.06	2.40
Urinsaya	Pahana Collana Pataca	109	368.45	350.33	378.37	11.48	3.12
Urinsaya	Pahana Taypi Pataca	54	365.00	347.61	383.18	16.57	4.54
Urinsaya	Pahana Cayao Pataca	78	325.38	315.95	339.51	9.55	2.94

Sources: Hanansaya: APY, Visita de Yanquecollaguas Hanansaya 1615–17, fols. 480v–611v; Urinsaya: APY, Visita de Yanquecollaguas Urinsaya 1604, fols. 208v–309r. Ayllus listed in order of registry in the visitas.

changes in their exact boundaries, the reconstructed ayllu land-tenure patterns probably closely approximate their actual distributions in the past. For clarity of presentation, in the figures that follow (Figures 7.6–7.9), only the average SDE of these five iterations along with one field location iteration is displayed for each ayllu.[7]

The Local Crop Mosaic

As a first measure of colonial land-use patterns, the visita declarations can be aggregated up to the village as a whole to display the overall distribution of crops over the local landscape. Visita declarations in Coporaque (Hanansaya and Urinsaya combined) indicate that the local crop mosaic was composed of 59 percent maize, 39 percent quinoa, and the remainder (2 percent) in other crops (potatoes, kañiwa [also declared as cañagua], and unspecified) (cf. Benavides 1986b; Benavides 1986c). Mapping out the declarations by reference to their modern toponymic counterparts provides a view of where these crops were grown. It also provides a measure for testing the accuracy of the method, since maize can only be grown on the terraced slopes below 3,600 m above sea level. While the terracing on these slopes creates warm microclimates and effectively sheds cool air descending at night (see chapter 3), frosts descend to the pampas surrounding Coporaque. Quinoa, potatoes, fava beans, and other more frost tolerant crops are cultivated in those areas today. A similar pattern in the past—maize on terraced slopes, frost-tolerant crops on the pampas—would therefore be expected, and deviations from it could signal lack of correspondence between ancient and modern toponym areas.

The dot-density map of Figure 7.2 displays this data by representing each field that could be located by toponym, color coded by the predominant crop declared in the visita.[8] The reconstructed distribution of crops is consistent with modern practices—maize cultivation was largely confined to complexes of bench terraces on the lower valley slopes, while quinoa cultivation was concentrated on broad-field terraces and valley bottom fields on the pampas of the Qal 4 and 5 geomorphic surfaces surrounding the village. The air photo detail in Figure 7.2 shows the intensively terraced slopes of the Waykiri, Ccayra, and Fayero areas below San Antonio/Chijra (CO-100). These toponym sectors are situated in a warm microclimate that results from their elevation, slope angle, orientation, and the terracing itself (Treacy 1989b:81–84). Situated just above the valley floor, these are some of the lowest-elevation terraces in Coporaque. Their southeasterly orientation promotes early warming in the morning sun—a beneficial effect accentuated by the mass and rock facings of the terraces. At night, the terraces radiate heat built up during the day and further reduce frost risk by shedding cool air, which instead settles

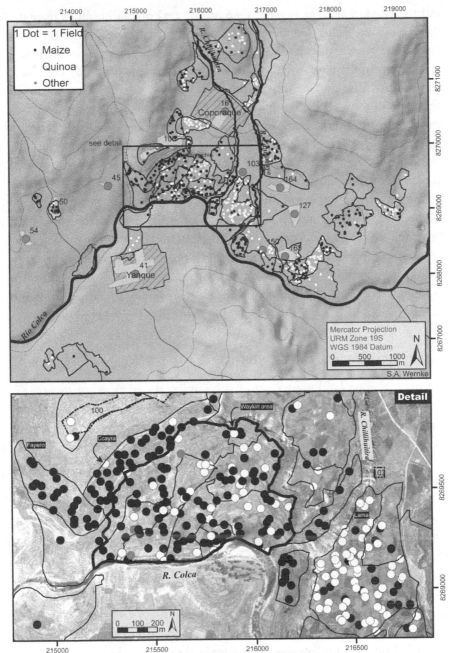

Figure 7.2. Dot-density map of crop declarations in Coporaque, 1604 and 1615–16.

downslope to the pampas and valley bottom (Treacy 1989b:81–84). As is evident in the dot-density overlay on the air photo, visita declarations of crops grown in the fields of these areas indicate that they were dedicated almost exclusively to maize production. Combining the declarations of Ccayra, Fayero, and the Waykiri area, 78 percent (186 out of 237) of landholdings were declared as maize fields. Coporaque villagers clearly preferentially cultivated this culturally valued crop over others in warm, fertile, low-frost-risk areas.

In contrast, the hardier, more nutritious quinoa was primarily cultivated on the more frost-prone pampas above the valley floor. For example, the air photo detail shows the predominance of quinoa fields declared in the Lama toponym sector on the pampa to the southeast of the Waykiri area (bottom right). Here, 79 percent (58 out of 73 fields) of landholdings were declared as quinoa fields. As a key subsistence crop, Coporaque villagers concentrated quinoa cultivation in the large broad-field terraces and valley bottom fields.

The distribution of crops therefore indicates that the toponym mapping method is accurate—the toponyms used to identify fields in the visitas that have modern matches did not significantly shift in their location or spatial extent during the intervening 400 years. This is not an unexpected result, given the apparent antiquity of the toponyms (many are Aymara terms) and since toponyms have been the primary means for distributing irrigation water and for making landholding claims (such as in the visitas themselves).

Moiety-Level Land-Tenure Patterning

Before analyzing land-tenure patterns by ayllu, it makes sense to first explore if there is patterning at the higher order grouping of ayllus by moiety. That is, if the landholding declarations of the households are aggregated to the scale of their respective moieties (ignoring for the moment their ayllu affiliations within the moiety) and spatially plotted, would we find distinct patterning? Given the widespread spatial associations between Hanansaya and Urinsaya moieties throughout the central Andes, this is reasonable first question to explore. Prior local research suggests that no such patterns were evident. Benavides (1986d) reconstructed the distribution of fields by moiety in Coporaque and found that Hanansaya and Urinsaya declarations in the visitas are not territorially discrete. Rather, households from both moieties share many toponym areas. Using similar methods, Robinson has also recently documented this kind of interdigitated moiety arrangement in Laricollaguas (Robinson 2003b). My findings are consistent with theirs. In the map of Figure 7.3, pie chart size is proportional to the combined field area declared by both moieties, and the pie charts display the percentage of field area declared by each moiety. Clearly, moieties as collectivities did not cultivate large discrete areas and did not control separate irrigation systems. Although moieties did not control separate sections of the canal network, the distribution of irrigation water could have been accomplished through a moiety- or ayllu-based turn-taking system similar to that employed today in Coporaque (Treacy 1994) and Cabanaconde (Gelles 1995, 2000). Canal maintenance was probably also coordinated and executed at the moiety level, as is the practice throughout the valley today (Guillet 1992; Valderrama Fernández and Escalante Gutierrez 1988).

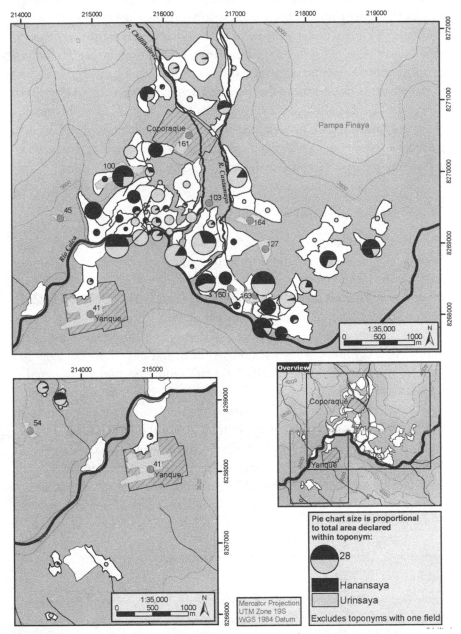

Figure 7.3. Landholdings by moiety, Coporaque 1604 and 1615–16.

This mixed-moiety land-tenure pattern has important implications for reconstructing terminal prehispanic residence patterns as well. It is highly unlikely that a single moiety made up the entire population of LIP/Late Horizon settlements, but rather that settlement populations were composed of both Hanansaya and Urinsaya members. Otherwise, one would have to imagine a scenario in which there was no correspondence between settlement pattern and land-use patterns. Moiety affiliation was likely more salient in irrigation apportionment and maintenance schemes, as is the case throughout the valley today (Gelles 1995, 2000; Guillet 1987, 1992; Treacy 1994; Valderrama Fernández and Escalante Gutierrez 1988).

But what can be said about the individual ayllus within each moiety? Residential and land-use use patterning could also be structured at this smaller scale. The landholding constellations of the constituent ayllus of each moiety are reconstructed below, which in turn enables a reconstruction of which ayllus inhabited particular settlements prior to reducción resettlement.

Ayllu-Level Land-Tenure Patterning

Like the mixed moiety–level pattern, ayllu-level land-tenure patterning in Coporaque was also generally dispersed. Ayllus in Coporaque, and almost certainly in the rest of the valley as well, did not control large, discrete areas of agricultural fields. Instead, households in each ayllu declared fields in a constellation of often non-contiguous toponym sectors. This is of course entirely consistent with the axiomatic pattern of dispersed land use in the Andes. As is common in high-altitude Andean settings where drought and frost are constant threats, the household risk-reduction strategy was to disperse many small holdings over different vertically distributed production zones rather than maximizing field size in any single area. Such a pattern also permits diversification of crops appropriate to local microclimates. Locally, such a pattern is hinted at simply in the average size of fields declared—just one-third topo (0.34 topos), or just over a tenth of a hectare.[9] However, while the dispersion of household landholdings would have minimized risk, household tenure rights to their scattered fields were also clearly mediated by ayllu affiliation.

Hanansaya: Articulating Dualistically Organized Ayllu Land-Use and Residential Patterns

As we will see, the plotted fields of Hanansaya ayllus show more discrete distributions than those of Urinsaya. Specifically, the fieldholdings of seven out of the eight Hanansaya ayllus are concentrated on either side of a prominent hydrological divide—the quebrada of the Chillihuitira River—which runs southward through the center of the Coporaque area (Figure 7.4). This quebrada divides Coporaque in two hydrologically, as water from the Chillihuitira feeds most of the canals for the fields to the west of the quebrada while water from the Sahuara/Cantumayo supplies the canals for most of the fields to the east (Figure 7.5).

At this point it is instructive to review the names of the ayllus as registered in the visitas. As discussed in the last chapter, the ayllus of Urinsaya predominantly conform to Inkaic tripartite and decimal onomastic conventions, while those of the Hanansaya moiety are predominantly Aymara terms that hint at an underlying dualistic structure based on a ranked, right-left concept. This is specifically manifest in the names of two groups of ayllus in the 1615–17 visita of Coporaque: Cupi (*cupi* means "right side") and Checa Malco (*checa* means "left side" and *malco* means "honored lord").[10] In the other documented cases of Aymara right-left dualism, the right side is higher ranking, associated with male gender traits and higher topography, while the left side is lower ranking, associated with female gender traits and lower topography (Albó 1972; Bouysse-Cassagne 1987). For example, ayllu

Figure 7.4. Panorama of the Coporaque area, showing the Chillihuitira drainage and "right" and "left" sides.

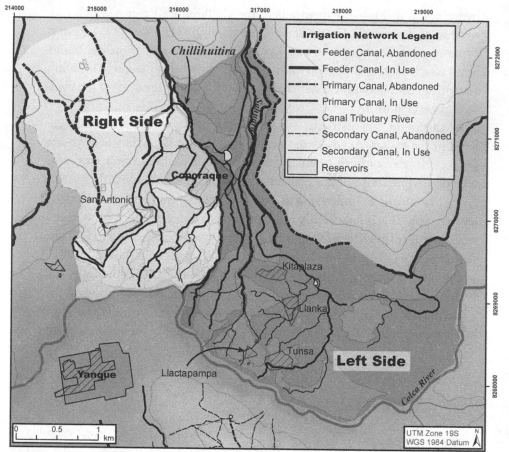

Figure 7.5. The irrigation system of Coporaque.

organization in Jesús de Machaca was also based dualistic division between groups of right (higher-ranking) and left (lower-ranking) ayllus separated by hydrologically axial division (Astvaldsson 2000). Two statistical measures are useful to provide measures of "sidedness" beyond impressionistic visual inspection: the SDE approach described above and a chi-square test comparing the observed (reconstructed) distributions against a scenario in which field placement would be unaffected by this sidedness. In the theoretical (null hypothesis) distribution, the landholdings of an ayllu would be distributed in direct proportion to the amount of land in the toponym areas on either side of the Chillihuitira River. This proportion can be derived by first summing the area of all the toponym areas, and then dividing that sum by the area on either side of the Chillihuitira dividing line. The total area of the toponyms is 432.7 ha, of which 294.3 ha are located to the east of the Chillihuitira and 138.4

are located to the west. In terms of proportions, 68 percent of the toponym area is located to the east (i.e., on the "left-hand side" according to the ayllu names) and 32 percent to the west (on the "right-hand side" according to the ayllu names). Expected values for the null hypothesis can therefore be generated by multiplying the total mapped area of the fieldholdings of a given ayllu by these east/west proportions (68 percent to the east ["left"] and 32 percent to the west ["right"]). A one-sample chi-square test was used to test for the statistical significance of the difference between the observed and expected values.

The reconstructed landholding patterns of the Hanansaya ayllus indeed show statistically significant concentrations to either the right or left side of the divide in four of eight cases, and all can be included in one of the two sides on the grounds of its SDE location and other grounds discussed below (Table 7.4). First, to start with the most obvious examples, the landholdings of the two explicitly named "right-side" ayllu (both named Cupi),[11] are located predominantly to the west of the Chillihuitira, while those of the explicitly named "left-side" ayllu Checa Malco are located predominantly to the east of this quebrada. In both cases, their land-tenure patterns are dispersed but their SDEs are discrete from one another, revealing how the risk-minimizing strategy of field dispersion was mediated by ayllu organization. Their SDEs show how the fields of the two "right-side" Cupi ayllus were distributed in a nearly identical fashion toward the west, while those of the "left-side" ayllu Checa Malco were concentrated to the east (Figure 7.6). Facing downstream (toward the Colca River), west is on the right-hand side and east is on the left (see Figure 7.4 above). This downstream directional orientation is consistent with the division between the conceptual right and left among Aymara populations in the Titicaca basin, where the higher-ranking, conceptual right-side Urcosuyu and lower-ranking, conceptual left-side Umasuyo are located to the right and left, respectively, relative to a downstream orientation along the Azangaro River–Lake Titicaca–Desaguadero River hydrological axis (Bouysse-Cassagne 1986:203).

Moreover, this right-left spatial duality is apparent not only for the explicitly named "left" (Checa) and "right" (Cupi) ayllus, *but for all of the other ayllus of Hanansaya*. On the one hand, the fields of the ayllus Collana Malco, Ila Tunga Malco, and Yumasca are all concentrated to the left side (east), while those of the ayllus Calloca and Oficiales Olleros (official potters) are concentrated to the right (west) (Figure 7.7).

When seeing these spatial distributions, it also becomes evident that the order in which ayllus were recorded in the visita is significant: The ayllus with the Malco honorific were listed in succession with the left-side ayllu

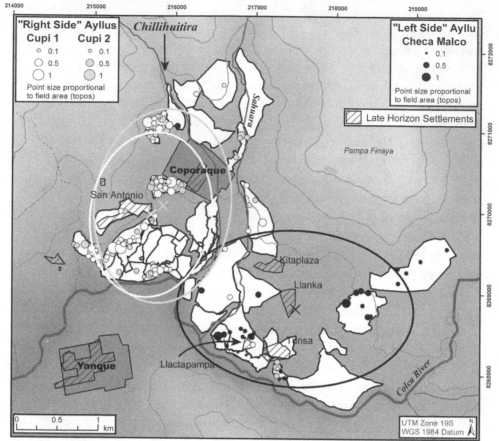

Figure 7.6. Landholding distributions, "right side" (Cupi) versus "left side" (Checa Malco) ayllus, Coporaque Hanansaya, 1615–17.

Table 7.4. Summary statistics, left/right predominance, Coporaque Hanansaya, 1615–16

Ayllu	Landholding Predominance	Observed "Left Side" (East)	Observed "Right Side" (West)	Expected Left Side	Expected Right Side	Chi-Square
Checa Malco	Left	10.75	0.5	7.65	3.6	3.92[a]
Collana Malco	Left (?)	8	1.5	6.46	3.04	1.15
Icatunga Mallco	Left (?)	15.25	3.75	12.92	6.08	1.31
Yumasca	Left (?)	25.25	5	20.58	9.67	3.32
Cupi	Right	7.25	17.5	16.83	7.92	17.06[a]
Aipi (Cupi)	Right	12	18.25	20.58	9.67	11.17[a]
Calloca	Right	5.75	12.75	12.58	5.92	11.60[a]
Official potters	None	1.5	2	2.38	1.12	1.02

Note: a. Statistical significance (a = 0.05) is met when $x^2 > 3.84$.

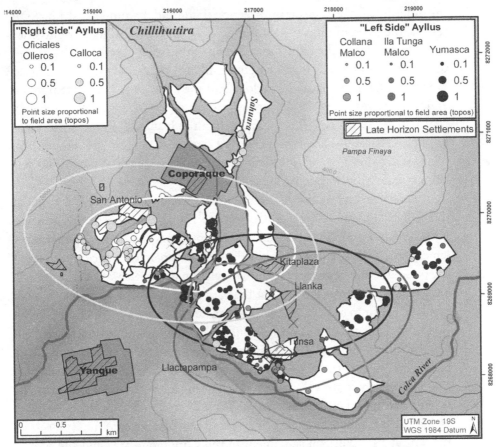

Figure 7.7. Landholding distributions, ayllus Collana Malco, Ila Tunga Malco, Yumasca, Oficiales Olleros, and Calloca, Coporaque Hanansaya, 1615–17.

Checa Malco (see Table 7.2). The distributions of their fields (Figure 7.7) reveal the spatial dimension of their relationship: They are all concentrated to the east or "left" side along with those of ayllu Checa Malco. The ayllu Yumasca, listed immediately after the Malco ayllus in the visita, also shows "left" or easterly landholding distribution (Figure 7.7). It is thus evident that all of the left-side ayllus lined up first to be recorded by the visitador. The ayllu that follows Calloca in the visita is Cupi, followed by another Cupi ayllu (referred to as "Aipi" in the ayllu header but Cupi in the ayllu summary in the visita), ushering in the right-side ayllus. The last two listed are the ayllu Calloca and an ayllu of official state potters (*oficiales olleros*). The SDEs of these show clear "right-side" or westerly distributions like the two Cupi ayllus (Figure 7.7). The chi-square test shows significant right-side predominance for Calloca but not for the ayllu of potters, but this is heavily influenced by the small sample size (see Table 7.4). Given the strong evidence for the ordering of ayllu registry by directional side and the similarly strong SDE results, the ayllu of official state potters was almost certainly a "right-side" ayllu. In summary, the Hanansaya moiety appears to have been composed of two groups of four ayllus: a (higher-ranking) right-side group composed of the two Cupi ayllus, ayllu Calloca and the ayllu of official state potters, and a (lower-ranking) left-side group composed of Collana Malco, Icatunga Malco, Checa Malco, and Yumasca. When the Hanansaya household field-holding declarations are thus aggregated into these two groups (Figure 7.8), the spatial pattern of the right-left duality is again clearly apparent in their aggregate distributions and SDEs.

This GIS reconstruction therefore makes manifest an underlying spatial dualism of the landholdings of Coporaque Hanansaya households and ayllus (see Figure 7.8). But how were these contrasting land-tenure patterns related to the prehispanic and colonial settlement patterns? A comparison of the pre-reducción settlement pattern in relation to these contrasting right-left land-tenure patterns suggests that they are rooted in contrasting patterns of residence prior to reducción resettlement, and by extension, illuminates how this local dualism articulated with Inka and Spanish administration (Table 7.5). In the case of the right-side ayllus, the center of their landholding distribution is closest to the settlement of San Antonio, the largest of the Late Horizon secondary centers (Figure 7.8). According to the reverse site-catchment framework, this suggests that the majority of ancestral population of these ayllus resided at that settlement. If we recall also that San Antonio (CO-100), the largest Late Horizon settlement in the Coporaque area and site of one of the early Franciscan doctrinas, was referred to as "Cupi" in ecclesiastical documentation (see chapter 5), the case becomes clearer still. Another piece of evidence further strengthens it: In the listing of villages that were resettled to Coporaque in the 1615–17 visita, one is listed as "Calocacupi" (APY Yanquecollaguas Hanansaya 1615–17, fol. 480v). This must be the same settlement as "Cupi" (San Antonio). Thus independent documentary evidence establishes that the site today known as San Antonio was a pre-Toledan Franciscan doctrina and that it originally was named after its main resident ayllu: the right-side Cupi and Calloca ayllus.

With such a clear case for the right-side ayllus, the contrasting, eastern-oriented constellations of the left-side ayllu landholdings must similarly represent an echo of pre-reducción residential patterns. The center of the aggregate distribution of the left-side ayllus (Checa Malco, Collana Malco, Ila Tunga Malco, and Yumasca) is adjacent to the large Late Horizon settlement of Llanka (CO-127) (Figure 7.8). This settlement is part of a cluster of four large Late Horizon settlements all within 500 m of one another, so the

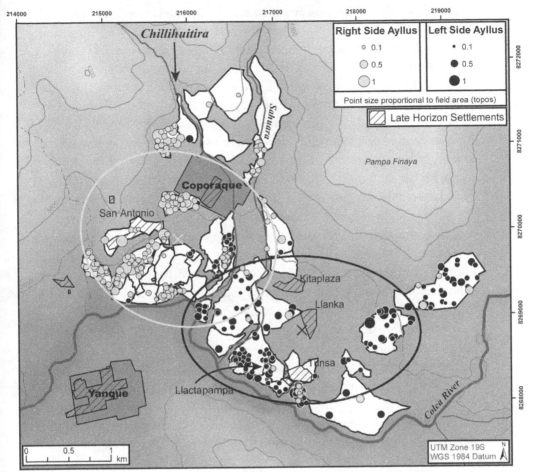

Figure 7.8. Aggregate "right-side" and "left-side" landholding distributions, Coporaque Hanansaya, 1615–17.

Table 7.5. Summary of pre-reducción ayllu residence patterns

Left-side ayllu: majority resided at CO-103, CO-127, CO-150/164, and CO-163		Right-side ayllu: majority resided at CO-100		Dispersed ayllu: population dispersed throughout most/all Late Horizon settlements in Coporaque	
Hanan	Urin	Hanan	Urin	Hanan	Urin
Checa Malco		Cupi	Collana	State potters	Pahana Collana Pataca
Collana Malco		Aipi/Cupi			Pahana Taypi Pataca
Icatunga Malco		Calloca			Pahana Cayao Pataca
Yumasca					

ancestral population of these ayllus could have resided at any one or several of these settlements. Among them, the site of Tunsa (CO-163), like San Antonio, housed local elite domestic architecture and an Inka great hall.

By extension, this reconstruction sheds light on the specific spatial mode of articulation between Inka imperial and local political structures. The Inkas grafted administration onto local bases of power, as the largest settlements on each side of this dualistically organized landscape became secondary administrative centers. Such a hybrid arrangement would have probably benefited local kurakas by stabilizing their rank and authority through their association with the state while also minimizing disruption and state investment. Franciscan friars subsequently erected a chapel at the principal settlement of the higher ranking of these two sides: Cupi, or right side. As we explored in chapter 6, this and other doctrinas grew during their brief occupation prior to resettlement to the reducciones (Echeverría y Morales 1952 [1804]:80). The influx of new households at San Antonio (Calocacupi) almost certainly came from the lower-ranking "left-side" ayllus and their settlements to the east. In this light, the establishment of the reducción of Coporaque can be seen as an intensification of centripetal trends that began under Inka administration, rather than a radical truncation of indigenous tradition.

The emplacement of the reducción of Coporaque also looks much more like a locally negotiated outcome than one of colonial domination. That is, the construction of Coporaque in a location that was virtually unoccupied during Inka times would seem to support the conventional interpretation that reducción effected an eradication of prehispanic patterns of settlement and land use. But in light of the reconstruction, it becomes clear that the village was specifically situated to balance the interests of local communities, since the village actually straddles the hydrological boundary between the two sides of the agricultural landscape. Such an arrangement would have thus minimized the disruptive effects of resettlement by situating the new village in a central location relative to established patterns of land use. In this sense, the specific location of Coporaque appears rational from the point of view of the state while also conceding to the agency of local communities in their negotiation of its *emplacement*.

Urinsaya: Land-Tenure and Residence Patterns of Inka-Engineered Ayllus

The onomastic land-tenure and residential patterns of Coporaque Urinsaya ayllus are different in every respect from their Hanansaya counterparts. As we recall from the previous chapter, the names of the ayllus of the Urinsaya moiety conform almost exactly to Inkaic ideals of tripartite ranking and decimal administration, suggesting a more penetrating reorganization by the state.

Of the nine ayllus that constitute the ideal structure of the Urinsaya moiety of Yanquecollaguas, segments of four were present in Coporaque: the high-ranking Collana (rank 1.1) and segments of all three of the pataca-level ayllus that make up the middle-ranking ayllu Pahana (in descending order of rank), Pahana Collana Pataca (rank 2.1), Pahana Taypi Pataca (rank 2.2), and Pahana Cayao Pataca (rank 2.3).[12] The reconstructed land-tenure patterns in relation to the Late Horizon settlement pattern indicates that the land-use and residential patterns of these state-engineered ayllus were very different from those of Hanansaya. Rather than discrete land-tenure and residential patterns to one side or the other of the Chillihuitira divide, those of Urinsaya ayllus were widely dispersed across both sides.

Figure 7.9 displays the land-tenure patterns of the Urinsaya ayllus. Their SDEs show how their landholdings are distributed more widely over both sides of the Chillihuitira than those of the Hanansaya ayllus. The centers of all but one of their distributions are closer to the Chillihuitira division itself than to any of the pre-reducción settlements. The one exception, ayllu Pahana Cayao Pataca, shows a central tendency nearer to the settlements to the east or left side of the Chillihuitira. But overall, their more dispersed patterns on either side of the axis that divided the two groups of Hanansaya ayllus signal correspondingly dispersed residential patterns among their prehispanic ancestral populations.

This dispersion could reflect a state strategy aimed at redistributing agricultural (and, by extension, hydraulic) interests. Such a policy might have been aimed at breaking up entrenched interests in the local landscape, which, based on the pattern of fortifications from the LIP, appear to have been charged and contested. Population dispersion away from LIP hilltop settlements and pukaras has been documented elsewhere in highland settings, both in the Cuzco heartland and a range of highland provincial settings, including highland Ecuador, the upper Mantaro Valley (D'Altroy 1992), and the Titicaca basin (Stanish 1997a, 1997b). Penetration of Inka administration to household-level patterns of agricultural production and consumption has been documented in other regionally important provincial settings (Hastorf 1990). Expansion and intensification of production were thus facilitated in part by occupying and developing areas that were previously unused or underused. What is clear is that the lands of the Urinsaya ayllus traversed the traditional boundary between the autochthonous Collagua ayllus. Considerable reordering of people and interests by the state could have resulted from the reshuffling of local population, state-ordered in-migration of mitmaq colonists from other areas, or a mix of the two. The answer is uncertain, though there are reasons to speculate that mitmaq colonists could have constituted

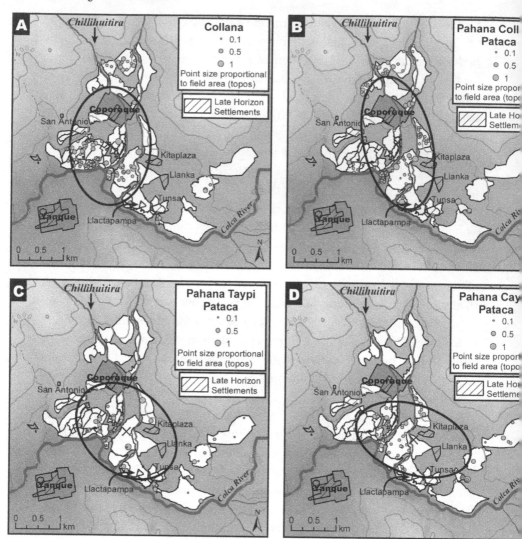

Figure 7.9. Ayllu landholding distributions, Coporaque Urinsaya, 1604.

at least a part of the Hanansaya ayllus. Mitmaq ayllus were often assigned decimal administrative designations (Espinoza Soriano 1975:387; Lorandi 1991; Salomon 1986:173). As a regional breadbasket, the Colca Valley was a major economic center, and the movement of mitmaq populations to other such locales on very large scales has been documented (Espinoza Soriano 1973; Wachtel 1982). Collagua mitmaq populations were recorded in the upper Mantaro Valley of the central Peruvian highlands, and so it is possible that resettled mitmaq households replaced local populations resettled by the state in other provinces (Levillier 1940:14–37). Archaeologically, scant architectural or artifactual indices point to an influx of a foreign population during

Inka times, but mitmaq colonies have proven surprisingly difficult to identify archaeologically (D'Altroy 2005).

In any case, reorganization on a similar scale to that of the reducción—whether through restructuring of land-tenure reorganization or the movement of people on a local, regional, or interregional scale—was also part of the local experience of Inka rule. Common state goals of reordering settlement and land use by the Inkas and Spanish were achieved via culturally specific solutions that are nearly mirror images of one another. The Inka project at once mapped onto the extant political landscape through the construction of ceremonial spaces at the principal settlements on each side of the autochthonous dualistic divide, while also attempting to "overwrite" that division by dispersing the households and agricultural interests of the reengineered Urinsaya ayllus on either side of it. The "solution" negotiated by Toledan administrators, in contrast, was centripetal: A new "center," the reducción of Coporaque, was built on the boundary line in the dualistic landscape. Though its layout embodied Spanish urban ideals, Coporaque was in this sense quite literally a "negotiated settlement." As discussed below, however, settlement reduction brought with it population decline, and the dereliction of large swaths of the agricultural landscape.

Legacies of Reducción: The Reduction of the Landscape

The effects of reducción—both in the routines of daily life and in the visible traces of abandoned agricultural features in the landscape—is very much a felt presence here and elsewhere in the Andean highlands today. The workday begins and ends with long hikes from the village to the chacras and back again, often with livestock. Large tracts of terraced agricultural fields and their associated irrigation systems are currently abandoned. In fact, over half of the bench terraces (about 61 percent) in the valley are not currently cultivated (Denevan 1988b:22, 28). Within Coporaque, where we can follow the trajectory of land use and settlement most closely, about 54 percent of fields—781 of a total of 1,315 ha—are abandoned at present. Of these, nearly two-thirds (65 percent, or 509 ha) are sloping fields and segmentary terrace systems that were abandoned during the shift to irrigated bench terracing, probably during Middle Horizon times (see chapter 3). But the remainder, 272 ha, are irrigated bench terrace complexes (Table 7.6). Production among these irrigated bench terraces reached their apogee under Inka administration, when the population was at its highest and production expanded and intensified. Thus virtually all irrigated bench terrace systems in a state of abandonment today must have fallen out of production during colonial or republican times.

Explanatory frameworks for such historic era agricultural deintensification have tended toward prime-mover models, focusing on drought (Guillet 1987), climate change (Brooks 1998), and colonial depopulation (Donkin 1979). Denevan (2001:205–10) has noted multiple correlations between terrace abandonment and these and other factors, though he suggests that depopulation and resettlement account for much of the observed pattern in the Colca Valley:

> Commonly, under conditions of depopulation, the most intensive forms of cultivation and the least accessible agricultural lands are abandoned. In the Colca Valley, with Spanish-controlled Indian settlements being located on the pampas near the river, and the population reduced, the higher terraces were indeed abandoned. (Denevan 2001:205–6)

Farmers are hypothesized to have taken land out of production in response to epidemic-induced demographic decline (a process augmented by the close living quarters of the reducciones) and as a consequence of moving people away from their fields into the new nucleated settlements. Epidemics clearly had major impacts on the communities of the valley from the sixteenth to eighteenth centuries: There was an estimated 87 percent decline from the pre-contact zenith (based on population retrodiction estimates) of 62,500–71,000 to a nadir estimate of 8,000–10,000 in 1721 (Cook 1982:82–85). In Coporaque, the local population fell from an estimated pre-contact (1530) high between 4,357 and 5,957 inhabitants to just 1,956 in 1604, a 55–67 percent decrease in three decades (Treacy 1994:167). The remoteness of some terrace complexes and their canal systems must have made them prohibitively expensive (in energetic terms) to maintain after resettlement, especially in the context of population decline. While this kind of cost-benefit calculus was clearly a factor in terrace abandonment, I argue that the changing physical and sociological structures of community organization mediated that calculus. That is, the altered relationship between settlement and agro-pastoral infrastructure in the valley after reducción produced a dialectic in which the farming and herding

Table 7.6. Areas (ha) and categories of abandoned and unabandoned fields in Coporaque

	Unabandoned	Abandoned, Unirrigated	Abandoned, Irrigated	Totals
Right side	166	5	46	217
Left side	368	504	226	1,098
Totals	534	509	272	1,315

practices of local communities had to either accommodate to or reconfigure the prehispanic and colonial features of the built landscape. One outcome of this dialectic was abandonment.

This explanation can account for the spatial distribution of abandoned canals and terraces in the survey better than strictly demographic or energetic models. Clearly, some abandoned irrigated terraces are located far from the reducciones as would be expected according to the risk minimization explanations. These include the abandoned terraces and canals of the undulating hills in extreme eastern Coporaque, as well as the abandoned canals and terraces and canals on the high slopes above Uyu Uyu and Llactarana in Yanque Urinsaya (both discussed in the previous chapter).

But just as clearly, there is no simple distance-from-reducción correlation for terrace abandonment as demographic/energetic explanations would predict. In fact, many abandoned terrace complexes in the survey area are very close to the reducciones. For example, to the adjacent east of Yanque, two large bench terrace complexes cover 27.5 ha on the north side of Cerro Pallaclle. The canal that irrigates these two clusters of terraces descended from the Waranqante canal into a small reservoir on the mesa-like top of Cerro

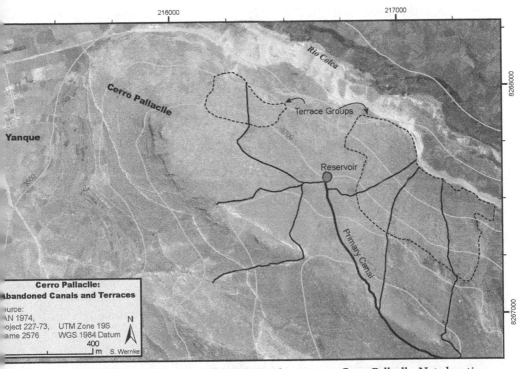

Figure 7.10. Abandoned irrigation features and terraces on Cerro Pallaclle. Note location adjacent to the southeast corner of the village of Yanque.

Pallaclle, and distribution canals radiate from the reservoir to irrigate each of the terrace groups (Figure 7.10). My survey and excavations in these terraces produced Late Horizon and Colonial Period ceramics, including in situ colonial sherds from a house floor. Therefore they appear to have been built during the Late Horizon and abandoned sometime during the colonial era, despite the fact that they are some of the closest canals and terraces to the village.

In Coporaque, abandoned canals and terraces flank either side of the village. To the immediate west of the village, a feeder canal network that drew water from the Chillihuitira and Wasamayo streams flowed into a large reservoir (Chilacotacocha) on the mesa-like upper reaches of Cerro Yurac Ccacca above the site of Chilacota (CO-154; Figure 7.11).[13] A secondary canal from one of the feeder canals fed a small complex of bench terraces on the steep slopes of the Chunancaya toponym sector to the adjacent west of the village, while the Chilacotacocha reservoir provided water to the terraces of the Chijra (CO-100) and Alto Ccayra sectors on the southern flanks of Cerro Yurac Ccacca. Given that San Antonio/Chijra (CO-100) continued to be occupied (and grew as a doctrina) during early colonial times, these canals and terraces appear to have been abandoned after reducción. To the adjacent east of the village, the abandoned "Inca" canal (as it is presently known) drew water from the Sahuara River and irrigated a narrow band (32 ha) of bench terraces on the western and southern slopes of Pampa Finaya (Figure 7.12). Although we observed no colonial-era sherds on these terraces, the abundant LIP/LH sherds on the surface provide a post quem date for their abandonment, so they were almost certainly abandoned during colonial times.

Building from these observations, I devised a multivariate approach to discriminate how demography, resettlement, climatic risk, and community organization differentially impinged on agricultural deintensification (Wernke 2010). Land tenure in the highly intensive, irrigated terrace systems such as those of the Colca Valley is at the more individuated end of the land-tenure spectrum in the Andes (Bolin 1993; Guillet 1981). But because terraces are dependent on their supporting irrigation systems for reliable yields in this semiarid climate, terracing and irrigation features are best considered complementary parts of a single agricultural infrastructure. Individual terraces can be maintained at the household level, but their necessary connections to canal and reservoir systems encompass them in supra-household schema of water distribution and infrastructural maintenance. Household decision making is thus impacted by suprahousehold management not only by day-to-day logistics of water distribution, but by seasonal and annual irrigation system management and maintenance operations. Primary feeder canals in the

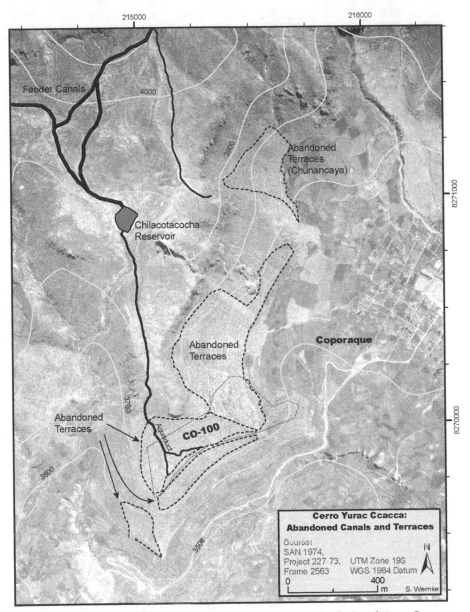

Figure 7.11. Abandoned irrigation features and terracing on the flanks of Yurac Ccacca, directly west of Coporaque.

central valley reach nearly 30 km in length, originating in the extreme heights, just below the catchment basins of the glaciated peaks. These lengthy and complex canal systems require regular maintenance, including annual cleaning and repair *faenas* (collective work festivals), which today are organized by community irrigation commissions and conducted by the beneficiaries

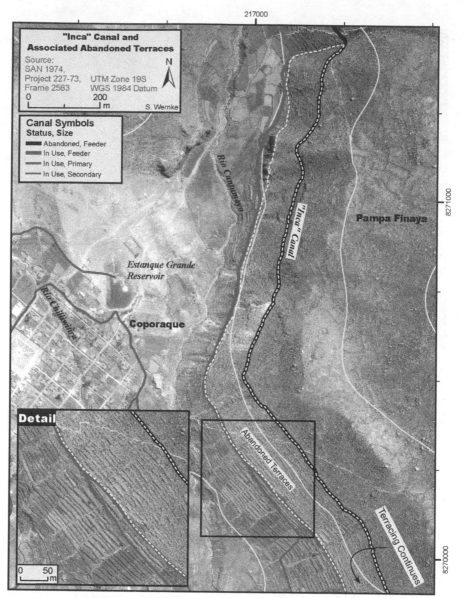

Figure 7.12. Abandoned "Inca" canal and associated terracing on the western slopes of Pampa Finaya. The canal and terracing continues out of the frame, around the southwest corner of Pampa Finaya.

of each respective irrigation system (Gelles 1990, 1995, 2000; Guillet 1987, 1992; Treacy 1994; Valderrama Fernández and Escalante Gutierrez 1988). Because reservoirs, which act as nodal points for storing water and regulating canal flow, infill with silt and also require annual cleaning, labor mobilization for infrastructural maintenance must have been a strong limiting factor as the population declined through the colonial period. As population declined—though theoretically leaving higher per capita landholdings among the surviving population—irrigation system maintenance must have become onerous, presenting irrigation authorities and their constituents with difficult decisions about how—and where—to cut their losses.

More than "adaptive" processes, then, *politics* must have been as central to agricultural deintensification under Spanish colonial rule as they were to agricultural intensification under Inka rule. A multivariate approach enables modeling of how demographic decline, resettlement, and climatic risk factors were all mediated by the kinds of community interfaces I reconstructed above. The methodology for this analysis was relatively straightforward, involving (1) digitization of abandoned field areas from aerial and satellite imagery, (2) simulation of field locations within unabandoned and abandoned field areas, and (3) implementation of an anisotropic walking model over a digital elevation model to and from the fields, using the center of the plaza of Coporaque as the starting point (see Wernke 2010 for a detailed discussion).

Digitizing abandoned field areas was accomplished through visual inspection and tracing of high-resolution aerial photos and satellite images (Figure 7.13). Abandoned fields are easily distinguished from unabandoned fields in such imagery (Denevan 1988b). As discussed above, unirrigated abandoned fields—that is, the rain-fed or runoff-capture field systems that were replaced by irrigated field systems much earlier (most likely during the Middle Horizon; Denevan 2001:198–99; Wernke 2010)—are thus excluded from this analysis. The resulting map of abandoned and unabandoned irrigated field areas shows an overall pattern of an unabandoned core area surrounded by a periphery of large contiguous sectors of abandoned fields (Figure 7.14). Two initial observations follow from simple inspection of the map. First, abandoned terraces were not interspersed with unabandoned ones, which would be more consistent with household-scale decision making. Instead, entire irrigation sectors were either allowed to lapse into dereliction or were shut down. Second, the peripheral distribution of the abandoned fields suggests that distance, elevation, or both were likely factors in the decision-making criteria.

Specific point locations for unabandoned and abandoned fields are required for this analysis. For the unabandoned fields, that is, for those fields declared in the visitas, the same random point location protocol was used: A random point location was generated for each field within its corresponding toponym. For abandoned field locations, a simulated 20 percent sample was produced by dividing each abandoned field sector area (first removing 10 percent of that area to account for field walls, trails, etc.) by the average

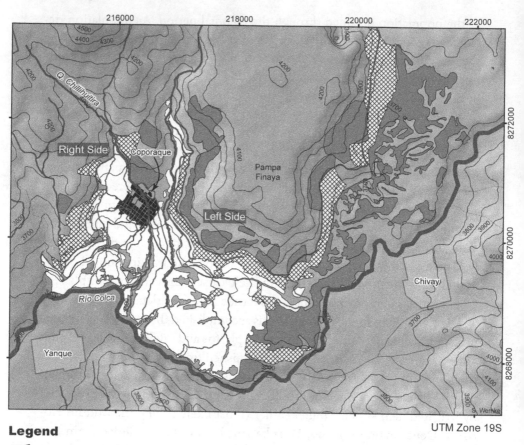

Figure 7.13. Unabandoned and abandoned field areas (including both irrigated and unirrigated systems).

field size (derived from the visita declarations) to produce a theoretical total field population within that area, and then assigning random point locations to a 20 percent sample of the total population. Five random point iterations for both abandoned and unabandoned fields were conducted to check for intersample errors introduced by the random sampling. No significant differences were found between samples. The difference between the actual and simulated field locations is therefore also not likely to be significant.

Viewing the resulting field distributions with least-cost paths in three-dimensional perspective (Figure 7.15) reinforces the impression that both distance and elevation were likely factors in abandonment decision making. Indeed, the results of the field location and walking simulation show that

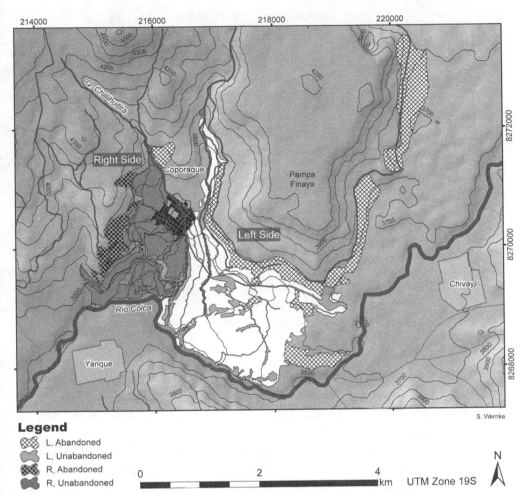

Figure 7.14. Unabandoned and abandoned irrigated field areas, showing right- and left-side division.

abandoned fields were both significantly farther away from Coporaque and higher in elevation than unabandoned fields (Table 7.7). The effect of distance is intuitive enough, though the distance calculus—what was or was not an acceptable or sustainable distance to walk to fields—must have also considered productivity, ecological zone, exposure to risks such as pests and frost, and other factors. The walking model, which employs least-cost paths to and from the fields, cannot capture such considerations but is intended as a heuristic and standardized measure that is a better alternative to simple Euclidean distance measures, which would be much less realistic in this high-relief environment.

That abandoned fields seem to be generally higher than unabandoned fields points to frost risk as a significant factor. Such risks were probably a

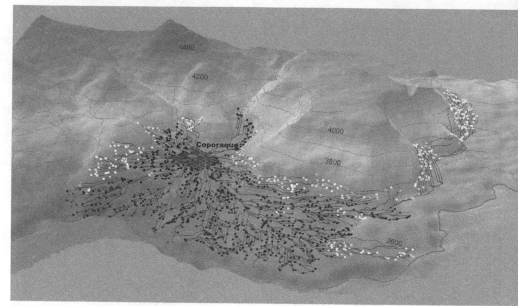

Figure 7.15. Three-dimensional view of unabandoned and abandoned fields, showing least-cost paths, from the south.

growing concern through the colonial period, as the sixteenth through mid-nineteenth centuries corresponds with the most severe era of the Little Ice Age (see Grove 1988; Rabatel et al. 2008; Thompson et al. 1986; Thompson et al. 1994). Even small average changes in temperature can have major local effects on frost-line elevations in high-altitude Andean settings. In the Mantaro Valley, crop cultivation lowered some 150 m below present upper limits during the Little Ice Age (Seltzer and Hastorf 1990:402). Locally, Brooks has argued that this kind of frost-line depression led to the abandonment of the upper 70–150 m of terraces in the upper reaches of the Japo drainage, located near Chivay on the south side of the valley (Brooks 1998:69–73, 384). Though these studies were concerned with the early phase of the Little Ice Age (the late thirteenth century), more widespread abandonment of the valley's upper terrace complexes might be expected during the most extreme phase of the Little Ice Age, between the mid-sixteenth and mid-nineteenth centuries (Thompson and Mosley-Thompson 1989:18).

The results of the walking model are presented graphically in the map of Figures 7.16–7.18. These results get us some way toward understanding that the irrigation communities of Coporaque made risk-minimizing decisions, both limiting exposure to frost risk (by preferentially abandoning higher altitude terrace complexes) and minimizing walking times (by preferentially abandoning more distant terrace complexes), but questions remain: Which

Table 7.7. Summary of average walking times and elevations of currently abandoned and unabandoned fields, separated by conceptual side

	Mean Walking Time, 1616 Visita (min.)	Mean Walking Time, Currently Unabandoned (min.)	Mean Walking Time, Abandoned (min.)	Mean Elevation, Unabandoned (m)	Mean Elevation, Abandoned (m)
Right side	37.8[a]	31.0[b]	38.1[c]	3,565	3,681.9[d]
Left side	45.8[a]	46.0[b]	109.4[c]	3,565	3,709.8[d]

Notes: a. $t(634.2) = -6.6, p < .001$.
b. $t(431.6) = -12.357, p < .001$.
c. $t(422.3) = -21.9, p < .001$.
d. $t(118.7) = -3.1, p = .002$.

factor mattered more, or were they equally important? And did they matter equally for both of the two "sides"—the right- and left-side ayllus—of Hanansaya?

Taking the last of these first, if we restrict analysis to unabandoned fields—those fields that were declared in the visitas which continue to be cultivated today—we see that walking times for the fields of the lower-ranking, left-side ayllu households were significantly greater on average than those of the right-side ayllu (Table 7.7). The same is true among abandoned fields. This suggests that the left-side ayllus were more significantly displaced by reducción resettlement and therefore had to bear a greater burden of its centripetal effects. Community organization—ayllu affiliation—was therefore probably a mediating factor in agricultural deintensification, as dwindling populations of the two "sides" were strained by the pressures of maintaining their differently distributed infrastructures. A binomial logistic regression using the conceptual side (right/left) as the dependent (response) variable and field state (unabandoned/abandoned) as the independent variable also shows that fields on the left side (to the east of the Chillihuitira) are more than twice as likely to be abandoned (odds ratio [OR] 2.18, 95 percent confidence interval [CI], 1.63–2.91). When both elevation and distance are held constant, with the state of fields (abandoned/unabandoned) as the dependent variable and conceptual side (right/left) as the independent variable, we find that fields on the left side are 61 percent less likely to be abandoned (OR 0.398, 95 percent CI, 0.231–0.685). Clearly distance, elevation, or both were important factors in the disproportionate abandonment of left-side fields.

But which factor, if either, mattered more? The fields of the left-side ayllus were not only more distant but higher on average than those of the right side. Binomial logistic regression allows us to measure which of these factors

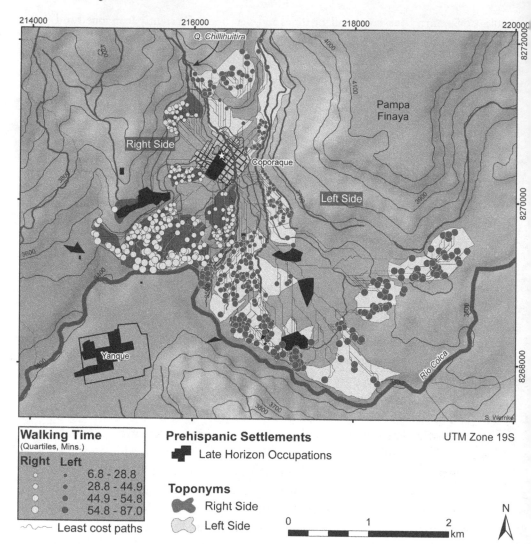

Figure 7.16. Least-cost paths to unabandoned right- and left-side fields.

was more important by running the model several times with one or more variables constant and comparing the odds ratio effects. First, the state of the fields (abandoned/unabandoned) can be modeled as the dependent variable and distance and elevation as the independent variables. Separate iterations for each side (right/left) tested for the effect of distance, distance adjusted for elevation (i.e., elevation held constant), elevation, and elevation adjusted for distance (i.e., distance held constant). Interestingly, the results show that different factors figured more prominently between the two sides. Specifically, elevation was the most important factor for the decision to abandon for the right side, while distance outweighed elevation for the left side. For

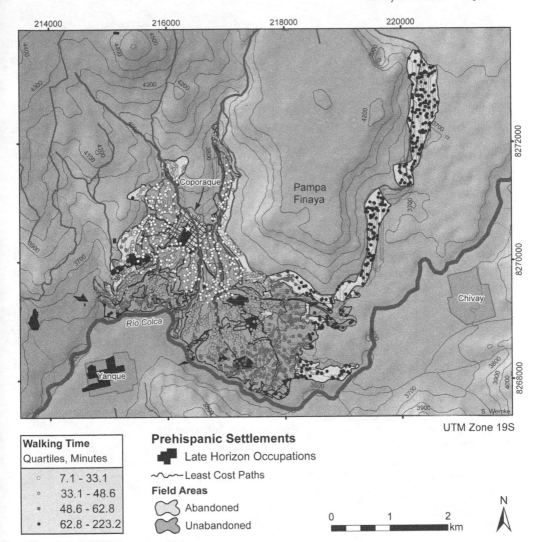

Figure 7.17. Least-cost paths to unabandoned and abandoned fields.

the right-side fields, if distance is held constant, abandonment becomes almost twice as likely (OR 1.962, 95 percent CI, 1.381–2.788), so some factor
other than distance must be at play. Conversely, if elevation is held constant,
they become 67 percent *less* likely to be abandoned (OR 0.328, 95 percent CI,
0.217–0.494). Thus, for the right-side ayllus, if the elevations of their fields
were not a concern, they would be significantly more reticent to abandon
their fields—by a margin of 67 percent—compared to a scenario in which
elevation did play a role in decision making. Elevation (a proxy for frost risk)
therefore outweighed distance in the decision-making process for aban-

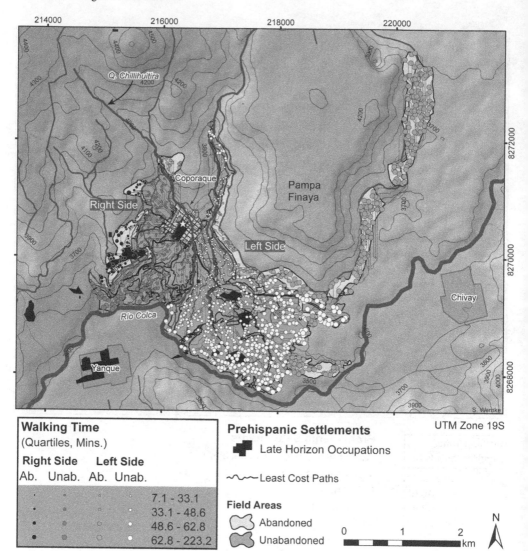

Figure 7.18. Least-cost paths to unabandoned and abandoned fields, showing right- and left-side division.

doning the fields and irrigation systems of the conceptual right side of the Coporaque landscape.

The reverse is the case for the fields and irrigation systems of the left-side ayllus: When the elevation of agricultural fields is held constant and only distance is considered, abandonment becomes 300 percent more likely (OR 3.053, 95 percent CI, 2.023–4.608). That is, when elevation is factored out in decision making for the people of the left-side ayllus, abandonment becomes significantly more likely—three times as likely. Some other factor (or factors) must account for the observed pattern of abandonment. The model holding walking time constant for left-side fields indicates that it was among those key factors: Abandonment becomes 51 percent *less* likely when walking time is held constant (OR 0.510, 95 percent CI, 0.359–0.724). Therefore, distance was clearly a significant concern for the people of the left-side ayllus, since their fields were significantly less likely to be abandoned—by a margin of 51 percent—if distance was not a factor in deciding whether to maintain or abandon a field.

How could it be that frost risk was the decisive factor for the right-side ayllus while distance was more important for the left-side ayllus? Here it is useful to recall that the fields of the right-side ayllus—whether or not currently abandoned—were closer overall than those of the left-side ayllus. Since the right-side ayllus were not as displaced by reducción resettlement, distance was not as big of an issue for them. Even their abandoned fields are within the walking distances of the *unabandoned* fields of the left-side ayllus. The households of the left-side ayllus, however, were moved farther from their original settlements by reducción, putting fields that were once within a tolerable distance out of reach. But again recalling the observations that started this discussion, not *all* of the fields of the left side were abandoned based on their distance, since some abandoned field complexes of the left side were very close to Coporaque—those irrigated by the "Inca" canal (see Figure 7.12 above). In that case, the pattern follows that of the right-side ayllus: Elevation appears to outweigh distance, since the Inka canal fields are the highest irrigated terraces on the western and southern slopes of Pampa Finaya. What was apparently operating, then, was a *sliding scale* of risk. The nearer the fields, the more frost risk weighed on the calculus to abandon, and the greater the distance, the more distance weighed in the calculus. Since all of the right-side fields were within the range of unabandoned fields of the left side, distance per se did not come into play. With fewer people to maintain their irrigation systems, frost risk was the more important factor in deciding which sectors to abandon (or allow to slowly lapse into dereliction) for them. For the left-side ayllus, frost risk outweighed distance for nearby fields, but distance eventually reached parity and ultimately outweighed it among their most distant field complexes as the prime factor.

We are now a fair way toward a more nuanced understanding of specifically how the factors of demography, climate, and space were mediated by the relations of community and state to produce the specific patterns of abandonment observed. "Causation" here was not a simple linear relationship: to say that terrace and canal abandonment was "caused" by colonial depopulation, resettlement, or climatic cooling during the Little Ice Age would be incomplete, even as each was an important factor. Instead, demographic decline can be seen as a *distal* causal factor—lowering the overall pool of available labor to maintain the canal and field systems. Frost risk and distance were more *proximal* factors, but all were mediated by the politics of community and state: how the reducción of Coporaque was pulled into place in the local landscape in the specific place that both straddled the boundary between the two sides and favored the higher-ranking right-side ayllus. Thus right-side ayllus, displaced less by resettlement, focused on maximizing productivity in their fields located in the warmest microclimates of Coporaque, allowing fields of higher frost risk on the upper slopes to lapse into dilapidation. Left-side ayllus, on the other hand, dealt with combined frost risk and greater distances to their fields by giving up their higher field and irrigation systems near the village while also taking their most distant ones out of production as the labor pool shrank. The legacy of reducción was a reduced landscape, reduced by the difficult—but rational—decisions of the communities that built, inhabited, and maintained it.

Discussion and Conclusion

This chapter illustrated how specific indigenous community structures continued to mediate and synchronize the land-use practices of local Coporaque households after conquest and resettlement. I have argued that the early colonial land-tenure patterns of the ayllus of Coporaque also reflect their terminal prehispanic patterns of residence and, by extension, provide insights into how Inka imperial administration articulated with local structures of community organization.

According to the visita declarations, Coporaque farmers continued to cultivate exclusively native crops three generations after conquest. Some villagers most likely also experimented with European cultigens, but they were not declared as the predominant crop grown in any fields in Coporaque during the first two decades of the seventeenth century. Coporaque farmers used the most productive, warmest production zones for cultivating maize, a frost-sensitive crop, while they planted the hardier quinoa in more marginal and frost-prone areas. This pattern shows the rationality of the local production regime not only in terms of minimizing risk but also in the culturally relative sense of preferentially cultivating maize—a less-nutritious but more culturally-esteemed crop than quinoa—in warm, fertile production zones.

Households also maintained access to multiple production zones and minimized their exposure to localized risks such as pests and frosts by distributing their landholdings among several small, dispersed fields. However, as reflected in the contrasting patterns of ayllu landholding distributions, these "microverticality" (Brush 1977) and risk-minimization strategies were mediated by ayllu affiliation. My land-tenure reconstructions demonstrate that ayllus did not control discrete field areas or "territories" but ayllu landholdings consisted of discontinuous and overlapping, but patterned, constellations of fields. The landholdings of all but one of the ayllus of Hanansaya, as well as the fields of the apical ayllu of the Urinsaya, were concentrated on either the "left" or "right" side of a hydrological dividing line running through the middle of Coporaque. In contrast, the landholdings of the other ayllus of Urinsaya, were more broadly distributed across the landscape of Coporaque on both sides of this dividing line. These distinct Hanansaya/Urinsaya ayllu patterns are also congruent with a parallel contrast in the naming patterns of the ayllus of each moiety. Hanansaya ayllu names generally do not follow the tripartite and decimpartite naming conventions of the ideal Inka sociopolitical organization of the province, and instead appear to be organized according to a left/right dualism, while those of Urinsaya conform more closely with the ideal Inka administrative structure (see chapter 6). Thus I have argued that the observed "left/right" landholding distributions of the Hanansaya ayllus represent vestiges of indigenous, perhaps pre-Inkaic, land-tenure patterns, while the dispersed patterns of Urinsaya ayllus, together with the ayllu of official state potters of Hanansaya, reflect greater Inka state intervention in the distribution of their fields.

Given this evidence for the prehispanic origin of the observed ayllu land-tenure patterns, I argued that they also reflect pre-reducción site-catchment patterns. By comparing the ayllu landholding distributions with the Late Horizon settlement pattern, therefore, I reconstructed pre-reducción ayllu residence patterns. These ayllu residence patterns provide a more culturally informed and nuanced view of the political organization of the local settlement system, both in terms of the supra-settlement organization of late prehispanic Collagua communities and in terms of how those communities articulated with Inka institutions.

As larger-scale communities, moieties were not residentially coterminous with settlements or groups of settlements, but were distributed over all of the settlements of Coporaque. Moiety affiliations cut across settlement and hydrological boundaries, and it appears that members from both moieties resided at all settlements (Table 7.5). Clearly, the hydrological interests of moieties as collectivities were widely dispersed. My analysis of hydrological relationships between feeder canals in chapter 6 suggested that water distribution was coordinated at a supra-settlement, watershed-scale during the LIP and Late Horizon. The land-tenure patterns I reconstructed in this chapter indicate that the households of many ayllus cultivated fields that were irrigated by several feeder canals, suggesting that they would have had an interest in maintaining and coordinating the apportionment of water between them rather than favoring one canal over another. Coporaque households also declared fields located on the opposite side of the Colca River near Yanque, as well as fields irrigated by the Misme canal, which draws water away from the settlements in the Coporaque area to irrigate the terraces surrounding the LIP/LH settlements of Uyu Uyu (YA-050) and Llactarana (YA-054) to the west (see chapter 4). This is especially true of the ayllus whose names and land-tenure patterns appear to be products of direct Inka state intervention: the ayllus of the middle-ranking Pahana macro-ayllu of Urinsaya. Their widely scattered land-tenure patterns may reflect an Inka state policy of dispersing hydrological interests in order to foment this kind of watershed-scale intensive water management regime, a policy enacted in neighboring valleys and regions (Trawick 2001; Zimmerer 2000). In contrast, the "right/left" land-tenure and residence patterns of the indigenous Hanansaya ayllus may reflect older, more localized hydrological interests that may have factored in the competition and conflict evident during the LIP.

The Inkas also appear to have attempted to subsume local political interests within a larger-scale hierarchy of settlements and ayllus. In chapter 4, I interpreted the association between elite Collagua houses and prominently situated Inka great halls at large LIP/Late Horizon settlements as indicative of the important intermediary role that local elites played in Inka imperial administration of the province. My reconstruction of pre-reducción ayllu residence patterns reinforces this interpretation because they indicate that an Inka administrative center was established on each side of the dualistic landscape: one at the right-side settlement of San Antonio (CO-100) and one at the left-side settlement of Tunsa/Llactapampa (CO-150/163). Inka administration appears to have been coordinated through the leaders of these ayllu segments at these secondary centers.

These local segments of larger ayllus would have been subsumed under the overarching authority of the paramount kurakas resident in Yanque (which was both the primary Inka administrative center and the location of the reducción and colonial provincial capital). This is consistent with what would be expected, since the Inka-era ancestor of the paramount lord—the kuraka of Collana of Hanansaya—would almost certainly have resided in the primary administrative center. The Inka-era paramount lord of Urinsaya may also have resided there, but it seems equally, if not more, likely that he resided at Uyu Uyu (YA-050), the other secondary administrative center located in present-day Yanque Urinsaya. In any case, it appears that the segments of the apical ayllus at San Antonio/Chijra and Tunsa/Llactapampa were subordinate to their counterparts in Yanque (and possibly Uyu Uyu). This reconstruction therefore reveals how supra-settlement, ranked communities were distributed over the local settlement system and shows in more culturally specific terms how the settlement hierarchy corresponded to the conceptual political hierarchy of the province.

The historically downstream effects of reducción are likewise illuminated by the land-tenure reconstructions presented above. Above all, they provide glimpses of what were surely complex negotiations in their emplacement and show how reducción was not simply a case of resettlement by colonial fiat— of an eradicative regime that brought prehispanic patterns of land use to their definitive end. We have already seen how the politically paramount reducciones of Yanque, Lari, and Cabanaconde were built atop or adjacent to Inkaic precursors, thus minimizing disruption by resettlement, but this analysis shows how even in a case of seemingly radical displacement, the *emplacement* of the reducción was figuratively (and literally) pushed and pulled into place by the longstanding and competing interests of the right and left-side ayllu communities in the local dualistic landscape. In this sense, the emplacement of this reducción was an improvised order that emerged from negotiating the dilemma of analogy or eradication.

To connect back to the theoretical discussion on the improvisation of colonial order through the interfaces of community and landscape, this reconstruction of land-tenure and residence patterns enables us to see specifically how specific indigenous schemas (ideal ayllu structures) recursively referred to and derived from tangible and durable features and interests in the resources of the built landscape. Seemingly abstract dualisms evident in ayllu naming conventions can now be seen to have emerged from daily practices of residing and cultivating in the local landscape, even as those practices were also structured by these schemas. The tangibility and durability of these interests and practices—the resistance of culture rather than resistance per se—substantially impinged on the terms of compromise in the negotiation of the dilemma of analogy or erasure in successive colonial projects.

Ironically, perhaps, such (otherwise obscure) compromises likely account for the durability of the reducciones in the Colca Valley, nearly all of which remain occupied through the present day. Their abandonment in other areas is likely a result of inattention or indifference to such local interests. In those cases, a more radically eradicative policy would have not only gained little cultural purchase, but likely endangered the very viability of local communities by fundamentally altering their basic compositions and distributions in their supporting landscapes. Indeed, locally, the detrimental effects of resettlement are abundantly evident even in this "attenuated" or negotiated case of reducción resettlement. Reducción exacerbated demographic declines caused by epidemic disease, stressing the surviving population further by lowering the overall labor pool needed to maintain irrigation and field systems. Thus even as land per capita likely increased with population decline, the stresses on the population and lack of labor required to maintain the systems they inherited from the Inka era (which were almost certainly at their most extensive and intensive in the history of the valley) resulted in the abandonment of large tracts of otherwise productive farmland. The analysis presented above shows the rationality of the process of abandonment: reducción also displaced lower-ranking communities more, leaving a legacy of greater walking distances and higher rates of abandonment for their fields. Higher-ranking ayllus, displaced less by reducción, abandoned only the least productive and riskiest field and irrigation systems.

These GIS-based spatial analyses and simulations thus enabled a more experience-near rendering of place, of living in and moving through this colonized landscape in the past. But the effects of these local-imperial compromises are also still very tangible today. The daily rhythm of life for farmers in the Colca Valley today is marked by long, sometimes grueling hikes between their reducción villages and their scattered fields. The landscape is a palimpsest of ancient and modern infrastructures, interspersed by expanses of abandoned fields and irrigation systems. Some abandoned fields and canals are seen as the work of Inkarrí, of a time of plenty when water was plentiful and the land was more productive (Pease 1978; Valderrama and Escalante 1997). While the vastness of some areas of relict fields lends itself to this kind of understanding, the area of cultivation is also expanding, as new terraces and canals are built every year (Guillet 1992; Treacy 1989a). Thus even as daily practices continue to be structured by inherited schema and resources, the ongoing work of "life in the fields" slowly expands the frontiers of cultivation.

Notes

1. I use these visitas because the Coporaque sections are complete in both, with the exception of a few missing folios (missing folios in the Coporaque section of the 1604 visita: 245r/v [ayllu Pahana Collana Pataca]; folios missing from the Coporaque section of the 1615–17 visita: 595r–596v [ayllu Cupi]). Coporaque appears in the fragment of the 1591 visita of Yanquecollaguas Urinsaya published in Pease (Verdugo and Colmenares 1977 [1591]), but the section is incomplete. The Coporaque section of the 1604 Urinsaya visita was recorded October 5–13, 1604, and the Coporaque section of the 1615–17 Hanansaya visita was recorded between December 5, 1615, and January 15, 1616 (APY Yanquecollaguas

Hanansaya 1615–17, fols. 480v–611v). All transcriptions by Laura Gutiérrez Arbulú. I thank María Benavides for providing me with the photocopies of the original archival documents and the transcriptions.

2. Both are housed in the Archivo Parroquial de Yanque (APY) of the Archdiocese Archives of Arequipa (AAA). The 1604 visita of Yanquecollaguas Urinsaya has also recently been published (Robinson 2005).

3. I conducted toponym surveys during 2000, 2002, and 2004, obtaining multiple identifications and cross-checking toponym locations whenever possible.

4. Some small plots were declared using other (less formal) measures, such as *pata* (patch/terrace), chacara (field), *pedaço/pedaçillo* (piece/small piece), *anden/andençillo* (terrace/little terrace), and *solar* (patio). Although the areas of these fields cannot be known, they were probably somewhat smaller than a quarter topo, the smallest fraction of a topo declared. I have equated them with one-eighth topo when reporting field areas in terms of hectares here.

5. Standard deviational ellipses and mean geometric center data were calculated using CrimeStat (version 2.0), a free spatial statistics application (Levine 2002).

6. Randomized intra-toponym field location simulations were generated using Hawth's Tools for GIS (http://www.spatialecology.com/htools/index.php/).

7. Average SDEs were derived from the mean length, rotational angle, and center of the major and minor axes of the five SDEs generated for each ayllu.

8. Given that toponym sectors are the minimal unit of provenience in the visitas, the location of the dots within each toponym is schematic—they are visual representations of the quantity of fields claimed within each toponym rather than their specific locations within them. The dot-density maps were generated using random point locations for each field within its respective toponym.

9. This figure is derived from the modern standardized area of a topo in the Department of Arequipa today: 3,496 m^2 (see chapter 4). Thus 3,496 × 0.34 = 1,189 m^2, or just over 0.1 ha.

10. Bertonio (1956 [1612]:79) defines Checa (Ccheca) as "left" and identifies its antonym (i.e., "right") as Cupi. Malco is glossed as "lord of vassals" (Bertonio 1956 [1612]:212).

11. Specifically, the first of these is listed as "Aipi" in the ayllu header (fol. 565v), but in the ayllu summary (fol. 585r) it is referred to as "Cupi." The name of the second "Cupi" ayllu (beginning on folio 585v) is referred to as such throughout.

12. Two ayllus of official state potters (olleros oficiales) listed as separate segments of the ayllus Pahana Collana Pataca and Pahana Cayao Pataca (APY Yanquecollaguas Urinsaya 1604, fols. 268v–269v, 309v–312r) are excluded from analysis due to insufficient sample size of mappable fields.

13. The topographic setting and configuration of the reservoir in relation to the terraces below mirror those of Cerro Pallaclle on the opposite side of the river in Yanque. Chilacotacocha and its associated canals were also documented previously by Treacy and Denevan (Treacy 1989b:154–55; Treacy and Denevan 1986).

CONCLUSION

By tracing the local historical trajectory from autonomous rule through the Inkaic and Spanish invasions, the goal of this book was to provide a grounded, emplaced perspective on the local experience of colonial rule. What comes to the fore in this perspective is the particular, irreducibly local manner in which new social orders were continuously improvised through the interfaces of community and landscape—orders in which lines of power between dominant and subordinate were not so clearly delimited. Tracing the historical arc in this manner shows in concrete terms how local peoples were quite accustomed to dealing with aggressive foreigners—not just reacting to them oppositionally, but pulling them into their *own* politics (to again paraphrase Ortner 1995:176–77) and all of the local categories of friction and tension that those politics entail. In the process, the institutions of Inkaic and Spanish colonialism were themselves significantly colonized.

The implications are not just local. "Community" in this sense was not just an unselfconscious byproduct of habituated interaction, it was a primary currency in these politics of articulation between Inkaic and Spanish colonial projects and local peoples. "Landscape" was not only the setting in which these negotiations took place, it was an emergent property of them, as the schemas of community (e.g., in local terms: Cupi/Checa; in Inka terms: Collana, Pahana, Cayao; in Spanish terms: reducción, policia) were at once materialized in durable features and interests (fields, canals, settlements, land-tenure systems) as they acted as models for directing their ongoing constitution and maintenance. These schemas and resources together—that is, *in place*—constituted the "resistance of culture" (Sahlins 2005:4) with which the Inkas and the Spanish necessarily contended. Thus colonialist plans of eradication and replacement reckoned with the practical necessities of collusion and analogy.

That much is the argument that ran through this book. The sections below provide a summary and synthesis of the substantive findings as they inform that argument.

Community and Landscape during the LIP and Late Horizon

Following the decline of the Middle Horizon states, several archaeological indices from the Late Intermediate period point to a major expansion of settlement and irrigated agricultural production associated with the development
of autonomous ethnic polities in the upper and lower reaches of the Colca
Valley. Collagua ethnogenesis during the LIP is marked by the appearance of
distinctive local domestic and mortuary architecture, extensive complexes of
irrigated bench terraces surrounding settlements, and a diagnostic ceramic
series of limited stylistic and formal continuity from the preceding Wari-influenced wares.

While these markers suggest an overarching unity of identity among the
Collaguas, I have argued that ethnic identification was not isomorphic with
political organization and was likely not as important as lower-order affiliations in everyday community life. In fact, material differences between the
areas later identified as "Cabana" in the lower valley versus "Collagua" in
the middle and upper stretches of the valley are scant. Though comparable
domestic architecture from Cabanaconde is lacking, the most marked differences relate to more noncentralized but overall more dense settlement
and more intensive land-use patterns in Yanquecollaguas and Laricollaguas
compared to Cabanaconde. Given the attested differences in language and
mythical origins between the two groups in colonial textual sources, it is exceedingly unlikely that such ethnic distinctions did not originate in the LIP,
but they were likely not as marked or as salient as they became under Inka
administration. This is consistent with an emerging consensus that much of
what has been imagined of the political landscape of the LIP—a balkanized
landscape of consolidated ethnic señoríos—is wrong because it has been
based on a retrospective projection of the *outcomes* of Inka imperial policies.
Those policies tended to reify ethnic boundaries and the political hierarchies
within them (see also Arkush 2010; Covey 2008). Ethnic identity during the
LIP here and elsewhere in the highlands was probably in this sense only the
most outwardly visible (Cohen's [1985:70–75] "public face" of community)
manifestation of a multiscalar, fractal-like structure of ayllu-based community identification—one compatible with Inka imperial interests (and those
of favored ethnic lords) in submerging lower-order conflicts, promoting ethnic identity, and preventing higher-order, inter-ethnic alliances.

As I have argued, then, autonomous political organization during the LIP
in the Colca Valley was heterarchical in nature, that is, composed of internally differentiated communities whose relative political rankings and relations were fluid. On the one hand, there is strong evidence for increasing
disparities of status during the LIP, such as intra- and intersite disparities in

the size and elaboration of domestic architecture, including major differences in tomb elaboration and mortuary treatment. On the other hand, political organization was apparently noncentralized; the LIP settlement patterns in all three areas of the valley markedly decentralized, and no settlement dominates the settlement pattern in terms of centrality or elaboration of architecture. Rather, an elite class resided at several large settlements in each area of the valley.

Within this heterarchical political structure, intrapolity community relations oscillated between coordination and competition. As illustrated in chapter 4, hydrological relationships between the long feeder canals that carry meltwater from the surrounding peaks and the distribution of settlements in relation to those canals illustrate that water apportionment was coordinated at a supra-settlement scale during the LIP and Late Horizon. This reveals an important aspect of sub-ethnic, but supra-settlement community organization, since irrigation water is the sine qua non of reliable agricultural production in the Colca Valley. However, frequent violent conflict between Collagua communities, and perhaps with external polities, during the LIP is also apparent in defensive site locations and pukaras. The common external threat of Inka incursion to the valley was likely a significant initial stimulus for activating high-order ethnic identification that continued through as the Inka occupation.

So the Inkas apparently sought to centralize and hierarchize the political organization of the Collaguas and Cabanas to establish a vertically integrated and horizontally compartmentalized administrative structure in which latent distinctions of rank between local ayllus were amplified, ossified, and reordered in the image of Inka ideals. As I have shown, these schema were articulated to analogous local counterparts and built forms in the landscape, resulting in an improvised order that does not conform to the heuristics of either "direct" or "indirect" strategies of imperial rule. Settlement in the valley during the Late Horizon reached its maximum extent and became locally centralized (but decentralized on a valley-wide basis) around primary administrative centers in each of Yanquecollaguas, Laricollaguas, and Cabanaconde. In the political nucleus of the province around Yanque and Coporaque, a more clearly defined second tier of administrative sites was also established at sites that were formerly at the top of the settlement hierarchy—Uyu Uyu (YA-050), San Antonio/Chijra (CO-100), and Tunsa/Llactapampa (CO-163/150)—where Inka great hall structures and their associated plazas were prominently situated in close association with elite Collagua domestic structures. By all indications, Inka rule was mediated through local elites at these sites. The repeated great hall–plaza couplet observed at similar nodes of Inka administration throughout the valley, combined with our excavation results at one of these complexes at Malata, signal that commensal ritual was a central currency in the local experience of Inka administration through these local elites. Inka rule was thus presented through analogous practices of affiliation—as an extension of traditional relations of reciprocity between ayllu commoners and their kurakas-cum-ancestors.

These interpretations derive not only from these archaeological corollaries but also from homologies reconstructed from the colonial visitas to the valley. The ideal structure of the Inkaic Collagua Province (reconstructed from the visitas to the valley) was composed of a nested hierarchy of ayllus that were ranked according to dualistic, tripartite, and decimal categories. Dualism was expressed by moiety divisions: Hanansaya (higher ranking) and Urinsaya (lower ranking). Within each moiety, macro-ayllus were ranked according to high-, middle-, and low-status categories (Collana, Payan, and Cayao), each of which was internally divided into three minimal ayllus of an ideal size of 100 households that were also ranked according to these same tripartite status categories. This recursive tripartite structure exactly parallels the nomenclature of the ceque system of Cuzco, clearly showing an attempt to implant an ideal schema of hierarchical order from above. But as shown in chapters 6 and 7, this schema was incompletely instituted, and in a way which left analogous local counterparts (the dualistic structure of Cupi/Checa, "right"/"left") more or less intact, though subsumed within the higher order moiety division. The names of the minimal ayllus of the Urinsaya moiety exactly parallel the nomenclature of the ceque system of Cuzco and have decimal administrative designations, suggesting a more comprehensive imperial reordering of community structures than among the ayllus of the Hanansaya moiety, which retained local Aymara names. In contrast to the tripartite- and decimal-dominated ranking system of the Urinsaya ayllus, the onomastic patterning among the Hanansaya ayllus indicate directional, dualistic principles structured autochthonous political organization and criteria of rank. The striking differences in ayllu onomastics between Hanansaya and Urinsaya suggest that the observed ordering was not moving toward a total state-imposed tripartite and decimal hierarchy but had stabilized between an autochthonous structure in the Hanansaya moiety and a state-ordered structure in the Urinsaya moiety.

The covariance of these naming patterns with their contrasting land-tenure patterns further suggest differential articulation of state and local institutions within the province. Reconstructed ayllu land-tenure patterns from the visitas provided a means for retrodicting the terminal prehispanic residence patterns of the ayllus of Coporaque and reveal how the imagined, hybrid local/imperial constructs of community discussed above were mapped onto the local settlement system. At the moiety level, the Inka-engineered ayllus of Urinsaya held highly dispersed landholdings, while the autochthonous ayllus or Hanansaya, consistent with their "right/left" dualistic naming patterns, held constellations of landholdings that were discretely distributed on either side of a prominent local hydrological divide (the quebradas Chillihuitira), thus revealing the spatial referent of their names. Through a variety of spatial analytics, the relationship between these colonial-era ayllu landholding distributions and the prehispanic settlement pattern allowed reconstruction of where those ayllus resided prior to reducción resettlement. This analysis shows that the higher-ranking right-side ayllus originally resided at San Antonio/Chijra (CO-100) (one of the largest LIP settlements that became a secondary Inka administrative center with a great hall and plaza), while the left-side ayllus originally resided at a group of settlements on the left (eastern) side of the Chillihuitira, the largest of which was Tunsa/Llactapampa (CO-163/CO-150) (again, one of the largest LIP settlements that became a secondary Inka administrative center with great hall and plaza). This spatial synthesis of archaeological and documentary data sets thus shows specifically how schema and resources—both of the Inkas and of autochthonous communities—articulated in situ. On the one hand, Inka administration reached down to establish a secondary administrative center at the primary settlements of each side of the autochthonous Collagua community structure, leaving existing schema and the durable features and interests it had established in the landscape largely intact. On the other hand, the dispersed land-tenure patterns of the ayllus of Urinsaya indicate that their members were originally dispersed widely over both sides of the right/left divide, thereby distributing agricultural and hydrological interests across boundaries that were likely contentious under autonomous rule. The Inkaic mode of articulating an ideal model of social order was the spatial mirror image of what was to come with the Spanish invasion: It was highly dispersed rather than "reductive."

This summary discussion bears importantly on the broader argument about improvised orders in colonial encounters. It shows how at once there was an envisioned colonial order—a simplified, idealized vision (schema) of a hierarchical social order—but in practice that colonial project was necessarily and significantly altered and adapted to existing resources of community and landscape. It therefore cannot be reduced to an outcome of "indirect" or "direct" imperial "strategies." It was improvised in place.

Religious Convergence during the Transition to Spanish Colonial Rule

Such was the situation on the ground when a handful of Franciscan friars reached the Colca Valley just a decade or so after the Spanish invasion of Peru. Chapter 5 explored how they established a series of doctrinas at the former places of articulation between Inka administration and local communities, in sites such as San Antonio/Chijra, Uyu Uyu, Yanque, Coporaque, and Malata. Working initially with minimal personnel and institutional structure and an ecclesiastical regime more open to pastoral experimentation than its post-Tridentine successors, the friars had chapels constructed in close association with—and sometimes literally recycling the same spaces as—the great halls and plazas that were central to the local experience of Inka rule.

Analysis of the growth and remodeling of domestic, public, and sacred space at the doctrina of Malata provides a window into how these spaces became new places, as new models of social order (reducción, policia) were brought to bear on the built environment of indigenous Andean settlements. It shows how new models of domestic space, in the form of rectilinear domestic structures laid out in rows edge of the site, were made to more directly communicate with the network of paths that funneled into a single entrance into the colonial plaza than the agglutinated patio groups of circular structures in the old site core. Comparing the spatial network models of foot traffic to the Inka great hall and plaza to the colonial plaza shows a shunting of traffic away from the Inka complex and toward the colonial plaza, as all paths led to a junction in front of the domestic compound that excavations show was an elite household—almost certainly the principal kuraka of the settlement. As under Inka rule, the kuraka served as the fulcrum of colonial rule. Simulation of surveillance patterns of traffic to the chapel presented in chapter 5 illustrates how the kuraka could observe the members of literally every household at the settlement filing in procession past his large patio adjacent to the plaza. So the deterministic view of the built environment and its role in the production of Christian subjects evident in the writings of clerics, policy thinkers, and the Crown during the early to mid-sixteenth century can be seen to be manifested in place even in this early post-conquest setting.

While this was likely the intent of the friars, I have questioned the effectiveness of that new spatial order because the relationship between built form and behavior is not so simple as the Spanish (or behaviorist theorists) would have it. More concretely in this context, this relationship is complicated by the analogies that must have inhered in it for the people of Malata, since ready material analogues to the communal focus of the doctrina (chapel/atrium/

plaza) were present in the village itself (great hall/plaza)—built spaces that were surely used in commensal events by some of the older individuals of the village just a short time previous. Thus even as all evidence points to an overall open disposition on the part of local communities to the aggressive inculcation of the rudiments of Catholicism, here is an example, I suspect, of how the same schemas and resources that can constrain the parameters of imagination and action can also provide the rudiments for questioning and altering them.

What kinds of analogies were produced through successive dwelling in the built forms of great hall/plaza and chapel/plaza? Obviously this is a difficult question to address directly, but in general terms it is important to keep in mind that over the longue durée, Catholic evangelization in the Andes did not in fact produce anything approaching the homogeneous set of practices and beliefs envisioned by the church, but instead created the myriad local Andean Catholicisms seen today (see Gose 2008). Equally revealing is the subsequent reactionary evangelical regime that accompanied the reducción and associated reforms of Viceroy Toledo in the 1570s, built on the intent of fundamentally remaking Andean communities. The revanchist politics of Toledo and the Third Lima Council in this sense ironically point to the success of early evangelization efforts to find cultural purchase through analogy, even as they misdiagnosed Andean assimilations of Catholicism as backsliding and demonically inspired "resistance."

Toledan Compromises and Their Legacies

But as much as the will to institute a tabula rasa politics would seem to have taken form in the reducciones and the associated institutional transformations of the Toledan era, I have emphasized how the new order (which set the basic institutional framework of the viceroyalty for over two centuries) was itself built on a series of uneasy compromises. While several dimensions of these compromises have been explored extensively by others (e.g., Larson 1998; Pease 1989; Saignes 1999; Spalding 1984; Stern 1982), the analyses in chapters 6 and 7 provide local and regional perspectives on the collusions that building and living in this new order required, and the legacies of them.

At the regional scale, the analysis of visita landholding and livestock declarations in chapter 6 illustrated how supra-local networks of ayllu affiliation and authority continued to synchronize diverse complementarity relationships between agriculturalists and pastoralists in post-Toledan times. At the level of domestic economy, commoner farming and herding households participated in direct exchange of their respective produce with their ayllu cohorts. In contrast, elite households declared fields and livestock in far-flung locales, thereby directly controlling the means of production in several production zones. Wealthy pastoralist households from the upper reaches of the valley declared maize fields in the central valley as well as in maize production enclaves in Huanca, Lluta, and the valley of Arequipa to the south. Wealthy agriculturalist households based in the central valley declared personal herds of livestock in the upper valley. As extractive agents, colonial Collagua kurakas of Yanque and Coporaque collected tribute from their far-flung ayllu segments and converted agricultural produce to sumptuary cumbi through attached specialists, as their predecessors would have done in Inkaic times.

At the local scale, we have seen how the reducciones themselves were negotiated settlements, and not a fiat imposition. Though the archaeological corollaries of direct rule would seem unassailable—the settlement pattern of terminal prehispanic and early colonial times was basically obliterated—a closer look at their emplacement reveals how they accommodated existing features and interests in the landscape. The reducción of Yanque (like Lari down valley) as principal settlement of colonial Yanquecollaguas (and the province as a whole) was built directly atop its Inka predecessor, minimizing disruptions of resettlement. But even in the case of Coporaque across the Colca River from Yanque, situated in a place where no significant terminal prehispanic settlement was registered by the survey, reconstruction of the land-tenure patterns of its constituent Hanansaya ayllus shows how it literally straddled the boundary between the right and left sides in the local dualistic landscape. The emplacement of Coporaque was not imposed, it was improvised relative to the embedded features (resources) and interests (schema) of the local landscape and the communities that dwelled there.

I have argued that it was this kind of balancing of the mandate to eradicate with the practical pressures to locate reducciones in locales that would minimally disrupt the productive and (socially reproductive) capacities that in part accounts for the longevity of the reducciones of the Colca Valley relative to many other Andean locales. But this is not to minimize the harmful effects of reducción, either for those who experienced it firsthand or those living its legacy today. The analysis of spatial patterning of abandoned agricultural complexes around Coporaque in the last chapter reveals how, even though the village is situated on the dividing line between the two sides of the local landscape, resettlement disproportionately displaced the peoples of the lower-ranking left-side ayllus, contributing to greater walking distances even among those fields that they continued to cultivate compared to their counterparts of the right side ayllus. Thus as the people of Coporaque suffered increasing mortality in the cramped quarters of the reducciones, the survivors of the two sides faced different matrices of endowments and risks in the maintenance of their agricultural infrastructure. The multivariate analysis presented in that chapter shows the specific spatial patterning of abandonment can be explained by the rationality of the decisions made in the face of the distinct mix of stressors that different ayllus faced in the wake of resettlement. Far from a reductive exercise, then, GIS-based simulation of the landscape surrounding the village enabled a more thickly described rendering of the experience of reducción and of the difficult decisions that community leaders faced in the wake of forced resettlement.

The people of the Colca Valley today live the legacy of those decisions, even as they make their own, on their way back and forth to their fields and pastures.

APPENDIX

Principal LIP/LH Settlements
in the Surveys of the Lower and Middle Colca Valley

The principal settlements occupied during the Late Intermediate period (LIP) and Late Horizon (LH) in the Yanque-Coporaque survey area are described below. For a complete listing of all sites registered, see Table A.1. Sites from Cabanaconde and Lari are also presented in Table A.1. These were recorded by Doutriaux (2004).

Table A.1. Site coordinates and areas by occupation, Late Intermediate period and Late Horizon

District	Site	UTM-E	UTM-N	Elevation	Area	Occupation
Cabanaconde	CA-002	180555	8270434	3299	Unknown	LIP
Cabanaconde	CA-006	821554	8270147	3113	0.600	LH
Cabanaconde	CA-013	181475	8268852	3542	1.300	LIP
Cabanaconde	CA-013	181475	8268852	3542	0.910	LH
Cabanaconde	CA-018	181858	8269967	3365	9.090	LIP
Cabanaconde	CA-018	181858	8269967	3365	13.650	LH
Cabanaconde	CA-019	182208	8268965	3476	0.900	LIP
Cabanaconde	CA-019	182208	8268965	3476	3.000	LH
Cabanaconde	CA-020	178623	8260385	4402	Unknown	LIP
Cabanaconde	CA-022	821073	8262388	4395	0.002	LH
Cabanaconde	CA-023	820776	8259917	4307	0.700	LIP
Cabanaconde	CA-023	820776	8259917	4307	5.550	LH
Cabanaconde	CA-028	181557	8270897	3348	0.090	LH
Cabanaconde	CA-029	182161	8270659	3443	Unknown	LIP
Cabanaconde	CA-029	182161	8270659	3443	0.075	LH
Cabanaconde	CA-031	179405	8271094	3257	Unknown	LIP

(*continued*)

District	Site	UTM-E	UTM-N	Elevation	Area	Occupation
Cabanaconde	CA-032	180160	8270857	3274	6.300	LIP
Cabanaconde	CA-032	180160	8270857	3274	8.370	LH
Cabanaconde	CA-033	179776	8271387	3078	3.270	LIP
Cabanaconde	CA-033	179776	8271387	3078	0.770	LH
Cabanaconde	CA-035	180604	8271508	3227	0.160	LIP
Cabanaconde	CA-035	180604	8271508	3227	0.300	LH
Cabanaconde	CA-037	181551	8272193	3165	7.855	LIP
Cabanaconde	CA-037	181551	8272193	3165	4.331	LH
Cabanaconde	CA-038	182300	8272060	3383	0.000	LIP
Cabanaconde	CA-038	182300	8272060	3383	0.060	LH
Cabanaconde	CA-040	182582	8270178	3518	0.800	LH
Cabanaconde	CA-042	182772	8270431	3545	0.000	LIP
Cabanaconde	CA-042	182772	8270431	3545	0.100	LH
Cabanaconde	CA-044	183346	8271821	3620	0.000	LIP
Cabanaconde	CA-045	182876	8271504	3526	0.000	LIP
Cabanaconde	CA-049	183843	8265846	3824	0.001	LH
Cabanaconde	CA-050	183976	8265752	3813	0.018	LIP
Cabanaconde	CA-050	183976	8265752	3813	0.018	LH
Coporaque	CO-061	213249	8272761	4320	2.830	LH
Coporaque	CO-098	215317	8270500	3725	Unknown	LIP
Coporaque	CO-100	215348	8269972	3631	8.650	LIP
Coporaque	CO-100	215348	8269972	3631	8.650	LH
Coporaque	CO-103	216622	8269577	3503	0.250	LIP
Coporaque	CO-103	216622	8269577	3503	0.250	LH
Coporaque	CO-105	217418	8276151	4293	0.060	LIP
Coporaque	CO-105	217418	8276151	4293	0.060	LH
Coporaque	CO-109	216403	8275673	4280	1.000	LH
Coporaque	CO-111	215685	8274320	4279	0.070	LH
Coporaque	CO-114	216953	8271034	3617	Unknown	LIP
Coporaque	CO-118	217006	8270976	3631	Unknown	LIP
Coporaque	CO-119	217088	8270660	3694	Unknown	LIP
Coporaque	CO-120	217049	8270321	3661	Unknown	LIP
Coporaque	CO-121	216548	8269211	3480	Unknown	LIP
Coporaque	CO-121	216548	8269211	3480	0.010	LH
Coporaque	CO-123	217059	8270556	3698	Unknown	LIP

District	Site	UTM-E	UTM-N	Elevation	Area	Occupation
Coporaque	CO-127	217416	8268928	3504	4.232	LIP
Coporaque	CO-127	217416	8268928	3504	4.230	LH
Coporaque	CO-128	218098	8269491	3548	Unknown	LIP
Coporaque	CO-147	218359	8268162	3522	Unknown	LIP
Coporaque	CO-148	218302	8268930	3520	Unknown	LIP
Coporaque	CO-149	217586	8268285	3492	Unknown	LIP
Coporaque	CO-150	216916	8268378	3455	1.401	LIP
Coporaque	CO-150	216916	8268378	3455	1.400	LH
Coporaque	CO-151	215101	8270357	3761	0.400	LIP
Coporaque	CO-151	215101	8270357	3761	0.400	LH
Coporaque	CO-153	215270	8270674	3837	0.010	LH
Coporaque	CO-154	215247	8270144	3709	Unknown	LIP
Coporaque	CO-156	214893	8275213	4407	0.010	LIP
Coporaque	CO-159	215155	8273897	4358	0.360	LH
Coporaque	CO-161	216353	8270521	3575	4.853	LIP
Coporaque	CO-161	216353	8270521	3575	4.850	LH
Coporaque	CO-163	217264	8268280	3462	5.746	LIP
Coporaque	CO-163	217264	8268280	3462	5.750	LH
Coporaque	CO-164	217199	8269331	3504	3.764	LIP
Coporaque	CO-164	217199	8269331	3504	3.760	LH
Coporaque	CO-165	217384	8268518	3489	Unknown	LIP
Coporaque	CO-166	217273	8268603	3487	Unknown	LIP
Coporaque	CO-167	217100	8268741	3487	Unknown	LIP
Coporaque	CO-168	217079	8269008	3487	Unknown	LIP
Coporaque	CO-169	217378	8269450	3519	Unknown	LIP
Lari	LA-003	203304	8271315	3369	48.1420	LH
Lari	LA-003–01	203254	8271596	3415	4.509	LIP
Lari	LA-003–02	202993	8271111	3353	3.380	LIP
Lari	LA-003–03	203368	8270815	3353	1.630	LIP
Lari	LA-005	206208	8270845	3751	Unknown	LIP
Lari	LA-005	206208	8270845	3751	0.003	LH
Lari	LA-006	205935	8270718	3694	0.007	LH
Lari	LA-007	205648	8270699	3600	0.014	LIP
Lari	LA-007	205648	8270699	3600	0.020	LH
Lari	LA-008	205437	8270739	3575	0.210	LIP

(continued)

District	Site	UTM-E	UTM-N	Elevation	Area	Occupation
Lari	LA-008	205437	8270739	3575	0.245	LH
Lari	LA-009	205556	8270965	3633	Unknown	LIP
Lari	LA-009	205556	8270965	3633	0.350	LH
Lari	LA-010	203618	8270423	3375	0.105	LH
Lari	LA-012	205177	8270870	3586	Unknown	LIP
Lari	LA-012	205177	8270870	3586	0.340	LH
Lari	LA-014	204884	8270485	3477	0.015	LIP
Lari	LA-014	204884	8270485	3477	0.035	LH
Lari	LA-015	202991	8270111	3262	0.420	LIP
Lari	LA-015	202991	8270111	3262	0.820	LH
Lari	LA-016	202943	8270760	3344	0.460	LIP
Lari	LA-016	202943	8270760	3344	0.670	LH
Lari	LA-017	203170	8270724	3348	Unknown	LIP
Lari	LA-017	203170	8270724	3348	0.049	LH
Lari	LA-020	202708	8271035	3345	0.031	LIP
Lari	LA-020	202708	8271035	3345	0.071	LH
Lari	LA-021	202486	8270861	3335	3.635	LIP
Lari	LA-021	202486	8270861	3335	3.635	LH
Lari	LA-022	202665	8271595	3362	0.090	LIP
Lari	LA-022	202665	8271595	3362	0.210	LH
Lari	LA-024	203815	8270722	3378	Unknown	LIP
Lari	LA-024	203815	8270722	3378	0.024	LH
Lari	LA-025	203797	8270561	3374	Unknown	LIP
Lari	LA-025	203797	8270561	3374	0.140	LH
Lari	LA-027	202150	8271287	3332	4.950	LIP
Lari	LA-027	202150	8271287	3332	6.705	LH
Lari	LA-028	202445	8270602	3333	0.036	LH
Lari	LA-029	202295	8270711	3329	0.036	LH
Lari	LA-033	201393	8270792	3271	0.180	LH
Lari	LA-034	202392	8271701	3380	0.280	LH
Lari	LA-035	202090	8272042	3415	0.011	LIP
Lari	LA-035	202090	8272042	3415	0.015	LH
Lari	LA-036	201748	8271865	3385	0.090	LH
Lari	LA-037	201155	8272061	3405	Unknown	LIP

District	Site	UTM-E	UTM-N	Elevation	Area	Occupation
Lari	LA-038	202058	8271653	3370	0.530	LH
Lari	LA-041	201202	8271323	3304	0.420	LH
Lari	LA-043	200375	8271123	3279	0.024	LH
Lari	LA-045	200438	8270817	3240	0.027	LH
Lari	LA-046	200575	8270673	3214	0.003	LH
Lari	LA-047	202979	8271950	3500	0.060	LIP
Lari	LA-047	202979	8271950	3500	0.200	LH
Lari	LA-048	202504	8272273	3551	0.018	LIP
Lari	LA-048	202504	8272273	3551	0.042	LH
Lari	LA-049	202425	8272016	3412	0.063	LH
Lari	LA-069	205790	8272172	3884	0.021	LH
Lari	LA-082	205115	8271134	3685	0.200	LH
Lari	LA-083	204409	8270584	3509	1.200	LIP
Lari	LA-083	204409	8270584	3509	1.200	LH
Lari	LA-095	205977	8270953	3657	0.735	LIP
Lari	LA-095	205977	8270953	3657	1.475	LH
Lari	LA-098	205876	8269375	3351	0.354	LH
Lari	LA-098	205876	8269375	3351	0.150	LIP
Lari	LA-099	200382	8272398	3407	1.194	LIP
Lari	LA-099	200382	8272398	3407	1.194	LH
Lari	LA-101	201185	8274479	3753	Unknown	LIP
Lari	LA-101	201185	8274479	3753	0.035	LH
Yanque	YA-001	216265	8268291	3408	Unknown	LIP
Yanque	YA-001	216265	8268291	3408	0.510	LH
Yanque	YA-002	215683	8268489	3436	Unknown	LIP
Yanque	YA-002	215683	8268489	3436	0.060	LH
Yanque	YA-004	215826	8269015	3363	Unknown	LIP
Yanque	YA-004	215826	8269015	3363	0.610	LH
Yanque	YA-006	215356	8268989	3399	0.040	LH
Yanque	YA-007	215513	8268241	3434	Unknown	LIP
Yanque	YA-007	215513	8268241	3434	0.010	LH
Yanque	YA-008	214855	8268977	3353	Unknown	LIP
Yanque	YA-009	214900	8268680	3415	Unknown	LIP

(continued)

District	Site	UTM-E	UTM-N	Elevation	Area	Occupation
Yanque	YA-010	215022	8268533	3426	0.030	LH
Yanque	YA-012	214079	8267557	3396	0.080	LH
Yanque	YA-014	214201	8266390	3477	Unknown	LIP
Yanque	YA-025	213472	8264813	3607	0.030	LH
Yanque	YA-029	214017	8265333	3554	Unknown	LIP
Yanque	YA-030	213605	8265689	3512	Unknown	LIP
Yanque	YA-032	214584	8265587	3601	1.861	LIP
Yanque	YA-032	214584	8265587	3601	1.860	LH
Yanque	YA-034	216578	8263465	4121	2.191	LIP
Yanque	YA-034	216578	8263465	4121	2.190	LH
Yanque	YA-040	216654	8263896	4083	0.150	LH
Yanque	YA-041	214962	8268034	3426	17.959	LIP
Yanque	YA-041	214962	8268034	3426	17.960	LH
Yanque	YA-042	214135	8268471	3388	0.010	LH
Yanque	YA-044	214611	8269129	3457	Unknown	LIP
Yanque	YA-045	214546	8269379	3505	1.505	LIP
Yanque	YA-045	214546	8269379	3505	1.510	LH
Yanque	YA-046	214467	8269045	3442	0.340	LH
Yanque	YA-047	214278	8268991	3446	Unknown	LIP
Yanque	YA-048	213784	8269166	3521	0.040	LIP
Yanque	YA-048	213784	8269166	3521	0.040	LH
Yanque	YA-050	213730	8269021	3478	4.265	LIP
Yanque	YA-050	213730	8269021	3478	4.260	LH
Yanque	YA-052	213617	8269209	3518	Unknown	LIP
Yanque	YA-052	213617	8269209	3518	0.030	LH
Yanque	YA-053	212937	8268836	3624	0.250	LIP
Yanque	YA-053	212937	8268836	3624	0.250	LH
Yanque	YA-054	213272	8268580	3518	1.754	LIP
Yanque	YA-054	213272	8268580	3518	1.750	LH
Yanque	YA-055	213583	8268638	3440	0.030	LH
Yanque	YA-056	213513	8268148	3468	Unknown	LIP
Yanque	YA-056	213513	8268148	3468	0.020	LH
Yanque	YA-059	214512	8270617	3762	Unknown	LIP
Yanque	YA-066	216288	8266268	3785	0.063	LIP

District	Site	UTM-E	UTM-N	Elevation	Area	Occupation
Yanque	YA-078	217557	8264939	4197	0.350	LH
Yanque	YA-082	218401	8262286	4559	0.010	LIP
Yanque	YA-088	216918	8262997	4223	0.697	LIP
Yanque	YA-089	216581	8262793	4168	0.260	LH
Yanque	YA-090	213417	8271951	4228	1.000	LH
Yanque	YA-093	212448	8272359	4264	0.749	LIP
Yanque	YA-093	212448	8272359	4264	0.750	LH
Yanque	YA-094	211952	8271998	4217	0.040	LH

Source: Data from Cabanaconde and Lari are from Doutriaux 2004.

YA-050, Uyu Uyu

Within the Yanque-Coporaque survey area, Uyu Uyu[1] (YA-050) shares the top tier of the settlement hierarchy with San Antonio/Chijra (CO-100) during the LIP and the second tier during the Late Horizon. No previous excavations or systematic survey have been conducted at Uyu Uyu. In 1959, Neira visited Uyu Uyu for part of a day during his brief reconnaissance of the valley (Neira Avendaño 1961), and based on its impressive domestic architectural remains, he subsequently described the site as the "original capital of the Collaguas" (Neira Avendaño 1990:172).

Uyu Uyu is located on a prominent mesa-like promontory on the north side of the river, within the agricultural sector of modern Yanque Urinsaya (see Figures 1.2, 4.23, and 4.24). The residential area of the site measures 4.26 ha in area and is composed of a dense concentration of 161 architectural spaces situated on low, broad domestic terraces. Based on differences in the size, distribution, and elaboration of domestic and Inka public architecture at the site, I argue that Uyu Uyu housed a diverse population of both Collagua elites and commoners and was a secondary administrative center under Inka rule.

Surrounding the site, the flanks of the promontory that Uyu Uyu occupies are covered by spectacular contour bench terraces that, due to their warm microclimate and frost-shedding properties, are especially valued by Yanque Urinsaya farmers today for their high maize productivity (fieldwork 1996, 2000). The overall site layout does not appear centrally organized but, instead, structured around the contours of domestic terraces that follow the local topography. The site forms a visually integrated whole with the agricultural terracing, and in this sense the site does not appear intrusive. Instead, the surrounding agricultural terracing accommodates the site, and their contours are followed by the domestic terraces in the settlement (see chapter 4, Figure 4.23). The initial construction of the current configuration of the surrounding bench terraces therefore probably coincides with the LIP occupation of the site. The primary canal for Yanque Urinsaya, the Misme canal, passes over a waterfall (Ccayra Cucho) just upslope of the northern end of the settlement before flowing westward to irrigate the bench terraces and valley bottom fields near Ichupampa to the west. A subsidiary canal branches from the Misme canal and runs alongside a path through the center of the site. Other feeder canals branch around the site to irrigate the surrounding terraces. Yanque villagers today plant crops on the former domestic terraces of Uyu Uyu, and crops are even cultivated inside of some large structures.

Several houses are grouped together on most terraces at Uyu Uyu, forming residential compounds such that multiple structures were probably used by individual households, or that several, perhaps related or extended family households shared a patio space. While their layout does not appear rigidly planned, two configurations of these compounds can be distinguished. In some cases, several houses are situated side by side, with doorways opening in the same direction. This arrangement is common among small to medium houses, as in Structures 21, 22, and 23 (Figure 4.23). In contrast to this more open, linear arrangement, other compounds form an L-shaped configuration, usually with large and elaborate houses forming the short axis of the L across the width of the terrace, as in Structures 30–35 and 121–26, both part of compounds that include large elite houses.

I categorized 143 of the 161 structures at the site as houses, 139 of which were dated to the LIP/LH, and of these, 91 were complete enough to measure building footprints. Variability in house sizes provide one index of social inequality within the settlement's inhabitants. The LIP/LH houses at the site range in size from small 15-m² dwellings to much larger and more elaborately constructed houses of up to 91 m², many of which have tenon supports for a second floor or attic. The midspread (interquartile) range of house sizes (footprint areas) at the site falls between 31.6 and 53.7 m², with a median size of 41.7 m². Only the midspread range of house areas at San Antonio/Chijra (CO-100) is this high (see below). Some of the largest and most elaborately constructed houses in the survey area are found at Uyu Uyu. Based on their size and quality of masonry, I identified twelve houses (Structures 13, 24, 26, 31, 42, 65, 66, 104, 112, 114, 125, and 126) as elite residences at the site. All but two of these houses are in the top quartile at the site in terms of size and stand apart for their fine masonry. Most have especially impressive facades and tenon supports for a second floor. For example, the facade of Structure 104, a large house with an adjoining annex near the center of the site, is composed of well-fitted split river boulders (Figure A.1). Structures 24, 31, and 125 all have belt courses of white stones forming decorative horizontal stripes around the building. The largest houses at the site are also unusually tall structures. For example, the gable of Structure 31, the second largest house at the site, is 6 m high. In short, based on these very large and elaborate houses present, I infer that an elite kuraka class was present at Uyu Uyu, and residents at the site, together with those from San Antonio/Chijra, were generally of high social status.

Furthermore, eight of the 12 elite houses (Structures 125, 126, 65, 66, 42, 114, 112, and 104) are clustered in the center of the site, situated either adjacent to one another or on the same terrace. These elite houses surround the north and west sides of a plaza, which is enclosed on its western side by an Inka

Figure A.1. Facade of Structure 104 at Uyu Uyu, from the east. Note tenon supports for second floor and clay plaster on interior wall surface.

great hall structure. This close spatial relationship between local elite residences and Inka architecture associated with public ritual and display of state largesse is suggestive of how local elites gained in status by their participation in Inka administration of the central valley.

CO-100, San Antonio/Chijra

Covering 12 ha, San Antonio/Chijra is the second largest settlement (after YA-041, Yanque) in the survey by aerial measure, and the second largest (after YA-050, Uyu Uyu) by prehispanic house count (n = 136). The site spans much of the eastern and southern flanks of Yurac Ccacca, a prominent peak reaching 3,817 m on the north side of the Colca River. The two toponym areas of the site are divided by a prominent ridge. San Antonio includes the terraces and buildings on a promontory and slopes on the eastern of the ridge, while Chijra encompasses the houses and terracing to the west of the ridge on the broad, basin-shaped southern slopes of Yurac Ccacca (Figure A.2). I have included both habitational sectors as a single site because all features are within 100 m of each other and the areas were occupied coevally.

Unlike Uyu Uyu, most of San Antonio/Chijra is situated on steep, terraced hillsides that today are divided between upper, abandoned bench

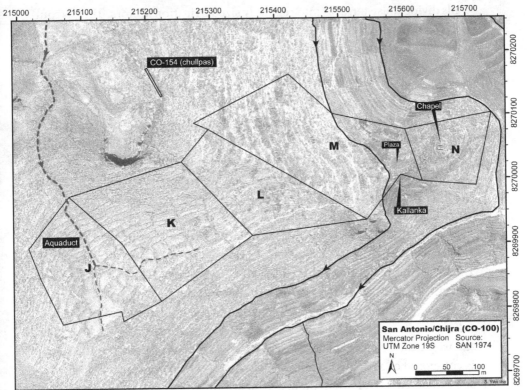

Figure A.2. Air photo of San Antonio/Chijra (CO-100).

terraces and lower, currently cultivated bench terraces. The lower terraces are irrigated by two canals, called the San Antonio and Ccayra. Virtually all of the architectural remains at the site are within the upper band of abandoned bench terraces. Prior to their abandonment during the colonial period (see chapter 5; cf. Denevan 1987), these upper terraces were irrigated by water from a reservoir to the northeast of the peak of Yurac Ccacca, flowing past Chilacota (site CO-151; see chapter 7) before running through Chijra as an aqueduct. This aqueduct splits near the center of Chijra to irrigate the terraces above the other two canals (Denevan 2001; Treacy and Denevan 1986). The terraces below these two canals are currently used primarily for maize cultivation, as they were during the colonial era. Downslope of the site lies the Waykiri area, a large basin of contour terraces and valley bottom fields situated in the warmest microclimate in Coporaque particularly valued today for its high productivity (Córdova Aguilar et al. 1986:64–65; Treacy 1989b). Immediately upslope of Waykiri are massive complexes of linear bench terraces (in the Alto Ccayra and Ccayra toponyms areas) that span the southern flanks of Yurac Ccacca just below Chijra. Vertical end walls divide these terraces into regularly sized irrigation sectors. Their layout was clearly centrally planned, perhaps dividing the irrigation sectors into regularly sized production units.[2]

These bench terraces continue upslope through San Antonio/Chijra and serve as domestic terraces for houses. But "domestic" terraces are not set apart as such; rather, houses were built on the surrounding agricultural terraces. As discussed previously, findings from excavations conducted by Malpass, de la Vera, and Neira in Chijra indicate that these terraces probably originate in the LIP, but their current configuration is most likely a product of subsequent modification during the Late Horizon (Denevan 2001; Malpass 1987; Treacy 1989b). Ceramic collections also indicate a larger occupation during the Late Horizon. Out of the total sample of 294 sherds we collected at the site, Late Horizon (Collagua III, Collagua Inka, and Inka) sherds outnumbered LIP (Collagua I and II) sherds by three to one—136 versus 46 sherds, respectively. I suspect, therefore, that most of the standing houses at the site were built during the latter part of the LIP or the Late Horizon.

During the survey, I divided Chijra into three sectors, registered as Sectors J, K, and L (Figure A.2).[3] Sector J encompasses a cluster of eight houses to the west near a relict aqueduct.[4] Sector K, located in the center of the slope, is composed of agricultural terraces with 18 dispersed (generally poorly preserved) houses and looted tombs. As an arbitrary measure, I demarcated the eastern side of Sector K just east of the massive Structure 17, the second largest house at the site (Figure A.2). Sector L, where we registered five houses, is the farthest sector to the east in the Chijra area and borders the ridgeline that separates it from the San Antonio area. Sector M is comprised of a dense cluster of 91 houses on the eastern-facing slope, and Sector N is the promontory topped by a the doctrina chapel (see chapter 5).

Previous research at the site consists of a brief initial visit to the San Antonio sector of the site by Neira in 1959 and a much more intensive investigation of the Chijra area as part of the Río Colca Abandoned Terrace Project. Neira initially described the large structures on and surrounding the promontory at the southeastern corner of the site. Apparently referring to the large structure on the top of the promontory, Neira has referred to San Antonio as the most important "sanctuary" in the valley (Neira Avendaño 1990:152).[5] In Chijra, research focused on understanding the construction, use, and abandonment sequence of agricultural terraces. Reconnaissance and test-pit excavations were conducted at one house and five terraces in Chijra (Malpass 1986, 1987; Malpass and de la Vera Cruz Chávez 1986, 1990; Neira Avendaño 1986; Treacy and Denevan 1986). Malpass (1987:51) reports seven houses on and around the terraces excavated by the Denevan team. Although they did not systematically survey the rest of the settlement, Treacy and Denevan report a total of 51 structures in the combined San Antonio/Chijra area.

In general, architectural preservation was not as good as at Uyu Uyu, in large part from more intense looting of worked cornerstones from structures, leaving their walls vulnerable to collapse.[6] We recorded 177 structures at San Antonio/Chijra, 136 of which I defined as LIP/LH houses—three fewer than at Uyu Uyu. Of these, 105 houses are densely packed on the terraced slopes and promontory of San Antonio and 31 are dispersed throughout the terraces of Chijra.

The architectural data from San Antonio clearly signal the presence of an elite class and marked social inequalities within the resident population. Forty-one (30 percent) of the 136 houses at San Antonio/Chijra were complete enough to measure building footprints—a lower percentage than at Uyu Uyu but a large sample nonetheless. House sizes vary widely between 14.0 and 136.5 m². This range is broader than at Uyu Uyu, and as discussed above, the two largest houses at the site, Structures 93 and 17, are the largest in the survey area. As a group, houses at San Antonio are very large, equaled only by Uyu Uyu. The midspread of house sizes ranged from 25.0 to 52.0 m², and the median house area of 37.5 m² is matched only by houses at Uyu Uyu, reflecting the generally large size of houses and high status of their inhabitants relative to the other sites in the survey.

Elite houses are concentrated on the eastern-facing terraced slopes of San Antonio in Sector M, as well as the promontory of Sector N. All of these elite houses are in the top house-size quartile (greater than 52.0 m²)[7] and are constructed of coursed, tabular (Type 5) masonry. However, these represent only structures complete enough to measure area and observe masonry style; among less-complete structures there are almost certainly more elite houses in Sectors M and N. In general, houses are larger in Sectors M and N than in the rest of the site (with a mean house area of 47.8 m² vs. 38.1 m² for Sectors J–L). Sixteen of the 19 houses in the third quartile (between 37.5 and 52.0 m²) are located in Sectors M and N. Small- and medium-sized houses are also interspersed throughout this sector, but it is clearly a high-status area of the site. Six of the seven houses I identified as elite residences are also located there. The largest house at the site (and in the survey), Structure 93, is situated on a 4.5-m-high terrace on the upper eastern slope of Sector M, overlooking the promontory and valley bottom below. Other elite houses, such as Structures 84, 85, and 87, are closely aligned side by side lower down on the hillside. The second largest house, Structure 17, stands out as an isolated structure in the center of the southern slope of the Chijra area, near its eastern end. This 14-x-12-m building is especially impressive for its tabular masonry on both exterior and interior wall facings and especially well executed corners. It was also probably a very tall structure, since there are tenon supports for a second floor on all four walls.

As at Uyu Uyu, these local elite houses are closely associated with at least one and possibly two prominently situated Inka great halls. As discussed above, the larger of the two (Structure 154) occupies the saddle between the promontory of Sector N and the terraced hillside of Sector M, thus straddling the point of access between the two sectors (see Figure 4.25). Also similar to its counterpart at Uyu Uyu, Structure 154 is fronted by a probable plaza— in this case, a level 18-x-28-m terrace that spans the remaining width of the saddle. A second rustic Inka structure (Structure 64) is situated just west of the ridgeline separating sectors Chijra and San Antonio. Like the other great halls, this structure opens to a terraced plaza or large patio space (26.5 × 15.0 m) just off the main path that runs along this ridge.

CO-127, Llanka

Llanka (CO-127) is a large, dispersed village to the southeast of Kitaplaza, on the Qal5 pampa to the north and east of the pukara fortifications discussed in chapter 4 (Figure A.3). The settlement is composed of 88 small- to medium-sized houses amid agricultural fields and terraces. The relative homogeneity of house sizes and the predominance of Inka polychrome ceramics suggest a strong state presence in the establishment and occupation of the site. The primary occupation of the site clearly dates to the Late Horizon; we collected only six LIP sherds, as opposed to 64 Late Horizon sherds, 16 percent of which were polychromes—the highest percentage of Late Horizon polychromes of any settlement in the survey.[8]

Houses at Llanka are distributed in various orientations at the site and there is no centralized planning apparent in its overall layout. Many of the houses adjoin one another, suggesting that households probably used more than one structure, forming small domestic compounds similar to those of Uyu Uyu. While the overall layout of the settlement suggest household-level planning, house sizes are much more homogeneous than at other sites and tend to be quite small. The midspread of house areas ranges between only 16 and 25 m². All but three are built of uncoursed Type 1 or Type 2 masonry. The larger structures at the site are discretely clustered on the south end of the site, but even these are only in the median size range of houses at Uyu Uyu and San Antonio.

Overall, Llanka appears to have been a settlement of commoner agriculturalists established (or at least considerably expanded) during the Inka

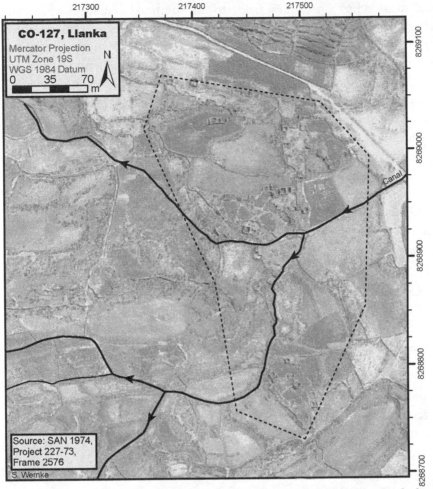

Figure A.3. Air photo of Llanka (CO-127), including canals. Path in upper right leads to Kitaplaza (CO-164) to the northwest, and to terracing and the settlement of Tunsa (CO-163) to the south.

occupation of the valley. Given the homogeneity of house sizes and high percentage of Inka polychrome ceramics, I suggest that this site may represent a settlement established with direct state management and oversight.

CO-164, Kitaplaza

Kitaplaza (CO-164) is located about 350 m northwest of Llanka (CO-127) along the modern road between Chivay and Coporaque. A major path diverges from the road and passes to the north of a central open space between the two distinct residential sectors of the site, leading eventually to Llanka and surrounding agricultural fields to the southeast (Figure A.4). To the adjacent north of the site are linear bench terraces that cover the southern flanks of Pampa Finaya—the Mosoqchacra ("new field") toponym sector. Surrounding the other sides of the site are valley bottom fields and terraces on the slopes between the Qal 5 and Qal 4 alluvial surfaces. Although the site produced a handful (n = 4) of Middle Horizon sherds, the primary occupations of the site are from the LIP and Late Horizon, and based on the predominance of Late Horizon ceramics, I suspect that the site grew considerably during under Inka occupation. We collected 23 LIP (six Collagua I and 17 Collagua II) sherds and 54 Late Horizon sherds (19 Collagua III, 32 Collagua Inka, and three Inka sherds).

Most of the standing architecture probably dates to the Late Horizon. Houses are not aligned by any overall site layout design but form residential compounds, with two or three houses oriented around small patio spaces. The 74 LIP/LH houses at the site are mostly in the small to medium size range; the largest houses only reach the median house size at San Antonio/ Chijra (CO-100) and Uyu Uyu (YA-050). All but two are of low-quality Type

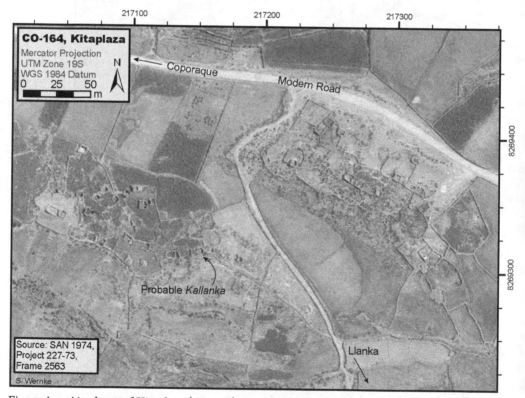

Figure A.4. Air photo of Kitaplaza (CO-164). Note two housing sectors separated by major path from the main road.

1 and Type 2 masonry. The two houses of higher quality masonry are made of coursed, rectangular, and ovoid worked blocks (Type 6 masonry). Together with these more elaborate houses in the southern residential sector is a possible Inka ceremonial or public structure at the site. As discussed above, a large (13.4-×-5-m) rectangular structure with windows on either side of its facade is not consistent with Collagua domestic architectural canons and may be an Inka structure, similar to the smaller of the two great halls at San Antonio/Chijra. As in the better-documented cases of Inka public architecture in the survey, this building fronts a small plaza-like space near the center of the site.F

Much like the nearby site of Llanka, Kitaplaza appears to have been a large commoner agriculturalist settlement occupied primarily during the LIP and Late Horizon. The site represents a typical mid-sized agriculturalist village within the local LIP/LH settlement pattern.

CO-150, Llactapampa, and CO-163, Tunsa

Llactapampa (CO-150) and Tunsa (CO-163) are both situated on the Qal 4 river terrace above the river gorge to the south of Coporaque, directly downslope and to the south of the three pukara fortifications discussed in chapter 4 (see Figure 4.26). They clearly housed a diverse population of agriculturalists, including local elites, and probably functioned as distinct sectors of a single large settlement, since they are less than 150 m apart and were coevally occupied. Combined, Llactapampa (20 houses) and Tunsa (70 houses) would form the fourth largest settlement in the survey.

With 70 houses dispersed over 5.75 ha, Tunsa is much larger than Llactapampa. The midspread range of house sizes at Tunsa (20–37 m²) is lower than that of Uyu Uyu and San Antonio (21–42 m² and 25–53 m², respectively), but there are also clearly elite houses at the site. As was the case at Uyu Uyu and San Antonio, the elite houses of Tunsa are situated near a great hall facing an open space that probably functioned as a plaza at the entrance to the site. This plaza area divides the settlement in two. Most of the houses are located to the east of the plaza, in valley bottom fields and surrounding low hillsides. Houses span the full range of size and quality of construction, including a very large (78 m²) house of fine Type 5 masonry on all sides. To the west, a smaller area with 15 houses occupies a low hill behind the great hall. Here, another very large house (72 m²) is situated along the north edge of the hill.

About 130 m to the northwest of the great hall at Tunsa, the 20 houses at the site of Llactapampa (CO-150) are generally large and well constructed, and the site as a whole may have functioned as an elite sector associated with the great hall of Tunsa. Only two houses at Llactapampa are of uncoursed, unworked Type 1 masonry, and the smallest house is 24 m²—considerably larger than the low-end range of other sites in the survey. Four houses are especially large and well made: two of coursed, tabular masonry (Type 5) and two of coursed, dressed fieldstone (Type 3). These structures are of similar quality and size as the elite houses of San Antonio/Chijra.

In sum, Tunsa and Llactapampa together probably formed a large town with an internally differentiated population that included both elites and commoners. The central placement of an Inka great hall between the elite houses of Tunsa and Llactapampa suggests the centrality of state public ritual in local Inka administration as well as the importance of local elites as mediating agents between local communities and the state.

YA-054, Llactarana

Llactarana is a small hamlet and associated ceramic scatter situated among irrigated bench terraces about half a kilometer to the southwest of Uyu Uyu (Figure A.5). The site is located just above the present course of the Misme canal, in a band of abandoned linear bench terraces that were previously irrigated by the canal when its course was slightly higher on the hillside. The present course of the canal thus forms the line between presently abandoned and cultivated terraces around the site. The site is covered by a dense ceramic scatter, and 254 diagnostics were recovered, including 54 LIP (15 Collagua I and 39 Collagua II) and 129 Late Horizon (23 Collagua III, 101 Collagua Inka, and 15 Inka) sherds. We divided the site into four sectors (Sectors A–D) based on surface features and artifact concentrations. Sector A is defined by a small rubble mound feature with possible cyst tombs (all badly eroded) in association with a dense ceramic scatter. The ceramic concentration continues downslope into abandoned terraces in Sector B. Sector C, to the adjacent north of Sectors A and B, is the architectural core of the site. We were able to map seven houses at the site (Figure A.6), but because of terrace wall collapse and heavy cactus growth, preservation of these structures was generally poor, and I suspect that other structures are no longer surficially visible. Six of the seven houses (Structures 1–5, and 7) are small to medium in size (20–37 m²), and the seventh (Structure 6) is poorly preserved but considerably larger. Several houses share single terraces at the site, and all face downslope to the east, but no residential compounds as such could be defined. Overall, the architectural evidence suggests that Llactarana was an undifferentiated hamlet

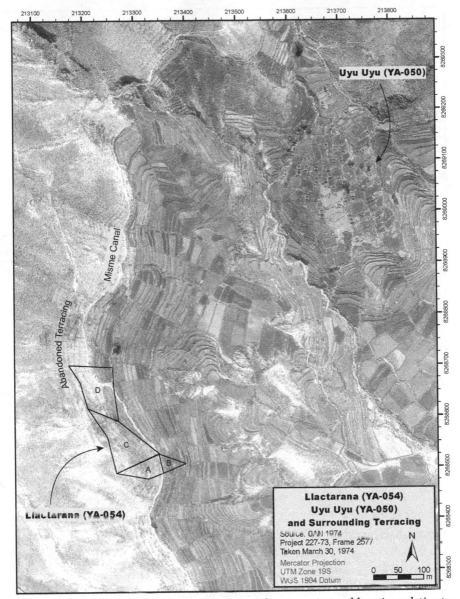

Figure A.5. Air photo of Llactarana with surrounding terracing and location relative to Uyu Uyu (YA-050). Note abandoned terraces above modern canal course.

with a handful of households that probably maintained close contact with residents of the neighboring major settlement of Uyu Uyu. Sector D consists of a ceramic scatter that continues across the abandoned terraces to the north of the residential area of Sector C.

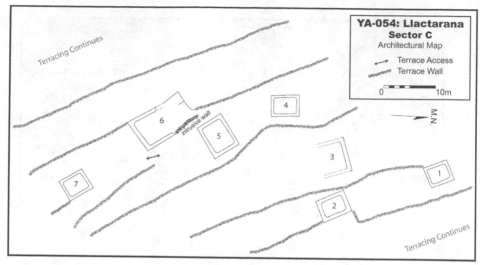

Figure A.6. Architectural map, habitational sector of Llactarana (YA-054).

YA-041 and CO-161, Yanque and Coporaque

Both reducción villages in the survey, Yanque (YA-041) and Coporaque (CO-161), are situated on top of LIP/LH settlements. Especially in the case of Yanque, the provincial capital of the Collaguas Province during the colonial era, the presence of what appears to have been the largest settlement in the central valley was probably the decisive factor regarding where to locate the reducción. Both are also located on the pampa of the Qal 4 alluvial surface—the broad, gently sloping terrace above the river gorge—and are surrounded by large expanses of valley bottom fields.

The settlement at Yanque was almost certainly the largest prehispanic settlement in the survey area. It also appears to have been the primary Inka administrative center for the central valley and possibly for the Collaguas province as a whole. The results of the street survey indicate that the prehispanic settlement of Yanque was concentrated in the northern half of the present reducción, where sherd densities are markedly higher. Collagua I (n = 7) and Collagua II (n = 19) sherds were too few and too dispersed throughout the reducción to reliably estimate a site area for the LIP. However, the site produced the largest collection of Late Horizon ceramics of any site in the survey, with 209 sherds (six Collagua III, 168 Collagua Inka, and 35 Inka). As another indicator of a strong Inka presence, 15 percent of Late Horizon sherds were polychromes—second only to Llanka in terms of percentage of polychromes in Late Horizon collections.[9]

Also, as I discussed above, architectural remains at Yanque include the

Figure A.7. Colonial/Republican era house in Yanque (YA-041) constructed with probable prehispanic (Type 6) masonry.

only examples of Inka cut-stone masonry in the survey. Assuming that these blocks were not moved a great distance from another settlement, their presence indicates that the settlement was an important political center under Inka rule. Dispersed throughout the northeastern quadrant of the village, other colonial- and republican-era buildings constructed of a conglomerate of unworked fieldstone and tabular and rectangular cut-stone blocks reveal the presence of what were probably large, elite Collagua houses. Many are identical to the Type 6 masonry of Collagua houses (e.g., Figure A.7), and other thin, tabular blocks interspersed in some house walls were probably from the corners, doorways, and wall heads of prehispanic houses.

By contrast, Coporaque appears to have been a much smaller settlement, and the late prehispanic occupations are much more ephemeral. These findings are contrary to expectations, since as discussed in chapter 4, Coporaque, based on the account of Oré (1992 [1598]:159 [41]), is widely cited in the literature as the Inkaic capital of Collaguas (Cook 1982, 2002; Málaga Medina 1977; Neira Avendaño 1990). Our ceramic collections were scant in Coporaque—the survey crew collected only 15 LIP and Late Horizon sherds. Architectural evidence of the LIP and Late Horizon occupations of Coporaque is also limited and somewhat ambiguous. On the one hand, no Cuzco Inka stonemasonry is present, and we identified only one house of probable prehispanic origin. This large house of tabular (Type 6) masonry is positioned diagonally

Figure A.8. Church of Coporaque from the north. This structure is built of thin tabular (Type 5) masonry that was probably mined from the surrounding LIP/LH sites.

relative to the street grid in the southeast corner of the village, breaking with the otherwise regular orientation of houses in relation to the streets.[10] It was modified after its original construction with an internal wall that separates the structure into two separate rooms. A handful of other houses, concentrated in the southern half of the village, incorporate tabular (Type 6) and rectangular (Type 7) worked blocks of probable prehispanic origin but were clearly constructed and used during colonial or even republican times. Also, the church of Coporaque (one of the only such original reducción churches stills standing in Peru) is built of tabular (Type 6) and rectangular (Type 7) masonry (Figures A.8 and A.9). Given the paucity of ceramic collections in Coporaque and the widespread evidence of cornerstone mining at the nearby sites of San Antonio/Chijra (CO-100), Tunsa (CO-163), and Llactapampa (CO-150), the vast majority of the blocks used to construct these buildings appear to have been transported from these sites.

YA-093, Jibillea, and CO-061

Jibillea (YA-093) and CO-061 are both small herding villages located in the puna to the north of the river. Jibillea is composed of 12 circular houses (4–7 m in diameter) and associated rock-walled corrals, and we registered eight circular structure foundations of similar size at CO-061, also in association

Figure A.9. Detail of masonry, northwest corner of church of Coporaque.

with corral features (Figure A.10). These two sites are representative of a broader pattern of expanded settlement and intensification of pastoralist production in the puna under Inka rule. As discussed in chapter 4, nine of the 16 Late Horizon settlements lacking LIP components are puna pastoralist settlements, but several other settlements with only small LIP components such as Jibillea clearly grew considerably during Inka rule.

The ceramic assemblages at both sites indicate that both Jibillea and

Figure A.10. Circular house and adjoining corral at Jibillea (YA-093).

CO-061 were either established or significantly expanded under Inka rule. At Jibillea we recovered 41 Late Horizon sherds but only one Middle Horizon and two LIP (Collagua II) sherds, while CO-061 produced no LIP ceramics and 40 Late Horizon sherds. Also, a large proportion of the Late Horizon ceramics are fancy Inka wares. Polychromes made up 15 percent of Late Horizon ceramics from Jibillea and 13 percent from CO-061, only slightly less than Yanque (YA-041), which had the highest proportion of Late Horizon polychromes (16 percent) and comparable to that of Llanka (CO-127) with 15 percent.[11]

Both settlements are also situated near large relict reservoirs. Two reservoirs are located near CO-061, one directly north of the residential area of the site and another 200 m southeast of the site. Another large reservoir is located to the immediate west of Jibillea. The general expansion of settlement in the puna during the Late Horizon and the close association between these two sites and large hydraulic features suggest that Jibillea and CO-061 were established as intensive herding settlements under Inka rule. The high percentage of elaborate polychrome Inka ceramics at these sites also hints at ties of reciprocity. Perhaps these prestige goods were mobilized by the state in exchange for labor service of these herding populations.

Notes

1. Alternate spellings: Ullullu, Uyo Uyo, also called Yanque Viejo.

2. Some of the terraces in Ccayra were reconstructed in the 1980s and 1990s by DESCO (a Peruvian NGO), but these are easily distinguishable from the surrounding ancient terraces.

3. Sectors A–I are composed of isolated tomb features and chullpas on the surrounding boulder-strewn ridges.

4. This is the area where the Denevan team focused most of their excavations in the early 1980s (see Malpass 1987).

5. Chapter 5 presents evidence indicating that this structure was an early colonial chapel built by Franciscans sometime between their arrival in the valley during 1540s and prior to the forced resettlement of the populations to the reducciones in the early 1570s.

6. I infer that cornerstones have been looted in part because the natural collapse pattern is the reverse—that is, because the corners are the strongest part of the building, especially if well executed with alternating headers and spanners, they are typically the last portion of a structure standing. Thus walls normally collapse inward first due to the batter (inward-leaning angle) of the walls, and the corners are left standing. This point is also illustrated for Inca architecture by Protzen (Protzen 1993:234, Fig. 13.21). Also, many of the cornerstones from San Antonio and other settlements around Coporaque were probably used to build the church there, which is the only sixteenth-century church in the reducciones of the Colca Valley that has remained largely intact. In contrast to the other churches of the valley, which, in the wake of earthquakes during the seventeenth and eighteenth centuries were rebuilt mostly or entirely of ashlar masonry of volcanic tuff (called sillar) brought to the valley from the puna heights to the south, the walls of the Church of Coporaque are constructed of thin, tabular masonry of the same characteristics as the Type 5 masonry of prehispanic houses at San Antonio, Tunsa, and Llactapampa in Coporaque. See the following chapter for further discussion.

7. Or, in the case of Structure 93, the largest house at the site (and in the survey) is an upper outlier in terms of area, measuring 13.0×10.5 m (136.5 m^2). Upper outliers are those 1.5–3 times the midspread range above the median.

8. Excluding sites with few (less than 20) Late Horizon sherds.

9. This excludes sites with small samples (less than 20) of Late Horizon sherds. The only site with a higher percentage of Late Horizon polychromes is Llanka (CO-127).

10. This structure has recently been encroached upon and damaged by the construction of a hotel complex. The hotel uses this "Inka" house as its centerpiece and is now surrounded by guest rooms.

11. Interestingly, both sites also produced probable Chucuito style rim sherds from plates, signaling trade ties between these herding settlements and those of the northwestern Titicaca basin.

REFERENCES CITED

Archive Abbreviations

APY   Archivo Parroquial de Yanque (housed in the Archivo Arzobispal de Arequipa)

ASFL   Archivo del Convento de San Francisco, Lima

Abbott, M. B., M. W. Binford, M. Brenner, and K. R. Kelts
     1997   A 3500 14c Yr High-Resolution Record of Water-Level Changes in Lake Titicaca, Bolivia/ Peru. *Quaternary Research* 47:169–80.

Abbott, M. B., G. O. Seltzer, K. R. Kelts, and J. Southon
     1997   Holocene Paleohydrology of the Tropical Andes from Lake Records. *Quaternary Research* 47:70–80.

Abercrombie, Thomas A.
     1986   The Politics of Sacrifice: An Aymara Cosmology in Action. Ph.D. dissertation, Department of Anthropology, University of Chicago. University Microfilms, Ann Arbor.
     1998   *Pathways of Memory and Power: Ethnography and History among an Andean People.* University of Wisconsin Press, Madison.

Albó, Xavier
     1972   Dinámica en la estructura intercomunitaria de Jesús de Machaca. *America Indígena* 32(3):773–816.

Aldenderfer, Mark S. (editor)
     1993   *Domestic Architecture, Ethnicity, and Complementarity in the South-Central Andes.* University of Iowa Press, Iowa City.

Aldenderfer, Mark S., and Charles Stanish
     1993   Domestic Architecture, Household Archaeology, and the Past in the South-Central Andes. In *Domestic Architecture, Ethnicity, and Complementarity in the South-Central Andes*, edited by Mark S. Aldenderfer, pp. 1–12. University of Iowa Press, Iowa City.

Anderson, Benedict
     1991   *Imagined Communities: Reflections on the Origins and Spread of Nationalism.* Verso, London.

Appadurai, Arjun (editor)
     1986   *The Social Life of Things: Commodities in Cultural Perspective.* Cambridge University Press, Cambridge.

APY Yanquecollaguas Hanansaya 1615–1617
   Visita de Yanquecollaguas Hanansaya. Jerónimo de Pamanes, visitador.
APY Yanquecollaguas Urinsaya 1604
   Visita de Yanquecollaguas Urinsaya. Juan de Rivero, visitador.
Arkush, Elizabeth N.
   2005   Colla Fortified Sites: Warfare and Regional Power in the Late Prehispanic Titicaca Ba-
           sin, Peru. Ph.D. dissertation, Department of Anthropology, University of California, Los
           Angeles.
   2008   War, Chronology, and Causality in the Titicaca Basin. *Latin American Antiquity* 19(4):
           339–73.
   2010   *Hillforts of the Ancient Andes: Colla Warfare, Society, and Landscape.* University Press of
           Florida, Gainesville.
Ascher, Marcia, and Robert Ascher
   1988   Code of the Quipu. 2 microfiches: negative; 11 × 15 cm vols. University Microfilms Interna-
           tional, Ann Arbor.
   1997   *Mathematics of the Incas: Code of the Quipu.* Dover Publications, Mineola, N.Y.
Ashmore, Wendy, and A. Bernard Knapp (editors)
   1999   *Archaeologies of Landscape: Contemporary Perspectives.* Blackwell, Malden, Mass.
Astvaldsson, Astvaldur
   2000   The Dynamics of Aymara Duality: Change and Continuity in Sociopolitical Structures in
           the Bolivian Andes. *Journal of Latin American Studies* 32(1):145–74.
Ayers, Edward L.
   2010   Turning toward Place, Space, and Time. In *The Spatial Humanities: GIS and the Future of
           Humanities Scholarship*, edited by David J. Bodenhamer, John Corrigan, and Trevor M.
           Harris, pp. 1–13. Indiana University Press, Bloomington.
Bakewell, Peter J.
   1984   *Miners of the Red Mountain: Indian Labor in Potosí, 1545–1650.* 1st ed. University of New
           Mexico Press, Albuquerque.
Balée, William L. (editor)
   1998   *Advances in Historical Ecology.* Columbia University Press, New York.
Balée, William L., and Clark L. Erickson (editors)
   2006   *Time and Complexity in Historical Ecology: Studies in the Neotropical Lowlands.* Columbia
           University Press, New York.
Bandy, Matthew S.
   2001   Population and History in the Ancient Titicaca Basin. Ph.D. dissertation, Department of
           Anthropology, University of California, Berkeley.
Barth, Fredrik
   1969   Introduction. In *Ethnic Groups and Boundaries: The Social Organization of Culture Differ-
           ence*, edited by Fredrik Barth, pp. 9–38. Allen & Unwin, London.
Bauer, Brian S.
   1992   *The Development of the Inca State.* University of Texas Press, Austin.
   1996   Legitimation of the State in Inca Myth and Ritual. *American Anthropologist* 98(2):327–37.
   1998   *The Sacred Landscape of the Inca: The Cuzco Ceque System.* University of Texas Press, Austin.
Bauer, Brian S., and Charles Stanish
   2001   *Ritual and Pilgrimage in the Ancient Andes: The Islands of the Sun and the Moon.* 1st ed. Uni-
           versity of Texas Press, Austin.

Bawden, Garth
1982   Community Organization Reflected by the Household: A Study of Pre-Columbian Social Dynamics. *Journal of Field Archaeology*. 9(2):165–81.

Benavides, Maria A.
1986a   Cambios en la tenencia y el uso de tierras desde el siglo XVI hasta el presente en el Valle del Colca (Caylloma, Arequipa). In *The Cultural Ecology, Archaeology, and History of Terracing in the Colca Valley of Southern Peru*, edited by William. M. Denavan, vol. 1, pp. 509–24. Technical Report to the National Science Foundation and the National Geographic Society. Department of Geography, University of Wisconsin, Madison.

1986b   Coporaque in the 1604 *Visita* to Yanquecollaguas Urinsaya. In *The Cultural Ecology, Archaeology, and History of Terracing and Terrace Abandonment in the Colca Valley of Southern Peru*, edited by William M. Denevan, vol. 1, pp. 406–25. Technical Report to the National Science Foundation and the National Geographic Society, Department of Geography, University of Wisconsin, Madison.

1986c   Coporaque in the 1615–1617 *Visita* of Yanquecollaguas Hanansaya. In *The Cultural Ecology, Archaeology, and History of Terracing and Terrace Abandonment in the Colca Valley of Southern Peru*, edited by William M. Denevan, vol. 1, pp. 509–24. Technical Report to the National Science Foundation and the National Geographic Society. Department of Geography, University of Wisconsin, Madison.

1986d   Coporaque Toponyms: Comparison and Analysis of Place Names in the 16th, 17th, and 20th Centuries. In *The Cultural Ecology, Archaeology, and History of Terracing and Terrace Abandonment in the Colca Valley of Southern Peru*, edited by William M. Denevan, vol. 1, pp. 450–92. Technical Report to the National Science Foundation and the National Geographic Society. Department of Geography, University of Wisconsin, Madison.

1986e   Introduction: Ethnohistorical Research for the Terrace Abandonment Project, Colca Valley. In *The Cultural Ecology, Archaeology, and History of Terracing and Terrace Abandonment in the Colca Valley of Southern Peru*, edited by William M. Denevan, vol. 1, pp. 386–93. Technical Report to the National Science Foundation and the National Geographic Society. Department of Geography, University of Wisconsin, Madison.

1987   Apuntes históricos y etnográficos del Valle del Río Colca (Arequipa, Perú) 1575–1980. *Boletín de Lima* 50:7–20.

1988a   La división social y geográfica Hanansaya/Urinsaya en el Valle del Colca y La Provincia de Caylloma (Arequipa, Perú). *Boletín de Lima* 60:49 53

1988b   The Yanque Parish Archive. In *The Cultural Ecology, Archaeology, and History of Terracing and Terrace Abandonment in the Colca Valley of Southern Peru*, edited by William M. Denevan, vol. 2, pp. 25–37. Technical Report to the National Science Foundation and the National Geographic Society. Department of Geography, University of Wisconsin, Madison.

1990   El Archivo Parroquial de Yanque. *Boletín del Instituto Riva Agüero* 17:47–70.

1991   Libro de Fábrica de la iglesia de Yanque. In *Actas del Primer Congreso de investigación histórica*, vol. 3, edited by Humberto Rodríguez Pastor, pp. 133–39. CONCYTEC, Lima.

1992   The Yanque Parish Archive. *Americas* 48, no. 4 (April): 519–35.

1997   Las batallas de Chachayllo: La lucha por el agua de riego en el Valle del Colca (Arequipa, Perú). *Boletín de la Sociedad Geográfica de Lima* 110:127–48.

Bender, Barbara
1992   Theorizing Landscape and the Prehistoric Landscapes of Stonehenge. *Man* 27:735–55.

1993   *Landscape: Politics and Perspectives*. Berg, Oxford.

Bertonio, Ludovico

    1956 [1612]   *Vocabulario de la Lengua Aymara*. Ediciones CERES, Cochabamba.

Binford, M. W., and Alan L. Kolata

    1996   The Natural and Human Setting. In *Tiwanaku and Its Hinterlands: Archaeology and Paleo-ecology of an Andean Civilization*, edited by Alan L. Kolata. Vol. 1, *Agroecology*, pp. 23–56. Smithsonian Institution Press, Washington, D.C.

Binford, Michael W., Alan L. Kolata, M. Brenner, Matthew T. Seddon, M. B. Abbott, and J. Curtis

    1997   Climate Variation and the Rise and Fall of an Andean Civilization. *Quaternary Research* 47:235–48.

Blaikie, Piers M., and Harold Brookfield

    1987   *Land Degradation and Society*. Methuen, New York.

Blom, Deborah E.

    2005   Embodying Borders: Human Body Modification and Diversity in Tiwanaku Society. *Journal of Anthropological Archaeology* 24(1):1–24.

Bodenhamer, David J., John Corrigan, and Trevor M. Harris

    2010a   Introduction. In *The Spatial Humanities: GIS and the Future of Humanities Scholarship*, edited by David J. Bodenhamer, John Corrigan, and Trevor M. Harris, pp. vii–xv. Indiana University Press, Bloomington.

    2010b   *The Spatial Humanities: GIS and the Future of Humanities Scholarship*. Indiana University Press, Bloomington.

Bolin, Inge

    1993   Levels of Autonomy in the Organization of Irrigation in the Highlands of Peru. In *Irrigation at High Altitudes: The Social Organization of Water Control Systems in the Andes*, edited by William P. Mitchell and David Guillet, pp. 141–66. Society for Latin American Anthropology Publication Series, vol. 12.

Botkin, Daniel B.

    1990   *Discordant Harmonies: A New Ecology for the Twenty-First Century*. Oxford University Press, New York.

Bourdieu, Pierre

    1973   The Berber House. In *Rules and Meaning: The Anthropology of Everyday Knowledge*, edited by Mary Douglas, pp. 98–110. Penguin Education, Harmondsworth, England.

    1977   *Outline of a Theory of Practice*. Translated by R. Nice. Cambridge University Press, Cambridge.

Bouysse-Cassagne, Thérèse

    1986   Urco and Uma: Aymara Concepts of Space. In *Anthropological History of Andean Polities*, edited by John V. Murra and Nathan Wachtel, pp. 201–27. Cambridge University Press, Cambridge.

    1987   *La identidad aymara: Aproximación histórica (siglo XV, siglo XVI)*. Travaux de l'institut Français d'Études Andines; T. 34. HISBOL-IFEA, La Paz.

Braudel, Fernand

    1972   *The Mediterranean and the Mediterranean World in the Age of Philip II*. Harper & Row, New York.

Bray, Tamara

    2003   Inca Pottery as Culinary Equipment: Food, Feasting, and Gender in Imperial State Design. *Latin American Antiquity* 14(1):1–22.

Brooks, Sarah Osgood
1998 Prehistoric Agricultural Terraces in the Río Japo Basin, Colca Valley, Peru. Ph.D. dissertation, Department of Geography, University of Wisconsin, Madison.

Brooks, Sarah Osgood, Michael D. Glascock, and Martín Giesso
1997 Source of Volcanic Glass for Ancient Andean Tools. *Nature* 386:449–50.

Browman, David L.
1981 New Light on Andean Tiwanaku. *American Scientist* 69(4):408–19.

Brown, Michael F.
1996 On Resisting Resistance. *American Anthropologist* 98(4):729–49.

Brush, Steven B.
1977 *Mountain, Field, and Family: The Economy of Human Ecology of an Andean Village.* University of Philadelphia Press, Philadelphia.

Bryant, R.
1992 Political Ecology: An Emerging Research Agenda in Third World Studies. *Political Geography* 11:12–36.

Burger, Richard L., Frank Asaro, Guido Salas, and Fred Stross
1998 The Chivay Obsidian Source and the Geological Origin of Titicaca Basin–Type Obsidian Artifacts. *Andean Past* 5:203–23.

Burger, Richard L., Karen Lynne Mohr Chávez, and Sergio Jorge Chávez
2000 Through the Glass Darkly: Prehispanic Obsidian Procurement and Exchange in Southern Peru and Northern Bolivia. *Journal of World Prehistory* 14(3):267–362.

Burger, Richard L., and Lucy C. Salazar
2004 *Machu Picchu: Unveiling the Mystery of the Incas.* Yale University Press, New Haven.

Burkhart, Louise M.
1998 Pious Performances: Christian Pageantry and Native Identity in Early Colonial Mexico. In *Native Traditions in the Postconquest World*, edited by Elizabeth H. Boone and Tom Cummins, pp. 361–81. Dumbarton Oaks, Washington, D.C.

Cardona Rosas, Augusto
1993 Características geográficas del patrón de asentamiento para el Valle de Chuquibamba— Arequipa, durante el Período comprendido entre el Horizonte Medio, y el Horizonte Tardío. Unpublished licenciate's thesis, Department of Archaeology, Facultad de Ciencias Históricu Arqueológicas, Universidad Católica Santa María, Arequipa.

Castro Pineda, Lucio
1963 La cátedra de Lengua Quechua en la Catedral de Lima. *Nueva Crónica* 1:136–47.

Caviedes, Cesar N.
1975 El Niño 1972: Its Climatic, Ecological, Human and Economic Implications. *Geographical Review* 65(4):493–509.
1984 El Niño 1982–83. *Geographical Review* 74:267–90.

Certeau, Michel de
1984 *The Practice of Everyday Life.* University of California Press, Berkeley and Los Angeles.

Chakrabarty, Dipesh
2000 *Provincializing Europe: Postcolonial Thought and Historical Difference.* Princeton University Press, Princeton.

Cieza de León, Pedro
1967 [1553] *El señorío de los Incas.* Instituto de Estudios Peruanos, Lima.
1985 [1553] *Crónica del Perú; segunda parte.* Pontificia Universidad Católica del Perú, Lima.

Cobb, Charles

2005   Archaeology and the "Savage Slot": Displacement and Emplacement in the Premodern World. *American Anthropologist* 107(4):563–74.

Coben, Lawrence S.

2006   Other Cuzcos: Replicated Theaters of Inka Power. In *Archaeology of Performance: Theaters of Power, Community, and Politics*, edited by Takeshi Inomata and Lawrence S. Coben, pp. 223–60. Altamira Press, Berkeley, Calif.

Cobo, Bernabe

1964 [1653]   Historia del Nuevo Mundo. In *Obras del Bernebé Cobo de la Compañía de Jesús*, vol. 2, edited by Francisco Mateos. Ediciones Atlas, Madrid.

1979 [1653]   *History of the Inca Empire*. Translated by Roland Hamilton. University of Texas Press, Austin.

Cock Carrasco, Guillermo

1976–77   Los kurakas de los Collaguas: Poder político y poder económico. *Historia y cultura* 10:95–118.

1981   El ayllu en la sociedad andina: Alcances y perspectivas. *Ethnohistória y antropología andina*, 231–53.

Cohen, Anthony P.

1985   *The Symbolic Construction of Community*. Key Ideas series. Routledge, New York.

Cole, Jeffrey A.

1985   *The Potosí Mita, 1573–1700: Compulsory Indian Labor in the Andes*. Stanford University Press, Stanford, Calif.

Comaroff, Jean, and John Comaroff

1986   Christianity and Colonialism in South Africa. *American Ethnologist* 13(1):1–22.

Cook, Alexadra Parma, and Noble David Cook

1991   *Good Faith and Truthful Ignorance: A Case of Transatlantic Bigamy*. Duke University Press, Durham, N.C.

Cook, Noble David

1975   Introducción. In *Tasa de la visita general de Francisco de Toledo*, edited by Noble David Cook, Alejandro Málaga Medina, and Thérèse Bouysse-Cassagne. Universidad Nacional Mayor de San Marcos, Lima.

1982   *The People of the Colca Valley: A Population Study*. Westview Press, Boulder, Colo.

1992   Luis Jerónimo de Oré: Una aproximación. In *Symbolo catholico indiano*, pp. 35–61. Lima.

1997   Cabanas y Collaguas en la era prehispánica. In *Arqueología, antropología e historia en los Andes: Homenaje a María Rostworowski*, edited by Rafael Varón Gabai and Javier Flores Espinoza, pp. 379–96. Instituto de Estudios Peruanos, Lima.

2002   "Tomando Posesión" Luis Gerónimo de Oré y el retorno de los Franciscanos a las doctrinas del Valle del Colca. In *El hombre y los Andes: Homenaje a Franklin Pease G. Y.*, edited by Javier Flores Espinoza and Rafael Varón Gabai, vol. 2, pp. 889–903. Pontificia Universidad Católica del Perú, Lima.

2003   Introducción. In *Collaguas II, Lari Collaguas: Economía, sociedad y población, 1604–1605*, edited by David J. Robinson, pp. xv–xxxv. Pontificia Universidad Católica del Perú, Lima.

2007   *People of the Volcano: Andean Counterpoint in the Colca Valley of Peru*. Duke University Press, Durham, N.C.

Cook, Noble David, Alejandro Málaga Medina, and Thérèse Bouysse-Cassagne (editors)

1975 [1582]   *Tasa de la visita general de Francisco de Toledo*. Universidad Nacional Mayor de San Marcos, Lima.

Córdoba y Salinas, Diego de
   1957 [1651]   *Chrónica franciscana de las Provincias del Perú.* Academy of American Franciscan History, Washington, D.C.

Córdova Aguilar, Hildegardo, Luis Gonzalez Ilizarbe, and Carlos Guevara Tello
   1986   Agriculture in Coporaque. In *The Cultural Ecology, Archaeology, and History of Terracing and Terrace Abandonment in the Colca Valley of Southern Peru,* edited by William M. Denevan, vol. 1, pp. 60–87. Technical Report to the National Science Foundation and the National Geographic Society. Department of Geography, University of Wisconsin, Madison.

Costin, Cathy L., and Timothy K. Earle
   1989   Status Distinction and Legitimation of Power as Reflected in Changing Patterns of Consumption in Late Prehispanic Peru. *American Antiquity* 54:691–714.

Covey, R. Alan
   2003   A Processual Study of Inka State Formation. *Journal of Anthropological Archaeology* 22(4):333–57.
   2006a Chronology, Succession, and Sovereignty: The Politics of Inka Historiography and Its Modern Interpretation. *Comparative Studies in Society and History* 48:169–199.
   2006b *How the Incas Built Their Heartland: State Formation and the Innovation of Imperial Strategies in the Sacred Valley, Peru.* University of Michigan Press, Ann Arbor.
   2008   Multiregional Perspectives on the Archaeology of the Andes During the Late Intermediate Period (c. A.D. 1000–1400). *Journal of Archaeological Research* 16:287–338.

Crespo, Juan C.
   1977   Los Collaguas en la visita de Alonso Fernández de Bonilla. In *Collaguas I,* edited by Franklin Pease, pp. 53–91. Pontificia Universidad Católica del Perú, Lima.

Crumley, Carole L.
   1975   Toward a Locational Definition of State Systems of Settlement. *American Anthropologist* 78:59–73.
   1979   Three Locational Models: An Epistemological Assessment for Anthropology and Archaeology. In *Advances in Archaeological Method and Theory,* vol. 2, edited by Michael B. Schiffer, pp. 141–73. Academic Press, New York.
   1987   A Dialectical Critique of Hierarchy. In *Power Relations and State Formation,* edited by Thomas C. Patterson and Christine W. Gailey, pp. 155–69. Archeology Section, American Anthropological Association, Washington, D.C.
   1994a *Historical Ecology: A Multidimensional Ecological Orientation.* School of American Research Press, Santa Fe, N.M.
   1994b *Historical Ecology: Cultural Knowledge and Changing Landscapes.* 1st ed. School of American Research Press, Santa Fe, N.M.
   1999   Sacred Landscapes: Constructed and Conceptualized. In *Archaeologies of Landscape,* edited by Wendy Ashmore and A. Bernard Knapp, pp. 269–76. Blackwell, Malden, Mass.

Cummins, Tom
   2002   Forms of Andean Colonial Towns, Free Will, and Marriage. In *The Archaeology of Colonialism,* edited by Claire L. Lyons and John K. Papadopoulos, pp. 199–240. Getty Research Institute, Los Angeles.

D'Altroy, Terence N.
   1987   Transitions in Power: Centralization of Wanka Political Organization under Inka Rule. *Ethnohistory* 34(1):78–102.
   2002   *The Incas.* Blackwell, Malden, Mass.

2005   Remaking the Social Landscape: Colonization in the Inka Empire. In *The Archaeology of Colonial Encounters*, edited by Gil Stein, pp. 263–96. School for Advanced Research Press, Santa Fe, N.M.

D'Altroy, Terence N., and Christine A. Hastorf

1984   Distribution and Contents of Inca State Storehouses in the Xauxa Region of Peru. *American Antiquity* 49(2):334–49.

de la Vera Cruz Chávez, Pablo

1987   Cambios en los patrones de asentamiento y el uso y abandono de los andenes en Cabanaconde, Valle del Colca, Perú. In *Pre-Hispanic Agricultural Fields in the Andean Region*, edited by William M. Denevan, Kent Mathewson, and Gregory W. Knapp.BAR International Series 359(I):89–128. Oxford.

1988   Estudio arqueológico en el Valle de Cabanaconde, Arequipa. Unpublished baccalaureate thesis, Department of Archaeology, Universidad Católica Santa María, Arequipa.

1989   Cronología y corología de la cuenca del Río Camaná—Majes—Colca—Arequipa. Unpublished licenciate's thesis, Department of Archaeology, Universidad Católica Santa María, Arequipa.

DeMarrais, Elizabeth, Timothy K. Earle, and Luis Jaime Castillo

1996   Ideology, Materialization, and Power Strategies. *Current Anthropology* 37(1):15–31.

Denevan, William M.

1980   Tipología de configuraciones agrícolas prehispánicas. *América Indígena* 40:610–52.

1986   *The Cultural Ecology, Archaeology, and History of Terracing and Terrace Abandonment in the Colca Valley of Southern Peru*. Vol. 1. Technical Report to the National Science Foundation and the National Geographic Society. Department of Geography, University of Wisconsin, Madison.

1987   Terrace Abandonment in the Colca Valley. In *Pre-Hispanic Agricultural Fields in the Andean Region*, edited by William M. Denevan, Kent Mathewson, and Gregory W. Knapp. BAR International Series 359(I):1–43.

1988a   *The Cultural Ecology, Archaeology, and History of Terracing and Terrace Abandonment in the Colca Valley of Southern Peru*. Vol. 2. Technical Report to the National Science Foundation and the National Geographic Society. Department of Geography, University of Wisconsin, Madison.

1988b   Measurement of Abandoned Terracing from Air Photos, Colca Valley, Peru. *Yearbook, Conference of Latin Americanist Geographers* 14:20–30.

2001   *Cultivated Landscapes of Native Amazonia and the Andes*. Oxford University Press, Oxford.

Denevan, William M., and Laura Hartwig

1986   Measurement of Terrace Abandonment in the Colca Valley. In *The Cultural Ecology, Archaeology, and History of Terracing and Terrace Abandonment in the Colca Valley of Southern Peru*, edited by William M. Denevan, vol. 1, pp. 99–115. Technical Report to the National Science Foundation and the National Geographic Society. Department of Geography, University of Wisconsin, Madison.

Denevan, William M., John M. Treacy, and Jonathan A. Sandor

1986   Physical Geography of the Coporaque Region. In *The Cultural Ecology, Archaeology, and History of Terracing and Terrace Abandonment in the Colca Valley of Southern Peru*, edited by William M. Denevan, vol. 1, pp. 47–59. Technical Report to the National Science Foundation and the National Geographic Society. Department of Geography, University of Wisconsin, Madison.

Dick, R. P., Jonathan A. Sandor, and N. S. Eash

1994   Soil Enzyme Activities after 1500 Years of Terrace Agriculture in the Colca Valley, Peru. *Agriculture, Ecosystems, and Environment* 50:123–31.

Dietler, Michael

2005   The Archaeology of Colonization and the Colonization of Archaeology: Theoretical Challenges from an Ancient Mediterranean Colonial Encounter. In *The Archaeology of Colonial Encounters*, edited by Gil Stein, pp. 33–68. School of American Research Press, Santa Fe, N.M.

Dillehay, Tom D. (editor)

1995   *Tombs for the Living: Andean Mortuary Practices*. Dumbarton Oaks, Washington, D.C.

2003   El colonialismo inka, el consumo de chicha y los festines desde una perspectiva de banquetes políticos. *Boletín de Arqueología PUCP* 7:355–63.

Dillehay, Tom D., and L. Núñez

1988   Camelids, Caravans, and Complex Societies in the South-Central Andes. In *Recent Studies in Pre-Columbian Archaeology*, edited by N.J. Saunders and O. de Montmollin. BAR International Series 421:603–34.

Donkin, R. A.

1979   *Agricultural Terracing in the Aboriginal New World*. Viking Fund Publications in Anthropology. University of Arizona Press, Tucson.

Doutriaux, Miriam

2002   Relaciones étnicas y económicas de poder: La conquista incaica en el Valle del Colca, Arequipa. *Boletín de Arqueología PUCP* 6:411–32.

2004   Imperial Conquest in a Multiethnic Setting: The Inka Occupation of the Colca Valley, Peru. Ph.D. dissertation, Department of Anthropology, University of California, Berkeley.

Durston, Alan

2007   *Pastoral Quechua: The History of Christian Translation in Colonial Peru, 1550–1650*. History, Languages, and Cultures of the Spanish and Portuguese Worlds. University of Notre Dame Press, Notre Dame, Ind.

Duviols, Pierre

1973   Huari y llacuaz: Agricultores y pastores, un dualismo prehispánico de oposición y complementaridad. *Revista del Museo Nacional* 39:153–91.

1986   *Cultura andina y represión: Procesos y visitas de idolatrías y hechicerías*. Centro de Estudios Rurales Andinos "Bartolomé de las Casas," Cusco.

Earle, Timothy K.

1994   Wealth Finance in the Inka Empire: Evidence from the Calchaquí Valley, Argentina. *American Antiquity* 59(3):443–60.

Eash, N. S., and J. A. Sandor

1995   Soil Chronosequence and Geomorphology in a Semiarid Valley in the Andes of Southern Peru. *Geoderma* 65:59–79.

Echeverría y Morales, Francisco Xavier

1952 [1804]   *Memoria de la Santa Iglesia de Arequipa*. Imprenta Portugal, Arequipa.

Ehrenreich, Robert M., Carole L. Crumley, and Janet E. Levy

1995   *Heterarchy and the Analysis of Complex Societies*. Archeological Papers of the American Anthropological Association, No. 6. American Anthropological Association, Arlington, Va.

Erickson, Clark L.

1999   Neo-Environmental Determinism and Agrarian "Collapse" in Andean Prehistory. *Antiquity* 73:281.

2000   The Lake Titicaca Basin: A Precolumbian Built Landscape. In *Imperfect Balance: Landscape Transformations in the Precolumbian Americas*, edited by David L. Lentz, pp. 311–56. Columbia University Press, New York.

Espinoza Soriano, Waldemar

1973   Las colonias de mitmas multiples en Abancay, siglos XV y XVI. *Revista del Museo Nacional* 39:225–300.

1975   Las mitmas Huayacuntu en Quito o Guarniciones para la represion armada, siglos XV y XVI. *Revista del Museo Nacional* 41:351–94.

Estenssoro, Juan Carlos

2003   *Del paganismo a la santidad: La incorporación de los indios del Perú al catolicismo, 1532–1750*. IFEA, Pontificia Universidad Católica del Perú, Instituto Riva-Agüero, Lima.

Femenias, Blenda

1997   Ambiguous Emblems: Gender, Clothing, and Representation in Contemporary Peru. Ph.D. dissertation, Anthropology, University of Wisconsin, Madison.

1998   Ethnic Artists and the Appropriation of Fashion: Embroidery and Identity in Caylloma, Peru. *Chungara* 30(2).

2005   *Gender and the Boundaries of Dress in Contemporary Peru*. University of Texas Press, Austin.

Fischler, Claude

1988   Food, Self and Identity. *Social Science Information* 27(2):275–92.

Flint, Richard, and Shirley Cushing Flint

2003   *The Coronado Expedition: From the Distance of 460 Years*. University of New Mexico Press, Albuquerque.

Foucault, Michel

1977   *Discipline and Punish: The Birth of the Prison*. Pantheon Books, New York.

1978   *The History of Sexuality*. Pantheon Books, New York.

Gade, Daniel W.

1967   Plant Use and Folk Agriculture in the Vilcanota Valley of Peru: A Cultural-Historical Geography of Plant Resources. Ph.D. dissertation, Department of Geography, University of Wisconsin, Madison.

Gade, Daniel W., and Mario Escobar

1982   Village Settlement and the Colonial Legacy in Southern Peru. *Geographical Review* 72:430–49.

Galdos Rodríguez, Guillermo

1984   Expansión de los Collaguas hacia el Valle de Arequipa. *El Derecho* 296:81–152.

1987   *Comunidades prehispánicas de Arequipa*. Fundación Manuel J. Bustamante De la Fuente, Arequipa.

Garcilaso de la Vega, El Inca

1966 [1609]   *Royal Commentaries of the Incas and General History of Peru*. 2 vols. University of Texas Press, Austin.

Garner, Richard L.

1988   Long-Term Silver Mining Trends in Spanish America: A Comparative Analysis of Peru and Mexico. *American Historical Review* 93(4):898–935.

Gelles, Paul H.

1990   Channels of Power, Fields of Contention: The Politics and Ideology of Irrigation in an Andean Peasant Community (Peru). Ph.D. dissertation, Department of Anthropology, Harvard University. University Microfilms, Ann Arbor.

1993   Cabaneño Ethnohydrology: The Cosmological Referents and Historical Roots of an

Andean Irrigation System. *Culture and Environment: A Fragile Coexistence: Proceedings of the Twenty-fourth Annual Conference of the Archaeological Association of the University of Calgary* 24:353–61.

1995   Equilibrium and Extraction: Dual Organization in the Andes. *American Ethnologist* 22(4):710–42.

2000   *Water and Power in Highland Peru.* Rutgers University Press, New Brunswick.

Giddens, Anthony

1979   *Central Problems of Social Theory.* University of California Press, Berkeley and Los Angeles.

Gieryn, Thomas

2002   What Buildings Do. *Theory and Society* 31:35–74.

Gillespie, Susan D.

2000   Beyond Kinship: An Introduction. In *Beyond Kinship: Social and Material Reproduction in House Societies,* edited by Rosemary Joyce and Susan D. Gillespie, pp. 1–21. University of Pennsylvania Press, Philadelphia.

Gisbert, Teresa, and José de Mesa

1985   *Arquitectura andina, 1530–1830: Historia y análisis.* Embajada de España en Bolivia, La Paz.

Given, Michael

2004   *The Archaeology of the Colonized.* Routledge, New York.

Gledhill, John

1988   Legacies of Empire: Political Centralization and Class Formation in the Hispanic-American World. In *State and Society: The Emergence and Development of Social Hierarchy and Political Centralization,* edited by John Gledhill, Barbara Bender, and Trolle Larsen Mogens, pp. 302–19. Unwin Hyman, London.

Goldstein, Paul S.

1993   House, Community, and the State in the Earliest Tiwanaku Colony: Domestic Patterns and State Integration at Omo M12, Moquegua. In *Domestic Architecture, Ethnicity, and Complementarity in the South-Central Andes,* edited by Mark S. Aldenderfer, pp. 25–41. University of Iowa Press, Iowa City.

2000   Communities without Borders: The Vertical Archipelago and Diaspora Communities in the Southern Andes. In *The Archaeology of Communities,* edited by Marcello A. Canuto and Jason Yaeger, pp. 182–209. Routledge, New York.

2005   *Andean Diaspora: The Tiwanaku Colonies and the Origins of South American Empire.* University Press of Florida, Gainesville.

González, Fernando Luis

1995   Fences, Fields and Fodder: Enclosures in Lari, Valle del Colca, Southern Peru. Master's thesis, Department of Geography, University of Wisconsin, Madison.

González Holguín, Diego, and Raúl Porras Barrenechea

1989 [1608]   *Vocabulario de la lengua general de todo el Perú, llamada lengua Qquichua o del Inca.* Universidad Nacional Mayor de San Marcos, Lima.

Gosden, Chris, and Chantal Knowles

2001   *Collecting Colonialism: Material Culture and Colonial Change.* Berg, New York.

Gose, Peter

1996   The Past Is a Lower Moiety: Diarchy, History, and Divine Kingship in the Inka Empire. *History and Anthropology* 9(4):383–414.

2003   Converting the Ancestors: Indirect Rule, Settlement Consolidation, and the Struggle over Burial in Colonial Peru, 1532–1614. In *Conversion: Old Worlds and New,* edited by Kenneth Mills and Anthony Grafton, pp. 140–74. University of Rochester Press, Rochester, N.Y.

2008   *Invaders as Ancestors: On the Intercultural Making and Unmaking of Spanish Colonialism in the Andes.* University of Toronto Press, Toronto.

Gregory, Ian, and Paul S. Ell (editors)

2007   *Historical GIS: Technologies, Methodologies, and Scholarship.* Cambridge University Press, New York.

Grove, Jean M.

1988   *The Little Ice Age.* Methuen, New York.

Guaman Poma de Ayala, Felipe

1987 [1615]   *Nueva corónica y buen gobierno,* edited by John V. Murra, Rolena Adorno, and Jorge L. Urioste. 3 vols. Historia 16, Madrid.

Guerra Santander, Ericka M., and Paúl A. Aquize Cáceres

1996   Patrón arquitectónico y patrón de asentamiento del sitio prehispánico de Uskallacta Chivay (Valle del Colca)—Arequipa. Unpublished licenciate's thesis, Department of Archaeology, Universidad Católica Santa María, Arequipa.

Guevara-Gil, Armando, and Frank Salomon

1994   A "Personal Visit": Colonial Political Ritual and the Making of Indians in the Andes. *Colonial Latin American Review* 3(1–2):3–36.

Guillet, David W.

1978   The Supra-Household Sphere of Production in the Andean Peasant Economy. *Actes du XXLe Congrés International des Américanistes* 4:89–105.

1981   Land Tenure, Ecological Zone, and Agricultural Regime in the Central Andes. *American Ethnologist* 8(1):139–56.

1987   Terracing and Irrigation in the Peruvian Highlands. *Current Anthropology* 28(4):409–30.

1992   *Covering Ground: Communal Water Management and the State in the Peruvian Highlands.* University of Michigan Press, Ann Arbor.

Guillet, David W., L. Furbee, J. A. Sandor, and R. A. Benfer

1995   On a Methodology for Combining Cognitive and Behavioral Research: The Lari Soils Project in Peru. In *The Cultural Dimension of Development: Indigenous Knowledge Systems,* edited by D. M. Warren, L. J. Slikkerveer, and D. Brokensha, pp. 71–81. Intermediate Technology Publications, London.

Gutiérrez, Ramón

1993   *Pueblos de indios: Otro urbanismo en la región andina.* Ediciones Abya-Yala, Quito.

Hastorf, Christine

1990   The Effect of the Inka State on Sausa Agricultural Production and Crop Consumption. *American Antiquity* 55:262–90.

Hemming, John

1983   *The Conquest of the Incas.* Rev. ed. Penguin Books, Harmondsworth, England.

Hollander, Jocelyn A., and Rachel L. Einwohner

2004   Conceptualizing Resistance. *Sociological Forum* 19(4):533–54.

Hyslop, John

1976   An Archaeological Investigation of the Lupaqa Kingdom and Its Origins. Ph.D. dissertation, Department of Anthropology, Columbia University, New York.

1990   *Inka Settlement Planning.* 1st ed. University of Texas Press, Austin.

Ingold, Tim

1993   The Temporality of Landscape. *World Archaeology* 25(2):152–74.

2000   *The Perception of the Environment: Essays on Livelihood, Dwelling and Skill.* Routledge, New York.

Isbell, William H.
  1997   *Mummies and Mortuary Monuments: A Postprocessual Prehistory of Central Andean Social Organization.* University of Texas Press, Austin.
  2000   What We Should Be Studying: The "Imagined Community" and the "Natural Community." In *The Archaeology of Communities*, edited by Marcello A. Canuto and Jason Yaeger, pp. 243–66. Routledge, New York.

Izaguirre Urbano, Lourdes E.
  n.d.   Estudio del subsistema agrícola del Distrito de Coporaque. Unpublished master's thesis, Facultad de Ingeniería Agrícola, Universidad Nacional Agraria, Lima.

Janusek, John W.
  1999   Craft and Local Power: Embedded Specialization in Tiwanaku Cities. *Latin American Antiquity* 10(2):107–31.

Jennings, Justin M.
  2002   Prehistoric Imperialism and Cultural Development in the Cotahuasi Valley, Peru. Ph.D. dissertation, Department of Anthropology, University of California, Santa Barbara.

Johnson, A. M.
  1976   The Climate of Peru, Bolivia, and Ecuador. In *Climates of Central and South America*, vol. 12, edited by W. Schwerdtfeger, pp. 147–200. World Survey of Climatology. Elsevier, New York.

Joseph, Miranda (editor)
  2002   *Against the Romance of Community.* University of Minnesota Press, Minneapolis.

Joyce, Rosemary, and Susan D. Gillespie (editors)
  2000   *Beyond Kinship: Social and Material Reproduction in House Societies.* University of Pennsylvania Press, Philadelphia.

Joyce, Rosemary A., and Julia A. Hendon
  2000   Heterarchy, History, and Material Reality: "Communities" in Late Classic Honduras. In *The Archaeology of Communities*, edited by Marcello A. Canuto and Jason Yaeger, pp. 143–60. Routledge, New York.

Julien, Catherine J.
  1982   Inca Decimal Administration in the Lake Titicaca Region. In *The Inca and Aztec States, 1400–1800: Anthropology and History*, edited by George Allen Collier, Renato Rosaldo, and John D. Wirth, pp. 119–51. Academic Press, New York.
  1983   *Hatunqolla: A View of Inca Rule from the Lake Titicaca Region.* University of California Press, Berkeley and Los Angeles.
  1985   Guano and Resource Control in Sixteenth-Century Arequipa. In *Andean Ecology and Civilization: An Interdisciplinary Perspective on Andean Ecological Complementarity*, edited by Shozo Masuda, Izumi Shimada, and Craig Morris, pp. 185–231. University of Tokyo Press, Tokyo.
  1988   How Inca Decimal Administration Worked. *Ethnohistory* 35:257–79.
  1991   *Condesuyo: The Political Division of Territory under Inca and Spanish Rule.* Bonner Amerikanistische Studien, Bonn.
  1998   La encomienda del Inca. In *Actas del IV Congreso Internacional de Etnohistoria*, vol. 2, pp. 489–516. Pontificia Universidad Católica, Lima.
  2000   *Reading Inca History.* University of Iowa Press, Iowa City.

Julien, Daniel G.
  1993   Late Pre-Inkaic Ethnic Groups in Highland Peru: An Archaeological-Ethnohistorical Model of the Political Geography of the Cajamarca Region. *Latin American Antiquity* 4(3):246–73.

Kagan, Richard L.

2000   *Urban Images of the Hispanic World, 1493–1793.* Yale University Press, New Haven.

Keane, Webb

2003   Semiotics and the Social Analysis of Material Things. *Language and Communication* 23:409–25.

2007   *Christian Moderns: Freedom and Fetish in the Mission Encounter.* University of California Press, Berkeley and Los Angeles.

Kirch, Patrick V., and Terry L. Hunt

1997   *Historical Ecology in the Pacific Islands: Prehistoric Environmental and Landscape Change.* Yale University Press, New Haven.

Knapp, A. Bernard, and Wendy Ashmore

1999   Archaeological Landscapes: Constructed, Conceptualized, Ideational. In *Archaeologies of Landscape,* edited by Wendy Ashmore and A. Bernard Knapp, pp. 1–32. Blackwell, Malden, Mass.

Knowles, Anne Kelly

2000   Introduction. *Social Science History* 24(3):451–70.

2002   *Past Time, Past Place: GIS for History.* ESRI Press, Redlands, Calif.

Knowles, Anne Kelly, and Amy Hillier (editors)

2008   *Placing History: How Maps, Spatial Data, and GIS Are Changing Historical Scholarship.* ESRI Press, Redlands, Calif.

Knudson, Kelly J., and Christopher M. Stojanowski

2009   *Bioarchaeology and Identity in the Americas.* University Press of Florida, Gainesville.

Kolata, Alan L.

1993   *The Tiwanaku: Portrait of an Andean Civilization.* The Peoples of America series. Blackwell, Cambridge.

1996   *Tiwanaku and Its Hinterlands: Archaeology and Paleoecology of an Andean Civilization.* Vol. 1, *Agroecology.* Smithsonian Institution Press, Washington, D.C.

Kolb, Michael J., and James E. Snead

1997   It's a Small World after All: Comparative Analyses of Community Organization in Archaeology. *American Antiquity* 62(4):609–28.

Kopytoff, Igor

1986   The Cultural Biography of Things: Commoditization as Process. In *The Social Life of Things: Commodities in Cultural Pe*

1944   *Peruvian Archeology in 1942.* Viking Fund Publications in Anthropology, Number 4. Viking Fund, New York.

La Lone, Darrell E.

1982   The Inca as a Nonmarket Economy: Supply on Command Versus Supply and Demand. In *Contexts for Prehistoric Exchange,* edited by Jonathon E. Ericson and Timothy K. Earle, pp. 291–316. Academic Press, New York.

Lamana, Gonzalo

2008   *Domination without Dominance: Inca-Spanish Encounters in Early Colonial Peru.* Duke University Press, Durham, N.C.

Lansing, John S.

1991   *Priests and Programmers: Technologies of Power in the Engineered Landscape of Bali.* Princeton University Press, Princeton.

Lara, Jaime

1997   Precious Green Jade Water: A Sixteenth-Century Adult Catechumate in the New World. *Worship* 71(5):415–28.

1998   The Sacramented Sun: Solar Eucharistic Worship in Colonial Latin America. In *El Cuerpo de Cristo: The Hispanic Presence in the United States Catholic Church*, edited by Peter Casarella and Raúl Gómez, pp. 261–91. Crossroad, New York.

2004   *City, Temple, Stage: Eschatological Architecture and Liturgical Theatrics in New Spain*. University of Notre Dame, Notre Dame, Ind.

Larson, Brooke
1998   *Cochabamba, 1550–1900: Colonialism and Agrarian Transformation in Bolivia*. Duke University Press, Durham, N.C.

Lentz, David L.
2000   *Imperfect Balance: Landscape Transformations in the Precolumbian Americas*. Columbia University Press, New York.

Levillier, Roberto
1935   *Don Francisco de Toledo, supremo organizador del Perú*. Colección de publicaciones históricas de la biblioteca del congreso argentino. 3 vols. Buenos Aires.

1940   *Don Francisco de Toledo, supremo organizador del Perú; su vida, su obra (1515–1582). Tomo II, sus informaciones sobre los Incas (1570–1572)*. Espasa-Calpe, S.A., Buenos Aires.

Liebmann, Matthew, and Melissa S. Murphy
2011   Rethinking the Archaeology of "Rebels, Backsliders, and Idolaters." In *Enduring Conquests: Rethinking the Archaeology of Resistance to Spanish Colonialism in the Americas*, edited by Matthew Liebmann and Melissa S. Murphy, pp. 3–18. School for Advanced Research Press, Santa Fe, N.M.

Lightfoot, Kent G.
1995   Culture Contact Studies: Redefining the Relationship between Prehistoric and Historical Archaeology. *American Antiquity* 60(2):199–217.

Linares Málaga, Eloy
1993   *Arequipa tierra mía*. Correo, Arequipa.

Llobera, Marcos
1996   Exploring the Topography of the Mind: GIS, Social Space and Archaeology. *Antiquity* 70(269):612–22.

Llosa, Hector, and Maria A. Benavides
1994   Arquitectura y vivienda campesina en tres pueblos andinos: Yanque, Lari, y Coporaque en el Valle del Río Colca, Arequipa. *Bulletin de l'Institut Français d'Études Andines* 23(1):105–50.

Lock, Gary
2010   Representations of Space and Place in the Humanities. In *The Spatial Humanities: GIS and the Future of Humanities Scholarship*, edited by David Bodenhamer, John Corrigan, and Trevor Harris, pp. 89–108. Indiana University Press, Bloomington.

Loomba, Ania
2005   *Colonialism/Postcolonialism*. Routledge, New York.

Lorandi, Ana María
1991   Evidencias en torno a los mitmaqkuna incaicos en el noroeste argentino. *Anthropológica* 9:213–36.

Low, Setha M., and Denise Lawrence-Zúñiga (editors)
2003   *The Anthropology of Space and Place: Locating Culture*. Blackwell, Malden, Mass.

Lumbreras, Luis G.
1974a   Los reinos post-Tiwanaku en el área altiplánica. *Revista del Museo Nacional* 40:55–85.
1974b   *The Peoples and Cultures of Ancient Peru*. Smithsonian Institution Press, Washington, D.C.

MacCormack, Sabine

1985   The Heart Has Its Reasons: Predicaments of Missionary Christianity in Early Colonial Peru. *Hispanic American Historical Review* 65(3):443–66.

1991   *Religion in the Andes: Vision and Imagination in Early Colonial Peru.* Princeton University Press, Princeton.

1993   Demons, Imagination, and the Incas. *New World Encounters,* 101–26.

2006   Gods, Demons, and Idols in the Andes. *Journal of the History of Ideas* 67(4):623–47.

Málaga Medina, Alejandro

1974   Las reducciones en el Perú (1532–1600). *Historia y Cultura* 8:141–72.

1977   Los Collagua en la historia de Arequipa en el siglo XVI. In *Collaguas I,* edited by Franklin Pease, pp. 93–130. Pontificia Universidad Católica del Perú, Lima.

1981   *Arequipa, estudios históricos.* Biblioteca Arequipa, Arequipa.

Malpass, Michael A.

1986   Late Prehistoric Terracing at Chirja in the Colca Valley, Peru: Preliminary Report. In *Perspectives on Andean Prehistory and Protohistory,* edited by Dan Sandweiss and P. Kvietok, pp. 19–34. Cornell University Latin American Studies Program, Ithaca, N.Y.

1987   Late Prehistoric Terracing at Chijra in the Colca Valley, Peru: Preliminary Report II. In *Pre-Hispanic Agricultural Fields in the Andean Region,* edited by William M. Denevan, Kent Mathewson, and Gregory W. Knapp. BAR International Series 359(I):45–66.

1988   Irrigated Versus Non-Irrigated Terracing in the Andes: Environmental Considerations. *Proceedings of the 7th Northeast Conference of Andean Archeology and Ethnohistory, Amherst, MA November 5–6, 1998,* 11.

Malpass, Michael A., and Pablo de la Vera Cruz Chávez

1986   Ceramic Sequence from Chijra, Colca Valley, Peru. In *The Cultural Ecology, Archaeology, and History of Terracing and Terrace Abandonment in the Colca Valley of Southern Peru,* edited by William M. Denevan, vol. 2, pp. 204–33. Technical Report to the National Science Foundation and the National Geographic Society. Department of Geography, University of Wisconsin, Madison.

1990   Cronología y secuencia de la cerámica de Chijra, Valle del Colca. *Gaceta Arqueológica Andina* 18/19:41–57.

Mannheim, Bruce

1991   *The Language of the Inka since the European Invasion.* University of Texas Press, Austin.

Manrique, Nelson

1985   *Colonialismo y pobreza campesina: Caylloma y el Valle del Colca siglos XVI–XX.* DESCO, Lima.

Masuda, Shozo, Izumi Shimada, and Craig Morris (editors)

1985   *Andean Ecology and Civilization: An Interdisciplinary Perspective on Andean Ecological Complementarity.* University of Tokyo Press, Tokyo.

Matienzo, Juan de

1910 [1567]   *Gobierno del Perú.* Compañía sud-americana de billetes de banco, Buenos Aires.

Mayer, Enrique

1985   Production Zones. In *Andean Ecology and Civilization: An Interdisciplinary Perspective on Andean Ecological Complementarity,* edited by Shozo Masuda, Izumi Shimada, and Craig Morris, pp. 45–84. University of Tokyo Press, Tokyo.

McGlade, J.

1995   Archaeology and the Ecodynamics of Human-Modified Landscapes. *Antiquity* 69:113–32.

Mendoza, Diego de
1976 [1664]   *Chronica de la Provincia de San Antonio de los Charcas del Orden de nuestro Seráfico P. S. Francisco en las Indias Occidentales, Reyno del Perú.* Editorial Casa Municipal de la Cultura Franz Tamayo, La Paz.

Mishkin, Bernard
1946   The Contemporary Quechua. In *Handbook of South American Indians,* vol. 2, pp. 411–70, edited by Julian H. Steward. Smithsonian Institution Press, Washington, D.C.

Mitchell, Timothy
1988   *Colonising Egypt.* University of California Press, Berkeley and Los Angeles.

Mitchell, William P.
1976   Irrigation and Community in the Central Peruvian Highlands. *American Anthropologist* 78(1):25–44.

Moore, Jerry D.
1996   Archaeology of Plazas and the Proxemics of Ritual: Three Andean Traditions. *American Anthropologist* 98(4):789–802.

Morante, José Maria
1939   Arqueología del Departamento de Arequipa; Condesuyos y Camaná precolumbinos. Unpublished Ph.D. dissertation, Department of Archaeology, Universidad Nacional de San Agustín, Arequipa.

Morris, Craig
1966   El tampu real de Tunsucancha. *Cuadernos de Investigacion* 1:95–116.
1982   The Infrastructure of Inka Control in the Peruvian Central Highlands. In *Inca and Aztec States, 1400–1800: Anthropology and History,* edited by George Allen Collier, Renato Rosaldo, and John D. Wirth, pp. 153–71. Academic Press, New York.

Morris, Craig, and Donald E. Thompson
1985   *Huánuco Pampa: An Inca City and Its Hinterland.* Thames and Hudson, London.

Morrison, Kathleen D.
2001   Coercion, Resistance, and Hierarchy: Local Processes and Imperial Strategies in the Vijayanagara Empire. In *Empires,* edited by Susan E. Alcock, Terence N. D'Altroy, Kathleen D. Morrison, and Carla M. Sinopoli, pp. 252–78. Cambridge University Press, Cambridge.

Muñoz, Lizette, and David Goldstein
2010   Paleoethnobotanical Studies in the Collesuyo Region: The Case of Malata. Paper presented at the 75th annual meeting of the Society for American Archaeology, St. Louis.

Murdock, George P.
1949   *Social Structure.* Macmillan, New York.

Murra, John V.
1956   The Economic Organization of the Inca State. Ph.D. dissertation, Department of Anthropology, University of Chicago. University Microfilms, Ann Arbor.
1962a   Cloth and Its Functions in the Inca State. *American Anthropologist* 64(4):710–28.
1962b   The Function of Cloth in the Inca State. *American Anthropologist* 64:710–28.
1964   Una apreciación etnológica de la visita. In *Visita hecha a la Provincia de Chucuito por Garci Diez de San Miguel en el año 1567,* edited by John V. Murra, pp. 419–44. Casa de la Cultura del Perú, Lima.
1968   An Aymara Kingdom in 1567. *Ethnohistory* 15:115–51.
1972   El control vertical de un máximo de pisos ecológicos en la economía de las sociedades andinas. In *Visita de la Provincia de León de Huánuco,* edited by John V. Murra, pp. 429–76. Universidad Hermilio Valdizán, Huánuco, Peru.

1980   *The Economic Organization of the Inka State.* JAI Press, Greenwich, Conn.

1985   "El Archipiélago Vertical" Revisited. In *Andean Ecology and Civilization,* edited by S. Masuda, Izumi Shimada, and Craig Morris, pp. 3–13. University of Tokyo Press, Tokyo.

Murra, John Victor, and Craig Morris

1976   Dynastic Oral Tradition, Administrative Records and Archaeology in the Andes. *World Archaeology* 7(3):269–79.

Nash, Donna J., and P. Ryan Williams

2009   Wari Political Organization on the Southern Periphery. In *Andean Civilization: A Tribute to Michael E. Moseley,* edited by Joyce Marcus and Patrick Ryan Williams, pp. 257–76. Cotsen Institute of Archaeology Press, Los Angeles.

Neira Avendaño, Máximo

1961   Los Collaguas. Unpublished master's thesis, Department of Archaeology, Universidad Nacional de San Agustín, Arequipa.

1986   Excavaciones arqueológicas en las ruinas de Chishra (Chijra), Coporaque. In *The Cultural Ecology, Archaeology, and History of Terracing and Terrace Abandonment in the Colca Valley of Southern Peru,* edited by William M. Denevan, vol. 1, pp. 167–97. Technical Report to the National Science Foundation and the National Geographic Society. Department of Geography, University of Wisconsin, Madison.

1990   Arequipa prehispánica. In *Historia general de Arequipa,* edited by Máximo Neira Avendaño, Guillermo Galdos Rodríguez, Alejandro Málaga Medina, Eusebio Quiroz Paz Soldán, and Juan Guillermo Carpio Muñoz, pp. 5–213. Fundación M. J. Bustamante de la Fuente, Arequipa.

Niles, Susan A.

1984   Architectural Form and Social Function in Inca Towns near Cuzco. BAR International Series 210:205–23.

1987   *Callachaca: Style and Status in an Inca Community.* 1st ed. University of Iowa Press, Iowa City.

1993   The Provinces in the Heartland: Stylistic Variation and Architectural Innovation near Inca Cuzco. In *Provincial Inca: Archaeological and Ethnohistorical Assessment of the Impact of the Inca State,* edited by Michael A. Malpass, pp. 145–76. University of Iowa Press, Iowa City.

Oficina Nacional de Evaluación de Recursos Naturales, Lima [ONERN]

1973   *Inventario, evaluación y uso racional de los recursos naturales de la costa: Cuenca de Río Camaná-Majes.* 2 vols. Oficina Nacional de Evaluación de Recursos Naturales, Lima.

Ohnuki-Tierney, Emiko

1995   Structure, Event and Historical Metaphor: Rice and Identities in Japanese History. *Journal of the Royal Anthropological Institute* 1(2):227–53.

Olivier, Laurent

2004   The Past of the Present. Archaeological Memory and Time. *Archaeological Dialogues* 10(2):204–13.

Oquiche Hernani, Alberto A.

1991   La ocupación collagua é inca en el sector de Achoma Valle del Colca. Unpublished baccalaureate thesis, Department of Archaeology, Universidad Católica Santa María, Arequipa.

Oré, Luis Jerónimo

1992 [1598]   *Symbolo catholico indiano.* Australis, Lima.

Orlove, Benjamin S., C. H. Chiang, and M. A. Cane

2000   Forecasting Andean Rainfall and Crop Yield from the Influence of El Niño on Pleiades Visibility. *Nature* 403:68–71.

Ortloff, Charles R., and Alan L. Kolata
  1993   Climate and Collapse: Agro-Ecological Perspectives on the Decline of the Tiwanaku State. *Journal of Archaeological Science.*

Ortner, Sherry B.
  1995   Resistance and the Problem of Ethnographic Refusal. *Comparative Studies in Society and History* 37(1):173–93.

Paerregaard, Karsten
  1993   Why Fight over Water? Power, Conflict, and Irrigation in an Andean Village. In *Irrigation at High Altitudes: The Social Organization of Water Control Systems in the Andes,* edited by William P. Mitchell and David Guillet, pp. 189–202. Society for Latin American Anthropology Publication Series, vol. 12.

Parsons, Jeffrey R., and Charles M. Hastings
  1988   The Late Intermediate Period. In *Peruvian Prehistory,* edited by Richard W. Keatinge, pp. 190–229. Cambridge University Press, Cambridge.

Parsons, Jeffrey R., Charles M. Hastings, and Ramiros Matos Mendieta
  1997   Rebuilding the State in Highland Peru: Herder-Cultivator Interaction During the Late Intermediate Period in the Tarama-Chinchaycocha Region. *Latin American Antiquity* 8(4):317–41.
  2001   *Prehispanic Settlement Patterns in the Upper Mantaro and Tarma Drainages, Junin, Peru.* Memoirs of the Museum of Anthropology, University of Michigan. Ann Arbor.

Pärssinen, Martti
  1992   *Tawantinsuyu: The Inca State and Its Political Organization.* SHS, Helsinki.

Patterson, Thomas C.
  1994   Toward a Properly Historical Ecology. In *Historical Ecology: Cultural Knowledge and Changing Landscapes,* edited by Carole L. Crumley, pp. 223–37. School of American Research Press, Santa Fe, N.M.

Patterson, Thomas C., and Christine Ward Gailey
  1987   *Power Relations and State Formation.* American Anthropological Association, Washington, D.C.

Pauketat, Timothy R.
  2000   Politicization and Community in the Pre-Columbian Mississippi Valley. In *The Archaeology of Communities: A New World Perspective,* edited by Marcello A. Canuto and Jason Yaeger, pp. 16–43. Routledge Press, New York,
  2001   Practice and History in Archaeology: An Emerging Paradigm. *Anthropological Theory* 1:73–98.

Pease G. Y., Franklin
  1977a   Collaguas: Una etnía del siglo XVI. In *Collaguas I,* edited by Franklin Pease, pp. 131–68. Pontificia Universidad Católica del Perú, Lima.

Pease G. Y., Franklin (editor)
  1977b   *Collaguas I.* Pontificia Universidad Católica del Perú Fondo Editorial, Lima.
  1978   Inkarri en Collaguas. In *Etnohistoria y antropologia andina,* edited by Amalia Castelli, Marcia Koth de Paredes, and Mariana Mould de Pease, pp. 237–40. Museo Nacional de Historia, Lima.
  1981   Ayllu y parcialidad: Reflexiones sobre el caso de Collaguas. In *Etnohistoria y antropologia andina,* edited by Amalia Castelli, Marcia Koth de Paredes, and Mariana Mould de Pease, pp. 19–33. Museo Nacional de Historia, Lima.
  1989   *Del Tawantinsuyu a la historia del Peru.* Pontificia Universidad Católica del Perú, Lima.

Peterson, Christian D., and Robert D. Drennan

    2005   Communities, Settlements, Sites, and Surveys: Regional-Scale Analysis of Prehistoric Human *American Antiquity* 70(1):5–30.

Pickles, John (editor)

    1995   *Ground Truth: The Social Implications of Geographic Information Systems.* Guilford Press, New York.

Platt, Tristan

    1982   *Estado boliviano y ayllu andino: Tierra y tributo en el norte de Potosí.* Instituto de Estudios Peruanos, Lima.

    1986   Mirrors and Maize: The Concept of *Yanantin* among the Macha of Bolivia. In *Anthropological History of Andean Polities*, edited by John V. Murra, Nathan Wachtel, and Jacques Revel, pp. 228–59. Cambridge University Press, New York.

Polo de Ondegardo, Juan

    1917 [1571]   Relación de los fundamentos acerca del notable daño que resulta de no guardar a los indios sus fueros. . . ." In *Colección de libros y documentos referentes a la historia del Perú* 1(3):45–188. Lima.

Pred, Allan

    1984a   *Making Histories and Constructing Human Geographies.* Westview Press, Boulder, Colo.

    1984b   Place as Historically Contingent Process: Structuration and the Time-Geography of Becoming Places. *Annals of the Association of American Geographers* 74(2):279–97.

Protzen, Jean-Pierre

    1993   *Inca Architecture and Construction at Ollantaytambo.* Oxford University Press, New York.

Quilter, Jeffrey, and Gary Urton

    2002   *Narrative Threads: Accounting and Recounting in Andean Khipu.* 1st ed. Joe R. And Teresa Lozano Long Series in Latin American and Latino Art and Culture. University of Texas Press, Austin.

Quilter, Jeffrey, Marc Zender, Karen Spalding, Régulo Franco Jordan, César Gálvez Mora, and Juan Castañeda Murga

    2010   Traces of a Lost Language and Number System Discovered on the North Coast of Peru. *American Anthropologist* 112(3):357–69.

Rabatel, Antoine, Bernard Francou, Vincent Jomelli, Philippe Naveau, and Delphine Grancher

    2008   A Chronology of the Little Ice Age in the Tropical Andes of Bolivia (16°S) and Its Implications for Climate Reconstruction. *Quaternary Research* 70:198–212.

Ramírez, Susan E.

    2005   *To Feed and Be Fed: The Cosmological Bases of Authority and Identity in the Andes.* Stanford University Press, Stanford, Calif.

Redfield, Robert

    1955   *The Little Community: Viewpoints for the Study of a Human Whole.* University of Chicago Press, Chicago.

    1956   *Peasant Society and Culture; an Anthropological Approach to Civilization.* University of Chicago Press, Chicago.

Reinhard, Johan

    1998   *Discovering the Inca Ice Maiden: My Adventures on Ampato.* National Geographic, Washington, D.C.

Restall, Matthew

    2003   *Seven Myths of the Spanish Conquest.* Oxford University Press, New York.

Ricard, Robert

1966   *The Spiritual Conquest of Mexico: An Essay on the Apostolate and the Evangelizing Methods of the Mendicant Orders in New Spain, 1523–1572.* Translated by Lesley Byrd Simpson. University of California Press, Berkeley and Los Angeles.

Rice, Prudence M.

1987   The Moquegua Bodegas Survey. *National Geographic Research* 3(2):136–38.

1994   Kilns of Moquegua, Peru: Technology, Excavations, and Functions. *Journal of Field Archaeology* 21:325–44.

Rice, Prudence M., and Sara L. van Beck

1993   Spanish Colonial Kiln Tradition of Moquegua, Peru. *Historical Archaeology* 27(4):65–81.

Robinson, David J. (editor)

2003a   *Collaguas II; Lari Collaguas.* Pontificia Universidad Católica del Perú, Lima.

2003b   Estudio. In *Collaguas II; Lari Collaguas,* edited by David J. Robinson, pp. xxxvii–cxii. Pontificia Universidad Católica del Perú, Lima.

2006   *Collaguas III; Yanque Collaguas.* Pontificia Universidad Católica del Perú, Lima.

2009   *Collaguas IV; Cabanaconde.* Pontificia Universidad Católica del Perú Lima.

Rossignol, Jacqueline, and LuAnn Wandsnider (editors)

1992   *Space, Time, and Archaeological Landscapes.* Plenum Press, New York.

Rostworowski de Diez Canseco, María

1978   *Señoríos indígenas de Lima y Canta.* Instituto de Estudios Peruanos, Lima.

1983   *Estructuras andinas del poder: Ideología religiosa y política.* Instituto de Estudios Peruanos, Lima.

1988   *Conflicts over Coca Fields in Sixteenth-Century Peru.* Studies in Latin American

1961   Stratigraphy and Seriation. *American Antiquity* 26(3):324–30.

Rowe, John H.

1946a   Inca Culture at the Time of the Spanish Conquest. In *Handbook of South American Indians,* vol. 2, pp. 183–330. Smithsonian Institution Press, Washington, D.C.

1946b   Inca Culture at the Time of the Spanish Conquest. In *Handbook of South American Indians,* vol. 2, pp. 183–330, edited by Julian H. Steward. Smithsonian Institution Press, Washington, D.C.

Sahlins, Marshall D.

1981   *Historical Metaphors and Mythical Realities: Structure in the Early History of the Sandwich Island Kingdom.* University of Michigan Press, Ann Arbor.

1985   *Islands of History.* University of Chicago Press, Chicago.

1995   *How "Natives" Think: About Captain Cook, for Example.* University of Chicago Press, Chicago.

2004   *Apologies to Thucydides: Understanding History as Culture and Vice Versa.* University of Chicago Press, Chicago.

2005   Preface. *Ethnohistory* 52(1):3–6.

Said, Edward W.

1978   *Orientalism.* Pantheon Books, New York.

Saignes, Thierry

1985   *Los andes orientales: Historia de un olvido.* Instituto Frances de Estudios Andinos, Lima.

1995   Indian Migration and Social Change in Seventeenth-Century Charcas. In *Ethnicity, Markets, and Migration in the Andes: At the Crossroads of History and Anthropology,* edited by Brooke Larson and Olivia Harris, pp. 167–95. Duke University Press, Durham, N.C.

1999   The Colonial Condition in the Quechua-Aymara Heartland. In *The Cambridge History of* the Native Peoples of the Americas, vol. 3, South America, Part II, edited by Frank Salomon and Stuart B. Schwartz, pp. 59–137. Cambridge University Press, New York.

Saignes, Thierry, Paul Garner, and Tristan Platt

1985   Caciques, Tribute and Migration in the Southern Andes: Indian Society and the 17th Century Colonial Order: (Audencia De Charcas). Occasional Papers 15. University of London, Institute of Latin American Studies. University of London Institute of Latin American Studies.

Salomon, Frank

1982   Vertical Politics on the Inka Frontier. In Anthropological History of Andean Polities, edited by John V. Murra, Jacques Revel, and Nathan Wachtel, pp. 89–117. Cambridge University Press, Cambridge.

1985   The Dynamic Potential of the Complementarity Concept. In Andean Ecology and Civilization: An Interdisciplinary Perspective on Andean Ecological Complementarity, edited by Shozo Masuda, Izumi Shimada, and Craig Morris, pp. 511–31. University of Tokyo Press, Tokyo.

1986   Native Lords of Quito in the Age of the Incas: The Political Economy of North-Andean Chiefdoms. Cambridge University Press, Cambridge.

1991   Introductory Essay: The Huarochirí Manuscript. In The Huarochirí Manuscript, pp. 1–38. Translated by F. Salomon and G. L. Urioste. University of Texas Press, Austin.

1995   "The Beautiful Grandparents": Andean Ancestor Shrines and Mortuary Ritual as Seen through Colonial Records. In Tombs for the Living: Andean Mortuary Practices, edited by Tom D. Dillehay, pp. 315–53. Dumbarton Oaks, Washington, D.C.

2004   The Cord Keepers: Khipus and Cultural Life in a Peruvian Village. Latin America Otherwise. Duke University Press, Durham, N.C.

Sandor, Jonathan A.

1986   Report on Soils in Agricultural Terraces in the Colca Valley. In The Cultural Ecology, Archaeology, and History of Terracing and Terrace Abandonment in the Colca Valley of Southern Peru, edited by William M. Denevan, vol. 1, pp. 235–75. Technical Report to the National Science Foundation and the National Geographic Society. Department of Geography, University of Wisconsin, Madison.

1987a   Initial Investigation of Soils in Agricultural Fields in the Colca Valley, Peru. In Pre-Hispanic Agricultural Fields in the Andean Region, edited by William M. Denevan, Kent Mathewson, and Gregory W. Knapp. BAR International Series 359(I):163–92.

1987b   Soil Conservation and Redevelopment of Agricultural Terraces in the Colca Valley, Peru. Journal of the Washington, D.C. Academy of Sciences 77:149–54.

1988   Investigation of Agricultural Soils at Lari, Colca Valley, Peru. In Cognitive, Behavioral, and Agronomic Studies of Soil Management in Lari, Colca Valley, Peru. Report to the National Science Foundation. Department of Anthropology, Catholic University, Washington, D.C.

1992   Long-Term Effects of Prehistoric Agriculture on Soil: Examples from New Mexico and Peru. In Soils in Archaeology: Landscape Evolution and Human Occupation, edited by V. T. Holliday, pp. 217–45. Smithsonian Institution Press, Washington, D.C.

Sandor, Jonathan A., and Neal S. Eash

1991   Significance of Ancient Agricultural Soils for Long-Term Agronomic Studies and Sustainable Agricultural Research. Agronomy Journal 83:29–37.

1995   Ancient Agricultural Soils in the Andes of Southern Peru. Soil Science Society of America Journal 59:170–79.

Sandor, Jonathan A., and L. Furbee

1996   Indigenous Knowledge and Classification of Soils in the Andes of Southern Peru. *Soil Science Society of America Journal* 60:1502–12.

Scarborough, Vernon L.

2003   *The Flow of Power: Ancient Water Systems and Landscapes.* SAR Press, Santa Fe, N.M.

Schama, S.

1995   *Landscape and Memory.* Random House, New York.

Schreiber, Katharina J.

1992   *Wari Imperialism in Middle Horizon Peru.* Museum of Anthropology, University of Michigan, Ann Arbor.

Sciscento, Margaret M.

1989   Imperialism in the High Andes: Inka and Wari Involvement in the Chuquibamba Valley, Peru. Ph.D. dissertation, Department of Anthropology, University of California, Santa Barbara. University Microfilms, Ann Arbor.

Scott, James C.

1985   *Weapons of the Weak: Everyday Forms of Peasant Resistance.* Yale University Press, New Haven.

1990   *Domination and the Arts of Resistance: Hidden Transcripts.* Yale University Press, New Haven.

Seddon, Matthew T.

1998   Ritual, Power, and the Development of a Complex Society: The Island of the Sun and the Tiwanaku State. Ph.D. dissertation, Department of Anthropology, University of Chicago.

Seed, Patricia

1991   "Failing to Marvel": Atahualpa's Encounter with the Word. *Latin American Research Review* 26(1):7–32.

1992   Taking Possession and Reading Texts: Establishing the Authority of Overseas Empires. *William and Mary Quarterly* 49(2):183–209.

Seltzer, Geoffrey O., and Christine A. Hastorf

1990   Climatic Change and Its Effect on Prehispanic Agriculture in the Central Peruvian Andes. *Journal of Field Archaeology* 17:397–414.

Sewell, William Hamilton

2005   *Logics of History: Social Theory and Social Transformation.* Chicago Studies in Practices of Meaning. University of Chicago Press, Chicago.

Shea, Daniel E.

1986a   The Achoma Archaeology Pilot Study. In *The Cultural Ecology, Archaeology, and History of Terracing and Terrace Abandonment in the Colca Valley of Southern Peru,* edited by William M. Denevan, vol. 1, pp. 313–62. Technical Report to the National Science Foundation and the National Geographic Society. Department of Geography, University of Wisconsin, Madison.

1986b   Preliminary Discussion of Prehistoric Settlement at Achoma. In *The Cultural Ecology, Archaeology, and History of Terracing and Terrace Abandonment in the Colca Valley of Southern Peru,* edited by William M. Denevan, vol. 1, pp. 313–62. Technical Report to the National Science Foundation and the National Geographic Society. Department of Geography, University of Wisconsin, Madison.

1987   Preliminary Discussion of Prehistoric Settlement and Terracing at Achoma, Colca Valley, Peru. In *Pre-Hispanic Agricultural Fields in the Andean Region,* edited by William M. Denevan, Kent Mathewson, and Gregory W. Knapp. BAR International Series 359(I):67–88.

1997   Discussion of Prehistoric Settlement at Achoma. In *Achoma Archaeology: A Study of Terrace Irrigation in Peru*, edited by Daniel E. Shea, pp. 49–58. Logan Museum of Anthropology, Beloit, Wisc.

Sherbondy, Jeanette E.

1982   The Canal Systems of Hanan Cuzco. Ph.D. dissertation, University of Illinois at Urbana-Champaign.

Silliman, Stephen

2005   Culture Contact or Colonialism? Challenges in the Archaeology of Native North America. *American Antiquity* 70(1):55–74.

Silverblatt, Irene

1988   Imperial Dilemmas, the Politics of Kinship, and Inca Reconstructions of History. *Comparative Studies in Society and History* 30(1):83–102.

Smith, Marvin T., and Mary Elizabeth Good

1982   *Early Sixteenth Century Glass Beads in the Spanish Colonial Trade.* Cottonlandia Museum Publications, Greenwood, Miss.

Smith, Marvin T., Elizabeth Graham, and David M. Pendergast

1981   European Beads from Spanish-Colonial Lamanai and Tipu, Belize. *Beads: Journal of the Society of Bead Researchers* 6:21–48.

Sofaer, Joanna R.

2006   *The Body as Material Culture: A Theoretical Osteoarchaeology.* Topics in Contemporary Archaeology series. Cambridge University Press, New York.

Soja, Edward W.

1989   *Postmodern Geographies: The Reassertion of Space in Critical Social Theory.* Verso, New York.

Spalding, Karen

1982   Exploitation as an Economic System: The State and the Extraction of Surplus in Colonial Peru. In *The Inca and Aztec States, 1400–1800: Anthropology and History*, edited by George Allen Collier, Renato Rosaldo, and John D. Wirth, pp. 321–42. Academic Press, New York.

1984   *Huarochirí: An Andean Society under Inca and Spanish Rule.* Stanford University Press, Stanford, Calif.

1999   The Crises and Transformations of Invaded Societies: Andean Area (1500–1580). In *The Cambridge History of the Native Peoples of the Americas*, vol. 3, *South America, Part I*, edited by Frank Salomon and Stuart B. Schwartz, pp. 904–64. Cambridge University Press, New York.

Spencer, J. E., and G. A. Hale

1961   The Origin, Nature, and Distribution of Agricultural Terracing. *Pacific Viewpoint* 2:1–40.

Staff, Soil Survey

1975   *Soil Taxonomy.* Agriculture Handbook 436. U.S. Department of Agriculture.

1990   *Keys to Soil Taxonomy.* SMSS Technical Monograph 19. Blacksburg, Va.

Stanish, Charles

1985   Post-Tiwanaku Regional Economies in the Otora Valley, Southern Peru. Ph.D. dissertation, Department of Anthropology, University of Chicago. University Microfilms, Ann Arbor.

1989a   An Archaeological Evaluation of an Ethnohistorical Model. In *Ecology, Settlement, and History in the Osmore Drainage*, edited by Don S. Rice, Charles Stanish, and Phillip R. Scarr. BAR International Series 545:–303–20.

1989b   Household Archaeology: Testing Models of Zonal Complementarity in the South Central Andes. *American Anthropologist* 91:7–24.

1992   *Ancient Andean Political Economy*. University of Texas Press, Austin.

1997a   *Archaeological Survey in the Juli-Desaguadero Region of Lake Titicaca Basin, Southern Peru*. Fieldiana. Anthropology, New Series, No. 29. Field Museum of Natural History, Chicago.

1997b   Nonmarket Imperialism in the Prehispanic Americas: The Inka Occupation of the Titicaca Basin. *Latin American Antiquity* 8(3):195–216.

2001   Regional Research on the Inca. *Journal of Archaeological Research* 9(3):213–41.

2003   *Ancient Titicaca: The Evolution of Complex Society in Southern Peru and Northern Bolivia*. University of California Press, Berkeley and Los Angeles.

Stanish, Charles, Richard Lewis Burger, Lisa M. Cipolla, Michael D. Glascock, and Esteban Quelima

2002   Evidence for Early Long-Distance Obsidian Exchange and Watercraft Use from the Southern Lake Titicaca Basin of Bolivia and Peru. *Latin American Antiquity* 13:444–54.

Stanish, Charles, Lee Steadman, and Matthew T. Seddon

1994   *Archaeological Research at Tumatumani, Juli, Peru*. Field Museum of Natural History, Chicago.

Stein, Gil (editor)

2005   *The Archaeology of Colonial Encounters: Comparative Perspectives*. School of American Research Press, Santa Fe, N.M.

Stern, Steve J.

1982   *Peru's Indian Peoples and the Challenge of Spanish Conquest*. University of Wisconsin Press, Madison.

1987   *Resistance, Rebellion, and Consciousness in the Andean Peasant World, 18th to 20th Centuries*. University of Wisconsin Press, Madison.

Stuiver, M., and P. J. Reimer

1993   Extended 14c Database and Revised Calib Radiocarbon Calibration Program. *Radiocarbon* 35:215–30.

Stuiver, M., P. J. Reimer, and T. F. Braziunas

1998   High-Precision Radiocarbon Age Calibration for Terrestrial and Marine Samples. *Radiocarbon* 40:1127–51.

Tandeter, Enrique

1981   Forced and Free Labour in Late Colonial Potosí. *Past and Present* 93:98–136.

Thompson, L. G.

1992   Ice Core Evidence from Peru and China. In *Climate since A.D. 1500*, edited by R. S. Bradley and P. D. Jones, pp. 517–48. Routledge, New York.

1995   Late Holocene Ice Core Records of Climate and Environment from the Tropical Andes, Peru. *Bulletin de l'Institut Français d'Études Andines* 24:619–29.

Thompson, L. G., M. E. Davis, E. Mosley-Thompson, and K.-b. Liu

1988   Pre-Incan Agricultural Activity Recorded in Dust Layers in Two Tropical Ice Cores. *Nature* 336:763–65.

Thompson, L. G., and E. Mosley-Thompson

1989   One-Half Millennium of Tropical Climate Variability as Recorded in the Stratigraphy of the Quelccaya Ice Cap, Peru. In *Climate Change in the Eastern Pacific and Western Americas*, edited by D. Peterson, pp. 15–31. American Geophysical Union Monograph 55. American Geophysical Union, Washington, D.C.

Thompson, L. G., E. Mosley-Thompson, J. F. Bolzan, and B. R. Koci

1985   A 1500-Yr Record of Tropical Precipitation in Ice Cores from the Quelccaya Ice Cap, Peru. *Science* 229:971–73.

Thompson, L. G., E. Mosley-Thompson, W. Dansgaard, and P. M. Grootes
　1986　The Little Ice Age as Recorded in the Stratigraphy of the Tropical Quelccaya Ice Cap. *Science* 234:361–64.

Thompson, Lonnie G.
　1993　Reconstructing the Paleo ENSO Records from Tropical and Subtropical Ice Cores. *Bulletin de l'Institut Français d'Études Andines* 22(1):65–83.

Thompson, Lonnie G., Ellen Mosley-Thompson, and Mary E. Davis
　1994　Glacial Records of Global Climate: A 1500-Year Tropical Ice Core Record of Climate. *Human Ecology* 22(1):83–95.

Tibesar, Antonine
　1953　*Franciscan Beginnings in Early Colonial Peru.* Academy of American Franciscan History, Washington, D.C.

Tilley, Christopher Y.
　1994　*A Phenomenology of Landscape: Places, Paths, and Monuments.* Explorations in Anthropology. Berg, Oxford.

Toledo, Francisco de
　1924 [1570–75]　Libro de la visita general del Virrey Toledo (1570–75). *Revista histórica: Órgano del Instituto Histórico del Perú* 7(2):114–216.

Toledo, Francisco de, María Justina Sarabia Viejo, and Guillermo Lohmann Villena
　1986　*Francisco de Toledo: Disposiciones gubernativas para el virreinato del Perú.* Publicaciones de la Escuela de Estudios Hispano-Americanos de Sevilla 320 (No. General), 347. 2 vols. Escuela de Estudios Hispano-Americanos; Consejo Superior de Investigaciones Científicas; Monte de Piedad y Caja de Ahorros de Sevilla, Sevilla.

Tord, Luis Enrique
　1983　*Templos coloniales del Colca—Arequipa.* Atlas, Lima.

Trawick, Paul
　2001　The Moral Economy of Water: Equity and Antiquity in the Andean Commons. *American Anthropologist* 103(2):361–79.

Treacy, John M.
　1989a　Agricultural Terraces in Peru's Colca Valley: Promises and Problems of an Ancient Technology. *Fragile Lands of Latin America: Strategies for Sustainable Development,* 209–29.
　1989b　The Fields of Coporaque: Agricultural Terracing and Water Management in the Colca Valley, Arequipa, Peru, Department of Geography, Ph.D. dissertation, Department of Geography, University of Wisconsin, Madison. University Microfilms, Ann Arbor.
　1993　Teaching Water: Hydraulic Management and Terracing in Coporaque, the Colca Valley, Peru. In *Irrigation at High Altitudes: The Social Organization of Water Control Systems in the Andes,* edited by William P. Mitchell and David Guillet, pp. 99–114. Society for Latin American Anthropology Publication Series, vol. 12.
　1994　*Las Chacras de Coporaque: Andeneria y riego en el Valle del Colca.* Instituto de Estudios Peruanos, Lima.

Treacy, John M., and William M. Denevan
　1986　Survey of Abandoned Terraces, Canals, and Houses at Chijra, Coporaque. In *The Cultural Ecology, Archaeology, and History O Terracing and Terrace Abandonment in the Colca Valley of Southern Peru,* edited by William M. Denevan, vol. 1, pp. 198–220. Technical Report to the National Science Foundation and the National Geographic Society. Department of Geography, University of Wisconsin, Madison.

Tripcevich, Nicholas

2007   Quarries, Caravans, and Routes to Complexity: Prehispanic Obsidian in the South-Central Andes. Ph.D. dissertation, Department of Anthropology, University of California, Santa Barbara.

2010   Exotic Goods, Chivay Obsidian, and Sociopolitical Change in the South-Central Andes. In *Trade and Exchange: Archaeological Studies from History and Prehistory*, edited by Carolyn D. Dillian and Carolyn L. White, pp. 59–73. Springer, New York.

Tripcevich, Nicholas, and Willy Yépez Álvarez

2009   La fuente de obsidiana "Chivay" y su posición en los Andes sur centrales. *Andes: Boletín del Centro de Estudios Precolombinos de la Universidad de Varsovia* 7:127–52.

Trouillot, Michel-Rolph

1991   Anthropology and the Savage Slot: The Poetics and Politics of Otherness. In *Recapturing Anthropology*, edited by Richard G. Fox, pp. 17–44. School of American Research, Santa Fe, N.M.

Tuan, Yi-fu

1977   *Space and Place: The Perspective of Experience*. University of Minnesota Press, Minneapolis.

Ulloa Mogollón, Juan de

1965 [1586]   Relación de la Provincia de los Collaguas para la descripción de las Indias que su Magestad manda hacer. In *Relaciones geográficas de Indias*, vol. 1, edited by Marcos Jimenez de la Espada, pp. 326–33. Ediciones Atlas, Madrid.

Urton, Gary

1984   Chuta: El espacio de la practica social en Pacariqtambo, Peru. *Revista Andina* 2(1):7–56.

1988   Arquitectura pública como texto social: La historia de un muro de adobe en Pacariqtambo, Peru (1915–1985). *Revista Andina* 6(1):225–61.

1990   *The History of a Myth: Pacariqtambo and the Origin of the Inkas*. University of Texas Press, Austin.

Valderrama, Ricardo, and Carmen Escalante

1997   *La doncella sacrificada: Mitos del Valle del Colca*. Universidad Nacional de San Agustín; Instituto Francés de Estudios Andinos, Arequipa.

Valderrama Fernández, Ricardo, and Carmen Escalante Gutierrez

1988   *Del Tata Mallku a la Mama Pacha: Riego, sociedad y ritos en los Andes peruanos*. Centro de Estudios y Promoción del Desarrollo, Lima.

Van Buren, Mary

1993   Community and Empire in Southern Peru: The Site of Torata Alta under Spanish Rule. Ph.D. dissertation, Department of Anthropology, University of Arizona. University Microfilms, Ann Arbor.

1996   Rethinking the Vertical Archipelago: Ethnicity, Exchange, and History in the South Central Andes. *American Anthropologist* 98(2):338–51.

1997   Continuity or Change? Vertical Archipelagos in Southern Peru During the Early Colonial Period. In *Approaches to the Historical Archaeology of Mexico, Central and South America*, edited by Janine Gasco, Greg Charles Smith, and Patricia Fournier-García, pp. 155–64. Institute of Archaeology, University of California, Los Angeles.

Van Buren, Mary, Peter T. Bürgi, and Prudence M. Rice

1993   Torata Alta: A Late Highland Settlement in the Osmore Drainage. In *Domestic Architecture, Ethnicity, and Complementarity in the South-Central Andes*, edited by Mark S. Aldenderfer, pp. 136–46. University of Iowa Press, Iowa City.

van de Guchte, Maarten

1999   The Inca Cognition of Landscape: Archaeology, Ethnohistory, and the Aesthetic of Alterity. In *Archaeologies of Landscape: Contemporary Perspectives*, edited by Wendy Ashmore and A. Bernard Knapp, pp. 149–68. Blackwell, Oxford.

Vargas Ugarte, Rubén

1952 [1551–52]   Primer concilio limense. In *Concilios limenses (1551–1772)*, vol. 1, edited by Rubén Vargas Ugarte, pp. 5–35. Tipografía Peruana, Lima.

Verdugo, Gaspar (visitador)

1977 [1591]   Fragmento de la visita a la Provincia de Collaguas, repartimiento de Yanque Collaguas, parcialidad de Hanansaya. In *Collaguas I*, edited by Franklin Pease, pp. 407–52. Pontificia Universidad Católica del Perú, Lima.

Verdugo, Gaspar, and Gaspar de Colmenares (visitadores)

1977 [1591]   Visita de Yanquecollaguas Urinsaya. In *Collaguas I*, edited by Franklin Pease, pp. 191–406. Pontificia Universidad Católica del Perú, Lima.

Wachtel, Nathan

1977   *The Vision of the Vanquished: The Spanish Conquest of Peru through Indian Eyes, 1530–1570*. Barnes & Noble, New York.

1982   The Mitimas of the Cochabamba Valley: The Colonization Policy of Huayna Capac. In *Inca and Aztec States, 1400–1800: Anthropology and History*, edited by George Allen Collier, Renato Rosaldo, and John D. Wirth, pp. 199–235. Academic Press, New York.

Wagstaff, J. Malcolm

1987   *Landscape and Culture: Geographical and Archaeological Perspectives*. Basil Blackwell, London.

Weaver, Brendan J. M., and Kathryn E. DeTore

2009   Colonial Crafts: Preliminary Investigations into Labor, Space, and Household Production of the 16th Century Community at Malata, Peru. Paper presented at the 73rd annual meeting of the Society for American Archaeology, Atlanta.

Wernke, Steven A.

2003   An Archaeo-History of Andean Community and Landscape: The Late Prehispanic and Early Colonial Colca Valley, Peru. Ph.D. dissertation, University of Wisconsin, Madison. University Microfilms, Ann Arbor.

2006a   Collagua "Eco-Logistics": Intermediate Elites and Hybrid Community Structures in the Colca Valley, Peru. In *Intermediate Elites in Pre-Columbian States and Empires*, edited by Christina M. Elson and R. Alan Covey, pp. 175–211. University of Arizona Press, Tucson.

2006b   The Politics of Community and Inka Statecraft in the Colca Valley, Peru. *Latin American Antiquity* 17(2):177–208.

2007a   Analogy or Erasure? Dialectics of Religious Transformation in the Early Doctrinas of the Colca Valley, Peru. *International Journal of Historical Archaeology* 11(2):152–82.

2007b   Negotiating Community and Landscape in the Peruvian Andes: A Trans-Conquest View. *American Anthropologist* 109(1):130–52.

2010   A Reduced Landscape: Toward a Multi-Causal Understanding of Historic Period Agricultural Deintensification in Highland Peru. *Journal of Latin American Geography* 9(3):51–83.

2011a   Asentamiento, agricultura, y pastoralism Durante el periodo Formativo en el Valle del Colca, Perú. *Chungará* 43(2):203–20.

2011b   Convergences: Producing Colonial Hybridity at an Early Doctrina in Highland Peru. In *Enduring Conquests: Rethinking the Archaeology of Resistance to Spanish Colonialism in the*

Americas, edited by Matthew Liebmann and Melissa Murphy, pp. 77–101. School for Advanced Research, Santa Fe, N.M.

2012a Households in Transition: Reconstructing Domestic Organization at an Early Colonial Mission in the Andean Highlands. In *Decolonizing Indigenous Histories: Exploring Prehistoric/Colonial Transitions in Archaeology,* edited by Maxine Oland, Siobhan M. Hart, and Liam Frink. University of Arizona Press, Tucson.

2012b Spatial Network Analysis of a Terminal Prehispanic and Early Colonial Settlement in Highland Peru. *Journal of Archaeological Science* 39(4):1111–22.

Wernke, Steven A., Teddy Abel Traslaviña, and Ericka M. Guerra Santander

2012 La transformación del espacio arquitectónico en una doctrina temprana en el Valle del Colca. In *Arquitectura prehispánica tardía: Construcción y poder en los Andes centrales,* edited by Kevin Lane and Milton Luján Dávila, pp. 543–78. Universidad Católica Sedes Sapientiae, Lima.

Wernke, Steven A., and Thomas M. Whitmore

2009 Agriculture and Inequality in the Colonial Andes: A Simulation of Production and Consumption Using Administrative Documents. *Human Ecology* 37:421–40.

Wheatley, David, and Mark Gillings

2002 *Spatial Technology and Archaeology: The Archaeological Applications of GIS.* Taylor & Francis, New York.

Whitehead, Neil L.

1998a Colonial Chiefdoms of the Lower Orinoco and Guayana Coast. In *Chiefdoms and Chieftaincy in the Americas,* edited by Elsa M. Redmond, pp. 150–63. University Press of Florida, Gainesville.

1998b Ecological History and Historical Ecology: Diachronic Modeling Versus Historical Explanation. In *Advances in Historical Ecology,* edited by W. Balée, pp. 30–41. Columbia University Press, New York.

Whitridge, Peter

2004 Landscapes, Houses, Bodies, Things: "Place" and the Archaeology of Inuit Imaginaries. *Journal of Archaeological Method and Theory* 11(2):213–50.

Williams, Patrick Ryan

1997 The Role of Disaster in the Development of Agriculture and the Evolution of Social Complexity in the South-Central Andean Sierra. Ph.D. dissertation, University of Florida, Gainesville. University Microfilms, Ann Arbor.

2002 Hydraulic Landscapes and Social Relations in the Middle Horizon Andes. In *The Reconstruction of Archaeological Landscapes through Digital Technologies,* edited by Mauricio Forte, Patrick Ryan Williams, James Wiseman, and Farouk El-Baz. BAR International Series 1151.

Winterhalder, Bruce

1993 Rainfall and Temperature Patterning and Predictability with Respect to Water Management in the Central Andes of Southern Peru. In *Irrigation at High Altitudes: The Social Organization of Water Control Systems in the Andes,* edited by William P. Mitchell, David Guillet, and Inge Bolin. Society for Latin American Anthropology, American Anthropological Association, Arlington, Va.

Wolf, Eric R.

1956 Aspects of Group Relations in Complex Society: Mexico. *American Anthropologist* 58:1065–1078.

Yaeger, Jason

2000   The Social Construction of Communities in the Classic Maya Countryside: Strategies of Affiliation in Western Belize. In *The Archaeology of Communities*, edited by Marcello A. Canuto and Jason Yaeger, pp. 123–42. Routledge, New York.

Yaeger, Jason, and Marcello A. Canuto

2000   Introducing an Archaeology of Communities. In *The Archaeology of Communities*, edited by Marcello A. Canuto and Jason Yaeger, pp. 1–15. Routledge, New York.

Zimmerer, Karl S.

1999   The Overlapping Patchworks of Mountain Agriculture in Peru and Bolivia: Toward a Regional-Global Landscape Model. *Human Ecology* 27(1):135–65.

2000   Rescaling Irrigation in Latin America: The Cultural Images and Political Ecology of Water Resources. *Ecumene* 7(2):150–75.

Zimmerman, Arthur F.

1938   *Francisco de Toledo, Fifth Viceroy of Peru, 1569–1581*. Caxton Printers, Caldwell.

Zorn, Elayne

2004   *Weaving a Future: Tourism, Cloth and Culture on an Andean Island*. University of Iowa Press, Iowa City.

Zuidema, R. Tom

1964   *The Ceque System of Cuzco: The Social Organization of the Capital of the Inca*. E. J. Brill, Leiden.

1973   Kinship and Ancestor Cult in Three Peruvian Communities. Hernandez Principe's Account of 1622. *Bulletin de l'Institut Français d'Études Andines* 2(10):16–33.

1977   The Inca Kinship System: A New Theoretical View. In *Andean Kinship and Marriage*, edited by Ralph Bolton and Enrique Mayer, pp. 240–92. Special Publication 7. American Anthropological Association, Washington, D.C.

INDEX

Page numbers in *italics* indicate figures and tables.

Steven A. Wernke is associate professor in the Department of Anthropology at Vanderbilt University.

CPSIA information can be obtained
at www.ICGtesting.com
Printed in the USA
BVHW030353150120
569558BV00003B/229/P